THE GRENADIER GUARDS
IN THE WAR OF
1939-1945

HIS MAJESTY KING GEORGE VI
Colonel-in-Chief of the Regiment.

THE GRENADIER GUARDS
IN THE WAR OF
1939-1945

BY

CAPTAIN NIGEL NICOLSON, M.B.E.

AND

PATRICK FORBES

VOLUME I

BY

PATRICK FORBES

THE CAMPAIGNS IN NORTH-WEST EUROPE

The Naval & Military Press Ltd

Published by
The Naval & Military Press Ltd
Unit 10 Ridgewood Industrial Park,
Uckfield, East Sussex,
TN22 5QE England
Tel: +44 (0) 1825 749494
Fax: +44 (0) 1825 765701
www.naval-military-press.com
www.military-genealogy.com
www.militarymaproom.com

Published for
The Grenadier Guards

THE GRENADIER GUARDS
IN THE WAR OF 1939-1945

VOLUME I

THE CAMPAIGNS IN NORTH-WEST EUROPE

Contents

PART II

THE NORTH-WEST EUROPEAN CAMPAIGN OF 1944-1945

Illustrations

Maps

Introduction

THE two volumes of this History deal with the campaigns of the six battalions of the Grenadier Guards in the war of 1939-45. They also describe how the Regiment was organized, trained and gradually expanded during the war years, and how the battalions were occupied in the months immediately following the German surrender of May, 1945. But in the main it is a story of battle, and preparation for battle.

Few people will wish to read a work of this kind from its first cover to its fourth, yet it can claim to be rather more than a mere book of reference, more than a compendium of the Regiment's successes, setbacks, hopes and fears. It is not by any means an account of the Second World War, but each chapter does reflect, like a convex mirror, more than the immediate background of this or that battalion. An attempt has been made to show the effect of strategic decisions upon the activities of the Grenadiers, and, conversely, the effect of their battles, whether won or lost, upon the general plans of campaign.

In writing of these campaigns the authors have had in mind two typical readers. The first is the Grenadier of 1949, who perhaps took part in some of the events described, and whose name may appear in the index. For him the main interest of these two volumes will lie in the account of his own battalion: he will perhaps be reminded of some events which he had forgotten, he will see others in the wider setting of which he was unaware at the time, and in many cases he will find new information about his battles which has come to light in the publication of official despatches or in the stories of released prisoners of war. To him this History is a record of what he himself suffered and achieved.

The second type of reader is a more nebulous character. He is the Grenadier of 1975 or 2045, whose name will not appear in the index (although it may contain his father's name, or his great-great-grandfather's): he is the young Grenadier of the future who wishes to find out what war and life in the Regiment were like in the 1940's, what were the structure and spirit of a battalion, what was the atmosphere of the campaigns in Africa or in Flanders, what the men ate and wore, and what weapons they carried in their hands. It is for his benefit that we have included much detail which may seem irrelevant to the contemporary reader; and it is for him that we have tried to answer the question "What was it like?" as well as the question "What actually happened?"

It has been far easier for the regimental historian to describe the 1939-45 war than it was for his predecessor to describe the war of 1914-18. There is a wider landscape to cover, a greater ebb and flow in the fortunes of the opposing sides, more variety in the operations in which the Grenadiers were engaged. Yet the two fundamental drawbacks of regimental history remain: the lack of unity between the operations of six different battalions; and the general similarity of all battles fought with the same weapons, by the same basic tactics, and against the same enemy. The first drawback tends to make a regimental history cumbersome and patchy; the second tends to make it dull.

We do not claim to have fully overcome these difficulties, for we considered that a full record was needed rather than one which was uniformly bright, but we have been assisted by two devices, which do something to relieve the tedium and awkward structure of the narrative. In the first place, we have linked together the operations of two or more battalions whenever they were taking part in the same phase of the same campaign. For example, the accounts of the 1st, 2nd and 3rd Battalions during the withdrawal to Dunkirk in 1940 have been welded into a continuous story, although the three battalions were split between two quite separate Corps: similarly, the advance by the 3rd and 5th Battalions up the spine of Italy in 1944 has been knit together, in spite of their widely differing experiences: and the adventures of the 1st and 2nd Battalions in North-West Europe in 1944-45 fall conveniently under the same chapter headings, as both were in the same brigade of the Guards Armoured Division. With these few exceptions and one or two others, the narrative tells separately the history of each battalion in each major phase of its campaigns, so that sometimes it is necessary to return several hundred miles in space and five or six months in time before the story of a sister-battalion can be resumed. At the time there was no great sense of unity within the Regiment, except a unity of sentiment; and in writing of the battalions it would be wrong to suggest a military unity which only rarely existed.

The second drawback, the tedious similarity of all battles, was obvious from the start. The variety of circumstance is infinite; the variety of atmosphere is not. Occasionally the magnitude of a battalion's triumphs or hardships raises a particular operation to the level of great drama. More often it is a local attack by a company, a patrol, or a period of rest behind the front line, which makes up the day-to-day narrative of events; and however exciting were the attacks or the patrols, however welcome the periods of relief, the interest of them to the reader, and even to the participants, wears thin after endless repetition. Yet to do justice to the Grenadiers who fought and perhaps gave their lives in these small engagements, it is very necessary to record them. To give each as much individuality as possible, we have been at pains to emphasize the points at which it differed from many such others—in its tactical setting, the appearance of the country, the attitude of the Germans, the details, perhaps, of some Guardsman's heroism, and so on. Scattered throughout the two volumes will also be found a description of those routine events which moulded a battalion's existence—a sea voyage, the approach to the front line, a ceremonial parade, the system of supply in mountains, the method of inter-battalion reliefs. By limiting the number of such descriptions we have tried to satisfy, without blurring, the reader's interest.

For the benefit of the regimental lecturer and the general reader we wish to suggest boldly which passages of this History they are likely to find of greatest interest. In making these suggestions we are not saying that this or that was the greatest battle fought by the Grenadiers during the war, or that this or that was their greatest achievement: we are only suggesting that in these sections the issues are most clear-cut, the actual events most dramatic, the results, one way or the other, most decisive. Of the battles we would list the following:

1. The 3rd Battalion at the River Escaut, May, 1940 (Vol. I, pp. 25-28).
2. The 6th Battalion at the Horseshoe (Mareth Line), March, 1943 (Vol. II, pp. 297-309).*
3. The 5th Battalion on the Tunisian Bou, April, 1943 (Vol. II, pp. 319-330).
4. The 6th Battalion at Monte Camino, November-December, 1943 (Vol. II, pp. 371-381).*
5. The 5th Battalion in the Anzio beach-head, January-February, 1944 (Vol. II, pp. 386-414).*
6. The 1st and 2nd Battalions' capture of the Waal bridge at Nijmegen, September, 1944 (Vol. I, pp. 124-140).*
7. The 4th Battalion at Meijel, November, 1944 (Vol. I, pp. 160-166).

Of other episodes, which did not involve very heavy fighting but are of the greatest interest in the history of the Regiment, we select the following:

1. The 1st, 2nd and 3rd Battalions' evacuation from Dunkirk, June, 1940 (Vol. I, pp. 40-46).
2. The 3rd and 6th Battalions at the final surrender of the German and Italian armies in Tunisia, May, 1943 (Vol. II, pp. 331-344).
3. The 1st and 2nd Battalions' advance through France, Belgium and Holland, September, 1944 (Vol. I, pp. 100-114).
4. The 4th Battalion's final advance into Germany, March-April, 1945 (Vol. I, pp. 211-225).
5. The 3rd Battalion's advance from the River Po to Austria, April-May, 1945 (Vol. II, pp. 505-523).

It remains to indicate the division of responsibility between the two authors, and the sources of their information. Captain Nicolson wrote the whole of Volume II (which deals exclusively with the Mediterranean campaigns), the account of the 1st, 2nd and 3rd Battalions in the B.E.F. campaign of 1940 (Chapter I, Volume I), and the sections of Chapter II of Volume I which deal with the 3rd, 5th and 6th Battalions. He is also responsible for the general editorship of both volumes. Patrick Forbes wrote by far the greater part of Volume I, including the formation of the Guards Armoured Division and the

---

*Those battles marked with an asterisk are probably the most suitable as subjects for lectures to troops.

6th Guards Tank Brigade, and the operations of the 1st, 2nd and 4th Battalions in 1944-45. Although we hope that this work shows no signs of bias in favour of any particular battalion, it should in fairness be stated where each of the authors saw active service during the war. Captain Nicolson joined the 3rd Battalion soon after Dunkirk, served as their Intelligence Officer during the early part of the Tunisian campaign, and remained closely associated with the 3rd Battalion until the end of the war as Brigade Intelligence Officer of the 1st Guards Brigade. Patrick Forbes joined the 4th Battalion in Holland and remained with them until the Armistice. He has previously written the History of the 6th Guards Tank Brigade.

The main documentary sources of information have been the War Diaries which were written daily by the adjutant of each battalion. On the few occasions when the threat of the enemy overrunning a battalion headquarters made it necessary to destroy the contemporary War Diaries (as with the 3rd Battalion on the Ypres—Comines Canal, and the 6th at Salerno), officers always took the trouble to reconstruct them from memory at the first opportunity. Some of these records are undeniably meagre; but others (such as Major-General Adair's and Colonel Colvin's B.E.F. narratives, Captain G. W. Chaplin's account of Anzio, and Lieutenant-Colonel C. M. F. Deakin's diary of the 4th Battalion) are extremely thorough and graphic. Wherever there are gaps they are amply filled by other contemporary documents—the reports of the commanding officers to the Lieutenant-Colonels of the Regiment, private letters written by officers and Guardsmen to their families and friends, the published despatches of Commanders-in-Chief, the accounts of war reporters, official citations, congratulatory messages, orders of the day, and so on. Of all these we have made the fullest use. But, in addition, we have tried to recapture the detail and atmosphere of the campaigns by interviewing many of the Grenadiers who took part in them, and by comparing one account with another to eliminate inaccuracy and distortion. This applies particularly to the battles where there were heavy casualties. A battalion headquarters often had no means of discovering exactly what had happened to their companies on these occasions: many of the leading figures were badly wounded, some were dead, others were taken prisoner, and often there was no time to interview the survivors. We *have* had the time : we have been able to interview the wounded when they recovered, the prisoners when they were freed : and we found that even after the passage of several years men do not easily forget the moments when they were in greatest danger: indeed, modesty was often a greater obstacle than failure of memory. There is no space to do more than thank all those who so generously gave their time and submitted to our interrogations—there were well over a hundred of all ranks—and those more senior officers who have kindly checked the typescripts of our accounts.

There were others who played a more direct part in the compilation of the History. Major M. Dawson collected much material concerning the 1st Battalion, and wrote a long and careful account of their operations in 1944-45 which has been an invaluable basis for many chapters of Volume I. Captain F. J. Jefferson did the same for the 2nd Battalion, and also spent long hours preparing the Appendices, to which Lieutenant J. Bayley added a valuable contribution. Captain Nicolson acknowledges with gratitude the help he received from Lieutenant M. J. Hussey in sifting the material which concerned the Mediterranean campaigns of the 5th and 6th Battalions, and from Major R. A. Paget-Cooke, M.B.E., in the preparation of the index. The Superintending Clerk, R.S.M. A. Douglas, M.B.E., and O.R.Q.M.S. E. C. Weaver, both of Regimental Headquarters, have generously put at our disposal their unrivalled knowledge of the Regiment's documentation; and Guardsman G. L. Dickinson was an invaluable secretary. Finally, Mr. J. Trotter, who drew almost all the maps from the rough tracings we gave him, has shown throughout eighteen months a patience and interest which have never flagged under a stream of suggestions, counter-suggestions and corrections.

NIGEL NICOLSON.
PATRICK FORBES.

LONDON.
May, 1948.

PART ONE

THE OPENING YEARS

CHAPTER I

THE BRITISH EXPEDITIONARY FORCE, 1939-40

1ST, 2ND AND 3RD BATTALIONS

1

MOBILIZATION AND THE MOVE TO FRANCE

*Outbreak of War—Mobilization—The three Grenadier Battalions
cross to France*

DURING the early part of the morning of Sunday, the 3rd of September, 1939
1939, the 3rd Battalion of the Grenadier Guards were reopening the Sept. 3
air-raid trenches which they had dug round their barracks at Aldershot
at the time of the autumn crisis of 1938. At 11 a.m. they downed their
tools, and the officers and men strolled back to their messes and
barrack rooms to listen to the Prime Minister's broadcast address.
At 11.15 they knew that Great Britain was once again at war with
Germany.

Mr. Chamberlain's statement had not come as a surprise; and it was
in a mood of slight sadness, tempered by excitement and wild conjec-
ture, that the British Army put into operation their careful plans for
mobilization. The Grenadier Guards knew exactly what was expected
of them. Their three regular battalions were put on a war footing
within a few days: their mobilization stores were unlocked and dis-
gorged a complete set of new equipment for each man: their ranks
were filled by officers and Guardsmen of the Regular Army Reserve
who had been called back from civilian life on the 31st of August.
From every quarter of the country the reservists poured into Wellington Barracks, some on foot, some driving their own cars: one of
them, a bus driver, left his protesting passengers standing in the
middle of Whitehall, and hurried round the corner to rejoin his
Regiment. At Wellington Barracks they were issued with uniforms
and equipment as fast as they came in, and marched in groups, rather
raggedly for want of practice, to Waterloo Station, headed by a subal-
tern officer wearing a blue greatcoat and sword. Coaches were re-
served for them on every train, and the men were dispatched as far as
it was possible to the same battalions in which they had lately served.

3

1939 When mobilization was complete, each of the three battalions of the Regiment was composed of about sixty per cent. regulars and forty per cent. reservists, leaving sufficient of the latter to form the Training Battalion at Windsor.

The order of battle of the relevant divisions and Guards Brigades at the outbreak of war was as follows:

1ST DIVISION
(Major-General H. R. L. G. Alexander.)

1ST GUARDS BRIGADE
    (Brigadier M. B. Beckwith-Smith, D.S.O., M.C.)
    3rd Battalion Grenadier Guards.
        (Lieut.-Colonel Sir John Aird, Bt., M.V.O., M.C.)
    2nd Battalion Coldstream Guards.
    2nd Battalion The Hampshire Regiment.
2ND INFANTRY BRIGADE.
3RD INFANTRY BRIGADE.

3RD DIVISION
(Major-General B. L. Montgomery.)

7TH GUARDS BRIGADE.
    (Brigadier J. A. C. Whitaker.)
    1st Battalion Grenadier Guards.
        (Lieut.-Colonel J. A. Prescott.)
    2nd Battalion Grenadier Guards.
        (Lieut.-Colonel G. M. Cornish, M.C.)
    1st Battalion Coldstream Guards.
8TH INFANTRY BRIGADE.
9TH INFANTRY BRIGADE.

The 1st and 2nd Battalions were stationed at Pirbright Camp; the 3rd Battalion at Barrosa Barracks, Aldershot.

The Grenadiers were ready to go overseas some time before the British and French staffs were prepared to receive them, and they occupied their days of waiting in sorting out their new companies and equipment, and in receiving official visitors. The Colonel of the Regiment (Field-Marshal H.R.H. The Duke of Connaught) inspected the 3rd Battalion on the 5th of September, and the 1st and 2nd Battalions on the 6th. His Majesty The King visited the 3rd Battalion on the 7th, and the 1st and 2nd Battalions on the 12th and 19th.

There was little training to be done, for both Brigades had just completed their autumn exercises, and as far as could be foreseen the

British Expeditionary Force would spend some time in static positions **1939**
on the French or German frontiers, leaving the initiative for attack to
the Germans. While the latter were already fully engaged in their
campaign against Poland, the French and British were given a breathing space in which to complete their mobilization, and assemble in
strength opposite the German frontiers. The start of the 1939 war
therefore lacked the atmosphere of extreme urgency in which the First
World War had begun. The Allied staff plans worked quickly and
smoothly, the troops were fed forward to their battlefields with efficiency and calm. It was to be 1914 all over again, without the rush.

The B.E.F. was transported to France in two Corps. The I Corps
(Lieutenant-General Sir John Dill), which included the 1st Division,
began to move across the Channel on the 20th of September; the
II Corps (Lieutenant-General A. F. Brooke), including the 3rd Division, a week later. The first unit of the Grenadiers to arrive in France
was therefore the 3rd Battalion, who were preceded on the 13th
of September by a small advance party under 2/Lieut. Crompton-
Roberts. They sailed from Spithead with a convoy of five troopships **Sept. 20**
and two destroyers, and landed at Cherbourg. The voyage was fairly
calm, highly secret, and quite uneventful. The men were crowded
below decks, hung about with lifebelts, and forbidden to smoke. On
arrival at Cherbourg they were bundled by staff officers into a train
which took them through Normandy to the B.E.F.'s assembly area
between the towns of Le Mans and Laval. The Battalion was directed
to march to the village of Tennie, and two companies were sent three
miles beyond to Bernay, to avoid the concentration of too many
troops in the same place, for the menace of heavy air attack governed
much of the B.E.F.'s planning at this stage. Their first billets on
French soil were extremely peaceful. The country was warm and
welcoming, the inhabitants most hospitable—all their own young men
had been called away to fill the French divisions—and the Battalion
settled down in their barns and cottages to enjoy a week of gentle
acclimatization. Their motor transport, under Capt. P. T. Clifton,
joined them from Brest.

The 7th Guards Brigade's journey was very similar. Moving up
from the 3rd Division's concentration area in Dorset, they left Southampton on the 29th of September and landed at Cherbourg, moving **Sept. 29**
from there by rail to the same concentration area at Tennie and
Bernay just after the I Corps had begun their journey to the north.

2

THE MAGINOT AND GORT LINES

The weakness of the Maginot Line—Occupation of the Gort Line on the Franco-Belgian frontier—The wet but bloodless winter of 1939-40 —Morale of the B.E.F.—3rd Battalion occupy a forward sector of the Maginot Line in February—Description of the Ligne de Contact— First patrolling against the enemy—Ringing of church bells in No Man's Land—Activity of the 7th Guards Brigade during the winter

1939   The Maginot Line, the most elaborate system of military defences ever built by man, extended along the Franco-German frontier between Switzerland and Luxembourg. That it was not prolonged by equivalent fortifications on the Franco-Belgian border was due in the first place to an unfortunate economy on the part of the French Government; secondly, to their belief that no German army would ever attempt to force a passage through the wooded mountains of the Ardennes; thirdly, to the difficulty of constructing a fortified zone through the flat, industrial area of Lille and Roubaix; and, fourthly, to the idea that Hitler would never wish to imitate the Schlieffen Plan of 1914 by advancing into France through the Low Countries. Yet, for all their optimism, the French High Command were not happy about their past decisions or their present situation in September, 1939. In all official and semi-official reports from the front it was suggested that the Maginot Line did in fact extend from the Swiss frontier to the sea, and popular war maps of this date showed a thick, black snake winding unbroken from Basel to Dunkirk. When they heard that their role was to line the Belgian frontier, many men of the B.E.F. vaguely expected to find fortifications of the Maginot type already prepared for them. And, though it would be incorrect to suggest that they were bitterly disappointed, they were certainly surprised at the inadequacy of the frontier defences which they found.

There was a single fortified line running about a mile south of the Belgian frontier, consisting of a half-completed anti-tank ditch, covered by concrete pillboxes at intervals of a few hundred yards, in which they placed their light French anti-tank guns. These defences had been thrown up in 1937 (at the expense of the ratepayers of Lille!) and were in only fair condition. It was not by any means a strong line. The frontage of each battalion was between 2,500 and 3,000 yards, more than twice the textbook width. There were no infantry trenches connecting the pillboxes, little wire, no mines or signal communications, no gun positions, and, above all, no secondary lines on

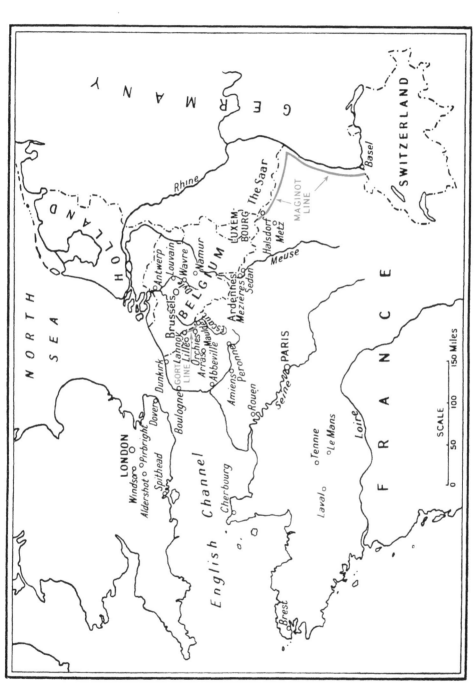

NORTHERN FRANCE

Face page 6

which to fall back if the front line was penetrated, or for the reserve 1939 brigades to occupy in static warfare. Still, it was a beginning, and during the long, cold winter of 1939-40 the B.E.F. had plenty with which to occupy themselves in elaborating the original French defences. It became known as the "Gort Line," named after the Commander-in-Chief, himself an old Grenadier, General The Viscount Gort, V.C.

The two British Corps moved up, one after the other, from their Normandy assembly areas through Rouen to the sector of the Franco-Belgian frontier which had been allotted to them north-east of Arras. In the early stages, the Gort Line was constructed and manned by three out of the four original British divisions. On the right, from *See Map* Maulde to near Orchies, was the 2nd Division; in the centre General *p. 6* Alexander's 1st Division; and on the left General Montgomery's 3rd Division, which extended as far north as Lannoy. The 4th Division was in G.H.Q. reserve near Arras. Within these general boundaries the 1st, 2nd and 3rd Battalions of the Grenadiers were each responsible for a small sector of the line. The 3rd was the first to move into posi- Oct. 3 tion, around the villages of Genech and Bachy, the latter about a mile from the Belgian border: its headquarters was in the Château du Fay. The 1st and 2nd Battalions followed ten days later and occupied the Oct. 13 villages of Annappes (1st Battalion) and Hem and Lannoy (2nd Battalion), where they remained until May.

All battalions set to work immediately. The border country was very slightly undulating, well wooded, and intersected by small streams. The Belgian frontier was not marked by any visible signs on the ground, but it was patrolled by Belgian guards, who had strict instructions to prevent the slightest infringement of their country's neutrality. A shopping or shooting expedition near the border involved the risk of sudden internment, if by chance the limit was overstepped, but from the Belgian side there was a constant traffic of civilians, who either worked legitimately in the French fields and factories, or had come to spy out the land on the enemy's behalf. Of all the front-line troops, the Field Security Police found that they alone were engaged from the start on the duties for which they had been trained. The infantry spent their whole time digging and draining and revetting, day after day. They soon discovered that the water lay very close to the surface, and their trenches became untenable after every shower of rain. To overcome this difficulty, they dug deep sump-pits at the corner of each trench; they made hundreds of wattle fences to shore up the crumbling trench walls; and in many places, especially in the sectors of the 1st and 2nd Battalions, they replaced the trench system by a series of breastworks, which gave them less

1939 protection against bullets but more against water-logging. Simultaneously, great progress was made by the Royal Engineers and reserve brigades on the construction of two reserve lines lying in rear of the Gort Line proper. A new series of concrete pillboxes sprang up, and a new anti-tank ditch was dug by mechanical excavators. By the end of the winter the Gort Line was more or less completed. It was still not strong enough by Maginot standards, and tactically its chief drawback was the lack of any dominating ground from which the artillery could observe, or behind which reserve troops could shelter or form up for counter-attack. But at least there was a continuous, triplicated obstacle; and a trench, a pillbox or a breastwork from which every man could fire his rifle or his gun.

During this period of preparation (the "sitzkrieg," as it was contemptuously called) the Guardsmen lived in whatever buildings lay nearest to their digging sites, marched out each morning to their work, and returned, usually soaked to the skin, just before nightfall. The autumn was terribly wet, the winter bitterly cold, yet their spirits remained extremely high. They knew that they were doing a useful job of work, its completion was within sight, and one day their own lives might depend upon their efforts now. If they were wet and cold, at least the food was good and hot, they had some shelter at night, and after a short time the purchase of hundreds of pairs of French workmen's trousers of blue canvas saved their service dress from the worst of the mud. They were never obliged to man the Gort Line tactically, except on infrequent exercises, when the carrier platoons would advance upon the trenches from the Belgian frontier in simulation of a German tank attack. They worked only in the day time, and at night either remained in their billets or visited the local towns, Lille, Douai or Arras, where the Army welfare services organized a series of clubs and concerts. It was not long before leave to the United Kingdom was allowed, and almost every man in each Battalion had returned at least once to his own home before the coming of spring.

The B.E.F. was therefore perfectly contented. It was half in the war and half out of it. It was a small force (though by May it had increased in size to ten regular divisions and three labour divisions), and it was still considered an exceptional honour to be serving overseas. Guardsmen returning home on leave would not be twitted on their inactivity, nor slyly asked if they had yet seen a German. They found themselves, much to their surprise, regarded with a certain awe, particularly if they had managed to retain on their boots a few splashes of Flanders mud. And although security was tighter than at any subsequent period of the war, they were closely questioned on their routine, their hardships, and the type of defences which they were digging. Out in France the Battalions received a series of highly important visitors. His 1939 Majesty The King toured the front in December, and at other times their sectors were inspected by the Duke of Gloucester, the Duke of Windsor, Mr. Chamberlain, the Secretary of State for War (Mr. Hore-Belisha), the C.I.G.S. (General Ironside), Lord Gort, General Georges (Commander of the Northern Group of Armies), General Giraud, and at frequent intervals by their own divisional commanders, Generals Alexander and Montgomery, whose names at that stage of the war were little known beyond Army circles. The B.E.F. could certainly not complain of neglect.

Early in December Lord Gort had arranged with the French High Command that a British infantry brigade should take its place on the Saar front, ahead of the main Maginot Line, where it would be in direct contact with the outposts of the German Siegfried Line. There were two main reasons for this innovation. First, to give British troops the experience of true active service conditions, of holding a line of trenches under fire, and patrolling forward across a No Man's Land; and, secondly, to counter the current German political propaganda which returned again and again to the last war theme that "the Englishman always fights to the last Frenchman."* One by one the brigades of the B.E.F. began to relieve each other at fortnightly intervals in the same sector of the Franco-German frontier, at Halsdorf, twenty miles north-east of Metz. The turn of the 1st Guards Brigade came in February. The 7th Guards Brigade did not have the same opportunity before the opening of active operations in May.

The Maginot system of defences in the Halsdorf sector consisted in 1940 four separate lines, extending in depth over about ten miles. The first line, the nearest to the enemy, was called the *Ligne de Contact,* which was little more than a line of observation posts, separated by about a mile from the nearest German outposts. The second, lying three miles behind, was the *Ligne de Recueil,* designed as a temporary delaying position, but no more. The third, four miles farther back, was the main Maginot Line—a chain of great subterranean forts. The fourth was a counter-attack line, in which reserve formations could form up to recapture any part of the main system which had fallen into enemy hands. It was the first two of these lines, the *Lignes de Contact et de Recueil,* which were manned by the British brigades. Most of the men

*When the 1st Guards Brigade arrived in the Saar they found the ground littered with German leaflets, which showed an Englishman and a Frenchman standing side by side at the edge of a blood-bath. "One, two, three, jump!" cries the Frenchman. The next picture showed the Frenchman swimming about in the blood-bath and the Englishman beginning to walk slyly away from the edge. "So long, old boy," he says. "Hope you like it."

1940 also had an opportunity to visit the main fortifications, particularly the great fortress of Hackenburg, where they were much impressed, not only by the ingenuity and labour which had gone to its construction but by the contrast between the calm efficiency of the French troops who manned it and the poor equipment and state of training of the field divisions they had met in Northern France. Each Guardsman was presented with the little Maginot medallion, which bore the molten legend "Ils ne passeront pas."

Feb. 11   When the 3rd Grenadiers tramped through the snow on the last stage of their journey to the front they found the *Ligne de Contact* in a deplorable condition. "The posts were ill-sited and badly constructed, not being even bullet-proof," wrote the Adjutant, Capt. C. Earle. The wire was so thin that a couple of rifles weighed it down sufficiently for a man to step across. The platoon posts were located at the outer edge of a wood where every movement showed up against the snow, and there was a quarter-of-a-mile gap between each platoon. There were few dug-outs, but one or two trenches had been covered over for protection against the cold. The Battalion could not do much to improve the defences while there was as much as fourteen degrees of frost and the ground was iron-hard. They did what they could, but for the greater part of each day and night they sat shivering in their slit trenches, looking out over a waste of snow at the German frontier, 1,500 yards away. It was the first time in the Second World War that the Grenadiers had directly confronted their enemies.

In front of them the ground sloped down towards a stream, and rose the other side in an apron of snow-clad fields and small woods, between which nestled the little village of Zeurange, the old French frontier post, which had been evacuated of all its inhabitants at the beginning of the war. A few hundred yards beyond the village was another wood, and at its bottom corner the Grenadiers would sometimes see the slight movement of a German observation post. Hours of patient watching at a telescope might be rewarded by other signs of German occupation. A shutter of a house, which was certainly closed last night, was now seen to have been swung open; a thin column of smoke rising in the early morning from behind the far wood suggested that the Germans were having breakfast, and a score of French shells were directed on the spot; and there was the startling occasion when a German motor-cyclist rode into Zeurange, to return a few moments later with a chicken strapped to his carrier. Otherwise the Germans were remarkably quiescent. They would occasionally shell the British line (the 3rd Battalion had two Guardsmen slightly wounded); and after the Grenadiers had been relieved, the Germans suddenly des-

Mar. 5 cended on a battalion of the Duke of Cornwall's Light Infantry under

cover of a box barrage, and neatly extracted an entire platoon, like a 1940
tooth. The Grenadiers were involved in no sharp conflicts of this sort,
but it was not for want of initiative on their part.

Every night patrols went forward into No Man's Land. In the later
stages of the war patrols were drawn from each company and each
platoon in turn, but during the Maginot period a special patrol force
of about twenty men, trained and led by Lieut. E. W. S. Ford, was
selected from the entire Battalion, and they alone, to the envy of their
comrades, carried out all the patrols. They lived with the equivalent
patrols of the other two battalions of the Brigade in a small frontier-
guard barracks. By day they slept, and observed the small stretch of
territory which was their hunting ground, criss-crossed by the tracks of
their own boots. At night they crept forward in groups, sometimes of
twelve or fifteen, sometimes of no more than three. They were dressed
in rubber boots and makeshift snow camouflage—the Intelligence
Officer, Capt. M. G. D. Clive, had scoured the cookhouses of Metz for
chefs' overalls—and carried grenades, bayonets, and the first American sub-machine guns to be issued to British troops. At first Lieut.
Ford did no more than watch the crossing places over the near stream,
lying out with his men for as long as six hours through a bitterly cold
night and a slow dawn, without the relief of a single movement, a
single word, or a single cough. Later he was allowed to move closer
to the German line. They evolved a careful system. Ahead would go
two men, L./Cpl. Nicholls (who won the Victoria Cross later in the
campaign) and Gdsm. Nash; behind them Lieut. Ford himself; and
behind him, spread out in arrowhead formation, the remainder of his
men. Every fifty yards the patrol would automatically lie down and
listen: then on again, another fifty yards. In this way they slowly
approached the German outposts. At times they were close enough
to hear the German sentries talking, and they noticed that whenever
they approached a certain wood, Ewig ("Earwig") Wood, an owl
would start hooting. Suspecting a German subterfuge,* they beat the
wood from end to end, but found nothing. And never during the entire
patrolling period were they involved in any clash with any Germans
at all. They were greatly disappointed.

It remains to recount one incident which caused a great stir at the
time. It had never been certainly ascertained whether the Germans Feb. 16
occupied the village of Zeurange, for, though Lieut. Ford had often
led his men through it and found nothing, there were indications that
the Germans might be using the church tower as an observation post.
On the last day of the Battalion's occupation of the line, Capt. L. S.

---

*General Alexander would later quote this incident to illustrate the duties of an
intelligence officer. He should find out, he said, whether owls were native to this part
of France or not.

1940 Starkey walked forward in daylight with another officer and one man, all dressed in white sheets, and entered the village at its western end They cautiously advanced up the street. Hearing a scuffle in an upper room of a house, Capt. Starkey crept up the staircase, a grenade ready in his hand, flung open the door—and found an old sow with a litter of piglets on the floor. The three men passed on to the far end of the village. They saw one German, and fired a few shots at him, which missed. On his way back Capt. Starkey entered the suspect church tower, and began ringing the bells in order to produce some sort of reaction from any Germans who might be lurking in the belfry. From above there was no reaction at all, although the bell-ringing continued for about ten minutes, but it soon had the effect of stirring into activity the artillery of both sides. The patrol returned safely, and the incident, which was witnessed by the Duke of Gloucester, and reported with much elation by the B.B.C., was one of the few which enlivened the Battalion's rather dull tenure of the Maginot Line.

The 3rd Grenadiers were relieved by the 2nd Coldstream, and for eight days worked on the defences of the *Ligne de Recueil* before the
Feb. 24 Brigade returned to Metz. The remaining winter months they spent either near their old sector of the Gort Line or training among the 1914-18 battlefields around Arras, or guarding aerodromes and ammunition dumps in the rear areas.

The 7th Guards Brigade had not moved from the Annappes— Lannoy sector which they occupied in October. Day after day and month after month their routine work on the Belgian frontier defences was varied only by the disheartening vagaries of the weather. Their carefully constructed network of trenches would at one moment be gripped in the dead hands of universal frost and snow, and at the next would be rendered useless by the floods which followed the thaw. Only a few events stand out. A German reconnaissance plane would pay infrequent visits to photograph their sector of the line; and the German wireless announced with fair accuracy the location of two out of the three Grenadier Battalions. From time to time small units were detached for guard duties on ammunition dumps, or sent to Paris to take part in international parades. They had little time for field training beyond periodic corps and divisional "manning exercises": and when the 1st Battalion varied the monotony by rifle and Bren-gun practice a complaint was received through diplomatic channels from a lady in Belgium that "a bullet from the west" had entered her bedroom window. The seven dreary winter months were scarcely the best preparation for the period of unprecedented activity which followed.

3

THE GERMAN OFFENSIVE OF 10TH MAY, 1940

*Decision to advance into Belgium if the Germans violated her neutrality—
Plan "D"—The German offensive comes as a surprise—Advance of the
B.E.F. to the River Dyle in Belgium—Occupation of Louvain by 7th
Guards Brigade—1st Battalion beat off the German attack on Louvain—
1st Guards Brigade at Huldenberg—Effect on the B.E.F. of the German
break-through at Sedan—General withdrawal ordered from the Dyle*

As early as the first month of the war the French and British Com- 1940
manders-in-Chief had decided that if the Germans attacked through
Belgium the Allied armies would not remain in the positions which
they had prepared on the Belgian frontier, but would advance into
Belgium to meet the enemy on one or other of the Belgian rivers.
At that time it did not strike the British battalions as strange that they
should be employed in constructing a line which would not be manned
against a German attack. It was not until much later that the regimental officer was even aware of the higher policy. If he did hear of it
he concluded that the object of the Gort Line was to provide a firm
base to which the B.E.F. and flanking armies could fall back if necessary, and still remain firmly linked with the Maginot Line. Furthermore, he appreciated that the strength of the B.E.F. would be more
than doubled during the course of the winter, and by the spring they
would be in a position to discard the original policy of static defence
and adopt the bolder policy of counter-offensive. That much was clear.
But behind General Gamelin's decision there were other reasons. The
Belgians, up to the moment of the German attack, had always refused
to engage in staff talks with the Allies, in order not to prejudice their
neutrality, but it was understood that if they were attacked they
would not only fight back with their own divisions but would immediately appeal for Allied co-operation. The same applied to the Dutch.
Therefore, in order to give maximum assistance to Belgium and
Holland (and, incidentally, to cushion the blow on Northern France,
and protect the Channel coast), General Gamelin prepared a series of
plans, ranging from Plan "A" to Plan "E," almost all of which involved the advance of the Seventh, Ninth and First French Armies
and the B.E.F. into Belgian territory as soon as it was invaded by
German armies from the east. In other words, the entire Allied force
on the Franco-Belgian frontier would swing into the Low Countries
on the pivot formed by the northern extremity of the Maginot Line.

1940
See Map
p. 46
At first the River Escaut (Scheldt) was chosen as the limit of this advance. But on the 16th of November it was finally decided to advance deeper into Belgium, to the line of the River Dyle. This was known as Plan "D," the plan which was actually put into effect. This sector of the Dyle allotted to the B.E.F. lay between Louvain and Wavre, both inclusive. On their left flank would be the Belgian Army, stretched between Louvain and Antwerp; on their right the First French Army, from Wavre to Namur. For the B.E.F. it meant an advance of sixty-five miles from the Gort Line to the Dyle Line.

By Christmas, 1939, Plan "D" had been worked out to its smallest detail, allowing for the refusal of the Dutch and Belgian staffs to discuss the extent of their own co-operation with the Allies in the event of a German attack. In the top-secret files of all three Grenadier Battalions were operation orders which told them exactly when and where they were to move. On one or two occasions during the winter months the B.E.F. had been alerted by strong rumours of an imminent German offensive, and all leave had been cancelled for short periods. But the actual opening of the attack in the early hours of the 10th of May, 1940, came as a surprise. "The tension which had been increasing during April," wrote Lord Gort in his official despatch, "had lessened somewhat during the early days of May. . . . It was not until the night of the 9th/10th of May that information was received of exceptional activity on the frontiers of Luxembourg, Belgium and Holland."

On that day the 3rd Battalion of the Grenadiers were in billets at Nomain on the Belgian frontier, and the 1st and 2nd Battalions at Annappes and Croix respectively. The 3rd Battalion was without its Commanding Officer, as Lieut.-Colonel Sir John Aird had given up his command three days before, and his successor, Major A. H. S. Adair, M.C., was still in England. Major O. W. D. Smith was in temporary command, and there were no more than twenty other officers present with the Battalion. The first they knew of the German attack was at 7 a.m. when the first of the Plan "D" code words was received at Battalion Headquarters. An hour later, as they listened to the B.B.C. news announcing the German invasion of the Low Countries, German bombers were streaming overhead towards Arras, and one or two bombs were dropped in the Battalion's area without causing any casualties.

May 10

The 7th Guards Brigade, fifteen miles away to the north, received the news in much the same way. Lieut.-Colonel J. A. Lloyd had just relieved Lieut.-Colonel G. M. Cornish in command of the 2nd Battalion, and the Commanding Officer of the 1st Battalion, Lieut.-Colonel J. A. Prescott, who was on leave in England, managed to

obtain a seat in the last passenger aeroplane to leave Hendon. At 1940
Croix officers of the 2nd Battalion realized that the rumour was true
only when they found the Chaplain breakfasting in steel helmet, gas-
mask and gas-detector sleeves.

Thereafter events moved quickly. The first British troops crossed
the Belgian frontier at 1 p.m. on the 10th and reached the Dyle un-
opposed at 10.30 that same night. Neither of the two Guards Brigades
was ordered forward until the following day. The 7th Guards Brigade May 11
began to move through Roubaix in troop-carrying vehicles at 7 a.m.
on the 11th, and penetrated deep into Belgium via Oudenarde, Alost
and Vilvorde to a village five miles east of Brussels, where they rested
for the night before continuing on foot the next morning to their
allotted sector of the Dyle Line at Louvain.

The 1st Guards Brigade left Nomain at 10 p.m. on the 11th, crossed
the frontier on foot at about midnight, and after marching twenty-one
miles all through the night via the Belgian town of Tournai reached
Velaines at 6.30 a.m. Here they found awaiting them their new May 12
Commanding Officer, Major Adair. He had left Victoria Station at
10.30 a.m. on the 11th, reached Boulogne at 3 p.m., caught, by the
skin of his teeth, a train to Douai, hired a taxi to drive him to the
Belgian frontier—it was driven by an ex-champion wrestler of France
—and from there took a lift in a British lorry to Velaines, where he
arrived about midnight, less than fourteen hours after leaving
London.

The leading divisions of the B.E.F. continued their advance
through Belgium both by day and by night, partly as a precaution
against air attack and partly because it was recognized to be a race
against time to man the Dyle Line before the German Army also
reached it in strength from the opposite direction. Of all their many May 13
marches during the May campaign this was perhaps the most exhausting. The Guardsmen's feet were still soft, and quickly blistered: their
muscles, unaccustomed to such sudden strain, soon stiffened. The
nights were hot and sultry; the roads crowded with transport which
edged the infantry on to the dusty verges. But at least for the first part
of the journey they were spared two other forms of hardship which
subsequently dogged their every footstep. There were few civilian
refugees moving against the stream of traffic, and the Germans, much
to everyone's surprise, refrained almost entirely from attacking the
long convoys from the air. The B.E.F. did not then realize the significance of this restraint. The Germans had no intention of interfering
with the execution of Plan "D." It suited perfectly their own intention
to break through the hinge of the Dyle and Maginot Lines at Sedan.

The B.E.F. sector of the Dyle was fully manned by the morning of

1940
See Map
p. 46
the 13th of May. Three British divisions were in the front line, six
others in reserve. On the right, as far south as Wavre, was the 2nd
Division (Major-General H. L. Loyd); in the centre lay Alexander's
1st Division (1st Guards Brigade), in the angle between the Rivers
Lasne and Dyle; and on the left Montgomery's 3rd Division (7th
Guards Brigade), which had been allotted the town of Louvain and a
stretch of the river to the south. Ahead of them was the bulk of the
Belgian Army, and a screen of French and British light armoured
columns, who were in contact with the German spearhead. All seemed
fairly peaceful on the 13th. There were disturbing reports of German
advances into Holland and across the Meuse, but when the enemy
first reached the Dyle on the evening of the 13th they seemed in no
hurry to press their attack. The Guards Brigades, after their exhausting march, had a few hours in which to rest, and then began to dig a
close network of slit trenches.

The 7th Guards Brigade, having struggled for the last few miles
against a flood of retreating civilians and Belgian soldiers, arrived at
Louvain to find a chaotic situation. The British had planned their dispositions with care; they intended to hold the line of the wide Dyle
Canal which ran through the centre of the town. But the Belgian
troops, the 6me Chasseurs, had very different ideas. To them Louvain
was not merely a strategic point; it was a city with deep patriotic
associations. They therefore refused to give place to the British
brigade, having received, they said, no orders to this effect, and insisted on manning the railway line which ran through the eastern
outskirts and was a far weaker defensive position than the canal. The
1st Grenadiers were consequently handicapped by a delicate political
situation and a weak tactical position which was not of their own
choosing. They made the best of it. Interspersed among the Belgian
troops, of whose intentions and morale they knew little, the forward
Grenadier platoons were deployed between the marshalling yards and
railway warehouses, both of which had already been heavily bombed.
Stretches of steel rail arched upwards from the track; a number of
goods wagons lay immovable among the wreckage and limited the
field of fire of most section posts to twenty-five or thirty yards. Close
behind them was the Dyle Canal, which could be crossed, when the
bridges were blown up, only by swimming or the use of small boats.
The Chasseurs did not appear at all confident; they had been mobilized only a few days before, and were shaken by the weight of bombs
which had already been dropped. They insisted upon remaining, yet
when the first German assault came they were unable to withstand it,
and by their lack of tactical sense and fighting spirit exposed both

themselves and the Grenadiers to dangers which could well have been 1940 avoided.

When, by the morning of the 14th, the 7th Guards Brigade had May 14 taken up this unpromising position, some sort of order, some sort of pattern, had emerged from the first few hours of chaos. The line was at least continuous and had some depth. On the right, east of the canal, and extending as far as the centre of the town, were the 1st Grenadiers, with No. 3 Company (Major Herbert) on the right, No. 4 Company (Capt. Sir Hugh Cholmeley) on the left, and the King's and No. 2 Companies (Capt. Sir John Little-Gilmour and Capt. D. Fisher-Rowe respectively) in reserve west of the canal. On the Battalion's left was the 1st Coldstream, and in reserve the 2nd Battalion of the Grenadiers. The Belgian troops were buffered between the British battalions.

Before the arrival of the first Germans on the Dyle there were many things to be done apart from the preparation of defensive positions. It was necessary to clear all civilians away from the expected battle zone; to take precautions against the fifth-column snipers and German parachute troops who were reported to be at large among the houses; to remove all advertisements outside cafés (for a rumour was in circulation that these had been carefully planted before the war as guides to enemy troops); but, above all, to institute a security inspection of the refugees who were flooding back across the Dyle, and to prepare the bridges for demolition.

> "The demolition of some of these bridges was a problem in itself," records one contemporary account. "Although the charges and firing equipment had already been placed in position, the constant stream of refugees and vehicles had displaced the wires and fuses. In addition, the task of deflecting the hordes of frantic people from a bridge which they were ardently desirous of crossing and which the Grenadiers were as ardently wishing to blow up, was no mean undertaking. It is regretfully recorded that, in one case, the fuse had been lit and everyone had taken cover when, from out of the blue, there came a Belgian lorry full of troops and ammunition. It was travelling at a high speed, and no one could stop it from reaching the centre of the span just when the charge exploded. The lorry with its cargo disappeared."

The battle of Louvain started on the night of the 14th/15th of May. German pressure was not at first very heavy, and it is doubtful whether the forward platoons were attacked by any larger body of men than a fighting patrol. However, these were sufficient to dislodge the raw Belgian troops, whose first experience this was of actual combat, and when No. 3 Company saw the Belgians gone and their own flank exposed they withdrew to better positions behind the canal. In this withdrawal Lieut. J. E. Seymour was wounded. Farther north, No. 4

C

1940 Company, though not directly attacked themselves, were left with
open flanks by the withdrawal of No. 3 Company and of the Coldstream, and were likewise ordered back to the west bank of the canal.
By midnight enemy pressure had relaxed. The Grenadiers had not
been hardly engaged, and now found themselves in the canal positions
which they had recommended to the Belgians from the start. In spite
of, or rather owing to, their withdrawal, the Battalion emerged from
this slight affair with increased confidence. No hint of a general withdrawal had yet reached them.

May 15   On the next day the enemy were seen to have moved up in strength
to the houses on the far bank of the canal, but the German pressure
was concentrated not on the Grenadiers but on the Coldstream, who
were forced to launch a strong counter-attack with light tanks in order
to regain the canal line. Following the success of the Coldstream, both
battalions retained their positions without difficulty, but were subjected to heavy German shell fire, which continued all through the
16th. At 5.30 p.m. that day Lieut.-Colonel Prescott received the totally
unexpected news that the B.E.F. had been ordered to withdraw west
of Brussels that very night.

Of the 2nd Battalion's activities at this stage little need be said, for
in their reserve positions behind Louvain they were not called upon
to meet their enemy face to face. The Battalion were, however, tactically deployed around the village of Winzele in the centre of the
Brigade's gun area and were subjected not only to air bombardment,
against which their own Bren-gun fire and the R.A.F.'s antiquated
Lysander aircraft were quite ineffective, but to sniping and treachery
by civilian fifth columnists. One example of this carefully planned
organization made a great impression on the Battalion. The occupants
of the farm where their headquarters was lodged decided to leave the
building as the German shelling became more intense. Madame, who
had greeted the Grenadiers two days before with warmth and a flood
of passable English, now bade farewell to her cows, horses and guests,
and left in tears. Two hours later the headquarters was very heavily
and accurately shelled. Their suspicion aroused, the Grenadiers
searched the immediate neighbourhood and found that arrows, point-
ing directly towards the house, had been ploughed into all the adjoining fields. Brigade Headquarters, a mile behind, had been similarly
indicated to spotting aircraft by arrows scythed out of the crops.
Telephone wires were cut as quickly as they could be laid; and
Germans dressed in British uniforms added to the danger and strain.

The 1st Guards Brigade, on arrival at Dyle, had been placed in
reserve to the 1st Division at Huldenberg, two miles east of the junc-

tion between the Dyle and the Lasne. Ahead of them, dug in on the 1940 very banks of the river, were the 2nd Brigade on the left and the 3rd Brigade on the right. The 3rd Grenadiers were disposed in Huldenberg itself, and across the spit of higher ground which separated the two rivers. They could not see the Dyle itself, but the companies dug positions on the reverse slopes from which they could block any German penetration of the river line. In addition to their slit-trench system, they put many of the houses in a state of defence and shored up their cellars. As they worked they were troubled by increasing German air attacks, and by the rumours of fifth columnists which were already beginning to circulate amongst the troops. Undoubtedly these rumours were much exaggerated, and every odd-looking civilian was immediately suspected to be an enemy agent. But there was one genuine case. A man ran through the Battalion's area on two successive nights yelling: "Gas! Gas!" and on each occasion the Guardsmen were made to put on their gas-masks until it was quite certain that the alarm was false. When an actual parachute was seen floating earthwards after a dog-fight overhead, it was too much for the men to resist it. Every Bren gun opened fire on it, and only after it had reached the ground was it discovered to be supporting a British Hurricane pilot, who was quite unharmed by the bullets, but broke his ankle on landing and was in an extremely bad temper. In compensation, the Bren gunners at the Battalion "B" Echelon claimed to have brought down a genuine German aircraft.

On the front of the 1st Division only one attempt was made by the Germans to cross the Dyle, and this was checked by artillery fire, but the 2nd Division on their right faced a more determined effort, and in one or two places the enemy gained a lodgement on the western bank. Less on account of this minor penetration than because of a more serious breach in the line of the neighbouring French division, the 2nd Division was withdrawn from the Dyle to the Lasne, and the 3rd Grenadiers were put temporarily under the command of the 3rd May 15 Brigade to plug any gaps which might open between the right of the 1st Division and the left of the 2nd. It was a depressing sight for the Grenadiers to see the 2nd Division withdrawing over a ridge on their right, and when a rumour of a general withdrawal reached them they thought it was quite impossible. It was nevertheless true.

They knew then only the bare outline of what had occurred. In the extreme north, after a five-day campaign, the Dutch Army had accepted terms of unconditional surrender. In the south the situation threatened to have even more serious consequences for the B.E.F. The Germans, attacking through Luxembourg and the "impenetrable" Ardennes, had crossed the Meuse on the 13th, and two days

1940 later had achieved a complete break-through between Sedan and Mezière. General Corap's Ninth French Army was breaking up into a disorganized rabble, and ten German armoured divisions were pouring through the twenty-mile gap and meeting almost no resistance farther west. The whole Dyle Line was already outflanked, and unless they withdrew immediately they were in danger of encirclement. On the evening of the 15th, when the panzer divisions were already south-*west* of Namur, General Gamelin ordered the withdrawal of the Northern Armies from the Dyle to the Escaut.

The first stage was carried out during the night of the 16th/17th of May. The particular role allotted to the 3rd Grenadiers was to cover the withdrawal of the 3rd Infantry Brigade, and then withdraw themselves, blowing up the Lasne bridges behind them. It was a nervous business, as the enemy were close on the heels of the 3rd Brigade and May 16 well forward on the Battalion's right flank. At 11.50 p.m. the forward companies began to thin out and successfully broke contact with the enemy after an exchange of a few shots in the darkness. The bridge at Huldenberg was blown up on schedule, and the Battalion tramped back to the Forest of Soignies, to be greeted by a swelling chorus of nightingales. "The Commander of the 3rd Brigade," recorded Major Adair, "almost wept with relief when I reported that the Battalion was safely away."

Simultaneously the 1st and 2nd Battalions were on their way back from Louvain. The 2nd Battalion had been ordered to cover the withdrawal of their own 1st Battalion and of the 1st Coldstream from positions of very close contact with the enemy. Major R. B. R. Colvin, as Second-in-Command of the 2nd Battalion, was waiting on the Louvain—Brussels road to check the units through. "It was a queer experience," he later wrote, "as one did not know if the first arrivals would be Guardsmen or Germans. I had two lambs with me who bleated pathetically, and all sorts of other animals turned up looking for a saviour who could give them food and water." The men were all very tired, and out of two Coldstream companies which had borne the brunt of the fighting in Louvain no more than one officer and sixty-three men survived. "The Belgians," continues Major Colvin, "had abandoned their line before the appointed hour, and we could see the German signals going up well behind our left flank. German aeroplanes were dropping flares, and everywhere from our deserted positions one saw spies signalling to the enemy. As one rocket was fired I caught sight of the leading company of the 2nd Battalion coming down the road."

It was four hours before all the British troops were safely through.

4

THE RIVER ESCAUT

First stage of the withdrawal—The situation worsens rapidly—All three Grenadier Battalions in line on the River Dendre—Further retreat to the Escaut—Experiences of the 7th Guards Brigade at Helchin—Attack on the 1st Guards Brigade at Pecq—Grenadier front line temporarily penetrated—Counter-attack by No. 3 Company— L./Cpl. H. Nicholls (3rd Battalion) wins the Victoria Cross—The Germans withdraw and position on the Escaut re-established

The sixty-mile withdrawal from the Dyle to the Escaut was carried 1940 out between the 17th and 19th of May in three stages. The first march took the battalions back to a line just west of Brussels; the second to the River Dendre; the third to the Escaut itself. It was not easy to explain to the troops why this monster withdrawal was necessary. They had barely seen the Germans; they had certainly had little opportunity to fight them face to face. And the experience of the 7th Guards Brigade in Louvain convinced them that they were retreating from in front of troops who were in no way their superior.

The officers had heard no more than vague reports of the southern break-through, and it was perhaps merciful that the full extent of the disaster was not known to them until later. The facts, as they developed after Plan "D" was finally abandoned, were briefly these. On the 18th of May, when the bulk of the B.E.F. was still on the Dendre, the tip of the German scythe had penetrated as far as Amiens. With five panzer divisions in that area they had only a short distance to cover before they reached Abbeville and the sea coast at the mouth of the River Somme. The bastion of Arras was still held by the 1st Welsh Guards (Lieut.-Colonel Copland-Griffiths), and Lord Gort gathered in all the spare units he could find to form a southern flank. (St. Pol, for example, was garrisoned by a mobile bath unit.) "In my opinion," Lord Gort later wrote, "there was imminent danger of the forces in the north-eastern area, that is to say, the French forces next to the sea, the Belgian Army, the B.E.F , and the bulk of the 1st French Army on our right, being irretrievably cut off from the main French forces in the South." With the German capture of Abbeville on the 20th of May, the day on which the Grenadiers occupied the Escaut Line, Lord Gort's apprehensions became a reality. "The picture," he wrote, "was no longer that of a line bent or temporarily broken, but of a besieged fortress."

The one consoling feature of a situation which was daily growing worse was that there was no great frontal pressure on the B.E.F. and

1940 no threat to their immediate line of retreat. They were cushioned between the Belgians and the French, with whom they withdrew in conformity step by step back to the Escaut. It was a terrible march. They felt upon their backs the accusing eyes of the Belgian civilians, as if they were a disgraced, defeated army, instead of an army which had been given no chance to show their worth. Some of them were marching back along the same roads up which they had advanced so confidently six days before. There had been cheers then, cheers of

May 17 welcome and encouragement, but now they met only with bitter looks of scorn and disappointment. A company of the 3rd Battalion which took a wrong turning in Brussels doubled back on their tracks for a short distance before they rejoined the right road, and during that brief space of time new hope gathered in the eyes of the Bruxellois; they began to cheer: the Allies were returning to the front. When they saw the company heading once more westwards, the cheers died away, and the Grenadiers did not see Brussels again until they entered the city at the head of the Guards Armoured Division on the 3rd of September, 1944.

For the greater part of the distance both Guards Brigades marched on foot twenty miles, on an average, in each day. When they reached their halting place it was not to rest but to dig a new line of trenches, only to be ordered back once more before they had time to put them to the test of battle. The long roads were crowded with transport, sometimes moving even slower than the infantry, sometimes halted for hours on end in paralysed blocks. On one side of the road was the military traffic, two or three vehicles abreast; on the other, all moving in the same direction, long lines of civilian refugees: old men and women pushing prams and wheelbarrows loaded with all their worldly goods; mothers with babies on their backs trudging wearily through the dust; small farm carts, crammed with twenty people apiece, fighting for a place among the luxury cars of the well-to-do. And in and out of the thin lanes left between the lines of traffic marched the British infantry, footsore and immensely tired. From time to time German aircraft would streak overhead, bombing and machine-gunning the column, soldiers and refugees alike, but mostly the refugees. To one officer, the chief memory of this march is the sight of an old woman, blood-stained and with a dead baby in her arms, rising from the ditch to shake her fist at the disappearing bombers. Another tells of a field where hundreds of crowded refugees had been cut to pieces by a dozen Dornier aircraft. It was the most terrible sight, he said, which he had witnessed throughout the war.

May 18   On arrival at the River Dendre, after their second march on two successive nights, all three Grenadier Battalions found themselves by chance side by side in the same sector of the line. The 3rd Battalion, 1940 in the outskirts of Ninove, was the left-hand unit of the 1st Division; the 1st Battalion the right-hand unit of the 2nd Division; and the 2nd Battalion, at Okhegem, were on the left of the 1st. There was a gap of a mile between the 1st and 3rd, and they made contact with each other only by liaison officers and patrols along the river bank.

The 3rd Battalion covered the two main bridges leading over the Dendre into Ninove, and were closely overlooked by two factories standing on the river bank nearer to the enemy. The Germans did not arrive until nightfall. The bridges were blown up ahead of them, and they made no attempt to press forward until daylight, when the Grenadiers were in the middle of their relief by a battalion of the Queen's Regiment.

There was a short period of anxiety before the Battalion was safely away. Enemy snipers with machine pistols harried the relief, and one of them killed 2/Lieut. P. Baring as he led the incoming platoon into position. He was the first Grenadier officer to lose his life in this war.

A few miles farther north the 1st Battalion were watching the stretch of the Dendre south of Okhegem, while the 2nd Battalion guarded the crossings at Okhegem itself. It was on the latter that the heavier responsibility was placed, for in the 1st Battalion's sector the river banks were too marshy to give the German assault troops a footing for attack. At 9 a.m. on the 18th the British cavalry screen withdrew west of the river, the bridge was blown, and the 2nd Battalion awaited confidently the appearance of the Germans. Surprisingly, the first arrivals were two German officers driving a blue saloon car, followed by twenty cyclists (pedalling, it was said, in step). The car was halted by an anti-tank rifle which Capt. Johnstone had at hand, and the cyclists, who took cover in a farm, were dealt with by the Battalion's 3-inch mortars. Soon afterwards German reconnaissance troops began firing across the river, and Okhegem itself was found to be filled with German sympathizers, who caused the Grenadiers great discomfort from the rear. R.S.M. Pratt was among those who were severely wounded by these fifth columnists. Half the Battalion were therefore obliged to turn their backs on the river and search the town for snipers, while the other half continued to engage their more orthodox enemy on the far bank and guard against any attempt to cross under cover of darkness. This uneasy situation continued until the Brigade withdrew early the next morning. The 2nd Battalion crawled back from their forward posts after daylight had broken, and, although they were not unduly harassed as they broke contact, their motor column was shelled continually for the first seven miles of the retreat. They were fortunate not to lose more than four men.

1940
May 19   So the retreat continued, from the Dendre to the Escaut. "It was a brilliantly fine day," wrote Major Adair, "and I suppose there has seldom been a more remarkable feat than the withdrawal of a whole Corps along completely open roads in broad daylight with enemy air superiority, but it had to be risked, and it was successfully accomplished. We were shelled and bombed a certain amount, but the casualties were light. We were carried in buses a part of the way, but the march was terribly long and tiring, owing to the congested roads, dust and heat. I have never seen the men more exhausted, and it was only by sheer will-power that they reached their positions on the Escaut."

The B.E.F. held the stretch of the Escaut between Oudenarde and Maulde on the Franco-Belgian border. The sector of the 1st Guards Brigade lay south of the village at Pecq: the sector of the 7th Guards Brigade at Helchin. The latter, whose experiences at this stage were the less trying of the two Brigades, were deployed in approximately the same positions as had been envisaged for them in the original Allied plans, when the B.E.F. was to have advanced no deeper into Belgium than the Escaut Line. "How wise we should have been," lamented one officer, "to have stuck to it!" Both the Grenadier Battalions were forward of the river, the 1st Battalion on the right, the 2nd, centred on Helchin itself, on the left. The Escaut ran through a wide stretch of flat, marshy ground, forcing the defenders to dig their trenches in sodden soil, unprotected by natural camouflage, and unapproachable in daylight except by ditch-crawling. The bridges were blown, and a dam opposite the 1st Battalion's sector was plugged with barbed wire, for they were advised that its total demolition would reduce the water up-stream to a dangerously low level.

May 20   Once again the Guardsmen waited for the first lappings of the grey German tide to beat against their makeshift defences; and once again it was opposite the sector of the 2nd Battalion that the enemy's main forces assembled. Our men were by this time so tired that their vigilance had relaxed. An officer, going forward to inspect the outer companies, suddenly saw three Germans crawling back undetected from within twenty yards of a Grenadier section post. He sounded the general stand-to, and half an hour later a German barrage of great intensity began to fall upon the western tip of the river. The subsequent attack was repulsed. Not a German soldier was allowed to set foot upon the near bank, and their storm troopers were withdrawn out of assaulting range, but not out of view. On the contrary, the Grenadiers were thereafter spectators of the assemblage of a large force on the far side of the Escaut. They watched the arrival of battalions of lorried infantry, the cumbersome erection of bridging materials, even the conferences of staff officers armed with flapping

THE DEFENCE OF THE RIVER ESCAUT** 25
THE DEFENCE OF THE RIVER ESCAUT

maps. Faced by these menacing preparations, the Grenadiers were 1940
then informed that there would be no more ammunition for their
supporting artillery for the next thirty-six hours, and probably no
more rations. The latter did not worry them unduly, for they could
live on the countryside, but the lack of ammunition was very serious
indeed. Fortunately, the enemy did not renew their attempts to cross
the Escaut, and the Grenadiers were more concerned with the ubiquitous civilian snipers, of whom the 2nd Battalion executed no fewer
than seventeen in one day.

At Pecq the 1st Guards Brigade were digging their positions during
the night of the 20th of May. The 2nd Coldstream guarded the *See Plan*
approaches from the river to the village itself, and the 3rd Grenadiers *p. 28*
were on their right, with three companies forward on the river bank,
and Battalion Headquarters and No. 3 Company a mile behind round
Bailleul. The whole sector was overlooked by Mont St. Aubert, which
lay in German hands two miles east of the river: from the monastery
buildings which crowned its summit the Germans could observe every
movement on the British side. However, at dawn all seemed quiet. A
heavy mist lay over the water. The men relaxed after the normal
morning stand-to, and some of them began to wash and prepare their
breakfasts. At that moment, at 7.30 a.m., the Germans attacked.   May 21

They had not been observed as they formed up, because the mist,
the high corn and odd clumps of trees had hidden their preparations
on the far bank. The first that the Grenadiers knew of the attack was
a sudden and very violent mortar and machine-gun barrage along the
whole width of the Brigade sector, and, though it was soon answered
by the British artillery, the Germans were already pouring across the
river (which was slightly wider than the Basingstoke Canal, and
abnormally shallow), and beached their rubber boats on the western
bank. The main assault fell at the boundary between the Grenadiers
and Coldstream. Swinging left-handed, the storm troopers overran
some of No. 4 Company's trenches, and pressed on, slightly inland, to
cut off No. 2 Company from their headquarters. The Grenadiers
immediately launched two counter-attacks. The first was led by Major
W. R. J. Alston-Roberts-West (No. 4 Company) in a great effort to
regain his lost trenches, but it failed. He himself and one of his
platoon commanders, 2/Lieut. A. N. Boyd, were killed in the attempt.
The second was a composite counter-attack by 2/Lieut. L. P. Aubrey-
Fletcher's platoon of No. 1 Company (Capt. P. T. Clifton) and a few
men of Nos. 2 and 4 Companies under Capt. P. J. C. Radford-Norcop.
They seized a ridge behind No. 4 Company's old position, but only a
handful reached the river bank, among them Lieut. C. G. Ford. Many

1940 others became casualties, including Capts. Clifton and Radford-Norcop, and Lieut. The Master of Forbes, who were all wounded.*

The situation was truly critical. An unknown number of determined and heavily armed Germans had already driven a wedge between the Coldstream and the Grenadiers, and were threatening to roll up the Battalion's entire line from north to south. There was only one reserve company, No. 3, and Major Adair took with him its commander, Capt. L. S. Starkey, to find out the extent of the damage. From the higher ground in rear they could see the Germans working round behind the front companies between the river and the main Pecq—Roubaix road. At intervals a whole line of figures in blue-grey uniforms would rise together from the corn (which was standing waist-high in the fields), double forward a few yards, and then sink down out of sight. No. 3 Company were sent forward from Bailleul with orders not merely to block the widening gap between the Coldstream and Grenadiers, but to drive the enemy back to their own side of the river.

At about 11.30 a.m. Capt. Starkey hurriedly assembled his men in their forming-up position in a road ditch, and began to advance under the cover of a thin smoke screen down to the square cornfield which was the centre of the German bridgehead. All went well at the start, for the Grenadier 3-inch mortars were ranged exactly on the German positions and effectively kept down the enemy's heads. Then the mortar crews stopped firing, thinking quite mistakenly that No. 3 Company was too close for safety; Capt. Starkey had no means of communicating with them except by runner, and in a situation of this sort a runner is far too slow. As soon as his men entered the western edge of the cornfield they came under heavy fire which they were unable to return. While they lay low among the corn-stalks they were hidden and fairly safe; but as soon as they raised their heads to fire back or double forward, a stream of bullets raked the corn-tops. After a short while, the company commander saw that there were two main groups of enemy machine guns, one down by the river among No. 4 Company's old trenches, and one farther west on a slight ridge backed by a line of poplars ("Poplar Ridge" on sketch map). He divided his company into two parties, with the intention of approaching each of the German groups from a different direction. A section of carriers under Lieut. H. Reynell-Pack covered the advance by machine-gun fire from behind and between the two converging arms. The right-hand party, of two Grenadier platoons, led by the company second-in-command, Capt. R. E. Abel Smith, rushed forward cheering, and

---

*Capt. Radford-Norcop did not recover from his wounds. He died nearly two months later in England.

**Lance-Corporal
H. NICHOLLS, V.C.**

Dunkirk, June, 1940.

Photo: Illustra

1940

made some progress towards the Escaut before they were over-whelmed by the intensity of the German fire. Their casualties were already very heavy. Capt. Abel Smith and one of his platoon commanders, Lieut. The Duke of Northumberland, who was last seen waving on his men with his ash stick, were killed outright, and the survivors could do no more than sink back into the corn, still about two hundred yards short of the river. At this moment Lieut. Reynell-Pack decided that he could best assist No. 3 Company by moving his carriers forward, as if they were light tanks, and charged the German machine-gun posts head-on. He almost succeeded. Unfortunately, the movement of the carriers over the rough ground made it impossible to fire from them with any accuracy, and they were soon caught in a cone of German bullets, some of which penetrated the steel sheeting of their sides. Lieut. Reynell-Pack himself was killed in the leading carrier, about fifty yards short of Poplar Ridge.

The left-hand party, consisting of Capt. Starkey, his headquarters and the remaining platoon, had seen the failure of this attack, and realized that the men who were still left alive in the centre of the cornfield would have little chance of escape if the machine guns on Poplar Ridge were not annihilated. The little group accordingly began to move forward nearer to the ridge. Among them was L./Cpl. H. Nicholls. He soon outstripped all his fellows except for his old comrade, Gdsm. Nash, who remained at his side to supply him with ammunition from his pouches. Nicholls, in the words of his citation, "picked up a Bren gun, and dashed forward towards the German machine guns, firing from the hip. He succeeded in silencing first one and then two machine guns, in spite of being again wounded in the head [he had received his first wound in the arm as he was moving up with his platoon]. He then proceeded to crawl forward on to a high piece of ground [above the poplars] and engaged the German infantry massed behind, causing many casualties, and continued his fire until he had no more ammunition left." He was wounded four times in all, and finally taken prisoner of war. Nicholls's action was not only superbly brave but it immediately affected the whole course of the battle. In the first place, he saved his comrades in the cornfield from almost certain annihilation; and in the second place (though this was not known until later), he alone had inflicted such losses on the enemy that they withdrew all their survivors across the river, no longer having the strength to press on or even to remain.

Nicholls was awarded the Victoria Cross, the first to be gained by any soldier in the Second World War. On the evidence of those who had seen him lying desperately wounded in German hands he was officially posted as "Missing, believed killed." His wife received his

1940 high decoration from the hands of His Majesty The King, but in September, 1940, he was reported to be alive and well in a German hospital, and survived the remainder of the war.

It was now about 1 p.m. The Battalion had sealed off the German penetration of the Escaut Line, but they were too weak to regain the lost trenches on the river bank. Capt. Starkey found himself with no more than four Guardsmen under his immediate control: the remainder were either dead, wounded, prisoners of war, or engaged in a grim game of hide-and-seek with the German snipers in the corn. Having exhausted his last reserves, Major Adair drew back the remnants of Nos. 2, 3 and 4 Companies to new positions between Bailleul and the main road, leaving No. 1 Company on the river bank, and bringing up two companies of the 2nd Hampshires, which were placed under his command, to positions of close support to the Grenadiers. Not much could be done at this stage to extricate the wounded. Major Starkey managed to load about half a dozen on to the only carrier which was still in running order, but of the remainder the majority lay out all that night.

Towards dusk Lieut. E. W. S. Ford led a patrol, composed of the Battalion tailor and other men of the headquarters, to the river bank. They found it deserted. The enemy had crossed back to their own side. There were several German bodies at the water's edge, and about thirty more round the poplars. Our own men who were taken prisoner later told how they had been ordered by their captors to dig graves for the German dead before they themselves were ferried back across the river. It cannot be doubted that it was the number of their casualties, and nothing else, which forced the Germans to withdraw. The Grenadiers had beaten back the storm troopers as effectively as if they had actually recaptured their own trenches. Our losses had also been very heavy: five officers were dead, three others wounded; and among the other ranks the total casualties were 180. It was the first serious battle in which the Grenadiers had been engaged since 1918.

May 22 That night and the next morning were comparatively quiet. The Grenadiers reoccupied the river line with two composite companies under Capts. Starkey and R. N. Brinckman. Every effort was made to bring back the wounded who were still lying out, and in this D./Sergt. Randall did particularly heroic work under heavy fire from across the river.

May 23 At 3 a.m. the 3rd Battalion withdrew from the Escaut on orders, and marched back across the French frontier to the Gort Line near Roubaix.

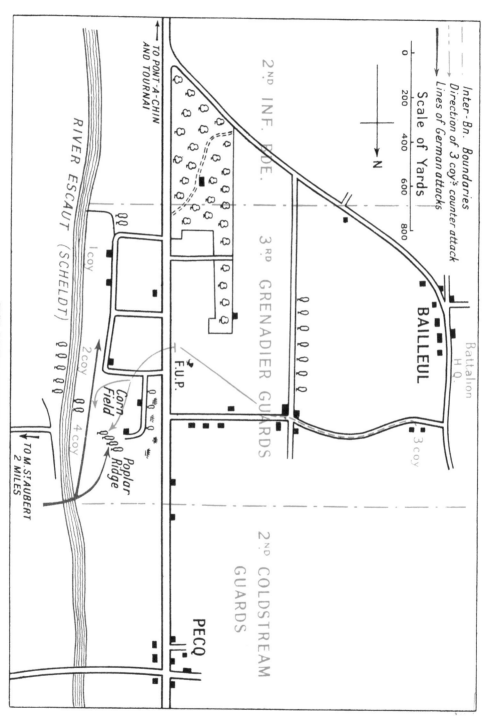

THE RIVER ESCAUT

5

THE YPRES—COMINES CANAL

General situation on 23rd May—Both Guards Brigades occupy the Gort Line—Orders received to retreat to Dunkirk—3rd Battalion suddenly switched to counter-attack the line of the Ypres-Comines Canal—A gallant and successful action—Capt. Brinckman's account—Battalion Headquarters attacked—Heavy casualties—Further withdrawal ordered

The Gort Line was at last put to its intended use, as a defence against **1940** a German attack through Belgium into Northern France. But how different, how fatally different, was the present situation from that which had been envisaged in September, 1939! Instead of confronting the enemy fairly and squarely, facing in one direction only, with their supply lines, their headquarters and reserves laid out neatly and securely behind them, the B.E.F. could not now regard their own line as anything more than a temporary delaying position. It was already deeply outflanked to the south, and unless the situation was very carefully watched the Gort Line might become a trap for the entire force.

Let us, as it were, stop the cameras and examine the general situation as it was on the evening of the 23rd of May, the day on which the two Guards Brigades filed back to the Gort Line. A French army was in position from the Scheldt estuary to the neighbourhood of Ghent: the line of the River Lys was the responsibility of the Belgian Army, which was very weak and much dispirited, but for the moment not under heavy attack. At Menin the B.E.F. with seven divisions, linked up with the Belgians, and manned the Gort Line (which ran almost at right angles to the Lys) as far as the area of Orchies. On their right was the French First Army in the quadrilateral Valenciennes—Douai—Orchies—Maulde. These four armies together held the eastern front. But there was also a southern front, manned by a scratch force of Lord Gort's lines-of-communication troops, which ran Douai—Bethune—St. Omer—Gravelines. It formed the northern flank of the great corridor which the Germans had driven from the Maginot Line to the sea. The southern side of this corridor, along which lay the larger part of the French Army, ran some ten miles south of a line Peronne—Amiens—Abbeville. The Welsh Guards were withdrawn from Arras on the 23rd. Boulogne, which was defended for forty-eight gruelling hours by two battalions of the 20th Guards Brigade (Brigadier W. A. F. L. Fox-Pitt), was completely encircled, and so was Calais. The Armies of the North were therefore cut off from the

1940 Armies of the South, and the Germans had at least five armoured divisions at the head of their corridor which at any moment might cut the Allies off from their two remaining ports, Ostend and Dunkirk.

While London and Paris urged on their field commanders the necessity for an immediate attack both north and south of the German corridor, Lord Gort knew on the 23rd that the time for that had already passed. He had used up all his reserves in manning the southern front; the Belgians were too far away; and the French First Army too exhausted. South of the German corridor only General Charles de Gaulle's armoured division had any punch left in them, and his attack, being almost unsupported, failed. The alternative idea of withdrawing the Allied forces through Dunkirk, to save what they could from the wreckage, had been suggested by Lord Gort to the British Cabinet as early as the 19th of May, and was considered in London to be "unlikely," a last desperate resort. Meanwhile it was through Dunkirk that the B.E.F. were now supplied, and their casualties evacuated by hospital ship. On the 23rd they were put on half rations, and their ammunition supplies in Belgium were sufficient for no more than four days more.

Very little of this was known even to the officers of the two Guards brigades as they returned to the Gort Line. The order which halved their ration scales caused some surprise, but the troops scarcely noticed the difference, because the Quartermasters of the three Grenadier Battalions (Lieut. R. S. Walker, 1st Battalion, Lieut. A. Aston, 2nd Battalion, and Lieut. G. F. Turner, D.C.M., 3rd Battalion) sent their butchers into the fields to round up the straying cattle, and many of the empty houses yielded abundant supplies of food, to which the Guardsmen were allowed to help themselves. Indeed, most of them admitted that they had never fed better. During these crucial days from the 23rd to the 26th of May, when the fate of entire empires was at stake, the part of the B.E.F. which lay in the centre of the Gort Line was hardly disturbed. For the first time since the 10th of May they had time to rest.

The 1st and 2nd Battalions were strung out between Wattrelos and Roubaix. The 1st were responsible for a series of canal bridges and cross-roads; the 2nd for the tangled slums of Roubaix itself. "The crowded population of this slum area was a terrible problem," wrote Major Colvin. "The civil authorities had fled several days before, leaving the people to starve. All the big factory owners had also decamped without paying the last week's wages, so we found a population which was tired, hungry, penniless, and very angry. When the sappers started to blow down whole rows of houses to clear our field of fire, and the German artillery came up within range, the civilians

began to move away. I have never been more sorry for anyone than 1940
these poor people, deserted by their country's leaders, starting off in a
westerly direction, knowing that all the roads would be bombed and
machine-gunned, and that the Germans were already across their line
of retreat to any other part of France."

Left to themselves, the Guardsmen set to work on a part of the Gort
Line which had been sadly neglected during the winter months, and
in a single night converted the industrial area into a reasonable state
of defence. The enemy did not attack. Bombing there was, and considerable shell fire (to which the British could answer with no more
than five rounds per gun per day), but only on the last of the three
days did German troops approach within patrolling distance. By this
time a further withdrawal had been ordered to Dunkirk. The Battalions were told to abandon all but their most essential equipment.
The 1st Battalion hid their surplus between the bales of wool in a
factory occupied by their headquarters, and the 2nd dumped all they
could spare, including new boots and uniforms never yet worn, into
the Roubaix Canal, "with the stealth of a murderer burying his kill."

The 3rd Battalion was at first in reserve to the 1st Guards Brigade, May 27
and when they moved up into the Gort Line proper on the outskirts
of Roubaix they, too, were disappointed to find that the state of the
defence works was far inferior to that of the sector which they themselves had built during the winter fifteen miles to the south-east. They
found little more than the block-houses and anti-tank ditch. However,
the line was never put to the test of battle. "One German," wrote
Major Adair, "crawled right up to the wire of our left block-house
with his bicycle. He then stood up and looked along the line of wire,
quite unconcerned, as if he did not realize that anyone was near. When
he recovered from his surprise our sentry opened fire, and the German
fell flat. Soon he was crawling away. . . . He was a lucky man, as
our marksmen had an off-day. There followed a considerable amount
of sniping, but the Germans did not press forward." The only other
incident of note was the sudden betrayal by fifth columnists. "One
bomb hit a glasshouse in the garden, shattering it to pieces, but the
golden pheasants in a cage a yard or two away escaped quite unhurt."
That night the Battalion were again withdrawn, no longer to the south-
west, for that way was barred, but north-west, towards Dunkirk. They
halted, after a twenty-mile march, on the far side of the River Lys, at
Le Touquet, north of Armentieres.

The reason which lay behind this further withdrawal was that the
Belgians were beginning to give way under German pressure at
Menin, the junction of the Lys with the Gort Line. "The pattern of

1940 the enemy pincer attack was now becoming clearer," wrote Lord Gort. "One movement from the south-west on Dunkirk had already devel oped and was being held: the counterpart was now developing on the Belgian front." He decided that in order to protect the B.E.F.'s vital communications with Dunkirk it was necessary to prolong the British lines along the old Ypres—Comines Canal, and beyond it as far as the River Yser, on which the Belgians might re-form. The only troops available were the British 5th and 50th Divisions, which had been earmarked for a counter-attack against the German corridor. Faced by the imminent collapse of the Belgian Army, the French agreed to cancel the southern counter-attack, and Lord Gort telegraphed to the War Office: "I must not conceal from you that a great part of the B.E.F. and its equipment will inevitably be lost even in the best circumstances."

For the moment, while naval and military preparations were acceler ated for the defence of Dunkirk, and for the evacuation of the armies from its port and neighbouring beaches, a great deal depended on the defence of the Ypres—Comines Canal. It was the first testing point of the strength of the Dunkirk perimeter. If the Germans were to reach Ypres before the bulk of the B.E.F. they might also be the first into Dunkirk, and that would be the end.

May 27   The 3rd Battalion had not been sent back from Roubaix to form part of the new line, and indeed only a few hours after they had arrived at Le Touquet, Major Adair received a written message from Brigadier Beckwith-Smith ordering him to march immediately to Dunkirk and embark. Only a few minutes later a staff officer of the II Corps dashed into Battalion Headquarters and told them that the line of the 5th Division had given way just north of Comines, and the Battalion, being one of the few immediately available, was to be put under the command of the 5th Division (Major-General Franklin) to retake the lost ground. The information was very vague. Nobody *See Sketch* knew the exact depth of the German penetration. The 6th Black *p. 36* Watch had already gone ahead between the railway and the Lys, but there was no news of their progress. The Grenadiers were to move up the centre, with a railway on their right and the 2nd North Stafford shires on their left. Zero hour was 8 p.m., and the start line the road running south-east from Messines. There were no other orders.

Consider the feelings of the Commanding Officer at this moment. During the previous night his Battalion had covered twenty miles which he described as "perhaps the most trying march of all," in single file, through stifling dust and along roads which were choked with British and French vehicles. On arrival they had begun to dig positions on the River Lys, only to be told to pack up and withdraw to Dunkirk. This news, depressing as it was, at least promised them 1940 some relief from the strain of endless marching and fighting. Then came the second message. Divorced from their own familiar Division and Brigade—whom they were not to see again until they reassembled in England—without even the time to snatch some food, the Battalion now had a further nine miles to march before they reached their start line, and from there it was a three-mile advance over unknown country to attack an enemy whose strength and exact positions were likewise unknown. It was a test of endurance and high morale to which the Guardsmen responded splendidly. An outside observer, a gunner officer, later wrote: "The Grenadiers seemed fresh and in good spirits . . . it was a lovely evening with a glorious sunset, and the Guardsmen marched away towards the line as if they were on parade at home." And another wrote: "A line of men appeared from behind the O.P. and advanced towards the enemy. They were followed by another line, who advanced through the first. I found out that they were the Grenadier Guards. I watched them until they disappeared into the trees and behind the hedges. They seemed to me to be carrying out a model attack. It was a fine and inspiring sight, and I shall never forget it."

Major Adair had deployed his Battalion in the form of a square. No. 2 Company (Capt. R. N. Brinckman, D.S.O.) was forward on the right; No. 1 Company (Lieut. R. Crompton-Roberts, M.C.) forward on the left; No. 4 Company (Capt. C. W. Norman-Barnett) right rear; No. 3 Company (Capt. L. S. Starkey) left rear. Battalion Headquarters and the mortar and carrier platoons were in rear of them. The "B" Echelon transport, under Capt. M. G. D. Clive and Lieut. (Qrmr.) Turner, were sent back to Dunkirk, and after many adventures rejoined the Battalion in England. The "A" Echelon transport, under Major A. S. P. Murray and Lieut. F. J. R. P. Needham, were stationed on the Lys at Warneton.

At 8.30 p.m. the Battalion crossed the start line. No. 2 Company used the railway line as a convenient guide to their objective, and the remainder advanced in a fairly compact group within sight of them. There was no sign of either the North Staffordshires on their left or of the Black Watch on their right. For the first two miles the advance was fairly smooth. Only odd shots were fired in their direction, and these were poorly aimed. But when it grew dark and they were approaching the canal the Battalion were drawn apart by the obstacles they encountered—the wire fences bordering the fields, the little woods, the streams and hidden ditches. As the leading companies topped the last rise before the canal they saw a farm blazing in front of Comines and the men of the Black Watch charging forward with

D

1940 fixed bayonets, silhouetted against the flames. The whole front was lit up by tracer bullets as Nos. 1 and 2 Companies began the ascent of the final slope up to the canal, and their casualties began to mount. Capt. Brinckman was hit by a piece of mortar bomb in the thigh, and soon afterwards twice more by machine-gun bullets. His two platoon commanders were killed. He was, however, still in touch with Lieut. Crompton-Roberts's company. "I ran across to him," wrote Capt. Brinckman, "and said that there was only one thing to do. 'We must charge these few Germans here at the point of the bayonet. When I get back to my company I will blow a whistle, and we will get up and go for them.' This we did and, getting amongst the Germans, we disposed of them all on our side of the canal. I received another wound in the left thigh at this time, but nothing to count."

Capt. Brinckman's account continues:

"I seemed to have practically no men left now; in fact, I had Sergt. Ryder (already wounded in the hip) and one Guardsman. There was a cottage on the canal which seemed to be the centre of activity of some German soldiers. I had five hand grenades on my haversack and four of these I threw into the window of the cottage. Those Germans who were not killed or wounded fled back across a small bridge on to the other side of the canal. I said to Sergt. Ryder: 'We are on our objective, but we must get hold of some more men.' I sent the Guardsman back to Major Adair along the railway line as I had previously arranged. Sergt. Ryder and myself then proceeded to crawl back to where I had left my reserve platoon. On the way back I was hit again through the back of the right knee and became unable to walk or crawl. I think Sergt. Ryder was also hit again, both of us by unlucky stray shots. I lay there for some time hoping that either my rear platoon commander would come forward or that, if my runner succeeded in getting back to Battalion Headquarters, we might perhaps receive some more support. I found myself bleeding very heavily and decided that my mortar wound was the worst. I put on my first field dressing, took off my tie and made a tourniquet above it. Probably due to fatigue and lack of sleep and also loss of blood, I think I must have fainted, because the next thing I remember was finding myself in daylight on a bed in the very cottage into which I had thrown the grenades the night before, with a German soldier, very much alive, standing over me, and two or three dead Germans lying on the floor around the bed. Through the door was another small bedroom, and on the bed I saw Sergt. Ryder, who was alive but evidently in great pain."*

Nos. 1 and 2 Companies had been all but annihilated by their splendid efforts. Lieut. R. Crompton-Roberts led a patrol forward to

---

*Before his wounds were properly healed, Capt. Brinckman escaped from a German hospital and made his way via Marseilles to Tunis. He was recaptured by French police in Algeria, but later released on the grounds that he would never be fit for further active service, and returned to England via Tangier and Gibraltar in the summer of 1941.

find No. 2 Company and bring back their wounded, but he was never **1940**
seen again, and much later it was discovered that he had been killed.
The only other officer in these two companies, 2/Lieut. L. P. Aubrey-
Fletcher, was wounded and taken prisoner. Capt. Brinckman's runner
never reached Battalion Headquarters with news of their success. The
Germans had time to recross the canal before the two rear companies
arrived, and the Battalion was obliged to take up a position a quarter
of a mile west of the canal. Having no tools with which to dig proper
trenches, they lined a field ditch, deepening it slightly with their
bayonets. No. 4 Company (Capt. Norman-Barnett) was on the right
flank, No. 3 Company (Capt. L. S. Starkey) on the left, and a little way
forward were the survivors of No. 1 Company, under Sergt. J. Wood,
D.C.M. In these positions the Battalion held off German attacks **May 28**
during the whole of the following day. In front of the ditch there was
a downward slope, open for about 150 yards, which the Battalion kept
covered by their machine guns pushed slightly ahead of the main
infantry line. The German method of attack, which was repeated
several times during the day, was to follow behind a heavy mortar
barrage in groups of fifteen to twenty, spaced out in wide, arrow-head
formation. The Grenadiers waited until they were close enough to see
the detail of their equipment (the Germans, strangely enough, were all
dressed in greatcoats) and then opened up with a stream of bullets
which could scarcely miss their mark. Gdsm. Diamond, for example, a
Bren gunner of No. 3 Company, bowled over ten or twelve men with
the first bursts of his gun. The enemy then withdrew out of sight, and
in a few moments a belt of fire descended on the Bren posts; but this
had been foreseen, and the gunners were back out of harm's way. The
same performance was then repeated. The Bren gunners returned: so
did the Germans; and a second and third time they were beaten back.
From behind, the 3-inch mortars, under P.S.M. H. Wood, D.C.M.,
supported the forward companies with an accurate torrent of bombs.

Casualties were not at this stage very severe (among them was
2/Lieut. J. H. Lane-Fox, who was wounded), and the Grenadiers felt
confident that they could hold their ditch indefinitely against such
futile tactics, provided that they had the ammunition. Food and water
they could do without, and did, but their precious supply of bullets
was sinking lower and lower. Finally Lieut. E. W. S. Ford attempted
to return to Battalion Headquarters with a carrier load of wounded.
Before he had gone very far, the carrier was set on fire by a German
anti-tank rifle. He reached the headquarters on foot, and two more
carriers were loaded with ammunition. These he successfully brought
back to the companies, only to find that the ammunition boxes had
been confused, and that the bulk of his load consisted of Very-light

1940 cartridges. They were not quite useless, for when they were fired over the battlefield the Germans mistook them for their own light signals, and the mortaring abruptly ceased. Lieut. Ford recalls how he emptied his pockets of the few grenades and bullets which were left to him, and laid them out in a thin row on the lip of the ditch, with his naked bayonet beside them. The Battalion, at that moment, were facing their greatest crisis of the campaign.

The Germans were not confining their efforts to frontal attacks against the three forward companies. Both the right and left flanks of the position were unprotected, and the enemy were infiltrating across the Lys into the outskirts of Warneton, where Major Murray and his truck drivers were under fire throughout the day. On the left the Germans passed through the wide gap which lay between the Grenadiers and the North Staffordshires to attack Battalion Headquarters itself. A carrier was set on fire and a barn at the back of the farm was also soon ablaze. All the secret papers were destroyed as a precaution, and the officers and headquarters staff fought off the Germans at a range of a few yards. Not a foot of ground was yielded, but to the other casualties were now added several men of the headquarters, including the Second-in-Command (Major O. W. D. Smith), the Adjutant (Capt. C. Earle) and the Intelligence Officer (Lieut. P. F. Thorne), all of whom were slightly wounded.

The Battalion were informed that they must hold the sector until 10 p.m. The first to move out were the "A" Echelon transport, which ran the gauntlet of a hail of shells and bullets before they were clear of Warneton, and assembled at Messines, having dumped all their surplus stores to make room for the Guardsmen. The companies successfully broke contact at the appointed hour, during a fortunate lull in the fighting, and also withdrew to Messines. From here they drove to Poperinghe. When they had time to call a roll, they found that the Battalion numbered no more than 9 officers and about 270 men.

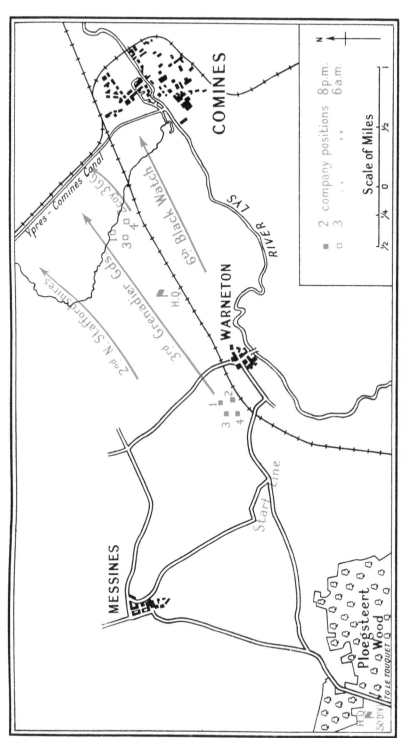

THE YPRES—COMINES CANAL

COMINES

RIVER LYS

Ypres - Comines Canal

6th Black Watch

No. 4 Coy. 3 Gds.

2nd N. Staffordshires

3rd Grenadier Gds.

H.Q.

WARNETON

MESSINES

Start Line

Ploegsteert
Wood

TO LE TOUQUET

H.Q.
50 DIV

N

2 company positions 8 p.m.
3 "   "   "   6 a.m.

Scale of Miles

½   ¼   0   ½   1

6

FURNES AND DUNKIRK

Effect of Belgian capitulation—7th Guards Brigade at Furnes—Com-
manding Officer of 2nd Battalion killed—Heavy fighting in Furnes—
Retreat of the three Battalions to the Beaches—Major Adair's account
of the 3rd Battalion's evacuation from Dunkirk—Major Colvin's
account of the evacuation from La Panne

By this time the general situation had been greatly worsened by the **1940**
decision of King Leopold of the Belgians to sue for an armistice.
When it came into force, at 4 a.m. on the 28th of May, the whole
north-east corner of the Dunkirk perimeter, which had previously been
the responsibility of the Belgian Army, was suddenly thrown open
to the influx of the German divisions opposing them. The attempt to
evacuate the whole of the B.E.F. from Dunkirk had never been one
which even Lord Gort had regarded with great optimism, but now,
with this extra burden thrown on his shoulders, success seemed even
less likely. It is an indication of the state of the B.E.F.'s communications that few officers heard of the Belgian capitulation until they
landed in England, although they were directly involved in its consequences. For example, Lieut. F. J. R. P. Needham, who acted as
Adjutant of the 3rd Battalion after Capt. Earle was wounded, learned
of the Belgian capitulation for the first time from a newspaper he
bought in Dover Harbour six days later. "It is still difficult to understand why we were allowed to reach the coast," is one officer's opinion
which is widely echoed; and Winston Churchill himself has said: "I
thought, and there were good judges who agreed with me, that perhaps
twenty or thirty thousand men might be re-embarked, but it certainly
seemed that the whole of the First French Army, and the whole of the
B.E.F. north of the Amiens—Abbeville gap, would be broken up in
open field or else have to capitulate for lack of food or ammunition."

How was it, then, that 220,000 British and 120,000 Allied troops
were successfully re-embarked? One explanation is that the Germans
were too exhausted to make the final effort which might have ended
the war then and there. Another, the efficiency with which the later
stages of the evacuation were organized. A third was undoubtedly the
refusal of the British troops to panic, and the patience with which they
waited their turn on the bomb- and shell-torn beaches. But to these
reasons one must add a fourth—the tenacity of those British brigades
which were hurried to plug the Belgian gap in the Dunkirk perimeter.

1940 Among them none fought with greater stubbornness than the 7th Guards Brigade at Furnes.

Since leaving the Escaut, the Brigade had passed through a series of exhausting and demoralizing experiences. On all sides they saw soldiers and civilians of three nationalities, leaderless and panic-stricken, some of them driven by selfish despair into mutiny, others actually in league with the enemy. As the ring tightened round the Dunkirk pocket, the very elaboration of Allied equipment became in itself one cause of their undoing. The roads were packed with guns, tanks, transport, and troops, muscle-bound for want of space in which to loosen their arms for fighting, starved of ammunition, disorganized by the disruption of communications and the consequent lack of clear orders. The Germans suffered from no such congestion; their only problem was to build up over long stretches of open road a sufficient weight of men and guns to administer the *coup de grâce*. Already the road from Roubaix to Ypres was under fire, and the two Grenadier Battalions, halted for hours on end, bombed and shelled continuously, knew that at any moment their further progress might be impenetrably barred. 2/Lieut. O. D. Bevan was killed, the first officer casualty in the 2nd Battalion.

May 28   For one day they remained at Oostvleteren in reserve, and then continued to Furnes, the site of their last and bitterest battle. The final stretch of their march was the hardest of all. The headquarters of the 2nd Battalion were only two hundred yards clear of their billet at Oostvleteren when the farmhouse was obliterated by a salvo of shells. Thereafter they made their way painfully towards Furnes, expecting to have at least a few hours in which to put the town in a state of defence. It was not to be. As they approached the outskirts they heard from within the sound of small-arms fire, and met harassed staff officers who told them that half of the town was already in enemy hands, that the British troops whom they were due to relieve were losing ground, but that, at all costs, the 3rd Division must hold the Furnes sector long enough to permit the embarkation of the I Corps. The Grenadier officers set out, with only one map between the two Battalions, to reconnoitre their positions.

It was then that the 2nd Battalion suffered a culminating blow. Their Commanding Officer, Lieut.-Colonel J. A. Lloyd, Major H. D. W. Pakenham and Capt. C. J. D. Jeffreys were shot by a sniper in the streets of Furnes. Colonel Lloyd was killed outright, and the two other officers severely wounded and left lying within seventy yards of a German fortified house. It was Lieut. J. A. P. Jones, M.C., assisted by Majors Bushman and Kingsmill, who recovered their bodies at very great risk, but both officers died of their wounds. Major

R. B. R. Colvin took over command of the 2nd Battalion. The Com- 1940
manding Officer of the 1st Battalion, Lieut.-Colonel J. A. Prescott,
was also slightly wounded by a shell splinter, and though he remained
in command he was unable to walk, and was assisted by Major C. M.
Venables-Llewelyn.

The 3rd Division were deployed astride the Furnes salient with the
8th Brigade north of the town, the 9th Brigade south, and the 7th
Guards Brigade between them. The 2nd Grenadiers held the central
part of the town, and the 1st Battalion its southern outskirts. Under
appalling difficulties the Grenadiers occupied the houses which overlooked a convenient stretch of canal running through the town's May 29
centre. Already many houses were ablaze, the streets and alleys were
alive with sharpshooters, Germans were creeping forward among the
ruins, and the bombardment was unceasing. The house on the Grande
Place where one battalion headquarters were lodged in the cellar was
soon reduced to rubble above their heads; and in the firing line each
section received orders to barricade their buildings and live and fight
there without coming into the open except to evacuate their wounded
and fetch their rations. Even as far back as Brigade Headquarters the
discomfort and danger were no less. Vital conferences were held in a
slit trench dug through the middle of a manure heap, with a straw-and-
dung roof for camouflage, and a cruel stench and crueller insects to
distract the commanders from their work.

The Germans made many attempts to cross the canal, and though May 30-
time after time their boats were sunk in mid-water they succeeded in 31
places in gaining a temporary lodgement on the near bank. So long as
their local penetrations were sealed off, no great danger resulted. But
when it was reported that the northern brigade was falling back, here
was a situation which might develop into a complete encirclement of
the town. On receipt of this news Major Colvin dispatched Lieut.
J. A. P. Jones with his carrier platoon to report on the situation and if
necessary to counter-attack. Lieut. Jones did even more than this. He
found that two British battalions had indeed fallen back, as they had
no ammunition, no communications with their headquarters, and only
two officers. With great initiative Lieut. Jones rallied the dispirited
troops, faced them towards the firing line, and led them back in person
to their old positions, with his carriers stiffening their resistance from
behind. Thereafter the line was never in such great danger. The left-
hand Grenadier company was very hard pressed, and its commander,
Capt. G. E. W. Potter, was wounded, but the front remained intact up
to the moment of withdrawal. Lieut. G. C. F. Gwyer, of the 1st Battalion, was also wounded.

The last Grenadier companies were clear of Furnes at 2.30 a.m. on June 1

1940 the 1st of June, and made their way on foot, some in the surviving vehicles, to the beaches at La Panne.

The 3rd Battalion meanwhile had destroyed all but a few of their vehicles, and marched through the flame-lit night to a point about ten miles south of Dunkirk. Having been separated from the remainder of their Brigade since the Escaut, the Battalion were not under direct orders of any particular headquarters, and were again seized upon to May 30 plug a new gap in the line. This time the threat was to the 151st Brigade of the 50th Division, who were holding the canal south of Moeres. At the Brigade Headquarters they found a fellow-Grenadier in Major A. F. L. Clive, who was the Brigade Major. There was not as yet any clean breach in the canal line, but enemy pressure upon it was increasing, and the 3rd Grenadiers were held back in readiness to counter-attack should it become necessary. Major Adair and his company commanders went forward to look at the ground over which they would be fighting. It was flat and intercepted by dykes, and they did not like the prospect at all. All that night and the following morn-
May 31 ing they waited in suspense, but when the order finally came it was not to counter-attack, but to fill a gap which had opened between the 151st Brigade and the 9th. The Battalion were rushed forward in some lorries which had escaped the almost universal destruction of trans-
June 1 port, and were in their position—their last—by dusk. They sent out their patrols in the dark, but the enemy did not attack. At 2.30 a.m. they blew up the bridges and withdrew to the lorries which the Commanding Officer had left under a strong guard. They motored back through Adinkerke towards Dunkirk.

The last phase of the Grenadier story in this campaign has been described in two graphic accounts, written on their return to England by the Commanding Officers of the 2nd and 3rd Battalions. There could be no more fitting conclusion to this chapter than to reproduce both *in extenso*.

The first is by Major Adair:

"When the 3rd Battalion reached Zuydcoote, three miles from Dunkirk, we were turned into a field and ordered to abandon all remaining transport. This field had line upon line of motor vehicles already dumped in it—the sight was indescribable. I managed to keep a carrier for myself and a three-ton lorry for the men's food and essentials. Then on we went. I met General Martel in Zuydcoote, and he was most grateful to the Battalion for having held the gap in the 50th Division's front. As we passed through the village it was being heavily shelled, and German aeroplanes were roaring overhead. There was a tremendous explosion as an ammunition dump went up just beside us. Major Murray had found a grand place for us to lie up in the sand-dunes.

Battalion Headquarters was perched up on a flat table of sand with a 1940 fine view out towards Dunkirk and the sea. Above us towered another fifty feet of sand, so we felt quite secure from the shells which constantly passed over our heads. We shared our tableland with a number of French officers, and directly we arrived all busily dug little trenches to give cover.

"It was now about 9 a.m., and after breakfast (consisting of tea, jam and biscuits) all settled down in the slit trenches for a bit of sleep, but we were not left long in peace. There was a roar in the sky and about thirty German bombers suddenly appeared overhead. They dived on two destroyers patrolling just in front of the beach, and dropped salvo after salvo of bombs. There was a tremendous explosion, and one of the destroyers blew up—a great mushroom of flame shooting hundreds of feet into the air. She settled down into the water, and in a few minutes disappeared entirely. The other destroyer heeled over on her side and sank. About ten minutes later another great mass of Heinkels appeared, this time sinking two transports, and so on through the morning: over 150 bombers came over before midday. The anti-aircraft fire was terrific—the whole sky was full of white puffs. Occasionally a German would swoop down and machine-gun us in our sand-pits. He got a hot reception—every Bren gun and machine gun in the neighbourhood blazed off at him: we were in more danger from this than from the aeroplane. Occasionally, too, a Hurricane would appear to chase off the bombers. There were some grand fights and several bombers crashed—one collided with a Hurricane, and both came tumbling down.

"About midday I was sent for to Brigade Headquarters (151st Brigade), and had a most unpleasant journey there: shells were falling pretty near, and the casualties on the outskirts of Zuydcoote had been very heavy. I got the cheering news that we were to move along the beach at 2 p.m., to the mole at Dunkirk, and embark that night: all our kit was to be left behind. The Battalion quickly prepared to move, my carrier was loaded up with food and all kit we could get aboard, and the Battalion set off for the beach. We took all our Bren guns and sufficient ammunition, in spite of the orders to dump them. It was a long and tiring march along the three miles of sand. I myself went ahead in the carrier, with Lieut. C. G. Ford, our Intelligence Officer, on a motor-cycle (the third he had picked up since breakfast). The litter on the beach was indescribable: rifles, Bren guns, kits, everything lying all over the place. Destroyers and large and small boats of every description were lying on the bottom quite close to the shore, with masts, bridges, and funnels standing right out of the water. One destroyer was actually beached, cut completely in two by the bombs.

"A heavy pall of smoke rose from the burning oil tanks near the harbour. When we arrived at the outskirts of Dunkirk a line of French sentries turned us off the sands, and the Battalion had to march a long detour through the town. The destruction was ghastly. Scarcely a house remained untouched, and the debris and litter made progress difficult. There had been no opportunity to clear up the streets or bury the dead. I went on to the dockyard entrance to find out where we were to halt.

There I met George Thorne, who gave me a most welcome cup of tea and a very smart tea-basket. General Alexander came along shortly afterwards. (He was left in command when Lord Gort had been ordered away the previous day.) He told us that there was now no question of embarking except in the short hours of darkness. He was very doubtful if the French could hold the Germans back another day. I then went on in my carrier to the base of the mole. The whole area was packed with ambulances bringing along the wounded. There were three anti-aircraft guns, but all the ammunition had been used up during the day, and I noticed that two of their barrels were being used to hold up a radio aerial. With some difficulty we squeezed the carrier on to the mole and unloaded the food and kit, placing them on the parapet, and leaving the driver in charge. We handed the carrier over to the Staff Captain, who was most grateful and promised to destroy it before leaving.

"It was now about 6.30 p.m. I walked along and met the Battalion. There were several other units on the mole itself, so there was nothing for it but to wait two or three hours, getting as much cover as we could from the shells. We sent forward a party to carry the stretcher cases along the pier: we also found a party to clear the mole of transport by pushing every motor vehicle into the canal. This was ordered by the senior staff officer, and was very necessary owing to the great congestion. The men thoroughly enjoyed this fatigue: one, two, three, heave —and a brand-new ambulance rolled down the slope into the water. There were plenty of biscuits and cigarettes lying about, so all had a bite of food. The doctor (Capt. W. H. Valentine) did a bit of paddling and foot-washing, much to our amusement. So the time gradually passed. One or two enemy planes came over, but dropped no bombs, and luckily there was no shelling.

"At last dusk came on, and the Battalion were ordered to move along the mole. This was a slow and nerve-racking business. There were several yawning gaps covered by loose boards where bombs had fallen. At length we reached the end of the pier. There were one or two ships in, and a sunken one on the farther side, which had been bombed all day—a nice waste of effort! We were told to get on board as quickly as possible. Our ship was the *Newhaven*, an old friend of mine from cross-Channel days. There was a great crowd on the decks, and soon the bells rang and we were away. As the ship left, a few parting shots from the shore guns fell near us.

"It was a beautiful, calm crossing, and when I woke up our ship was lying off Dover in brilliant early morning sunshine. We hung about outside the harbour, and did not finally tie up until 11 a.m."

The second account, by Major R. B. R. Colvin, commanding the 2nd Battalion, tells in vivid terms the adventures of his own party of Grenadiers from the moment of their arrival on the beaches at La Panne on the 1st of June:

"Of ships there were plenty, but they were a long way off-shore and the tide was only just starting to flow. Of staff officers or N.L.Os. there was no sign, and consequently nobody knew what was expected of them. Some kept walking, others cast off every stitch of clothing and **1940** started to swim out to the ships. There were very few small boats available to ferry men out to the destroyers, and what there were we tried to keep available for the wounded. We were up to our necks in the sea for an hour helping the wounded, and in the middle of it all the Messerschmitts arrived and flew up and down the beaches machine-gunning this enormous mass with tracer ammunition and cannon. Considering that the target was ideal, it was extraordinary how few men were hit, but as everyone was returning their fire with rifles, revolvers and Brens, and the naval vessels were firing their guns at low angle, it was a network of shot and shell. I submerged myself in the sea with the wounded chap I was helping, and we just kept our heads above water.

"The destroyers were now signalling for us to move westwards towards Dunkirk, as they could take no more off those shallow sands. It was an amazing sight to see these thousands of men trekking across the sands, more or less a solid mass five miles in length and about one hundred yards broad. Squadrons of Messerschmitts periodically attacked, and there were many unpleasant sights of wounded men left on the sands to die or be drowned by the flood tide which runs at a great speed on that coast. As we proceeded westwards we picked up quite a lot of our own Battalion and made several unsuccessful attempts to launch boats, only to find that they had been perforated by bullets. The German guns were now ranging on the sand-dunes and the beaches, and at any moment one expected to see their infantry arrive; they had only four and a half miles to come and by driving a few armoured cars up and down the beach they could have wiped out our entire force. We were now faced with the alternative of marching to Dunkirk, which was another six or seven miles, and there wait our turn to embark for perhaps another twenty-four hours; or else wait where we were for high water at 8.30 a.m., when the destroyers could run in. I decided on the latter course, and we waded out again to an old steamer, which was grounded, in the hope of being ferried from there to the destroyers.

"The water was up to our armpits, and by the time we clambered on board we were feeling the cold after four hours in wet uniforms. Enemy bombers now appeared in great numbers, and the Junkers dive-bombed our stationary destroyers and sank two by direct hits. It was a most depressing sight. We made rather desperate signals to the destroyers, but I knew they could not run up to our hulk, which was lying on a sandbank. After some time a motor-boat towing a chain of empty ship's boats came out to us. Now that we had a motor-boat we intended to run a ferry service to and from the destroyers. As we neared the destroyer it was attacked by Junkers dive-bombers and hit in the engines. She put to sea as quickly as possible with clouds of smoke pouring from her and was subsequently abandoned. We expected to be machine-gunned to pieces in our crowded boats, but they were too busy trying to kill off our sailors who were struggling in the oil and unable to swim.

"Our motor-boat conked out with a cracked cylinder, so we had to cut adrift from her and shape our own course. Luckily we had a set of sweeps in our boat, but not one of the fourteen men in her knew how to row. I did what I could to organize a crew and pulled stroke myself, but it was hopeless, and had there been any breeze we might have drifted anywhere. We eventually reached an Admiralty tender which was picking up the sailors who were now being carried along the coast on the flood tide. Most of them were practically dead with cold, being coated in thick oil and some were terribly injured. The tender picked us up and I found Capt. Berthon, R.N., in command, with Lieut.-Cmdr. Hughes, whom I also knew slightly. No sooner were we on board than three Heinkels appeared and started to bomb us. We retaliated with our Lewis guns, which seemed to upset their aim. Apart from being covered in spray, no harm betook us.

"We then got under way and for half an hour or so kept jinking and altering course without shaking off our pursuers. The wounded sailors on deck were in a terrible plight, but the soldiers whom I had collected were mostly screaming with fright and one man was actually vomiting with sheer terror. The one R.A.M.C. doctor on board was doing yeoman service with the wounded, aided by a Padre, who said to me: 'I have never prayed so hard before.' There were a few lifebelts on board, but not enough to go round sixty or seventy people, and we were jammed tight on the decks. A wounded soldier next door to me died, so I took his lifebelt and had hardly got it over my head when a bomb hit us right amidships. I remember being knocked down and trying to get up again, only to find I had one leg out of action. The ship then heeled right over and everything came crashing down. Everyone made a rush for the side, and I remember a horrid feeling of going down and down into a bottomless pit. I took a deep breath, said a short prayer, and thought this was the one end I least desired. I had the sensation of being pushed through the water at great speed, everywhere surrounded by coal. The next thing that I realized was that my head was above water and that I was some fifty yards away from a lot of wreckage and struggling people. This probably saved my life, as most of the soldiers drowned each other through panic, though a lot must have been killed by the bomb.

"The sailors, with their usual ingenuity and pluck, were clinging to every piece of wreckage and helping their wounded comrades as best they could. There was nothing for it now but to hope to be picked up by another boat, as the shore was two miles distant and the strong tide was carrying us due east. Some more Messerschmitts then appeared and put down a burst of tracer among us, but then cleared off. After what seemed an eternity a large motor-boat hove in sight and passed within a quarter of a mile of us, but despite shots and signals from the sailors on the wreckage they did not see us, and proceeded on their course. Men were now dying every moment from cramp, and their cries for help were pathetic. It was the second time that day that many of these sailors had faced death by drowning.

"We were all very near the end of our tether when we realized that the tide was carrying us towards a wrecked steamer which was lying with her stern nearly under water. I remember discarding my Sam

Browne belt and wishing I could do the same with my boots, and then 1940 striking out as best I could towards the ship. As good fortune would have it, the tide took us right under the hull of the ship, only I was on the opposite side to the sailors. I grabbed a rope ladder hanging from the fo'c'sle, but owing to my damaged leg the tide race carried my legs away and I couldn't get a footing on the bottom rung, so I had to give up my last hope and cast away. The tide washed along the side of the ship very fast, and as I passed under her stern I saw an old gangway hanging in the water. This I got hold of and was able to drag myself up on to the bottom rung. It was so smashed about that I doubted if it would bear my weight, and great was the relief when I pitched over on to the deck. Cramp in both legs made it impossible to move, and the cold was so intense that I couldn't even speak.

"After we had recovered ourselves a couple of sailors gave me a hand into a bunk in the deck-house and found some blankets and dry clothes, which were a godsend to all of us.

"Presumably the Germans could see us moving on the decks and they came and bombed us again, but failed to score a direct hit. One simply prayed for a quick end or anything rather than be cast into that cold water again.

"After an hour we recovered our circulation and the sailors discovered some tinned pears and biscuits, which were a great help. As this ship still had a boat on her davits, Capt. Berthon decided to load it with food and men, and the remaining twelve of us would try to pull across the Channel. We did not dare wait for darkness, as the bombers would surely return before long, or we might be shelled from the shore. We were just about to start when a Thames lighter answered our signals of revolver shots and came alongside. There were two men very badly wounded and the way the strong arms of the sailors and the bargees passed all three of us down the ship's side was wonderful. Capt. Berthon ordered the old lighter to go full speed for home (three and a half knots!), but the master said, 'No.' He had been ordered to go back to the beaches to pick up some wounded soldiers who had been left there—so back we went amongst the bombs and shells, which were now landing in the sea. However, we took on another twenty-five men and laid them out in the hold where the timber is usually stacked. Most of these poor chaps were in a very bad way, but bearing their agonies bravely. We put off again unharmed and started for home. After running with a fair tide for half an hour we struck a sandbank. After violent efforts, and thanks to our flat bottom, we pulled off and tried another way out against a foul tide which reduced our speed to nothing. There was nothing to do but lay on our backs and watch the bombers circling around, but they never attacked our little craft again.

"Luckily for us it was a flat calm, not even a ripple on the sea, and after about two hours we spotted two dinghies making signals to us. One contained four Belgian soldiers and the other two Grenadiers from my own Battalion. We were packed very tight and the iron decks were extremely hard after a few hours' lying in one position. We were all praying for the cover of darkness, but at 10 p.m. it was still quite light and to our horror we saw three aircraft overtaking us and skim-

1940   ming along only fifty feet high. As there had not been another ship in sight for hours, this I felt was one of the worst moments of the whole business. We flattened ourselves and waited for the first rip of bullets, but only got a cheerful wave of the hand from our own pilots flying Lockheed Hudsons on their coastal patrols.

"As darkness fell Capt. Berthon sent an order round the boat that everyone was to be ready to repel any attack by German armoured T.Bs., as they had been active in the Channel. What a hope! But I admire this indomitable fighting spirit of the Royal Navy. We were presently investigated by a French destroyer, which gave us renewed courage but nearly capsized us with its wash!

"About 2 a.m. we ran into a lot of shipping off Margate, but as we didn't know the harbour signals we were told to go to Dover. In the first light of a glorious June morning the white cliffs of England had never looked more attractive."

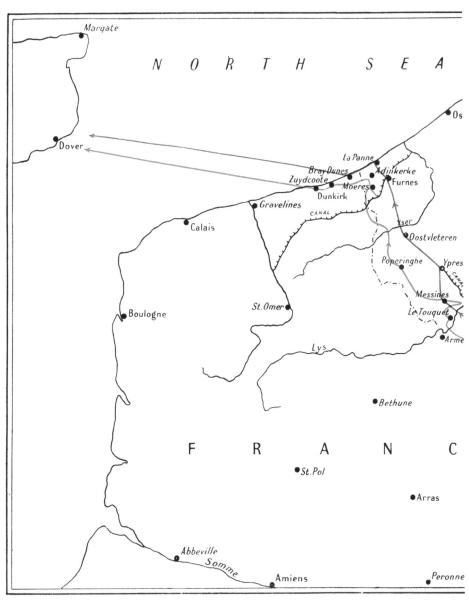

THE WITHDRAWAL

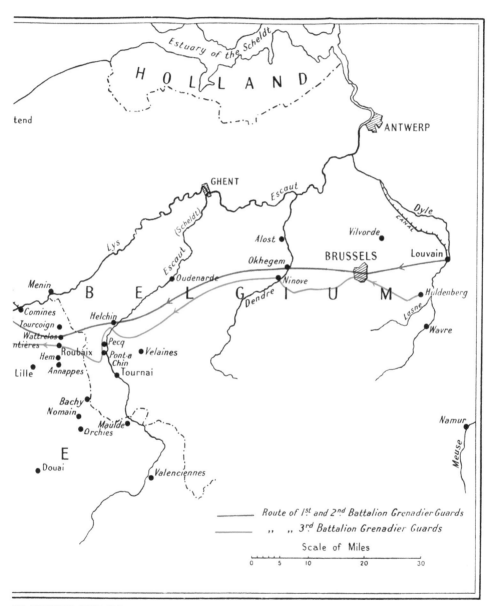

Estuary of the Scheldt

H O L L A N D

tend

ANTWERP

GHENT

Escaut

Dyle

Lys

(Scheldt)

Escaut

Alost

Vilvorde

Canal

Okhegem

BRUSSELS

Louvain

Menin

B E L

Oudenarde

Ninove

Huldenberg

Comines

Helchin

Dendre

G I U M

Lasne

Tourcoign

Wattrelos

Pecq

Wavre

ntières

Roubaix

Velaines

Hem

Pont-a

Chin

Lille

Annappes

Tournai

Bachy

Nomain

Namur

Maulde

Orchies

E

Meuse

Douai

Valenciennes

——————— Route of 1ˢᵗ and 2ⁿᵈ Battalion Grenadier Guards

——————— ,,   ,, 3ʳᵈ Battalion Grenadier Guards

Scale of Miles

0   5   10   20   30

TO DUNKIRK, MAY, 1940

CHAPTER II

THE WAITING YEARS

1

THE THREAT OF INVASION

*The Battalions reassemble in England—7th Guards Brigade ordered to
return to France—Orders cancelled on collapse of the French Army—
Manning the coastline in Sussex and Lincolnshire—Atmosphere of the
months of waiting for a German invasion—Climax on 7th September, 1940*

ON arrival from Dunkirk at the harbours of South-East England, the
struggling little boats gave up their soldier passengers to the willing
hands waiting to receive them on the quays. There was no sense of
disgrace, only a sense of immense relief. Though their equipment was
mostly lost, the men were safe. They had landed at many separate
ports, and a few days were still to elapse before the units could be
reconstituted and the divisions reassembled. As fast as the men came
off the boats they filled the first available trains, irrespective of their
destinations or regiments, and were taken to makeshift camps in
scattered parts of the country. Here their names and units were noted,
and within a short while the commandants began to receive from the
War Office information about the new concentration area of each
division. So the little groups of Guardsmen gradually coalesced, to
find that many of their comrades whom they had thought dead were
living, and that the corporate spirit of each battalion would not be
allowed to fade.

In this way the 1st and 2nd Battalions (7th Guards Brigade) reassembled near Salisbury, the 3rd Battalion (1st Guards Brigade) at
Wakefield. At both places their own refound companionship, the welcome of the civilians, and the peace and quiet of the English countryside were sedatives for their tired nerves and bodies, stimulants to the
revival of their self-esteem.

There was also a very great deal to be done in a very short space
of time. Not many of the men, even after so great an ordeal, could be
spared to revisit their families. Apart from the absorption of reinforcements arriving daily from the Training and Holding Battalions, the
reorganization of the companies and their complete re-equipment, the

1940 strategical situation which followed the evacuation from Dunkirk demanded decisions which made an immediate impact upon the smallest units of the Army. As early as the 7th of June, five days after the completion of the evacuation, General Montgomery informed the 7th Guards Brigade that the 3rd Division would be the first to return to France to assist in the salvaging of what remained of the country. The Brigade was inspected by His Majesty The King, and on the 19th of June moved down to the part of Sussex around Littlehampton and Arundel to complete their preparations. On the 28th of June secret orders were received for immediate embarkation. Two days later, when the collapse of France seemed complete, the plan was abandoned. The 3rd Division remained in Sussex, and for a fortnight took over a stretch of the coastal defences. At about the same time, the 3rd Battalion moved from Wakefield to Louth, near the coast of Lincolnshire.

The scheme which was hurriedly evolved for defence against a German invasion was based upon a pitiably thin screen of coast-watching battalions, backed by a mobile force held several miles inland. The 1st Battalion in Sussex was an example of the first type; the 3rd Battalion in Lincolnshire an example of the second. On the coast the companies dug and manned trenches and erected obstacles at points which commanded the beaches. Inland, the battalions held
Summer themselves in readiness to move in commandeered buses to counter-attack at any point where the enemy might gain a foothold, and to recapture any of the coastal aerodromes which might be seized by airborne troops. The inadequacy of our equipment and the alarming shortage of troops were evident to every soldier, and indeed to every civilian, who had any knowledge of the military dispositions in his own area. A visit to the actual coastline filled even the most ignorant observer with alarm. Spaced out at intervals of a hundred yards or more, linking the few coastal batteries of antiquated guns, small section posts were sited to watch a vast stretch of sand, across which straggled limp loops of barbed wire, festooned with seaweed after every high tide, and a cold, grey sea washing ashore beyond the reach of their Bren guns. This, one grimly pondered, might be the very spot selected for attack.* Returning along the leafy lanes in that splendid summer of 1940, past the concrete road blocks, past the heaps of steel girders left lying ready beside the bridges, and the fresh trenches dug by the villagers in each other's back gardens, one saw how makeshift, how amateurish, were Britain's methods of self-defence: how dogged courage, ingenuity, more improvisation, and the Royal Navy were our

*We now know that the Sussex coastline was to have been invaded in the projected German operation, but not the coast of Lincolnshire.

only real safeguards. What only a few realized was that the Army, in those earliest days, had not more than three days' ammunition supply, and less than a hundred light tanks. **1940**

Yet it would be wrong to suggest that the months of waiting were filled with anxiety for those in the ranks or in subordinate command. The imagination, boggling at the scale of events which might soon occur, seldom strayed farther than immediate local problems. The Guardsmen, secure and fairly comfortable in a score of farms and cottages, found a pleasant novelty in the unfamiliar parts of their own country to which the fortunes of war had bound them so intimately and unexpectedly.

> "Many years hence," wrote a Grenadier officer, "people will ask us what it was like to be waiting on or near the beaches for an invasion which might come at any moment. I fear that in retrospect we may make it sound more romantic and exciting than it actually is. For what happens day by day? In the morning we drill on the road : we are told that our hair is too long, our trousers too short. For an hour afterwards we learn for the twentieth time about the inside of a Bren gun. And in the afternoon the company may go for a march over the Downs. The only moment when the heart beats any faster is just before dawn, when we take out our patrols through the sleepy countryside. We are ordered to watch for dropping parachutes, winking lights, 'suspicious-looking' people—any civilian astir at that hour therefore becomes suspect—but, though we have drawn a blank so far, we come back to our breakfasts wet with dew from the orchards and the corn, and glowing with a sense of duty well performed."

As summer passed into autumn the invasion scare grew no less acute. In London the men of the Holding Battalion built sandbag emplacements in Parliament Square, under Admiralty Arch, and at other nodal points in the heart of the capital; at Windsor the Training Battalion, inexperienced as they were, were given an operational role for the defence of the Castle. The Grenadier field battalions were fortunate to receive their new equipment among the first battalions of the remodelled Army, and by the late summer they were better equipped for battle than in May, 1940.

The climax came in September, 1940. German attacks on the airfields and communication centres of the Home Counties had reached their height : the assembly of invasion barges in the cross-Channel ports seemed complete, and the weather was all too propitious. On the evening of the 7th of September the code word "Cromwell" ("Invasion is imminent") was flashed to every unit in the Home Forces. Here is one close-up of the effect of that message upon a company of the 3rd Battalion : **Sept. 7**

E

1940 "I went round the billets, doubled the sentries, released the men in arrest, and ordered the drummer to sound the alarm in the streets of Louth. I told the men that the Germans might already have landed, but where I had no idea. Our country buses purred quietly in the field outside, their civilian drivers talking quietly to the Guardsmen, drinking cups of tea. Then, for there was nothing else to do, we returned to the billets, wrote our last letters, and waited. When, the next morning, we learned that no invasion had taken place, we relaxed, feeling slightly ashamed of our heroics the night before."

2

EXPANSION AND PREPARATION
(3RD, 5TH AND 6TH BATTALIONS)

The year 1941 the turning point in the Regiment's history—The special role of the 3rd Battalion—3rd, 5th and 6th Battalions—Eight projected operations which never took place—Formation of the 5th and 6th Battalions—Their early history

1941 With the approach of the winter of 1940-41, the threat of a German invasion diminished, and the hope of repelling it, if it came, more certain. In April, 1941, the Germans unleashed their forces against Greece and Yugoslavia, but as only a small part of their colossal Army was involved in these new operations the spring weather revived the invasion scare in England. In more than one War Diary of the period we observe how keenly even a battalion headquarters noted the conjunction of a favourable moon, a favourable tide and a fair-weather forecast. The beaches were still fully manned; the arming and training of the Home Guard were approaching completion; road blocks sprang up deeper and deeper inland; and in a thousand billets scattered over the length and breadth of Great Britain soldiers still slept in their boots, and their lorries waited ready outside.

Yet there was a great difference in mood between 1940 and 1941. A "breathing space" had become a "margin of safety," and a margin of safety an opportunity to hit back. Without relaxing their precautions for defence, the British Army began simultaneously to look forward to the day when they might themselves once more take the offensive. It was at this period (the late winter of 1940-41) that the first models of assault landing craft were secretly tested on remote Scottish lochs: that the detailed study began of the enemy coastline from Norway to Southern France; it was also the period when certain units and divisions of the Home Army were relieved from the stultifying duty of coast guarding, and were trained in those special offensive tactics which sooner or later, in one place or another, would begin 1941 to loosen the German grip on Europe. A full-scale invasion of the Continent was no more than a dream. But the Army was reviving, fast rearming, swollen by new recruits, inspired by a new sense of enterprise. It was a period of long-range preparation and short-range experiment.

The Grenadier Guards were affected by the change in atmosphere in three particular ways. In the first place, to the original three Battalions three more were added in the course of a single year—from October, 1940, to October, 1941. In the second place, the 3rd, 5th and 6th Battalions began to train for specialized forms of warfare, chiefly combined operations and desert fighting: they were earmarked for early employment overseas, and did in fact all leave this country before the spring of 1943, to engage in the operations which form the subject of Volume II of this History. In the third place, the 1st, 2nd and 4th Battalions were also released from their immediate counter-invasion commitments, and began the long process of training for armoured warfare.

The year 1941 therefore marks the turning point in the war record of the Regiment. It was in that year that it reached its maximum strength: and in that year that each Battalion set its feet along one of the many separate paths which led to victory four years later.

Let us first trace the story of the 3rd Battalion during 1941 and 1942, a story which differs widely from that of all the others: for not only were they set geographically apart, being billeted in Scotland during most of this period but they were concerned with the preparations for more than half a dozen separate adventures, none of which took place but all of which, following each other with startling rapidity, maintained the spirit of the Battalion at a high pitch of expectation and gave them a distinct status in the eyes of the Regiment and indeed the whole Army.

Few people, even in the 3rd Battalion itself, knew what lay behind the closed doors of the countless planning conferences. The Commander of the 1st Guards Brigade (Brigadier F. A. V. Copland-Griffiths, D.S.O.), with his Brigade Major (Major C. Earle and, later, Major G. E. Pike) and Intelligence Officer (Capt. R. M. C. Howard), would receive a sudden message to report to the War Office. There, as they entered an inner room, they would be told: "You are to form part of a small invasion force which is to land at ———." Having received their general instructions, they would begin to plan in the greatest detail the landing of the assault craft, the system of supply and communications, and the gaining of a beach-head. Meanwhile,

1941 back in Scotland, based on Glasgow, Dumfries or Perth, the Battalions would be launched on elaborate exercises centring round some hidden island or the depth of a Highland loch, reproducing as closely as possible—though they did not know it—the conditions they would shortly find on a foreign shore. Even the commanding officers were sometimes unaware of the actual objective: the junior officers and men never knew, and all their ingenuity failed to extract the secret.*

Even now it is not possible to reveal the destination of each project. In all, there were eight such schemes, as listed below. The name of the commanding officer responsible is given in each case:

1941-42   1. February, 1941 (Lieut.-Colonel R. B. R. Colvin). Invasion of *Sicily*. The battalions of the 1st Guards Brigade were to have landed at different points in the neighbourhood of Palermo, and linked up inland with other units coming from the United Kingdom and the Middle East. For this operation the Brigade practised on the shores of Loch Fyne, opposite Inverary, landing in assault craft from a fleet of motor vessels moored in the upper reaches of the loch. The project was abandoned owing to shortage of troops.

2 and 3. June-August, 1941 (Lieut.-Colonel R. B. R. Colvin). These two operations, originally sponsored by Mr. Churchill, were cancelled at short notice owing to diplomatic difficulties, and for the same reason it would be impolitic to describe them here. For the first operation the 3rd Grenadiers and 2nd Coldstream, together with a Marine Commando battalion, were mobilized at Pollock Camp, Glasgow. Strict secrecy covered, and still covers, the planning stages, and it was not until long afterwards that a junior officer of the Battalion discovered that he was to have led his platoon ashore on the very beach where he had spent much of his childhood. In the second operation the Brigade formed part of a much larger force, known as 110 Force (commanded by Lieutenant-General H. R. Alexander), which later became the nucleus of the First Army.

4. December, 1941 (Lieut.-Colonel R. B. R. Colvin.) The invasion of *Pantellaria*. In the late summer the Brigade had moved to Dumfriesshire, and the 3rd Grenadiers were split between Castle Douglas and Dalbeattie. In preparation for the Pantellaria operation, they took part in exercises on the Isle of Bute, landing at dawn, up to the waists in ice-cold water. This scheme was abandoned before the planning had entered its final stages. During the winter the close association which had by this time developed between the Grenadiers and the Royal

---

*For instance, it was supposed that Lieut. R. H. Whitworth, the Battalion Intelligence Officer, was in the secret of one projected invasion: it was also known that he was given to talking in his sleep. Therefore a group of young officers would creep nightly to his bedside and listen anxiously to a stream of mumbled remarks. They listened fruitlessly, for Whitworth was not, after all, in the secret.

Sun Photos, Perth

H.M. The King inspects the 3rd Battalion at Perth.   Summer, 1942.

Officers (L. to R.): Capt. H. W. O. Bradley, Brig. F. A. V. Copland-Griffiths, Lt.-Col. A. G. W. Heber-Percy, Capt. K. E. M. Tufnell, H.M. The King.

The 2nd Battalion in England.   Summer, 1943.

Centre: Lt.-Col R. N. Brinckman, D.S.O., M.C.   *Gale & Polden Ltd*

Navy was further strengthened by the inclusion of small parties of 1942 Grenadiers on H.M. destroyers escorting coastal convoys between the Firth of Forth and Chatham.

5. January, 1942 (Lieut.-Colonel R. B. R. Colvin). Landing on the coast of *Norway*. A most hazardous scheme. The intention was to seize a naval base, and either withdraw after a few days or exploit an early success. The operation was cancelled, much to the relief of the few officers who knew about it, owing to the risk of immediate counter-attack by a German armoured division known to be stationed close to the spot selected for attack.

6. May, 1942 (Lieut.-Colonel A. S. Hanning). The invasion of the *Isle of Alderney*. The 1st Guards Brigade were moved for this operation from the area of Perth, where they had been billeted since the end of the winter, to the Isle of Wight. It was the most ambitious, and perhaps the most daring, of all their projects, for Alderney was one of the most heavily defended places on the whole enemy coastline. They would have landed inside the small harbour, and swept on to occupy the whole island under cover of an intense air bombardment, and remained in occupation for two or three days. The plan broke down on the failure of the Army and Royal Air Force to agree on the timing of the air attack.

7. May, 1942 (Major A. G. W. Heber-Percy). After the abandonment of the assault on Alderney a raid on the French coast near *Boulogne* was projected for two of the Grenadier companies. While the remainder of the Battalion returned to Perth, these companies were actually embarked on their ships off Cowes, and were within a few hours of sailing, when a heavy sea began to run which made it impossible to carry out the raid.

8. November, 1942 (Lieut.-Colonel A. G. W. Heber-Percy). Landing at *Bone,* as part of the First Army's invasion of North Africa. The plan, and the reasons for its cancellation, are fully discussed in the opening of Volume II.

On the 11th of October, 1941, the 5th Battalion of the Regiment was formed at Chigwell, in Essex, and a week later, on the 18th, the 6th Battalion was raised at Caterham Barracks. It was the time when the German Army was at the height of its power. The ports of North-Eastern France were still choked with invasion barges; Moscow was already threatened with encirclement; the Balkans were overrun; and even the situation in Libya seemed to favour the Axis Powers. These events had little effect upon the early months of the two new Battalions.

Their experiences were so diverse that it is necessary to separate

1942 them from the moment of their birth, and treat them not like twins but as individuals, sprung fully armed from the head of the same parent, with separate characteristics and separate destinies. As the 6th Battalion were the first to go overseas, it will be more convenient to tell their early story first.

The 6th Battalion grew under the care of Lieut.-Colonel A. F. L. Clive, M.C. The nucleus came from the Chislehurst Detachment of the Holding Battalion, and two hundred additional men came from Windsor. Few of the men, and only thirteen of the thirty-two officers, had seen previous active service, and the majority had been engaged during the past year in guarding vital points in the Home Counties and London area, where they had had few opportunities for training and had forgotten much of what they had learned at the Guards Depot. The enthusiasm of the Battalion's early months was therefore tempered by the dull necessity for recovering behind barrack walls the elementary principles of tactics and weapon training. At the same time, the Battalion had a definite function in view. From the start they were a motor battalion, whose war establishment suited them for operations inside an armoured division, particularly in desert warfare. And they were not placed under the command of a specific brigade or division: they were directly under the orders of the War Office, and expected to go overseas very soon.

The dormitory areas of Surrey were poorly suited for experimenting with tactics designed for use on Libyan sands, and the shortage of equipment added further to their difficulties. There was also the uncertainty of the future. From the 31st of January, 1942, when they received their first order to mobilize, until the 16th of June of the same year, when they finally embarked at Liverpool, there was scarcely a fortnight without its order, counter-order or postponement.

In slow stages, punctuated by periods of false alarms and embarkation leave, the Battalion began to learn their difficult role. They were assisted by attachments to specialized units, including the Guards Armoured Division, and by a generous allotment of vacancies at the Army and Command schools. At one time as many as three hundred officers and men were away under various forms of instruction.

In May, 1942, they were half-trained, and if not yet ready for battle at least ready for embarkation. The Battalion, the youngest of the Regiment, were honoured by the first visit which their new Colonel, Her Royal Highness Princess Elizabeth, had paid to any of her battalions. On the 14th of June they left Caterham for Liverpool on the first stage of their long journey to join the 201st Guards Brigade in the Middle East.

The 5th Battalion were formed at Chigwell by Lieut.-Colonel

J. B. G. Hennessy. Their early history falls into two phases—before 1942 and after they joined the 24th Guards Brigade in June, 1942.

The Battalion were at first part of the 32nd Guards Brigade, whose immediate tasks were to prepare the defences of North-East London, and to assist in the training of the Home Guard. These occupations were unenlivening compared with the more dramatic future promised to the 6th Battalion, and their static functions gave many of the men the impression that the 5th Battalion was intended merely for service at home, and that in the end it might become no more than a holding and reinforcement unit. This was far from so, but the growth of a corporate spirit came slowly, and was not assisted by their distribution over a built-up area of Essex four miles square which was quite unsuitable for training. In May enthusiasm was stimulated by short visits to camps in the West of England, and on their return they were transferred to Uxbridge, to join the 24th Guards Brigade Group (Brigadier R. B. R. Colvin).

The atmosphere now changed completely. The Brigade Group were a highly mobile force, originally designed to cover the southern approaches to London, and now under notice for service overseas. They were one of the most highly trained brigades in the British Army: there was a sense of urgency, to which the 5th Battalion immediately responded. They set themselves to train in earnest, first in the lovely parkland round Uxbridge, then at Blandford Camp in Dorsetshire, and later in a bivouac camp near Marlborough.

In the late summer of 1942 they went to Caterham, and Lieut.-Colonel R. H. Bushman took over command. They continued their training intensively. Part of the Battalion had their first experience of combined operations in Argyllshire, and part in the Isle of Wight. The whole Battalion then moved, in December, to Catrine, in Ayrshire, where they remained until they embarked, in February, 1943, to join the First Army in Tunisia.

By March, 1943, the Grenadiers therefore had three Battalions—the 3rd, 5th and 6th—serving on Tunisian soil. We now turn to the early history of the other three Battalions.

3

FORMATION OF THE GUARDS ARMOURED DIVISION AND THE 6TH GUARDS TANK BRIGADE

(1ST, 2ND AND 4TH BATTALIONS)

Early movements of the Battalions—Decision to form a Guards Armoured Division—Separation of the Armoured Division and Tank Brigade—Early training—2nd Battalion equipped with Sherman tanks, 4th Battalion with Churchill tanks—Training perfected in Yorkshire—Preparations for invading the Continent—Move to the South Coast in April, 1944—D Day—The three Battalions sail for Normandy

1940-44　　Of the three Grenadier Battalions which formed part of the original Guards Armoured Division, the 1st and 2nd were regular Battalions of the Regiment and the 4th was newly raised. The history of the year which preceded their transformation from infantry into armoured troops need not detain us long, but for the sake of completeness a record of their movements during this year must not be omitted.

The 7th Guards Brigade (1st and 2nd Battalions) left the Sussex coast in July, 1940, for the borders of Oxfordshire and Gloucestershire, and from there went to Marston Bigot and Castle Cary in Somerset, where they remained until the end of November. The winter, spring and early summer of 1940-41 were spent in Dorset—by the 1st Battalion at Swanage, and by the 2nd Battalion at Parkstone and later at Weymouth.

The 4th Battalion were raised at Wanstead, outside London, on the 15th of October, 1940, under the command of Lieut.-Colonel O. W. D. Smith. They did not move from Wanstead for the next eleven months. Their duties, as part of the 30th Guards Brigade (Brigadier A. H. S. Adair, D.S.O., M.C.), were to prepare a sector of the London defences and to hold themselves in readiness to help the police in the event of rioting or severe bombing in the East End of London.

For all three Battalions it was a year of aimless monotony. Unlike the 3rd, 5th and 6th Battalions, their only prospect of action was through an enemy invasion of this country. They were still short of equipment, and the men grew not unnaturally weary of endless training with the scanty equipment they had. The very normality of their country, suburban or seaside billets, the very regularity of their home leave once in every three months, added to their sense of remoteness from the war.

For those in charge of Great Britain's affairs, these same twelve 1940-44
months contained some of the most trying moments of the whole
war. Not once during the winter of 1940-41 did the Soviet Union
or the United States display any intention of entering the conflict. The volume of *matériel de guerre* which reached the country
through Lend-Lease channels was never more than a trickle. Shipping
losses mounted and German bombing raids began to affect the nation's
industrial production. Above all, the threat of invasion did not dimin-
ish, but rather, as the summer of 1941 approached, increased.

As they reviewed this sombre situation the Army Council focused
their attention on the alarming amount of armour which they knew an
enemy invasion would contain. To combat it they had only a handful
of tanks scattered throughout Southern England; a force that would
surely crumble under the superior might of the enemy. They therefore
decided that a number of infantry formations—among them elements
of the Brigade of Guards—would have to be put into tanks. High
officers of the Brigade were consulted and found to welcome the pro-
posal. The King gave his approval. And so it was that in May, 1941, a
Guards Armoured Division was formed.

It was a far-sighted and an extremely bold decision: far-sighted
because, besides ensuring that the Army would have more armour to
resist invasion, it created a formidable striking force for future offensive operations; bold because the Brigade of Guards had had no previous experience of armoured warfare. But bolder still because there
were many responsible persons who predicted that Guardsmen, on
account of their height and of their discipline and training, would
never be successful in tanks.

The new Division was officially formed on the 15th of September,
1941, by Major-General Sir Oliver Leese. Its main body consisted of
two armoured brigades, the 5th (Brigadier W. A. F. L. Fox-Pitt) and
the 6th (Brigadier Allan Adair), whose orders of battle were:

HEADQUARTERS, 5TH GUARDS ARMOURED BRIGADE

    1st (Motor) Battalion Grenadier Guards.
    2nd (Armoured) Battalion Grenadier Guards.
    1st (Armoured) Battalion Coldstream Guards.
    2nd (Armoured) Battalion Irish Guards.

HEADQUARTERS, 6TH GUARDS ARMOURED BRIGADE

    4th (Armoured) Battalion Grenadier Guards.
    4th (Motor) Battalion Coldstream Guards.
    3rd (Armoured) Battalion Scots Guards.
    2nd (Armoured) Battalion Welsh Guards.

1940-44   Before long, however, several of these battalions, and others too, were moved about like pieces in a jigsaw puzzle and fitted into different frames.

First, during the autumn of 1942, in the light of experience gained in the Middle East, it was decided that armoured divisions should consist of one infantry and one armoured brigade, instead of two of the latter. The 32nd Guards Infantry Brigade was therefore brought into the Guards Armoured Division and the 6th Guards (Armoured) Brigade, after a few weeks of uncertainty, was put into the 15th (Scottish) Division, leaving behind its battalion of Welsh Guards, but with the 4th Coldstream as an armoured battalion instead. Then in the autumn of 1943 the status of the 6th Guards Tank Brigade, as it was called, was again changed. It left the 15th (Scottish) Division and became an independent heavy tank brigade. So in the end the Brigade of Guards was responsible for two entirely separate armoured bodies: the Guards Armoured Division, commanded by Major-General Allan Adair, and the 6th Guards Tank Brigade, commanded by Brigadier G. L. Verney and later by Brigadier W. D. C. Greenacre. The orders of battle of the two formations were:

GUARDS ARMOURED DIVISION

HEADQUARTERS, 5TH GUARDS ARMOURED BRIGADE

1st (Motor) Battalion Grenadier Guards.
2nd (Armoured) Battalion Grenadier Guards.
1st (Armoured) Battalion Coldstream Guards.
2nd (Armoured) Battalion Irish Guards.
2nd (Armoured) Battalion Welsh Guards.

HEADQUARTERS, 32ND GUARDS INFANTRY BRIGADE

5th Battalion Coldstream Guards.
3rd Battalion Irish Guards.
1st Battalion Welsh Guards.

6TH GUARDS TANK BRIGADE

HEADQUARTERS, 6TH GUARDS TANK BRIGADE

4th Tank Battalion Grenadier Guards.
4th Tank Battalion Coldstream Guards.
3rd Tank Battalion Scots Guards.

It was thus arrayed that the Division and the Brigade set sail for France in the summer of 1944.

The requirements of this volume do not permit a long and detailed 1940-44 description of the Battalion's training for armoured warfare. To trace their progress week by week, or even month by month, might enlighten Grenadiers who may one day be called upon to serve in a second Guards Armoured Division; but for others it would be tedious. So a brief summary of the cardinal features of this period must suffice.

Of the three Battalions which the Regiment provided for the armoured venture, only two, the 2nd and 4th, became fully armoured battalions; the other, the 1st, underwent a less drastic transformation to a motor battalion.* But for all of them, inclusion in the new Division was a stroke of fortune. It gave them just that change of environment, that reawakening of interest and that renewal of opportunity which, after a year of negative action, they so sorely needed.

The magnitude of the task which confronted them was indeed immense. For every man who knew how to drive a tank, there were a hundred who had never even driven a car. For every officer who understood the mysteries of a carburettor or a final drive, there were a dozen who were never quite sure where to find the dip-stick in a car engine. Few members of the Battalions had heard of "hull-down positions," "power traverses" or "induction manifolds"; and those who had could not claim to know their exact meaning. To have asked the average man in the spring of 1941 to show you how to change a broken tank track would have been like asking a Civil Servant to mend a railway line. And to have demanded to be shown the whereabouts of a tank cupola would have met with the same response as a question on Patagonia. The Battalions were starting from scratch and the process of training had to begin at the very roots of each of them.

First, the five men who make up a tank crew—tank commander, gunner, wireless operator, driver and co-driver—had to be taught how to handle and look after their tank. Then the four tank crews (sometimes three or five) that make up a troop had to be taught elementary armoured tactics. Later they had to learn how to co-operate with infantry, and so the process continued, the problems of tactics and control becoming greater at every stage, until each of the squadrons were sufficiently sure of themselves to take part in battalion, brigade and, finally, divisional exercises.

In the year which followed their entry into the field of armoured warfare, the three Grenadier Battalions passed through all these exacting stages of training. In the autumn of 1941, when the 1st Battalion (Lieut.-Colonel J. A. Gascoigne) was at Piddlehinton Camp, near

---

*The decision to motorize the 1st Battalion was influenced by the height of the King's Company. Although the six-foot-two-inch minimum had been waived, the height of the Company was still above the average of the rest of the Brigade of Guards.

1940-44 Dorchester, the 2nd (Lieut.-Colonel W. V. Dilwyn Venables Llewel-
lyn) at Sherborne, and the 4th (Lieut.-Colonel O. W. D. Smith) at
Mere, the majority of the men of both armoured battalions were sent
away to train as gunners, wireless operators and drivers with the
Royal Armoured Corps at Tidworth. When they came back, in early
November, the 1st Battalion moved to Mere, the 2nd Battalion to
Warminster, and the 4th to Codford, and they set about building
model rooms and wireless and gunnery centres in which to learn the
principles of armoured tactics. Soon the first Crusaders arrived and
by the spring of 1941 the Battalions were practising on the muddy
slopes of Salisbury Plain what they had learnt indoors. In April, 1942
—Major E. H. Goulburn succeeded Lieut.-Colonel J. A. Gascoigne
as Commanding Officer of the 1st Battalion at this time—training on
an armoured troop-motor platoon basis started and before the summer
was up all three Battalions had taken part in brigade and divisional
exercises. They had also spent days away from Salisbury Plain, firing
their guns on the ranges at Linney Head, in Wales, and perfecting their
driving along the twisting lanes of Somerset.

The Battalions were handicapped to a considerable extent during
this first year of their training by shortage of equipment. Terse entries
in the War Diaries, such as, "The following kit has been received:—
Pistols 289, Machine Carbines Sten 202, Binoculars 98 pairs," show
how acute the problem was. There is even a passage in the 1st Battalion Diary which reads: "An anti-tank gun platoon was formed
with *borrowed* 2 pounders"! But whether they had the right equipment or not, the Battalions always had something new to learn or
practise and the months passed rapidly. Frequent lectures on such
subjects as "The United States" and "How I escaped from Poland"
helped to break up the routine, while Saturday drill parades ensured
that the Battalions escaped from grease-guns and petrol fumes to
smarten themselves up at least once a week. There were also a number
of big parades to brighten the monotony of perpetual training. On the
21st of April each Battalion sent a party to Windsor to parade in front
of big parades to brighten the monotony of perpetual training. On the
week before, the Prime Minister, the Right Hon. Winston Churchill,
and General Marshall, Chief of Staff, United States Army, had reviewed the 5th Brigade, and on the 20th of May His Majesty, with
the Queen, inspected the King's Company at Warminster.

The beginning of the Division's second year of life coincided with
numerous changes of command and equipment. The 4th Battalion
left the Division with the rest of the 6th Guards Tank Brigade, and
Lieut.-Colonel H. R. H. Davies took over command from Lieut.-

*See Appendix I.

Inspection at Windsor Castle by H.R.H. Princess Elizabeth, 21st April, 1942.

Back Row.—R.S.M. M. Young, R.S.M. J. Brown, R.S.M. W. Hagell, Suptg. Clerk A. Douglas, R.S.M. W. Povey, R.S.M. D. Hobbs, R.S.M. W. Cutts, R.S.M. H. Robinson, R.S.M. F. Hufton.

Third Row.—Lt. F. E. J. Carver, Lt. T. W. Garnett, Lt. E. V. Philpott, Lt. E. R. Randall, Lt. H. N. Lucas, Major R. Beard, Capt. A. Aston, Lt. B. H. Pratt.

Second Row.—Major E. H. Goulburn, Capt. E. C. W. M. Penn, Capt. J. G. S. Gammell, Capt. J. D. Buchanan, Capt. A. H. Penn, Major G. A. I. Dury, Capt. D. V. Bonsor, Capt. T. A. Gore-Browne, Capt. R. G. Briscoe, Capt. R. B. St. Q. Wall, Capt. The Master of Forbes.

Front Row.—Lt.-Col. C. M. Dillwyn-Venables-Llewelyn, Lt.-Col. A. S. Hanning, Lt.-Col. O. W. D. Smith, H.M. The Queen, H.M. The King, H.R.H. The Princess Elizabeth, Col. J. A. Prescott (Lieut.-Colonel Commanding), H.R.H. The Princess Margaret, Lt.-Col. G. M. Cornish, Lt.-Col. Hon. J. B. G. Hennessey, Lt.-Col. A. F. L. Clive.

Colonel O. W. D. Smith. The 2nd and 4th Battalions began handing 1940-44
in their Crusaders, and by late October, when Lieut.-Colonel R. N.
Brinckman assumed command of the former, they were being re-
issued with Covenanters. Early in October the 1st Battalion joined the
2nd Battalion in Warminster and moved into luxurious "Belisha"
barracks—to the envy of the rest of the Division, who were mostly
housed in Nissen huts.

These events momentarily disrupted the Battalions' training, but
by the end of October they were all making up for lost time. The 5th
Brigade held day and night exercises almost every week-end—the
gunners used the big training areas during the week—and the 1st and
2nd Battalions took part in them all. For the 4th Battalion there
were many new problems. They remained at Codford, but as the
Churchills with which they were to be re-equipped did not begin to
arrive until the early part of 1943, they had to accustom themselves
to their new role as a heavy tank battalion while still using Covenanters. After the New Year they began exchanging officers and non-
commissioned officers with the 15th (Scottish) Division, who were in
Northumberland, and the foundations of their co-operation with this
division, later to reach great heights in Normandy, were firmly laid.

In the spring of 1943 two events of note took place. The first was
Exercise "Spartan," which was designed to test the stamina of all the
troops in England. Each Battalion took part, and although the sun
shone the whole time, taking the edge off the exercise's real object,
they all gained a great deal of experience. Lieut. H. Pritchard lost his
life during the exercise when his tank ran over a railway embankment
and overturned. The second event of importance was the visit of Her
Royal Highness The Colonel to the 4th Battalion on the 13th of March
—the first public engagement Her Royal Highness had fulfilled alone.

As soon as Exercise "Spartan" was over, both the Guards Armoured
Division and the 6th Guards Tank Brigade left Salisbury Plain. The
4th Battalion went to Wensleydale, in Yorkshire, where they spent
six months training on the Wolds. This rich farming country had
recently been requisitioned, and it afforded the best possible facilities
for every type of manœuvre. In June the Guards Armoured Division
moved to Yorkshire, too. The 1st Battalion took up residence round
Ampleforth, with two companies at Gilling East and one company in
a hutted camp at Oswaldkirk; the 2nd Battalion moved into Dun-
combe Park, near Helmsley. They had spent the previous two months
at Thetford, in Norfolk, taking part in exercises on the Stamford
Common battle area which were considerably enlivened by the use of
live ammunition.

Events now began to move more swiftly. The Division and the

1940-44 Brigade were mobilizing and their equipment was being brought up to the most modern standards. In Norfolk the 1st and 2nd Battalions had exchanged their Covenanters for Shermans, the latest and fastest type of tank yet produced in America. And the 4th Battalion received a new version of the Churchill which was infinitely more reliable than the early models. All through the summer training continued at top speed, and in the middle of July the Division spent a month in tented camps on the Wolds to be nearer the training area: the King's Company were with the 2nd Battalion at West Lutton; No. 2 Company with the 2nd Battalion of the Irish Guards at Fimber; Battalion Headquarters and No. 3 Company with Brigade Headquarters at Huggate; and No. 4 Company with the 1st Battalion Coldstream Guards at Stedmere.*

The summer training reached a climax in a Corps exercise—"Blackcock"—which, for the 1st Battalion, ended in an assault crossing over the River Derwent. Shortly afterwards the 4th Battalion moved to Welbeck Abbey, in Nottinghamshire, and the 2nd Battalion went for ten days to Kirkcudbright to try out the 75-mm. guns with which the Shermans were equipped. During this visit Lieut. J. R. Boyd was killed when his tank ran into a crater and overturned. The 1st Battalion spent October carrying out amphibious training in Scarborough Harbour.

The next six months saw the Division and the Brigade putting the finishing touches to their training. Under all sorts of weather conditions they would practise crossing river obstacles, passing through gaps in minefields, night moves, artillery co-operation, vehicle recovery, petrol and ammunition supply, and the evacuation of casualties. They had been training now for over two and a half years, and as the winter wore on the prospect of action seemed as far away as ever. Cut off from the invigorating atmosphere of big towns, with very few opportunities for recreation, the Battalions began to grow weary of the continual manœuvres. The bigger the exercise the harder it was to keep interest alive. But the repeated efforts of the officers to teach him how to break out of a bridgehead must have convinced the most unresponsive guardsman that when the Division and the Brigade were ordered to move south in April, 1944, the move was not being undertaken merely for the sake of his health.

At the Three Power Conference which was held at Teheran in September, 1943, the leaders of Great Britain, the United States and Soviet Russia agreed that the supreme operation of the war—the inva-

---

*These groupings of an armoured battalion to a motor company had been started in Norfolk and continued until after the first battle in Normandy.

sion of the Continent and the final attack on Germany herself—would 1940-44 have to be launched from the British Isles. They had originally hoped that it would be possible to take advantage of the foothold which the Mediterranean forces had gained in Italy, and start the drive to Berlin from Southern Europe—the Balkans, the French Riviera or Italy. But at Teheran they decided that the difficulties of supply and terrain in that region were too great for the huge forces which would be needed for the operation and so, for the second time in the war, Great Britain became the focal point of Allied strategy.

Long before the decision was taken to use Great Britain as the platform from which the invasion of Europe would be launched, a planning staff in England had been drawing up the blue-prints of the operation. After the Teheran Conference the many varied details of the undertaking were carefully pieced together. General Eisenhower, the Allied Commander in the Mediterranean, was appointed Supreme Commander of the expedition and, under him, General Montgomery was given command of the British and Canadian invasion forces.

By the spring of 1944 Great Britain had become one enormous armed camp. The advance contingents of four separate armies—the First, Third, Seventh and Ninth—had arrived from America with naval and air support as well as huge supplies of petrol, ammunition and food. From the Mediterranean area had come several famous British divisions to provide a nucleus of battle-proved men to tackle the first vital weeks after D Day. All over England, in parks, fields and even on the fringes of main roads, vast quantities of trucks, guns, transporters and ambulances—everything that might conceivably be needed for the invasion—lay waiting to be used. In the south more than a dozen English villages were denuded of their inhabitants to allow the finishing touches of invasion training to be carried out under the most realistic conditions.

March turned to April. The suspense began to affect the whole country. Rumours swept from home to home; all leave for non-operational units was stopped, huge transporters carrying landing barges were seen going towards the South Coast, war correspondents arrived in England announcing that they were here to cover the invasion, and the Government refused to grant exit permits to civilians of any nationality to leave the country. It was an anxious period for the civilian population.

For the Army it was different. There had been waiting, long and tiresome months of waiting, but they had been training all the while. Now they were fully trained, magnificently equipped and their morale was high. They knew they would not have to wait much longer before their chance of retribution came.

During the last few days of April and in early May the move to the South Coast began. Squads of Military Police erected innumerable signs to direct the long convoys which rumbled incessantly along the roads leading to the ports. The railways were loaded to capacity with *matériel de guerre*. Transit camps sprouted up around the harbours and in the towns and villages near the sea; and hotels, schools, halls and private houses were requisitioned to accommodate troops. The coming invasion loomed ahead as the most hazardous adventure in all military history.

When the Guards Armoured Division and the 6th Guards Tank Brigade left the North of England in April, 1944, nobody in the Battalions was allowed to know where they were heading. One Battalion advance party was left in the dark until they were within thirty miles of their destination. But when the veil of secrecy was finally lifted no one could have felt disappointed: billets had been arranged for the 1st Battalion at Hove, for the 2nd (commanded since January by Lieut.-Colonel J. N. R. Moore) at Brighton, and for the 4th in the Kentish village of Otterden.

The Battalions were destined to remain in Southern England for the greater part of two months. It was a period which contrasted greatly with the austere time they had spent in the Yorkshire Wolds and the Nottingham Dukeries putting the finishing touches to their training. The 1st and 2nd Battalions were particularly well situated. There were countless theatres, cinemas and dance halls in Brighton, the county ground at Hove could be used for cricket matches, the beach was sufficiently clear of mines to make bathing possible, there was an ice rink near by, and greyhound racing took place every Saturday. Moreover, to put the seal on every man's happiness, twenty-four hours' leave was allowed each week.

Life soon took on the appearance of a continuous Waterloo Ball; but there was much hard work to be done as well. The most urgent task which faced the Battalions was the water-proofing of the tanks and wheeled vehicles. Every single one of the armoured Battalions' seventy-odd tanks as well as the wheeled vehicles of all three Battalions had to be made proof against travelling in anything up to five feet of water, since it was expected that the landings from the various types of landing craft would have to be made some distance off shore. The Technical Adjutants—Capt. A. J. Shaughnessy (1st Battalion), Capt. B. A. Johnston (2nd Battalion) and Capt. J. D. Stobart (4th Battalion)—and their staffs were probably worked harder at this time than at any other, during either training or operations. Vehicles kept arriving right up to the last minute, and each one had to be completely sealed up, even to the point of plugging the bolt and rivet joints with 1940-44 grease and wrapping the electrical components with waterproof silk. By the time a tank was ready the gun had a mackintosh cover, the fan opening and the rear of the engine had cast-iron chutes, and a quick-release explosive wiring ran to the major water-proof components. The crews worked night and day to complete the task and at Brighton there were frequent processions of tanks moving along the sea-front to the local swimming baths, where the preliminary tests were made.

While the vehicles were being water-proofed the administrative departments of the Battalions were making the final touches and adjustments to bring everything up to the standards and down to the minimums required for battle. The Quartermasters—Capt. F. E. J. Carver (1st Battalion), Capt. T. W. Garnett, M.B.E. (2nd Battalion) and Lieut. E. R. Randall (4th Battalion)—were getting rid of surplus equipment; the Signal Officers—Lieut. G. B. Palau (1st Battalion), Lieut. F. J. Jefferson (2nd Battalion) and Capt. P. A. Walker (4th Battalion)—were composing codes to last a month; while the Intelligence Officers—Lieut. J. R. M. Rocke (1st Battalion), Lieut. A. N. Breitmeyer (2nd Battalion) and Lieut. J. N. R. Hearne (4th Battalion) —were closeted in the map rooms pondering over charts of the landing beaches. Everyone was trying desperately to remember what they were certain they had forgotten.

On Wednesday, the 17th of May, Her Royal Highness Princess Elizabeth, the Colonel of the Regiment, came to make her first inspection of the 1st and 2nd Battalions on parade. A site for the ceremony was found on a large, flat sports ground on the top of the steep hill overlooking Hove and the sea. Tarmac was out of the question, and the thin grass surface was coated with dust, but the setting was ideal and the Welsh Guards kindly lent the Battalions a pipe band. Several full-dress rehearsals were held and at 11 o'clock on the appointed morning the 1st Battalion was drawn up in review order for inspection. Her Royal Highness was greeted on her arrival by a Royal Salute, and she then walked round the entire Battalion speaking to all the officers and many of the old soldiers. The Battalion finally marched past and then the officers of both Battalions entertained their Colonel to lunch at the Dudley Hotel. In the afternoon Her Royal Highness inspected the 2nd Battalion, while members of the 1st Battalion lined the streets.

Before the Battalions moved to the South Coast censorship of letters had started, and by the middle of May everyone was very security-minded indeed. As long as a single civilian remained in Brighton or Hove it was impossible to disguise the fact from the outside that over half the Guards Armoured Division was stationed in the two towns, but everyone tried hard and officers returning from their short leave

F

1940-44 would yell "Euston" or "King's Cross" to taxi drivers in the full hearing of their families, only to redirect their puzzled drivers to Victoria when round the first corner. These precautions seemed a trifle far-fetched, but when at the end of May the Government took the drastic step of forbidding diplomats to leave or enter Great Britain, it was realized that no security measures could be too carefully enforced.

On the 6th of June the news for which the whole world had been waiting anxiously arrived—suddenly—in the middle of the morning. The much-delayed invasion had at last taken place and assault troops were already fighting on the Normandy beaches. In the evening personal messages from the Supreme Commander of the Allied Expeditionary Force, General Eisenhower, and from the Commander-in-Chief of the Anglo-Canadian 21st Army Group, General Sir Bernard Montgomery, were read out to each Battalion. And at Brighton, two days later, the Commander of the Guards Armoured Division, Major-General Allan Adair, addressed all ranks of the 5th Brigade, giving them the broad outline of the Allied plan, telling them of the progress that had already been made and wishing them good luck in the future.

For the next week the air was pregnant with rumour. There were those who thought that before the week was up each of the Battalions would be racing to the nearest port. But, although soon after the landings the many beach-heads were linked into a single bridge-head, there could be no question of a quick break-out, and infantry rather than armoured formations were top priority in the build-up of forces in the bridgehead. The Battalions waited patiently. Eve-of-battle parties followed one another with bewildering rapidity. Nearly every troop and platoon had its celebration, but the beer supply of Brighton and Otterden withstood the onslaught gallantly. On the 8th of June the senior officers of the 1st and 2nd Battalions entertained a party of officers of the Canadian Grenadier Guards, an armoured regiment which was destined to play a leading part in the advance of the Canadian First Army. The final party was given on the evening of the 12th of June, when the Commanding Officer of the 1st Battalion and the Adjutant, Capt. R. Steele, entertained the officers of H.Q. Company and the warrant officers of the Battalion. An impending movement order, contained in the single code word "Sugar," did its best to wreck the evening, but this order, like so many experienced in training in the past, was quickly cancelled.

"Sugar," for the 1st Battalion, reappeared in earnest two days later, and at tea time on the 15th of June Capt. Steele returned from Divisional Headquarters at Heathfield Park with the news that the Battalion was to move to Tilbury early the next day. And so, puzzled but excited, the 1st Battalion left its comfortable billets which practically faced the Normandy bridgehead, and drove slowly north 1940-44 throughout the 16th of June. All their motor-cycles were securely strapped to the vehicles and the control of the long column was left in the capable hands of the Military Police. At Caterham, that happy hunting ground of all Guardsmen, the Battalion caught its first glimpse of a flying bomb speeding north towards London, but it was hit some three miles farther on and burst in the air. Near Caterham the Battalion was met by squads of Metropolitan Police, who guided the unwieldy column with skill and precision to the docks. The people of London's East End gave the convoy an unforgettable send-off: many found it more moving than subsequent Continental receptions for "les liberateurs." Cakes, cigarettes and bottles of beer were showered into the vehicles and messages of good will were chalked on the blitzed walls by men and women who had suffered more at the hands of the Luftwaffe than the Battalion was ever likely to suffer at the hands of the Wehrmacht.

The Battalion were to travel in two ships, the s.s. *Ocean Strength* and the s.s. *Fort Tremblant,* American Liberty ships of some 7,500 tons. They left Tilbury at midday on the 19th of June, but before they sailed out of the Thames estuary they spent three days riding at anchor off Southend Pier.

The 2nd Battalion did not leave England until the 30th of June and the 4th Battalion were delayed a further three weeks. Being armoured battalions, they were carried in tank landing ships and in a smaller variety of the same vessel, known as tank landing craft. But although each Battalion travelled separately and at long intervals, these voyages across the Channel were remarkably similar. The sea was calm in each case, German bombers did not interfere with their passage, and when they arrived off the coast of Normandy, at the Gold and Juno Beaches, they were able to land in such shallow water that only a small percentage of their water-proofed vehicles became immersed.

PART TWO

THE NORTH-WEST EUROPEAN CAMPAIGN OF 1944-45

CHAPTER III

NORMANDY

1ST, 2ND AND 4TH BATTALIONS

1

RETURN TO FRANCE

First impressions of Normandy—General Montgomery's strategy—The Guards Armoured Division captures Cagny—The Division reorganized

THE Normandy campaign was divided into three phases: first the assault; then the securing of the bridgehead and the build-up of sup- porting forces; finally—the most spectacular operation of all—the break-out. When the three Battalions of the Regiment landed in France the campaign was still in its infancy, so even the 4th Battalion, who were the last to arrive, had over ten days to wait before taking part in the fighting. 1944
June-
July

The three Battalions spent these opening days of their new life on the Continent in fields and orchards east of Bayeux near the village of Esquay-sur-Seulles, which had emerged unscathed from the first turbulent hours of the landings. There was plenty for the Battalions to do. All their vehicles had to be completely de-water-proofed and then camouflaged, their weapons needed cleaning and all their ammunition and equipment had to be inspected and checked. Once these jobs had been done, arrangements were made for observer parties of officers and senior non-commissioned officers to go forward in jeeps and watch the battles taking place. There was much in the bridgehead to interest three almost green Battalions, and as they moved about examining burned-out Tiger tanks, snipers' crow's-nests and the assortment of enemy equipment which littered the countryside, they gradually formed valuable impressions of what warfare in Normandy would be like.*

As the days dragged by, and the prospect of action seemed as remote as ever, the smallest things took on an exaggerated importance: the arrival of the mail and the newspapers, the next meal and the next

---

*Three 1st Battalion officers, Lieuts. A. B. Wodehouse, J. N. McEwen and R. W. Humphreys, together with the Battalion's twelve snipers, spent forty-eight hours in the line with the Royal Welch Fusiliers. They went out on day and night patrols, but never had the chance of firing a shot.

1944 bath—the essentials and the little luxuries of life which normally pass unnoticed. Their very existence in the throbbing, overcrowded bridge-head seemed little short of a miracle. For less than a month before the soil of France had not known the tread of a British soldier's boot for four long years.

By the middle of July the campaign had reached its most critical stage, both for the Germans and the Allies. For nearly six weeks both sides had been battering the bridgehead perimeter, but neither had gained any spectacular success. After a bitter struggle the Allies had captured Caen and the Americans had forced their way up the Cher-bourg Peninsula, but in the central sector villages had changed hands frequently and still the front line did not move.

With nearly a million men across the Channel the Allies were by now admirably situated to launch a major offensive. Indeed, it was imperative that they should attempt to break out of the bridgehead soon, because with such an enormous force in an area not much larger than the county of Rutland they were finding it excessively difficult to manoeuvre to advantage or to create deception. Nowhere in the neigh-bourhood of the bridgehead perimeter could tanks be successfully employed; if they were to make proper use of their superiority in numbers they would have to fight the Germans in flatter and less cumbersome country.

The Germans were fully aware of the Allied predicament, and in an endeavour to keep them contained within the bridgehead they decided to take a risk. Finding that their Seventh Army, grouped opposite the bridgehead, was incapable of bearing the weight of Allied attacks alone, they brought down to the Normandy battlefields their Fifteenth Army, which until then had been waiting in the area of Calais, prepared to oppose an attempt to capture the flying-bomb sites. This meant that if the Allies succeeded in breaking out of the bridge-head and surrounding the two armies there would be no troops left in Northern France to bar the way to a thrust towards the Rhine.

At his headquarters at St. Germain, on the outskirts of Paris, von Kluge, the German Supreme Commander, foresaw the two ways in which the Allies could surround his forces: they could either thrust out into the Falaise Plain or sweep round to the Brittany Peninsula; both routes offered excellent country for tank warfare. But as the main strength of the Allied armies was grouped round Caen, von Kluge had no alternative but to position the greater part of the Fifteenth Army near Caen too.

This was exactly what General Montgomery had hoped would happen. For as long as the bulk of the German armour was pinned down at Caen he could safely launch the Americans towards Brittany **1944** in a wide sweep behind the German forces facing the bridgehead. An operation to ensure that the Germans would not start moving their tanks across to the western edges of the bridgehead was therefore planned forthwith.

As Caen was in the British sector, General Dempsey, the Commander of the British Second Army, took charge of the operation. Having at his disposal three full armoured divisions—the 7th and 11th and the Guards—he decided to mass them all in the VIII Corps and to move them secretly to the eastern part of the bridgehead. To the I Corps he allotted the task of throwing additional bridges across the Orne Canal and of forcing gaps in the minefields lining the enemy defences; the XXX Corps was to make a diversionary attack southwest of Caen; and a new method of synchronizing heavy bomber and artillery support was used for the first time during the operation in the hope that when the force of some five or six hundred tanks broke out into the Falaise Plain they would be protected in front and on both flanks by a wall of explosive. It was a plan that depended for success on perfect timing. How far it succeeded can be judged by the experiences of the 1st and 2nd Battalions of the Regiment, who went into action for the first time in Normandy during this operation.

The offensive was scheduled to begin at 6 a.m. on the 18th of July, **July 17** so throughout the 17th the armoured divisions wended their way across country to the ridge overlooking Caen, where they were to concentrate. Rough tracks had been hewn through the fields and orchards by bulldozers, but as they were only marked with white tapes which were soon turned an indifferent colour by the dust the tank commanders and drivers had the greatest difficulty in finding their way. However, few tanks went astray and by 6 p.m. the Caen Ridge was swarming with the armoured might of the VIII Corps.

Promptly at 6 a.m. the next morning the air was filled with the roar **July 18** of a thousand heavy and medium bombers flying in from the sea. Within a few minutes the south-western suburbs of Caen, still held by the Germans, and the villages beyond were shrouded in a thick cloud of smoke and dust. Anti-aircraft tracer shot into the sky, but the German gunners had evidently been taken by surprise; only seven Lancasters were shot down.

As soon as the bombing raid was over the ground artillery opened up, and the tanks started to move off down the farther side of the ridge in the direction of the Orne Canal. The 11th Armoured Division led, with the Guards Armoured Division close behind; the Desert Rats were farther to the right. Before long the 11th Armoured Division *See Map p. 76* were across the Orne Canal, but on the farther bank they found the

1944 gaps through the minefield dangerously narrow. A number of their tanks went up on mines, making it difficult for others to pass. Soon a bottleneck developed—a misfortune which had a fatal effect on the rest of the operation, as it gave the Germans time to recover from the shock of the aerial bombardment. The 11th Armoured Division had not gone two miles beyond the minefield on the farther side of the canal before they were fired on by anti-tank guns surrounding Cagny, a village on the Caen—Paris highway. Rather than hold up the whole of the advance while dealing with this opposition, they veered off to the south-west and left Cagny to be cleared by the Guards Armoured Division. A little later the 11th Armoured Division ran into the main force of enemy tanks and could not proceed. So, scarcely four hours after the bombing raid, the offensive petered out into a series of local engagements which prevented the armour from gathering sufficient momentum to burst forth into the Falaise Plain.

CAGNY

It took the Guards Armoured Division the rest of the morning and the whole of the afternoon to capture Cagny. The main responsibility for this task fell on the 2nd Battalion of the Regiment, who led the Division through the minefields and were therefore first to fall foul of the German anti-tank guns. Every advantage lay with the defenders: the ground haze was thickened by the dust churned up by the armour, and thick hedges and belts of tall trees limited the vision of the tank commanders as they peered through their field-glasses, trying to pick out the enemy guns in the corn and root fields. Three tanks of the leading squadron, No. 2, were hit when they were still over a mile from Cagny, and as it was impossible to escape the fire by manœuvring to left or right the squadron was brought to a standstill. The Commanding Officer, Lieut.-Colonel J. N. R. Moore, seeing that a frontal assault on the village was out of the question, went up to confer with Major Sir Arthur Grant, the squadron leader of No. 2 Squadron; but he had only just returned to his own tank some hundred yards in rear of the squadron when Sir Arthur Grant's tank was hit and, although the crew survived, Sir Arthur himself was killed outright. At much the same time Lieut. T. O. Ruggles-Brise's tank was knocked out, but all the crew escaped alive, with the exception of the officer, who was posted as missing and is presumed to have been killed.

Reports had reached the Commanding Officer that Tiger tanks were operating to the left and left rear of the Battalion, so he ordered No. 3 Squadron to take up a position guarding this flank. The squadron continued in this role throughout the day, fighting several sharp engagements with the enemy armour, in one of which Lieut. The Hon.

J. P. Corbett's tank was hit, and the whole crew were killed. While **1944**
No. 3 Squadron were holding back the Tigers, half of No. 1 Squadron,
consisting of two troops under the command of Capt. J. A. P. Jones,
were dispatched round the left flank towards Cagny. Their progress
was bitterly opposed by the Germans. Although Capt. Jones's tank
itself was hit and the whole crew were severely burned through manning their posts long after the tank had begun to blaze, the leading
troop, less two tanks which stuck in bomb craters, reached the outskirts of the village by 4 p.m. This achievement enabled Lieut.-Colonel
Moore to call up the King's Company (Major N. E. W. Baker), who
entered Cagny soon afterwards. The Germans had withdrawn, leaving
behind a mass of guns and equipment, around which were littered
quantities of paper, like confetti at a carnival. The company jumped
to the conclusion that a brigade headquarters must have been operating in the extreme front line, but whenever they came upon abandoned German equipment in the future there was always a similar
profusion of paper near by.

While the 2nd Battalion was engaged in front of Cagny, the progress of the rest of the Division farther back had necessarily been
slow. The King's Company, moving forward with the reserve squadron of the 2nd Battalion, was mortared and shelled continually and
could do no more than accept the surrender of little parties of enemy
who, dazed by the air and gun bombardment, had little inclination to
continue fighting.

The remainder of the 1st Battalion, operating with the 2nd Battalion
Irish Guards and the 1st Battalion Coldstream Guards, still farther
back, spent an equally frustrating afternoon. They were able to send
out small parties into the cornfields to collect prisoners, but they had
no opportunity of taking a direct part in the action. They were
mortared all the afternoon: one shell hit an anti-tank gun of No. 3
Company which had just taken up position, and Lieut. A. P. St. C.
Raynor was seriously wounded in the stomach. Earlier, Lieut. R. W.
Humphreys (King's Company) had been run over by a carrier and
was incapacitated for the rest of the campaign.

As soon as Cagny was captured two companies of the 1st Battalion
took part in small attacks designed to carry the advance beyond the
village. With the 2nd Battalion Irish Guards, No. 2 Company pushed
south-west down the Caen—Paris highway; but the open country on
either side was too well defended by enemy anti-tank guns for the 2nd
Irish to go far and, although the company managed to reach a cross-
roads about half-way between Cagny and Vimont, it was dark by the
time they got there, and they were ordered to return. No. 4 Company
patrolled down the side of a large wood directly south of Cagny, and,

having reached the railway running north of the village of Le Poirier, remained there until relieved by the 32nd Brigade the next morning.

The attack was not resumed the next day. The 2nd Battalion waited in reserve to the north of Cagny until the 21st, when it received orders to move for a rest to Mondeville, the industrial quarter of Caen. On the 19th the 1st Battalion took up position around Cagny to free the 5th Coldstream for an attack east of the village on the following morning. It had been intended originally that they should be relieved on the night of the 20th by a battalion of the Argyll and Sutherland Highlanders, but a violent rainstorm played havoc with the roads and disrupted the arrangements for the change-over. In the wake of the downpour came hordes of mosquitoes, and these, coupled with increasingly accurate mortar bombardments and an attack by German fighters, made life extremely unpleasant for the 1st Battalion. They had to spend most of the time taking cover in water-logged and mosquito-ridden trenches. The night before they were finally relieved Capt. J. H. Lane-Fox, second-in-command of No. 2 Company, went to investigate a light which was flashing in Cagny village some three hundred yards from his company headquarters, and was shot in the leg; the wound would not have been serious had it not been in close proximity to another he had received when serving with the 3rd Battalion in 1940. On the 22nd of July it became possible for the Argyll and Sutherland Highlanders to come up, and the 1st Battalion drove back to join the 2nd Battalion in Caen, from the neighbourhood of which, five days before, they had set forth with high hopes of breaking out into the Falaise Plain. As a newspaper correspondent put it, they had broken "in"—but not "out."

Opinion varied considerably on the reasons why the armoured thrust had not met with greater success. General Dietrich, the Commander of the I S.S. Panzer Corps which opposed the attack, was later captured and awarded the credit to an old trick he had learnt in Russia; by putting his ear to the ground, he claimed, he had heard the British tanks advancing from some miles away and had thus been able to strengthen his defences in the path of the attack. Some believed that the pause between the bombardment and the attack on Cagny, caused by the bottleneck in the minefields, was responsible. But whatever the causes of failure, the fact remained that the majority of the troops taking part were green and the experience they gained during the operation saved many lives later on. Considering that the 1st Battalion had been in the line for four and a half days and that the 2nd Battalion had borne the brunt of the attack on Cagny, the two Battalions of the Regiment had not paid an unduly high price. In the 1st Battalion six officers—Capt. J. H. Lane-Fox and Lieuts.

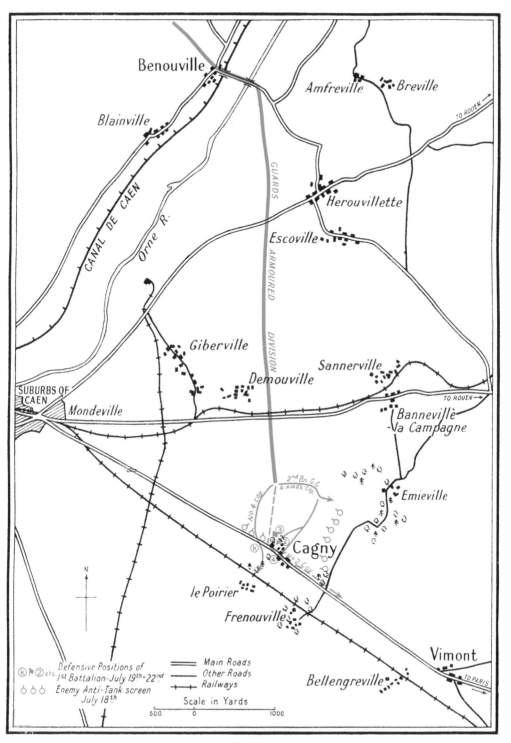

CAGNY

A. P. St. C. Raynor, R. W. Humphreys, J. F. L. Denny, J. H. W. **1944** Huggins and K. C. Boles—had been wounded, and fifteen other ranks had been killed. The 2nd Battalion had lost twenty-two tanks; two officers and ten other ranks had been killed, one officer and twenty-five other ranks had been wounded, and one officer and two other ranks were missing.

One immediate result of the battle was that the Commander of the Guards Armoured Division, Major-General Allan Adair, decided to make changes in the organization of the Division. During training in England and in the recent battle the Division's four armoured battalions had been pooled in the 5th Brigade, and each (with the exception of the Welsh Guards, who were mounted in Cromwells) had been supported by a highly mobile motor company of the 1st Battalion of the Regiment; the 32nd Brigade contained only infantry. The armour of the 5th Brigade went into action first, relying on the motor companies to deal with anti-tank guns, guard the prisoners and protect the harbour areas at night, while the 32nd Brigade came forward to mount major infantry attacks and consolidate the gains of the tanks. This formation had been devised when a comparatively rapid advance across good tank country had been envisaged, but in Normandy, where anti-tank gunners and bazooka-men could conceal themselves with ease and where advancing troops frequently left whole pockets of unseen and undamaged enemy behind them, it was clearly impracticable. General Adair therefore decided that in future each brigade should be composed of two armoured battle groups, each consisting of an armoured battalion and a motor or lorried-infantry battalion. The effect of this reorganization was to increase the Division's mobility, and to split it up into four component parts, each of which was able to fend for itself against strong opposition. In the 5th Brigade the 1st and 2nd Battalions of the Regiment formed the "Grenadier Group."* There were also the Coldstream, Irish and Welsh Groups, one of which (usually the Coldstream Group) joined the Grenadiers in the 5th Brigade, leaving the other two to form the 32nd Brigade. This new combination resulted in perfect tank and infantry co-operation: it had the advantage over normal methods that the same armoured battalion always fought alongside the same infantry battalion; and both were battalions of the same regiment.

---

*It was arranged that the Group would be commanded by the senior commanding officer, Lieut.-Colonel E. H. Goulburn (1st Battalion), and that Lieut.-Colonel J. N. R. Moore (2nd Battalion) would be the Second-in-Command. The Group Commander always gave out orders direct to companies and squadrons.

2

THE ADVANCE TO THE SOULEUVRE VALLEY

*American Third Army break out towards Brittany while the British pin
down German armour near Caen—6th Guards Tank Brigade ordered to
capture Caumont Ridge in support of Americans—4th Battalion in action
for first time—A resounding victory—Guards Armoured Division advance
towards Vire—Lessons of the early battles*

1944
July 22-30
The 1st and 2nd Battalions remained in the suburbs of Caen until the 30th of July. From D Day onwards the R.A.F. had been drenching the whole area with bombs, and there was scarcely a building left that was not a burnt-out shell. Victims of the bombardments, German soldiers and French civilians alike, lay in the streets unburied; there were gaping holes in all the drains, and smashed furniture and the filthy refuse of many weeks of chaos lay scattered all over the town and its outskirts. These conditions made it difficult enough for the Battalions to clean their vehicles, weapons and equipment, but their worries were further increased by German shells which landed with increasing precision where they were working. During one bombardment the Padre of the 2nd Battalion, the Rev. Walter Berry, and Lieut. P. G. Rawlings were killed.

On the 25th another attempt was made to break out into the Falaise Plain by cutting the enemy line due south of Caen, between the villages of St. Martin de Fontenay and Tilly la Campagne. The 2nd and 3rd Canadian Infantry Divisions were to open the attack and the 7th Armoured Division and the Guards Armoured Division were to follow through. But the 2nd and 3rd Canadian Infantry Divisions met stiffer opposition than had been expected, and the attack was cancelled before the greater part of the Guards Armoured Division had moved. It had been even less successful than the attempt to reach Falaise in the previous week.

This second setback might well have had a serious effect on the rest of the Normandy campaign, but, happily, on the other side of the bridgehead, events had taken a turn for the better. General Montgomery had decided that the time had come to launch the Americans and after one of the most costly and determined battles of the war General Bradley, who controlled the American armies under General Montgomery, had forced his way into St. Lo, the key to Brittany and the Loire Valley. General Patton's Third Army had already taken over and was heading boldly for Avranches. The German line had at last begun to give way.

Bertram Park

MAJOR-GENERAL A. H. S. ADAIR, D.S.O., M.C.
Commander of the Guards Armoured Division.

For three days the Americans made excellent progress, but on the 1944 28th they sent word to the British Second Army that they were being constantly harassed by Germans firing from the high ground on their left flank. As this ground was directly in front of the Second Army's position, they asked that an offensive be launched immediately to capture it. The manœuvre would at the same time forestall any enemy attempt to form a pivot some ten miles ahead of the central sector of the bridgehead, between Caumont and Villers Bocage. If the British armoured divisions were successful, they could push forward to Vire. As the Canadians were about to make a third attempt to reach Falaise from the western side of the bridgehead, there was every chance that the German armies would be cut into three slices by these triple attacks to the south.

The British army's forward positions were at that time on the Caumont Ridge, over twenty miles south-west of Caen. The heights from which the Germans were firing on the Americans lay six miles farther south. The ground in between was typical of what was known locally as the bocage. Narrow, twisting lanes, concealed by banks of anything up to ten feet high, divided cider-apple orchards and woods into a thousand different patterns. There were only a few white, stone farmhouses to dispel the illusion that the valley was part of the "purple land" of Peru. It was obvious that only Churchill tanks, with their broad tracks and powerful engines, could hope to cross it. The 6th Guards Tank Brigade, which contained the 4th Battalion of the Regiment, was therefore ordered to move up to the Caumont Ridge. Early on the 30th of July it was to support the infantry of the 15th (Scottish) Division in an attack on the heights beyond.

CAUMONT*

When they received the order to move at 7 o'clock on the evening of the 28th, the 4th Battalion were still in the orchards near Bayeux. The tanks were hurriedly packed and by 9 o'clock they were on the move. It was a fine evening, but when it grew dark there was no moon, and, as the exact destination had not been disclosed, the only means of steering was by the light of small green lamps which had been placed on the ground to mark the way. These became less and less frequent as the journey continued, but after winding backwards and forwards through what seemed an eternity of orchards, sunken lanes

---

*This description of the 4th Battalion's engagement at Caumont, as well as certain other passages relating to the 4th Battalion in this book, has already appeared in "The 6th Guards Tank Brigade," by Patrick Forbes (Sampson Low & Marston Co. Ltd.). The author wishes to acknowledge Messrs. Sampson Low's permission to reprint them.

1944 and tortuous tracks the Churchills reached the ridge overlooking Caumont by dawn the following morning.

July 29   The plan was unfolded that afternoon. The 4th Battalion, with Flails* and Crocodiles† in support, were to open the attack by capturing Lutain Wood and the little village of Sept Vents, both just below *See Map* the Caumont Ridge. Then the 4th Coldstream and the 3rd Scots *p. 82* Guards were to run across the valley side by side, the former to take some high ground slightly to the east, and the latter to capture Hill 309, the dominating feature of the whole area. Finally, the Guards Armoured Division was to pass through and push farther south still. Heavy artillery and heavy bombers were to pave the way for the attack and the 43rd Division and the 11th Armoured Division were to protect the flanks.

The only essential feature of the plan that could not be revealed during the afternoon was exactly when zero hour was to be. When the 4th Battalion settled down for the night they were under the impression that it would definitely not be earlier than 10 a.m. By 2 o'clock no message to the contrary had arrived, but for safety's sake a runner was sent to Brigade Headquarters. The man had not returned by 4 o'clock, so another runner was sent to the 4th Coldstream to see if they had any information. An hour later word reached the Battalion that zero hour had been brought forward and that the barrage was to begin at 7.30 a.m.! So they had precisely two and a half hours in which to get up, have something to eat, pack up the tanks, check their wirelesses, warm up the engines, contact the infantry and move to their positions on the ridge before the bombing began.

July 30   Somehow they managed it. At 8 a.m., a few minutes after the last of the bombers had banked away, the leading tanks of the 4th Battalion rumbled slowly over the skyline and drove down into the valley below. As the tank commanders peered through the thick early morning mist they could see smoke billowing upwards from Sept Vents, and farther to the left they could just pick out the outline of Lutain Wood. Passing through the gaps in the minefields they fanned out and began firing their guns in deadly earnest for the first time.

It was all over remarkably quickly. The Germans had been told that they were faced by one battle-weary American division, and the sight of fifty Churchills supporting the formidable 15th (Scottish) Division convinced them at once of the folly of standing their ground. As soon as the flame-throwers squirted the edges of Lutain Wood, Germans emerged from it in droves. It was the same at Sept Vents— a few shots of high explosive from the tanks, a few bursts of machine-

*Sherman tanks equipped with a device for clearing minefields.
†Churchill tanks equipped with flame-throwing apparatus.

gun fire and then out of the ruins of the village came a long line of 1944 quivering prisoners. There were Poles, Russians and even two reputed Japanese among them, but not many officers. Most of them had run away as soon as they caught sight of the Churchills.

Both Sept Vents and Lutain Wood were in the hands of the 4th Battalion by 8.30, only half an hour after the attack began. But for this speedy victory the Battalion paid the price of two officers, Capt. G. C. Grey, M.P., for some time the youngest Member of the House of Commons, and Lieut. J. G. Marshall-Cornwall, both of whom were killed by snipers. There were no other casualties, although five tanks went up on mines: Major J. C. Gascoigne's, while he was dealing with a sniper on Sept Vents church tower; Lieut. H. A. Verney's, while he was moving towards Lutain Wood; and the tanks commanded by Lieut. A. MacR. Collie, Lieut. J. R. C. Higgins and Sergt. Bowen.

As soon as the 4th Battalion had punched a hole in the enemy defences at Sept Vents and Lutain Wood, the 4th Coldstream and the 3rd Scots Guards passed through it. German resistance soon became fiercer and the battle raged all day—ending in a daring tank dash by the Coldstream on to Hill 309. The 4th Battalion, moving behind the Coldstream, brought up their infantry and then harboured for the night in a field near La Ferriere au Doyen. In the course of the next twenty-four hours the Germans made many attempts to dislodge the Coldstream from Hill 309, but the Coldstream repelled each of the attacks and held firm.

The Battle of Caumont opened up the road to Vire, and cost the German 326th Division an entire brigade. The 6th Tank Brigade won praise from many quarters. The Higher Command, as was their custom when troops went into action for the first time, had provided all the support possible in the form of heavy bombers and heavy artillery. But they evidently had not expected such a resounding victory, and messages of congratulation reached Brigadier G. L. Verney from all over the world. The Commander of the VIII Corps, Lieutenant-General Sir Richard O'Connor, sent a message in which he said: "No tank unit has been handled with greater dash and determination." And nearly a year later General Dempsey told the Brigade that he considered the Battle of Caumont to have been one of the most important events of the campaign in North-West Europe.

The 30th of July was a day of victories on all parts of the front. The Americans, on the right, reached Rennes and St. Malo, and their armoured spearheads started to fan out behind the German forces facing the bridgehead. But, although it was evident that the whole defensive front was crumbling, there were still a number of pockets of enemy directly to the south of Hill 309. At first it seemed unlikely

G

1944 that they could hold out for long, but they made such good use of the succession of steep, wooded ridges which separated Caumont and Vire—country which has been called the "Norman Switzerland"—that they caused the heavy fighting to continue for another ten days.

The 4th Battalion renewed the offensive south of Caumont on the **July 31** evening of the 31st of July with an attack designed to capture the high ground just north of the Bois du Homme. It was not mounted until a quarter to seven, and the preparations were considerably enlivened by an attack on the Battalion harbour area by rocket-firing Typhoons. Fortunately no damage or casualties resulted, but, to add to the delay, artillery from another Corps proceeded to smoke and bombard the whole of the ground over which the Battalion were to advance. When the attack finally began, the tank commanders saw what they thought were German Panthers in the distance, but, to their great relief, these turned out later to be only wooden dummies. They met only slight opposition and were soon on the high ground, although the thick smoke which enveloped it made the infantry's task harder and the support which could be given by the tanks much less effective. Just as No. 1 Squadron arrived on the objective at about 10 o'clock, eight Typhoons dropped sixteen bombs, probably 500-pounders, on top of them and these were immediately followed by a further eight aircraft firing rockets and cannons. Again good fortune prevented any casualties.

While the 4th Battalion were fighting this battle the Grenadier Group were moving up towards the front line. They had left Caen on the 30th and had spent one day and a night near Bayeux, coming up to some large cornfields on the Caumont Ridge earlier that day. During the night they harboured in fields adjoining the Caumont—Vire road, about four miles south of Caumont. For this move the new formation was used for the first time, and the companies and squadrons harboured in groups which worked together until the end of the war: the King's Company with No. 2 Squadron; No. 2 Company with No. 3 Squadron; and No. 4 Company with No. 1 Squadron.

The 2nd Irish Guards and the 5th Coldstream had preceded the Grenadier Group and spent the night just behind the leading troops of the 15th (Scottish) Division. The next morning this Group was ordered to pass through the infantry and secure the high ground two or three miles farther south. If they met with success the Grenadier Group could then pass through them down the Caumont—Vire road, force a crossing over the River Souleuvre and swing east to Vassy.

The Grenadier Group had only just harboured for the night when **Aug. 1** the Commanding Officer of the 1st Battalion, who, as senior com-

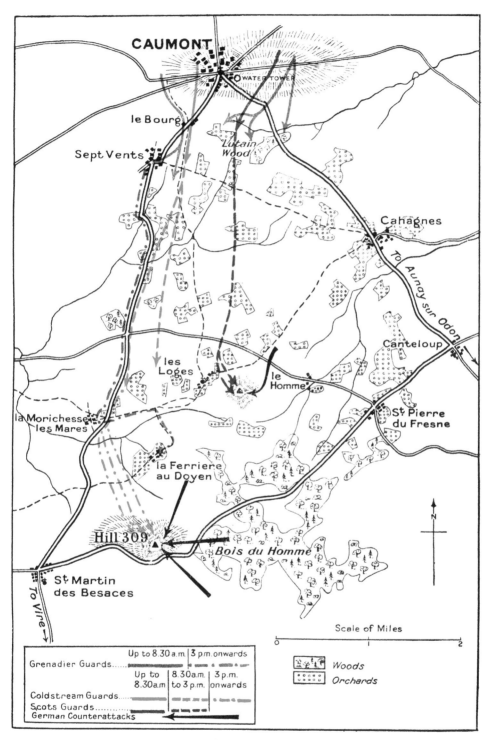

CAUMONT

manding officer, was in command of the Group, received orders that 1944 the two Battalions were to move at dawn to St. Martin des Besaces, a village about a mile and a half north of the high ground which the Irish Guards Group were to capture. These orders aroused hopes of a swift advance; but they were short-lived. Soon after dawn the Irish Guards sent word that they were unable to make headway beyond the dominant feature of the high ground, Point 192. The danger of a counter-attack seemed so acute that the Grenadier Group were ordered to take up positions in and around the village to defend the important road junctions and to keep in close contact with the Irish Guards in case they needed help. With the exception of the King's Company, they remained around the cross-roads at St. Martin des Besaces for a period of twenty-four hours, during which time no general offensive action took place, although patrols were sent out frequently both to make contact with other formations on the flanks and to locate in greater detail enemy outposts. The companies in the village provided the Germans with excellent targets and they suffered a number of casualties from shelling.

In the middle of the morning Capt. The Hon. V. P. Gibbs, second-in-command of the King's Company, went forward to discuss the situation with the Irish Guards, and he was asked to bring up the company to help in the defence of Point 192. After occupying Point 192 for nearly six hours, Major N. E. W. Baker, the company commander, was ordered to go south through Le Tourneur and to capture the bridge beyond, being given a troop of tanks from the 2nd Irish Guards to support him. A short distance down the road the company was fired on by two enemy tanks and by infantry of unknown strength positioned just north of Le Tourneur. Major Baker gradually forced the enemy to fall back by sending small groups of men armed with Piats* round the enemy flanks, but when night fell the company was still some way away from the bridge. The tank troops were unable to give proper support owing to the high banks and hedges, and as it was almost impossible to pin-point the enemy positions Major Baker decided that it would be suicidal to try to rush the bridge without more infantry support. He therefore withdrew and took over the positions of two Coldstream companies which were dispatched soon after midnight to capture the bridge.

On that day the 4th Battalion remained stationary. No. 1 Squadron was on the high ground which had been captured the day before; and the rest of the Battalion in a harbour area. In the evening a troop was called out to help the King's Own Scottish Borderers to put in an attack on a wooded ridge running north-east from the Bois du

*Anti-tank weapons used by British infantry.

1944 Homme, into which it appeared German infantry had been infiltrating during the day. Sergt. Berresford's troop of No. 2 Squadron was chosen for this action and, although there was considerable opposition and Sergt. Berresford came so close to a German sniper that he was able to shoot him with a revolver, the attack was successful.

With the leading units of the 6th Guards Tank Brigade thus firmly entrenched on the heights of the Bois du Homme and the leading units of the Guards Armoured Division dominating the valley of the Souleuvre, the two formations were now half-way between Caumont and Vire. The events of the past few days had provided ample evidence of the difficulties confronting armoured forces in the bocage country, but, nevertheless, it seemed reasonable to suppose that a final determined attack might overwhelm the German forces defending the road to Vire. A plan with more ambitious intentions than those of the previous day was therefore drawn up during the night.

The Battle of Cagny and the advance to the Souleuvre Valley formed the connecting link between the three Grenadier Battalions' training in England and their service as combatant units from Normandy to the Baltic. What, then, did these battles teach the Battalions? What was it like to be fighting in Normandy during that fateful summer of 1944?

In the few weeks of grace which each of the Battalions were given before their first battles, they all had time and opportunity to gather a good deal of second-hand information about the peculiarities of fighting in Normandy. They knew, for instance, that they would always be short of sleep, because daylight lasted from 5 o'clock in the morning until 11 o'clock at night. They knew that the dust thrown up by the powdery tracks and lanes would make the legendary "fog of battle" more potent than ever. They knew that the little meadows and copses and trees which screened the roads would create innumerable difficulties in pin-pointing targets.

They had been told a lot about the Germans. That the German was still a good soldier, that he had an excellent eye for country, and that he was using his weapons, especially his machine guns, to good advantage, had been drummed into them unceasingly. They knew that to reduce casualties the Germans were holding their main lines of resistance thinly, but that as soon as the artillery barrages lifted they would bring up their reserves again. Reports had reached the Battalions about the German prisoners. They had been told that as a breed they showed far less confidence than they had in the desert— no doubt largely owing to the fact that their company commanders

and even their commanding officers were now in the habit of dis- 1944
appearing in the face of danger.

On the subject of our own methods of fighting in Normandy the
Battalions' instruction had been no less thorough. The distinguished
part that heavy bombers were playing in almost every battle had been
made plain to them daily since their arrival in Normandy. Even the
least observant had been able to see how flexible our heavy artillery
had become: they knew that it would have been possible in an emergency for the artillery of a whole Corps to be brought down to aid a
platoon. They had been told that the close support given to the
forward troops by rocket-firing aircraft was proving every whit as
devastating as the German dive-bombers during the period prior to
the collapse of France. They knew that tanks were playing a vital part
in driving the Germans back—despite the unsuitable country. Other
armoured formations had told them that a few rounds of high explosive fired into the base of a stubborn bank or a forbidding tree worked
wonders.

These and many other points the Battalions had grasped before
they went into action in Normandy. But there were three lessons, the
implications of which they could not fully grasp second-hand. Their
first battles brought these home to them in full measure.

The first was geographical. No matter how long a tank commander
pored over his maps or listened to the accounts brought back by
people who had experienced them, he could not visualize the compli-
cations of fighting over Norman country until he had done so himself.
In Yorkshire there had been many an exercise on the moors when
tanks stuck in gullies or overturned in quarries. But in Normandy it
was infinitely worse. The Battalions realized in their very first battle
that they would often be frustrated and that they would miss innumerable golden opportunities because a tank, let alone a carrier, could
not climb up an almost perpendicular bank or crash through a tree-
lined hedge at a vital moment.

The second lesson concerned the German tanks. The 2nd and 4th
Battalions had been warned time and time again about the giant
Panther and Tiger tanks which the Germans were using, but when
they actually came to meet them in battle the Battalions began to
feel an even greater respect for them. They saw their own perfectly
aimed shots bounding off the frontal armour of the enemy tanks like
ping-pong balls, and they learnt once and for all that there were only
two effective methods of dealing with them: either to move round to
the flank of the Hun tank and shoot at its sides at a range of no more
than five hundred yards, or to call on the medium artillery to deal
with it from behind. Furthermore, it had been shown that neither the

1944 Sherman nor the Churchill (which was the most heavily armoured tank yet produced by either Britain or America) was capable of withstanding a direct hit from a German 88-mm. anti-tank gun.

The third lesson concerned snipers. Snipers were ubiquitous in Normandy, and the very first battles made it abundantly clear that drastic measures would have to be taken to find an antidote for them. For the tanks a partial answer was found in the form of an armoured plate, about ten inches high, welded to the back of the turret cupola; but the last word was obviously in the hands of the tank commander himself. For only if he resolved never to show his head above the cupola need he have no fears of high-pitched "pings" peppering the side of his turret.

3

LAST BATTLES IN THE BOCAGE

King's Company clear the road to Vire—Enemy attempts to recapture Drouet Hill resisted—All three Grenadier Battalions combine for attack on hills near Arclais—4th Battalion's unsuccessful attack on Estry—1st Battalion occupy Viessoix after heavy fighting—The Germans, having failed to retake Avranches, stream out of the Falaise pocket towards Seine

Aug. 2   At sunrise on the 2nd of August the Cromwells of the Welsh Guards led the Guards Armoured Division down the northern slopes of the Souleuvre Valley. They reached the main Caen—Vire road without much difficulty and found the bridge over the Souleuvre intact. One *See Map* squadron then went straight on towards Vire and continued to find *p. 102* the going easy, but the squadron that turned left along the Vassy road, which ran beside the river, was soon brought to a halt by small-arms and anti-tank-gun fire coming from either side of the valley. The valley was just like a Devonshire combe, deep, narrow and twisting—a hiker's paradise, but quite unsuitable for a tank attack. The Welsh Guards were therefore told to withdraw slightly and the Commander of the Grenadier Group was ordered to clear the high ground on either side of the Vassy road.

It was hoped that the advance could then continue along it, or at least that the Irish Guards would then be able to pass unhindered over the river and down the less-treacherous main road towards Vire. But as soon as the various companies and squadrons took up their positions for the attack, it was realized that the enemy were in far greater numbers than had previously been supposed. Gradually what was intended to be an offensive sweep towards Vassy developed into a

August, 1944.   Sherman and Churchill tanks negotiating a typical lane in the Normandy Bocage.

Tanks of the Guards Armoured Division and the 6th Guards Tank Brigade in a valley near Vassy, Normandy.

bitter defensive action to allow the rest of the Division to make for **1944**
Vire. And in the resulting traffic jams the 6th Guards Tank Brigade
was unable to move down from the Bois du Homme to take part in the
fighting.

DROUET AND ARCLAIS

When the Grenadier Group was called forward the Commanding
Officer of the 1st Battalion decided to use two companies for the
operation, one on either side of the road and river. No. 2 Company,
on the right, were to drive the enemy off the Drouet Spur which overlooked the Vassy road and then clear the village and the northern
edges of the two big woods to the east. On the left, a motor platoon
of No. 4 Company, supported by a section of carriers and a troop of
tanks from No. 2 Squadron, was to seize the high ground about a mile
due east of Catheolles, whereupon the whole company was to establish
itself on a more dominating feature another mile farther east, which
was marked on the map as Point 260. The King's Company and No. 2
Squadron were to be used more locally; they were given the task of
driving away an enemy tank which the Welsh Guards had spotted and
which was threatening the main Caen—Vire road. Ostensibly a battalion operation, the nature of the country and the consequent difficulty of control and communications reduced liaison between the
companies to a minimum, so that in effect the engagement, like the
Battle of Cagny, became a series of entirely separate company and
squadron actions.

Although it was the smallest of the three, the most satisfactory of
these actions was that of the King's Company and No. 2 Squadron.
Moving off from Catheolles at midday, they contacted the Welsh
Guards and then tried to work round the flank of the Panther which
was holding up the advance down the main road to Vire. The enemy
tank soon decided to retreat and in the resulting rush to engage it the
company discovered that it was supported by two other tanks as well
as by a party of infantry. They immediately aimed their Piats and
were still hoping to catch the enemy force when suddenly another
party of infantry and five more tanks started to counter-attack. Some
very confused fighting followed and No. 2 Squadron, who were unable to get forward because of the hedges and ditches, began shelling
a wood only a hundred yards in front of the company, having mistaken
them for enemy. Eventually the enemy were made to withdraw and
Major N. E. W. Baker took his company back to Catheolles, having
by that time successfully rid the main Vire road of enemy fire. It was
thanks to their efforts that the 4th Battalion and the 15th (Scottish)
Division were able to attack the next morning.

No. 4 Company's attempt to secure the high ground near Arclais was doomed to failure. Less than half-way up the hill the motor platoon was met by a curtain of fire and while trying to rush the enemy position the platoon commander, Lieut. J. N. McEwen, was badly wounded and his servant killed. More fire then appeared from another direction, and, try as they would, the platoon found it impossible either to work their way round to the flank or to evacuate their wounded officer. The troop in support was stuck at the bottom of the valley, so the platoon was forced to withdraw, covered by the courageous fire of L./Sergt. Everin, who had dismounted from his tank and had taken his Browning gun up the hill. Lieut. McEwen was posted as "Missing, believed wounded and a prisoner," and was finally "liberated" by the Americans in a German hospital in Paris three weeks later.

All the fighting which took place in the neighbourhood of the Vassy road was heavy, but it reached a peak on No. 2 Company's front. Both on the 2nd and the 3rd they had to contend with one crisis after another. The action began badly when Capt. R. H. M. Marriott, second-in-command of the company, who had been left in charge of the transport just below the Drouet Spur, was severely wounded in the thigh by enemy shelling; but the situation did not become difficult until the company had cleared Drouet and was starting to advance along the northern edge of the first big wood beyond. Here the left-hand platoon, moving through scrub on the edge of the wood, was halted by heavy automatic fire which wounded the platoon commander, Lieut. A. B. Wodehouse, and inflicted several other casualties. These particular Spandau parties did not last for long because the right-hand platoon managed to get through to the eastern side of the wood and rush them off their feet; but shortly afterwards other parties began firing from the other side of the Souleuvre Valley, heralding not only the return of the Germans to the wood which had just been cleared but also the approach of German tanks. For this the leading platoon were ill-prepared: they were cut off from the rest of the company, and as the small wireless sets would not function properly in the woods Major R. H. Bromley, the company commander, who was with them, had had himself to return to bring up the reserve platoon—a journey which took a considerable time.

No. 3 Squadron, of the 2nd Battalion, had been sent forward to deal with the contingency—Lieut. P. N. Whitley was wounded *en route*—but owing to the appalling country they were unable to get farther forward than the village of Drouet, with the result that, when the counter-attack arrived, consisting of several huge enemy tanks and a strong party of infantry, the leading platoon had no hope of repel-

ling it. After a while the reserve platoon managed to filter their way 1944
up to the leading platoon's area, but, with the enemy all round and
the position rapidly becoming untenable, the leading platoon commander, Lieut. M. Dawson, sent both platoons back to a farmhouse
east of Drouet which was being used by the company as a firm base.
Although fired on all the way, the platoons got back safely, only to
find that the farmhouse, which was at the bottom of the valley and
dominated by the big wood, was being swept by automatic fire at a
range of less than a hundred yards. As casualties were mounting,
Major Bromley decided to withdraw the company and No. 3 Squadron on to Drouet Spur and to dig in there for the night. As dusk fell the
company picked up the sound of enemy vehicles moving about; it
took little imagination to realize that, sooner or later, the enemy meant
to regain the spur, without which they could not hope to prevent the
passage of the remainder of the Division down the main Caen—Vire
road.

The night passed comparatively peacefully, disturbed only by a Aug. 3
German who bowled grenades into the leading platoon's position.
At dawn a patrol was sent out to find the German, but its departure
unfortunately coincided with the first of a series of enemy counter-
attacks on Drouet Spur, and the patrol had great difficulty in getting
back. This first counter-attack was beaten off by the combined fire of
the company and No. 3 Squadron, and for three hours there was a
lull in the fighting. At about 10 o'clock the enemy cascaded the company's position with shells, and these turned out to be the prelude to
a much heavier counter-attack, supported directly by one tank and
indirectly by several others. The shelling was severe, and 2/Lieut.
J. A. Barry, second-in-command of the carrier platoon, was killed.
The counter-attack failed to drive the company off the spur, but a
section of the right forward platoon, which was on the slope above the
village, was overrun and two men were taken prisoner. The enemy
then established themselves just below the crest of the hill and for the
remainder of the day were within thirty yards of No. 2 Company's
leading platoon. The small, bare hilltop was surrounded on three sides
by fields of growing corn, and the German machine gunners and
even an enemy tank managed to get to within a few yards of the
company's position unobserved. Bombardments and counter-bom-
bardments continued all through the morning, afternoon and evening.

It was at 8 p.m. that the enemy made his most determined attempt
to capture the Drouet Spur. For half an hour before, the company's
small area was shelled unmercifully and at the same time parties of
enemy infantry worked round the flanks of the position, through the
standing corn, firing their Spandaus from all sides. Against this in-

1944 visible foe the tanks of No. 3 Squadron and the small arms of the company responded magnificently: every weapon that could be mustered fired down on to the village of Drouet, which was the forming-up point for all these attacks, so relentlessly that the enemy was at no time able to show his head over the spur, and shortly before dark he retired. Major A. M. H. Gregory-Hood decided not to withdraw the tanks, as was the usual practice at night, because he felt that the enemy would immediately plague them with mortar shells. His decision was rewarded by the sight of hundreds of shells passing overhead, few of which landed on the tanks.

Although Drouet Hill was the focal point of all the enemy attacks on the 3rd of August and No. 2 Company lost fifty men holding it, the remainder of the Grenadier Group did not have an easy day either. Catheolles and the area near the bridge over the Souleuvre were shelled accurately all day, and each company and squadron suffered a few casualties.

In the afternoon the 4th Battalion of the Regiment moved up from the Bois du Homme to some fields close by Grenadier Group Headquarters in preparation for a joint attack on the high ground near Arclais, where No. 4 Company had had trouble on the previous day. The Churchills of the 4th Battalion were to take the hill while the 3-inch mortars of the 1st Battalion and the Shermans of the 2nd Battalion formed a protective screen between them and the enemy— this being the only occasion during the North-West European campaign on which all three Battalions of the Regiment worked together. For various reasons, the attack could not begin until 9.15 p.m., leaving only forty minutes of daylight. The Churchills were expected to find their own way across the virtually impassable valley below Arclais Hill, so there seemed little hope that they would make much progress that night. As was expected, the first troop to move down into the valley became bogged at once, and only one troop, Sergt. Blake's, managed to get across. The moral value to the infantry of this one troop was immense and they were able to drive the Germans off the hill during the night. The crews of the tanks bogged in the valley spent a hair-raising night being stalked by the enemy. One in particular was bogged so deeply that the water came into the turret. The enemy surrounded it and told the crew to surrender. When they refused to do so the enemy boarded the tank and tried to open the engine doors, but they were luckily locked and the crew escaped unscathed.

Aug. 4   Early the next morning the 4th Battalion were ordered to proceed at top speed to Montcharivel, a distance of some eight miles, where they were to join up with the 8th Battalion Royal Scots Fusiliers. They had nearly completed the journey when Lieut. G. A. G. Selby-

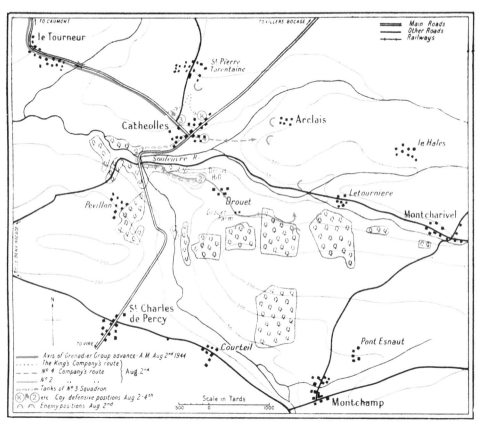

Main Roads
Other Roads
Railways

TO CAUMONT
TO VILLERS BOCAGE
le Tourneur
St Pierre
Torentaine
Catheolles
Arclais
le Hales
Souleuvre R.
Drouet
Hill
Letourniere
Drouet
Pevillon
Drouet
Farm
Montcharivel
St Charles
de Percy
TO VIRE
Courteil
Pont Esnaut
Montchamp

Axis of Grenadier Group advance·A.M. Aug 2nd 1944
The King's Company's route
Nº 4 Company's route ⎰ Aug 2nd
Nº 2 ,, ,,
Tanks of Nº 3 Squadron
K 2 etc Coy defensive positions Aug 2·4th
Enemy positions Aug 2nd

Scale in Yards
500   0   1000

ARCLAIS AND DROUET HILL

Lowndes, who was with the Royal Scots Fusiliers, called up on the 1944 wireless to say that the infantry had been held up by mines and machine guns and wanted help immediately. Lieut. A. MacR. Collie was ordered to risk the mines and push straight through to the village, but he soon reported that the road was blocked, and the squadron leader, Major J. C. Gascoigne, decided to take two troops and try to find a way round on the right. After a journey which took them most of the afternoon, the party contacted the Royal Scots Fusiliers and a plan was made to capture Montcharivel. So far as was known, the enemy were just behind the village occupying a position manned by several machine guns and supported by a Mark IV tank, so it was decided to send two platoons and the two tank troops round the left flank. They set off at 9.30 under the command of Lieut. H. A. Verney. Almost at once Lieut. Verney reported that a flame-thrower was approaching, but this turned out to be a haystack which he himself had set on fire with his Besa gun. Three or four machine-gun positions were engaged in the fading light, and by the time it was dark the Germans had been driven out of Montcharivel.

For the next twenty-four hours there was a lull in the fighting and Aug. 5 both the Guards Armoured Division and the 6th Guards Tank Brigade took advantage of it to rest and overhaul their vehicles. Everybody was beginning to feel the strain of the non-stop fighting of the past few days, and certain officers were sent back to the rear echelon for a period of rest. With them went Major R. H. Bromley, who had been badly wounded and had lost his hearing during the last counter-attack on Drouet Hill, but had refused to be evacuated until all danger had passed.

ESTRY

By the 6th of August the war in France had become a blitzkrieg. Aug. 6 American tanks had reached Brest and the River Loire, forty miles to the south-west of Rennes. Brittany was almost cut off and the ports of Lorient and St. Malo had been isolated. The whole defensive front appeared to be crumbling and it was thought that the Guards Armoured Division would be able to reach Vire without undue difficulty. Before they made an attempt to do so, however, it was decided that the 6th Guards Tank Brigade and the 15th (Scottish) Division should capture the ground on the left of the Caen—Vire road and thus dispose of any enemy interference on the left flank. An attack for this purpose was planned for the 7th of August. It was intended that No. 2 Squadron of the Grenadiers, who were then attached to the 3rd Battalion Scots Guards owing to the severe casualties that battalion had suffered at Caumont, should proceed down the main Aunay-sur-Odon

1944 —Vire road and capture Estry, a small village half-way between the two towns, while the Coldstream and Scots Guards battalions of the Brigade attacked in the direction of Vassy.

Aug. 7   The attack began at dawn on the 7th. No. 2 Squadron had been told to expect little, if any, opposition, and indeed, until they reached a point about fifty yards from the cross-roads at Estry, a thick fog which was covering the countryside that morning hindered them more than the German opposition. Near the cross-roads the advance was brought to a complete standstill. The tanks and the infantry were subjected to severe shelling and mortaring, and Lieut. H. W. Wollaston reported that the cross-roads was not only mined but covered by an anti-tank gun. Capt. H. J. Gould, the acting squadron leader, conferred with the infantry commander and it was decided that, while Sergt. Berresford's troop endeavoured to reach the cross-roads by going straight on, Lord Oliver Fitzroy's troop and a platoon of infantry should move off the road to the left and head for the church. Both these attacks were supposed to have been preceded by an artillery bombardment, but it never materialized and the task of the two troops was further complicated by a rumour that an enemy tank was in the village threatening their line of advance.

See Map p. 94

Lord Oliver Fitzroy's troop managed to get to within twenty yards of the orchard which contained the church and were starting to cover the infantry as they moved forward towards the cross-roads, when the German tank opened up and knocked out one of the tanks of the troop. Lord Oliver Fitzroy engaged it until all his ammunition had been expended and then tried to back out of the orchard; while so doing he was shot in the neck by a sniper and died at once. Shortly afterwards the troop lost the rest of their tanks and were forced to retire, having, nevertheless, achieved the task allotted to them. Sergt Berresford's troop were less successful. They made one attempt to destroy the anti-tank gun at the cross-roads, but this proved so costly that they were forced to retreat under cover of smoke and remained for the rest of the day on the road itself, giving what support they could, mainly moral, to the infantry.

Capt. Gould tried once more to get into Estry by sending two troops, under the command of Capt. J. A. Cannan, along a sunken lane on the left of the main road, but this too was a failure. The leading Churchill received a direct hit which killed three members of the crew, and the troop leader, Lieut. G. C. B. Gidley-Kitchin, was severely burned shortly afterwards by a phosphorus bomb which landed on his engine cover. By 7 o'clock the squadron had suffered fourteen casualties—among them Capt. Cannan and Lieut. Wollaston, who were wounded—and it was withdrawn. Later in the

evening a squadron of the Scots Guards made another attempt to take 1944
Estry, but this again was doomed to failure. The plan of battle had
been designed to deal with the weakening opposition of a crumbling
line of beaten soldiers; it had met instead the enemy's best fighting
troops in their most determined mood, showing, almost for the last
time in Normandy, a real co-ordinated defence.

Renewed attacks on Estry from the north-west by all three squad- Aug. 8
rons of the 4th Battalion during the next four days were no more
successful. On the 8th of August, after the Corps artillery had ham-
mered at Estry for a full hour, No. 3 Squadron, the Royal Scots
Fusiliers and the King's Own Scottish Borderers did their best to help
six Crocodiles and six Avres* manœuvre into position so that they
could hurl their missiles against the enemy defences. As far as was
known, however, not one of these special tanks was able to get near
enough to fire its weapon because as soon as they approached Estry
the banks and sunken lanes made it quite impossible for them to
proceed. After the second attempt to take Estry had failed No. 3
Squadron remained in close support of the infantry and for many
hours was given a very unpleasant reception by the dug-in Tigers,
snipers and mortars.

During the early hours of the 9th No. 1 Squadron took over from Aug. 9
No. 3. They also found it impossible to advance and spent a long and
tiring day, being continually attacked by mortars, bazookas, 150-mm.
self-propelled guns, and snipers; one of the last-mentioned seriously
wounded Lieut. H. A. Verney in the head. Just as No. 1 Squadron
were about to rally a few hundred yards behind the front positions,
they were ordered by the Brigadier of the 44th Brigade to remain
where they were, since he felt that the Germans would counter-attack
if they heard the tanks withdrawing. The infantry therefore provided
a company to guard the Churchills against tank-hunting parties.
Small-arms fire and innumerable eerie noises helped to keep everyone
on the alert throughout the night. When No. 2 Squadron took over
from them at dawn the next morning, No. 1 Squadron had been in the
line for eighteen hours.

As it had now become obvious that the Germans intended to fight
to the last man, the 4th Battalion was ordered merely to cover the
enemy's line of escape and wait until he withdrew, which was inevitable in the near future. A whole infantry brigade, a tank battalion,
Flails, Crocodiles, Avres, Corps artillery and air bombardment had
failed completely to drive the Germans away from Estry. It remained
for their supplies to run out before they would give in. The sleepless

---

*Churchill tanks equipped with a large mortar for blasting concrete pillboxes. They
were always manned by Royal Engineers.

1944 nights, the exhausting hours spent in the tanks with all hatches closed and the sickening smell of dead cows scattered all over the fields combined to make this vigil over Estry one of the most unattractive tasks of the whole campaign.

As a result of the unforeseen hold-up at Estry the ground to the left of the Caen—Vire road between the Souleuvre and Vassy was not cleared until the 10th of August, and the Guards Armoured Division's final attack in Normandy had to be postponed until the 11th. In the interval the Division edged slowly forward on either side of the main road, testing the enemy's strength and occupying hilly features whenever opportunity occurred. These moves—the first of which took the Grenadier Group to St. Charles de Percy and the second to the high ground at La Bottrie,* eight miles farther south—were not eventful in themselves, but they were made very trying by the choking and blinding dust caused by so many vehicles travelling along roads which were designed for nothing faster than agricultural traffic. Each tank and half-track as it went along raised a cloud of dust so thick that it completely obscured the view of vehicles following behind. No goggles could really be effective in such conditions, and many men had inflamed eyes which sometimes called for temporary evacuation. And, apart from the acute discomfort, to travel more than two miles an hour meant creating a swirl of dust which gave away the position to the enemy artillery.

At La Bottrie there was a view over a wide sweep of country to the rear and it could clearly be seen how well the enemy had been able to overlook the country over which the Division had been fighting during the previous week. On the 9th the enemy shelling died down and it did appear at last that the enemy, conscious of the fast-moving American advances to the south, was pulling back to the east; and that the hard-slogging match which had gone on since Caumont might be replaced by a more congenial pursuit for which an armoured division is better suited.

VIESSOIX

Aug. 10 The 1st Battalion patrolled extensively on the 10th of August in order to give the Divisional Commander information about the enemy and thus assist him in making a plan. At 4.30 p.m.—a short time after Lieut. J. F. Lascelles had been wounded by a shell—the Group Com-

---

*The Group took over the high ground at La Bottrie from a battalion of the King's Shropshire Light Infantry, who were supported by a squadron of tanks commanded by Major Borwick, of the Royal Scots Greys. Owing to congestion on the roads, the leading squadron of the 2nd Battalion did not arrive until after dark. Major Borwick refused to leave the 1st Battalion until the tanks arrived, saying that he had frequently supported Grenadiers in Italy and certainly would not leave them unprotected now.

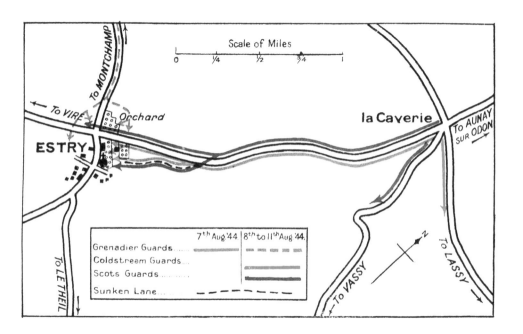

mander went to Brigade Headquarters and orders were given out for 1944
the ambitious advance of the next day. The 32nd Brigade, which was
then north-east of La Bottrie, was to put in an attack at dawn on some
high ground in front of its leading positions. The Irish Guards Group
were then to pass through the 32nd Brigade and move south, parallel
with and to the left of the Grenadier Group, who were to move down
the La Bottrie—Viessoix road. When both Groups reached the Vire
—Vassy road the Irish Guards Group were to swing west of Viessoix
and then continue the southward advance, followed by the Grenadier
Group. The ultimate objective was Mont de Cerisi, an imposing
feature some twelve miles away and a few miles north-west of the
town of Flers.

Patrolling continued during the night and there was little sign of Aug. 11
the enemy. In fact, the only place where patrols reported that there
might be serious opposition was a road block about a mile and a half
south of the Grenadier Group position and about half a mile short of
the village of Viessoix. As a preliminary to the attack, the 3-inch
mortars of the King's and No. 4 Companies were therefore sighted on
the enemy's position closely covering the road block, but, just before
the attack began, it was discovered that the enemy had vanished
during the night and the mortars were never used.

No. 4 Company and No. 1 Squadron reached the road block without mishap, and the leading carrier neatly side-stepped the trees felled
across the road—only to go up on a mine buried in the road on the
bridge just beyond. No. 1 Squadron immediately split into two, and
the force commanded by Capt. The Lord Carrington was sent off to
see if a bridge farther to the left was passable. It ran into yet another See Map
minefield and two tanks were blown up, while a third, Lieut. J. W. E. p. 98
Scott's, was bazookaed. On the original route, meanwhile, Capt. H. F.
Stanley had ordered the two leading motor platoons to debus, and,
accompanied by a troop of tanks (Lieut. The Hon. Martin Fitzalan-
Howard), this force went round the mines and entered the village of
Viessoix, but found it empty. The third motor platoon then started
to sweep for the mines with mine detectors, but almost at once heavy
and accurate shell and mortar fire descended on the bridge and its
immediate environs and caused casualties. What little doubt existed
that the bridge was under the enemy's direct observation was soon
dispelled when the enemy opened up with well-directed small-arms
fire from the direction of Le Val, a hamlet to the east. This fire continued all day almost without interruption, and it was found impossible to clear the mines, although a party of sappers did manage to
pull the block to the side of the road by hitching a cable to the trees
and pulling them clear with a tank.

1944 The two motor platoons in Viessoix ran into trouble as soon as they showed themselves in the forward part of the village, and they were heavily shelled and mortared indeed. Although, with the exception of a few snipers, the enemy had vacated the village, he held strong positions on the high wooded ground to the south-west. One troop of tanks under Lieut. Sir Howard Frank, Bt., did succeed in bypassing the road block at the bridge and got through to assist the infantry, but within three-quarters of an hour the two platoons, which had entered the village thirty-six strong, had suffered twenty-five casualties. With his force thus whittled down, Capt. Stanley could obviously do little, but he managed to form a strong-point in buildings in the middle of Viessoix and then returned to see the Group Commander.

The Group Commander decided to try to find a way round for the wheeled transport and sent a troop of tanks from No. 1 Squadron to reconnoitre a route through Le Val. Approaching the village, one of the tanks reported that it had exploded a mine, but by then Lieut.-Colonel Goulburn had sent the third motor platoon* to assist in the capture of Le Val. This was done with little trouble, although the road through the hamlet was found to be mined. The motor platoon and the troop of tanks then established themselves in Le Val, and the Commanding Officer sent another troop of tanks to the eastern edge of Viessoix to protect the left flank of the force in the village.

With the enemy dominating Viessoix and with Le Val liberally strewn with mines, the Group Commander called a conference and made a fresh plan. He decided that the only possible course was for a route to be forced between the two villages and, as No. 4 Company were now fully committed and could clearly do no more, he ordered them to hold on to their hard-won possessions. The King's Company and No. 2 Squadron were ordered to advance between Viessoix and Le Val and to rejoin the original route at the village of La Coquerie. If this was successful, they were to push on to a cross-roads a further mile down the road and form a strong-point there.

The time was now about 3 p.m. and an hour later the company moved up to the road block and left their transport. The area of the bridge was still being heavily mortared and the company suffered a few casualties as they started to move forward on foot behind the tanks and carriers. The advance continued steadily as far as the main Vire—Vassy road east of Viessoix, and here Major N. E. W. Baker called for a prearranged artillery bombardment on two woods some five hundred yards south of the road. Unfortunately, this plan did not

---

*This platoon was capably handled by L./Sergt. Harper, who was killed three days later. He received the posthumous award of the Military Medal for his gallantry at the road block.

include an orchard much closer to the road, from which well-con- **1944** cealed and dug-in enemy fired on the company and caused casualties. Fire from 25-pounders was eventually brought to bear on the orchard, and the tanks fired high-explosive shells from their 75-mm. guns while the company attacked the orchard from the other flank. By this means a footing was gained in the orchard and a number of Germans were killed. As soon as the covering fire ceased, however, the Germans put in a counter-attack, heavily supported by artillery. The King's Company and No. 2 Squadron held firm and inflicted casualties on the enemy, but they were now so close to them that they could not call on their supporting weapons as before. The tanks in turn were having a most unpleasant time in the very close country.

The enemy, part of the 5th Parachute Regiment from the 3rd Parachute Division, fought with skill and determination, and used the terrain to the best advantage, both to close in on tanks and infantry with bazookas and automatic weapons and also to equip themselves with excellent observation posts for their mortars and heavier weapons. No. 2 Squadron lost several tanks to bazookas, and Lieut. H. Misa was killed when his Sherman was hit.

During the engagement the enemy flagrantly breached the rules of war. A German ambulance was seen driving towards the tanks, and, as it was plastered with red crosses, was not fired at. It drove up to within ten yards of Lieut. J. Utterson-Kelso's tank and then the doors were flung open and ten desperadoes, armed with bazookas and grenades, leapt into a ditch near by. They then hit the tank with a bazooka and killed the troop leader with a grenade.

By 6.30 p.m. the company alone had suffered twenty-seven casualties, and as further progress was obviously impossible the company and squadron were withdrawn a few hundred yards to the main road. Shortly afterwards Lieut.-Colonel E. H. Goulburn went back to the Brigadier's command post, then situated with Combined Group Headquarters at La Bottrie. There he saw the Divisional Commander, Major-General Allan Adair, who told him that the Irish Guards Battle Group had been even less successful and had not moved off at all, as the preliminary 32nd Brigade attack by the Coldstream Group had made little headway. But, farther to the west, the 3rd Division, with whom the Battalion had fought in Belgium in 1940, were making steady progress in their advance south. They were responsible for clearing the woods on the high ground south-west of Viessoix, from which No. 4 Company had met such trouble earlier in the day; so it was vital that the Grenadier Group should hold Viessoix.

Acting on this information, the Group Commander ordered No. 2 Company, who were still in position near La Bottrie, to move forward

H

1944 on foot at dusk and to form a strong-point round the cross-roads at the north of Viessoix. The King's Company were left east of the village and at dusk they compressed their positions in order to give better protection to the tanks of No. 2 Squadron. By midnight No. 2 Company, without Lieut. A. Tyser, who had been wounded while making a reconnaissance, were in position round the cross-roads. Shortly afterwards the tanks of No. 1 Squadron were able to lift Capt. Stanley and the remains of his two motor platoons back to where his company had concentrated near Battalion Headquarters. The Group had had a rough day at the hands of determined opponents, but the Germans were evidently none too happy either, as, at dusk, nearly all shelling and mortaring died down and the night passed peacefully.

Aug. 12   Patrols the next morning proved that the main body of the enemy had withdrawn, and mine-clearing parties at the bridge near Viessoix were able to operate unimpeded. At about midday a civilian walked down the main road straight into one of No. 2 Company's positions. The platoon commander, Lieut. M. Dawson, realized at once that the civilian's French accent was rather odd and that his claim to be an Alsatian on his way to Vire was unconvincing. Searched and partly stripped, the man proved to be a beginner at the art of espionage; he had in his possession a compass, a small map on the back of a handkerchief and a much larger map showing German positions east of Viessoix. These were less easily explained away than the guttural accent, and he was subsequently shot.

At 5 o'clock that evening a conference was held at Brigade Headquarters from which the Group Commander returned with important information. A revolutionary change had overtaken the situation during the past forty-eight hours. The German High Command, faced with the imminent threat of the Americans linking up with the Canadians at Falaise and thus surrounding their entire forces, had decided not to extricate them to the east before the gap closed—as had been expected—but to make a desperate attempt to cut the encircling American armies in two by breaking through to the Brittany coast at Avranches. As all the American supplies had to pass through Avranches and the Germans were scarcely twenty miles away from the town, General Montgomery had ordered every available unit to move into a position of defence in the path of the German attack—an order which necessitated the Grenadier Group breaking contact with the enemy and moving back to the high ground four miles to the north-west of Viessoix.

Aug. 13   The Group moved on the morning of the 13th, forming a strong-point astride the Vire—Estry road. They naturally expected soon to be engaged in heavy fighting, but, apart from an occasional shell and

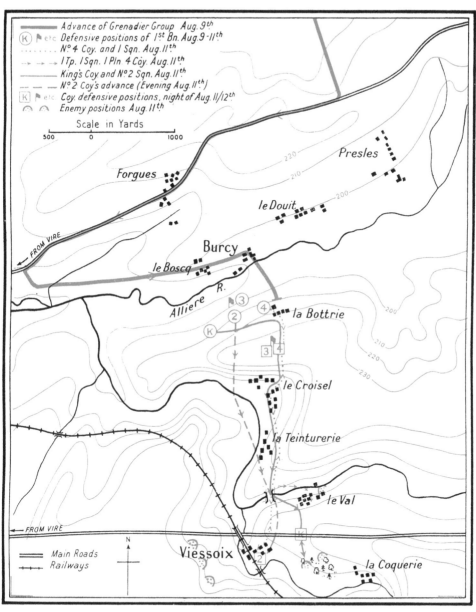

Advance of Grenadier Group Aug. 9th
Ⓚ ♦ etc Defensive positions of 1st Bn. Aug. 9-11th
N° 4 Coy. and I Sqn. Aug. 11th
1 Tp. I Sqn. I Pln. 4 Coy. Aug. 11th
King's Coy. and N° 2 Sqn. Aug. 11th
N° 2 Coy's advance (Evening Aug. 11th)
☒ ♦ etc Coy. defensive positions, night of Aug. 11/12th
◉ ◉ Enemy positions Aug. 11th

Scale in Yards
500   0   1000

Presles

Forques

le Douit

FROM VIRE

Burcy

le Boscq

Alliere R.

la Bottrie

le Croisel

la Teinturerie

le Val

FROM VIRE

N

Main Roads
Railways

Viessoix

la Coquerie

VIESSOIX

one unfortunate attack by American Thunderbolt fighter-bombers **1944** which killed three other ranks and wounded Lieut. R. B. Joly, their position was never molested. Before the day was out the Americans, ably supported by British Typhoons, had routed the panzer divisions trying to reach Avranches and had thus turned what at one moment had seemed an ugly situation into a brilliant victory.

That night the Germans, having missed their chance to retreat through the Falaise Gap before it closed, embarked on their disastrous retreat towards the Seine. The Grenadier Group and the 4th Battalion, which had concentrated near Flers after the battle at Estry, were not called upon to fight again in Normandy. Instead, they settled down under the hot August sun to rest and reorganize in preparation for the next phase of the North-West European campaign.

CHAPTER IV

THE PURSUIT TO BRUSSELS AND NIJMEGEN

1ST AND 2ND BATTALIONS

1

NORMANDY TO BRUSSELS

A sudden change of atmosphere—Guards Armoured Division directed on the Somme crossings—Advance across the Seine to Beauvais—Liberation of Beauvais by Grenadier Group—Co-operation of French Partisans— Somme crossed almost without opposition—Guards Armoured Division's rapid advance to Arras and Douai—Orders received to liberate Brussels— The great advance of 3rd September—Battle of Pont-a-Marcq—Grenadier Group enter Brussels—A remarkable acclamation

1944 THE six weeks which followed the fighting in Normandy were the most momentous of the whole North-West European campaign. After nearly three months of static warfare, of shorter duration, it is true, but, at the same time no less demoralizing, than the long-drawn-out trench fighting of the First World War, the vast war machine which the Allies had massed on the Continent changed, almost overnight, from bottom to top gear and sped across Europe in the fastest military advance history has ever recorded. First, Northern France was liberated, the very country over which veterans of the B.E.F. had fought in such tragic circumstances in 1940. Then, in one historic week, the Germans were routed from Belgium, and Brussels was liberated. Finally, aided by British and American paratroopers, the advance continued across Holland to the Rhine at Nijmegen. By the end of these few weeks the war had been brought up to the enemy's front door; although the windows might be shuttered and barred, and all the entrances firmly locked, such progress had made it certain that before long sufficient men and material could be brought up to blow the whole structure to pieces.

Aug. 13-27 The most formidable obstacles in the path of the advance were a succession of water barriers, the first of which was the Seine. While the tide of battle moved forward to this river, the Guards Armoured Division and the 6th Guards Tank Brigade waited in the Normandy bocage. The fields in which the three Battalions of the Regiment were situated stood like pleasant oases in a countryside dulled and scorched

100

by war. Grass that was green, trees that did not harbour snipers— 1944
such things had seemed to belong to the distant past during the fighting
in Normandy, and the pattern of life soon became more normal. Tents
of all shapes and sizes were erected. Up went yard upon yard of signal
cable, laid to catch the unwary traveller after dark. For the first time
since leaving England fresh vegetables, real bread and leaf tea took
the place of the tinned and dehydrated products of the fourteen-man
packs issued by the Quartermasters during the fighting. At the Battalion canteens the Guardsmen could buy cakes and tea to their
hearts' content. In the 4th Battalion footballs emerged from the depths
of the Quartermaster's trucks, and matches were arranged with the
local inhabitants which were vociferously supported by neighbouring
football fans. E.N.S.A. used all its ingenuity to convert the few undamaged playhouses in the vicinity and performed to packed and
appreciative audiences. When the weather was fine the men went to
bathe in the River Souleuvre, for which all three Battalions had
fought only a few days before. And every day parties set off on sight-
seeing tours all over Normandy.

After a fortnight* of such comparative luxury the novelty began
to pall. The war was moving on. Each day the enemy were another
twenty miles farther away until the whole of Northern France was
freed as far as the Seine. Each day the reports from General Patton's
armies streaking towards Paris became more remarkable. Anglo-
American forces had already landed on the Riviera and they were
proceeding at a good pace up the Rhône Valley towards the Swiss
border. The whole fabric of German resistance in France was gradually being split by the advancing armies. There were now seven in
France, deployed in the following order from north to south: the First
Canadian, Second British, First, Ninth, Third and Seventh American,
and the First French. All were on the move.

On the 28th of August Major-General Allan Adair was informed Aug. 28
that the Guards Armoured Division was to come under the command
of the XXX Corps. He flew to see Lieutenant-General Horrocks, the
Corps Commander, at his headquarters near Vernon on the banks of
the Seine. The 43rd Division had just finished a crossing operation,
and the 11th Armoured Division, the 50th Division and the 8th
Armoured Brigade were moving over the two Bailey bridges which
had just been built. The Corps Commander was most anxious to push
on to the River Somme at the earliest possible moment and asked
General Adair when the Division could be up. He replied that the

---

*During this period Lieut.-Colonel E. H. Goulburn reorganized the Support
Company of the 1st Battalion. Handing in six of his twelve anti-tank guns, he formed
two motor platoons with the personnel and acquired half-track vehicles for them.

1944 Division was still at Conde, a hundred miles away, and that the earliest that it could be concentrated north of the river was on the night of the 30th of August. "Then we will start tomorrow," said General Horrocks. "The 11th Armoured Division will be directed on Amiens, the 8th Armoured Brigade on Beauvais. You will come on as quickly as you can, moving by night if necessary, pass through the 8th Armoured Brigade and seize crossings over the River Somme." General Adair flew back to the Division, gave out his orders and the advance began.

The Grenadiers of the 4th Battalion remained where they were. It was considered that a heavy tank brigade was unsuited to lightning advances and, as it turned out, they had to wait until the following year to experience the thrill of a gigantic break-out.

Aug. 28-29 The distance from the fields near Flers, where the 1st and 2nd Battalions were situated, to the River Seine is about ninety miles as the crow flies, and in peace time, in a civilian car whose driver has only his private responsibility, such a journey would have been neither remarkable nor difficult. But the movement of soldiers has never been a simple operation and never more complicated than in the case of a modern armoured division. The 1st and 2nd Battalions' move to the Seine was made against time and in pouring rain, over roads that had been pummelled both by the retreating Germans and the British *See Map p. 122* advance guards following on their heels. From Flers, where the tanks were driven on to the transporters, to Laigle, where they were met by three officers rejoining their battalions after three days' leave in Paris which they had entered with the liberating troops, and finally to the hills east of Vernon, where they assembled for battle, was a forty-eight-hour journey: over an indicated route, at an ordered speed, in a fixed density of so many vehicles to the mile. Supply points and staging areas had to be arranged, advance parties had to be briefed, road pickets detailed, motor-cyclists sent forward at such-and-such a time. The huge assortment of vehicles had to be marshalled according to their purpose and kind: three-ton lorries and Bren carriers, half-tracks and cooking trucks, company vehicles and jeeps, water trucks, ambulances and the vehicles mounted for anti-aircraft de-fence. Owing to the secrecy of the move, the drivers were forbidden to show even the flicker of a light, so that at times tank transporters overturned in the ditches or knocked down telegraph poles, which endangered the passage of the lighter vehicles behind. Yet the journey was completed speedily and with few breakdowns.

Aug. 30 Across the Seine the 8th Armoured Brigade had already broken out of the bridgehead held by the 43rd (Wessex) Division and were pursuing the retreating enemy northwards. Seventy miles beyond lay the

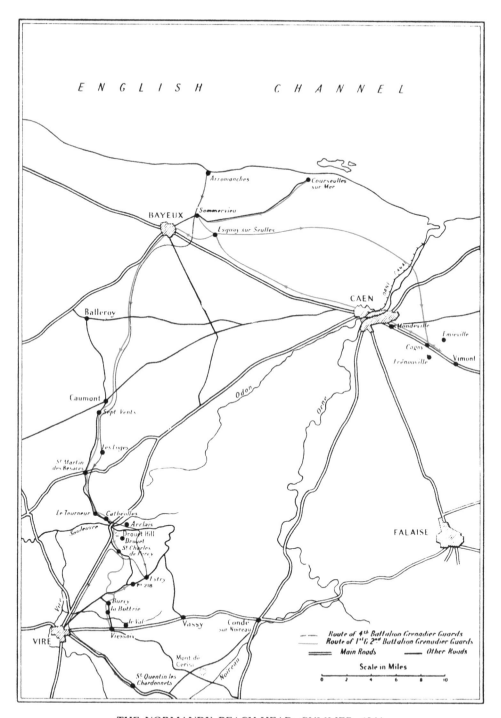

ENGLISH CHANNEL

Arromanches
Courseulles sur Mer
BAYEUX
Sommervieu
Esquay sur Seulles
CAEN
Mondeville
Émiéville
Balleroy
Cagny
Frénouville
Vimont
Caumont
Odon
Sept Vents
Orne
Les Loges
St Martin des Besaces
FALAISE
Le Tourneur
Cathéolles
Arclais
Drouet Hill
Drouet
St Charles de Percy
Estry
Pt 218
Burcy
la Bottrie
le Val
Vassy
Condé sur Noireau
Viessoix
VIRE
Mont de Cerisi
Noireau
St Quentin les Chardonnets

Route of 4th Battalion Grenadier Guards
Route of 1st & 2nd Battalion Grenadier Guards
Main Roads   Other Roads
Scale in Miles
0   2   4   6   8   10

THE NORMANDY BEACH-HEAD, SUMMER, 1944

Somme, and as a heavier formation would be needed to seize crossings **1944** over the river the Guards Armoured Division, less than three hours after crossing the Seine, were ordered to begin moving again to catch up with the 8th Armoured Brigade before nightfall. Gisors was the town allotted to the Grenadier Group, and for the rest of the day they crawled towards it. All efforts they made to go quicker were frustrated by the congestion caused by the tail-end of the 8th Armoured Brigade. By nightfall they were through the town and, a few miles to the north, the Battalions drove off the road. As the 8th Armoured Brigade was held up, they expected to spend the night there, but at 10.30 all hopes of sleep were shattered when the Group Commander was summoned to Brigade Headquarters and told that the Group were to bypass the opposition at 2 o'clock in the morning. For the next three hours the Grenadier camp bristled with activity: patrols were whisked off into the night to find a bypass; petrol tanks were replenished, the drivers checked their engines; and anyone who could be spared from an urgent task was detailed to cook a hurried meal. By 2 o'clock the wireless sets were humming and the giant engines of the Shermans had spluttered and choked to life, invading the stillness of the night like angered tigers roaring in the jungle.

A night drive in tanks is seldom a pleasant experience, but on this **Aug. 31** particular occasion it was little less than a nightmare. An officer wrote: "It was one of those drives when sleep comes over one in great waves, at times almost impossible to fight off. The strain of trying to follow the route on the map and pick out the road with only the thin pin-pricks of side-lights to help, brought before one's eyes strange hallucinations of barriers and bridges and herds of cattle that were not there." Fired by the immense urgency of their task, the drivers kept going and, as dawn was just beginning to break, the Group found themselves on the outskirts of Beauvais, half-way between the Seine and the Somme.

It was in this town, in 1472, when it was surrounded by Charles the Bold of Normandy, that the women had taken up arms and fought with such courage and skill that the siege was raised in a matter of days. On the 31st of August, 1944, there was no need for a single shot to be fired, as the enemy had fled the night before. But the Grenadiers were the first British troops the town had seen for four long years, and, as they entered, the doors of the houses were flung open and from every direction people rushed headlong into the streets, mad with excitement, screaming, shouting and waving flags. This was liberation—the day the local population had prayed for and dreamed of ever since a terrible week in 1940 when Nazi armies had swooped down to plague them. Now, at long last, they could give vent to the

1944 emotions which four years of prison life had engendered in them. The
scenes that took place in Beauvais were to be repeated many times as
the advance across the Lowlands continued. It was always the same.
The girls would clamber on to the tanks begging kisses off the Guardsmen. Mothers would hand up their babies to be petted by "les liberateurs." Old women would cry, old men shout and young men burst
forward to shake a British soldier's hand, while the children asked for
autographs. Every soldier might have been a prince, every mud-
stained vehicle a glittering coronation coach. The sense of joy was
irresistible and the Guardsmen would enter into the spirit of the
occasion with as much verve as the liberated themselves. Only when
the mounting spirit of the crowd led to a craving for revenge and
screaming women—collaborators—were dragged away to have their
hair shorn off, would they remain aloof.

Intoxicated with excitement though they were, the citizens of
Beauvais were sufficiently level-headed to notice that the Grenadiers
kept on glancing up towards the sky. This puzzled them, and one
elderly Frenchman tackled an officer on the subject. "Why," he
asked, "are you so worried about being attacked from the air when
you have air superiority?" The reason was simple. Bitter experience
had taught the Battalions that friendly planes, especially in forward
areas and during swift advances, were often to be feared more than
those of the enemy. Each vehicle was provided with a canister of
yellow smoke—the prearranged signal to warn British pilots off their
own troops—and on many a short halt the whine of a diving plane
caused the column to be obscured in a cloud of yellow smoke before
the aircraft was identified. Enemy pilots who occasionally did come
over, especially later on in Holland and Germany, must have been
agreeably surprised to see the Grenadiers so readily marking themselves as prey. But the troops had learnt that a Typhoon attack was
far more nerve-racking than anything the Luftwaffe could produce.

There was slight confusion over the route beyond Beauvais and the
column halted for a short time on the farther side of the town. The
tank crews just had time to brew some tea—this they could do far more
quickly than any housewife—and then they moved off again. Not a
shot was fired all the morning and the only Germans the Group saw
were parties of prisoners being proudly displayed by their captors, the
local Maquis. As soon as the Maquis heard that the British were
approaching, they would don their armbands, take up rifles and
tommy-guns which had been hidden for many a long month, and
become the hunters instead of the hunted. They were amateur soldiers
and very light-hearted, but they devised means of searching the woods
and fields for wandering Germans which were extremely effective.

Never once were the Grenadiers asked to guard or transport the 1944 prisoners of the Maquis; in fact, these patriots would have been indignant had they offered to do so.

The countryside between the Seine and the Somme is rich and green, a land well watered by many streams, thinly patched with forest and sprinkled with orchards and numerous villages. The Grenadiers had now had virtually no sleep for three nights running, but the welcome they were given in the villages through which they passed rekindled their energy in the same way as applause in a theatre stimulates an actor. Their destination was Corbie, a few miles upstream from Amiens, where the Household Cavalry had reported the bridge to be intact. By 3 o'clock they were approaching Villers-Bretonneux, the last village before the Somme, and here the Group halted while the commanding officers went forward to a ridge overlooking the river to prepare a plan for the crossing.

Standing in a 1914-18 war cemetery, which contained the graves of hundreds of Australian soldiers, the commanding officers had a magnificent view across the Somme to the hills on the far side. The Household Cavalry had reported that there were enemy on the lower slopes of these hills, near the bridge, so the commanding officers drew up an elaborate plan for the crossing. No. 2 Company and No. 3 Squadron would go over first and seize the ground which the Household Cavalry had reported held. The King's Company would cross next. Then both groups would proceed two or three miles farther north.

But not a shot was fired at the tanks as they crossed the Somme. Apparently the Germans on the slopes could not see the bridge and they awoke too late to the danger. On the farther bank the King's Company were fired at from a churchyard by enemy concealed behind tombstones, but they soon gave in and the King's Company and No. 2 Squadron climbed the hill without difficulty. There was only one anti-tank gun on the entire hillside, and, although it knocked out two of No. 3 Squadron's tanks, it was soon destroyed and the rest of the opposition gradually melted away. Thus, in a few hours, the Grenadiers gained a foothold over the river which, in the other war, had been the scene of hard and bitter fighting for many months on end.

That night, in their harbour areas on the high ground on the eastern bank of the Somme, the Group heard the B.B.C. giving them anonymous credit for their day's work. Encouraged by this, they settled down to a spell of well-earned sleep. But the peace of the night was disturbed by a burning farmhouse to which enemy planes were attracted like moths to a candle.

No time was wasted the next morning in continuing the advance Sept. 1 towards Arras. The Welsh Guards, performing their function of divi-

1944 sional reconnaissance with great skill, brushed aside the few pockets of enemy that remained on the route, and the Division had a clear run all day. As they sped across the rolling, open countryside, dotted with the British graveyards of the First World War, the cheering people and an occasional German lorry abandoned in the middle of the road, sometimes slowed them down, but never for more than a few minutes. At times it was like driving through an elongated dump of condemned vehicles. In the ditches, on the pavements and in the fields beside the road lay the wrecks of the mechanized transport of the German Army —lorries, half-tracks, volkswagen,* staff cars. The Germans had had no time to destroy or take away the contents, and several enterprising officers ended the day with a good haul of brandy, cigars and choco-late. One fortunate Guardsman came upon a German canteen wagon stacked with the whole gamut of soldiers' comforts. By 2 o'clock they bypassed Arras and were approaching Neuville, where a strange sight awaited them. The local Maquis had rounded up nearly two hundred prisoners—an extraordinary collection of men, a cross-sec-tion of the German occupation army in the West. There were smart and sulky S.S. troops, old men of over fifty from field bakeries, Russians from Turkistan, men who had fought in submarines, near-sighted clerks, men with half-healed wounds, deaf men, men with stomach ailments, and even children of fifteen or sixteen. In a last desperate effort to prevent the Allies chasing them out of France the Germans had mobilized everybody and anybody, given them weapons and told them to fight to the last round. But the majority of them had taken matters into their own hands, believing a prison camp prefer-able to a glorious death for the Fuehrer.

On the way to Arras No. 2 Company and No. 3 Squadron had been ordered to swing east from the main road and, if possible, capture the town of Albert, which was believed to be garrisoned, as it contained a big store depot. The two leading tanks were knocked out as they entered the suburbs, and it was realized that there were S.S. troops in the buildings, who were prepared to make a stand. One platoon and one troop were able to work their way round as far as the railway level-crossing in the western half of the town, but the road here was mined and a self-propelled gun hit Lieut. The Hon. C. E. Stourton's tank, wounding him and his crew. The company commander, Capt. The Duke of Rutland, decided that the road was too thickly mined for the tanks to pass through and sent two platoons off to try to cross the railway at a different place. But when they reached the railway embankment they were met by heavy fire, so a plan was made to contain the town until the evening, when an infantry battalion from

---

*German counterpart of a jeep.

the 50th Division made a concerted attack which the company and 1944 squadron supported with fire. They rejoined their Battalions late that night, in time to hear the announcement that the Grenadier Group would move the following morning to the aerodrome at Douai, which had just been captured by the Irish Guards. The afternoon had passed quietly near Arras, disturbed only by two British fighters, which machine-gunned the area and set a Welsh Guards lorry on fire. "Vive la R.A.F." had been chalked on several vehicles by overjoyed civilians: after this incident the Divisional Commander's A.D.C., Capt. The Hon. A. D. Tryon, walked over to his scout car and added the words "except two Spitfires."

If the Germans had sent a strong force of bombers over Douai Sept. 2 aerodrome on the 2nd of September the number of tanks and motor vehicles that the 5th Guards Armoured Brigade would have been able to operate the next day would probably have been very small indeed. For, at midday, the Grenadier and Irish Groups assembled on the long runways, and there is no possible way of camouflaging tanks and carriers so that they blend with a huge expanse of concrete. The danger was fully realized—in fact, there was a double risk because no one was sure that the Air Ministry had received word that Douai aerodrome was in British hands—but it had to be accepted because the tanks were beginning to feel the strain of the long mileages of the past few days, and, if they were to be quickly and efficiently maintained, it was essential for them to be parked on concrete. The Shermans had stood the test extremely well—owing in no small measure to the efforts of Capt. B. A. Johnston, the Technical Adjutant, and his staff—but without careful and frequent maintenance all tanks are as unreliable as human beings without sleep, and the drivers were kept fully occupied all day.

This was the first time that any of the battalions in the Division had been allowed more than a few hours in the same place since leaving Flers, and now that they had occasion to collect their thoughts they began to realize that what they had done in the past week and what they hoped to do in the future had suddenly been lifted from the realms of daily routine—of intense interest to themselves but only vaguely interesting to the outside world—into the heights of a drama which was headline news in the world's Press. During the advance itself they had begun to take for granted the cheers of the crowds, the almost complete absence of the enemy and the consequent saving of life, but they had only to remember Normandy to grasp the dramatic quality of the situation. Then the Seine had seemed the horizon of war, behind which lay an eternity of hard, costly battles like Cagny or Drouet Hill. That things had turned out differently and that the coun-

1944 try beyond the Seine had provided them with the chance of leading a lightning dash through the enemy lines—the role for which they had trained so hard in England—were the reward of the decisive Battle of Normandy. But the contrast between the two was so great that it was almost like slipping overnight from the era of the penny-farthing bicycle into that of the transatlantic airliner.

While the Group was reorganizing itself on Douai aerodrome, plans were being hatched for a superlatively ambitious advance the next day. The I Airborne Corps had been waiting impatiently in England for several weeks and it was intended to drop them at 11 o'clock the next morning near Tournai, on the Belgian frontier. At this same hour the Guards Armoured Division was to leave Douai, pass through them and then go right on to Brussels. Describing the excitement that this news caused among the Grenadiers of the 1st and 2nd Battalions, an officer wrote: "When we heard that we were to take Brussels the following day our spirits soared. It was one of those occasions when anything seemed possible. If we had been told to put the tanks into Dakotas and fly to Berlin I don't think we would have turned a hair." There was only one regret. It had been stated that, if the weather turned out to be too bad for the paratroopers to be dropped, the Division would start at 6 instead of 11 o'clock. This would provide a comfortable margin for error and raise the odds on the Division reaching Brussels before nightfall. As the general feeling throughout the Division was that it was quite unnecessary to employ airborne troops at all and that the Division was perfectly capable, given reasonable luck, of getting to Brussels without any outside assistance, to forfeit the extra five hours seemed unfortunate. But it was for the meteorologists to decide the issue. At 2 a.m. they conferred with the High Command and presented them with such bad weather reports that the airborne operation had to be abandoned. And so it was that at 6 a.m. on Sunday, the 3rd of September, the fifth anniversary of the declaration of war, the Guards Armoured Division started on the road to Brussels—alone.

The main road from Douai to the Belgian capital passes through **Sept. 3** Ath, Enghien and Hal. The Welsh Guards, who were to lead the 32nd Brigade, were given this route, and the 5th Guards Armoured Brigade, with the Grenadier Group in the lead, moved along secondary roads farther to the north through Beaumont, Pont-a-Marcq, Tournai, Lessines and Herinnes. Although the northern route was the longer of the two, it was felt that there would probably be less opposition on it and that an equal handicap would be imposed on each brigade. It was not known how many Germans had been left to defend the gateway to Brussels, but aerial reconnaissance had revealed that for the past twenty-four hours German transport had been sneaking out of Bel- gium's capital by the back door, and it seemed unlikely that more than token detachments had been left behind in the ancient provinces of Hainault and Brabant, through which the Division was to pass.

For the first part of the morning this appreciation of the situation turned out to be entirely correct. As the Group drove across the industrial area of Northern France—true Black Country—the cheering crowds which thronged the streets and blocked the corners were the sole obstacles in the path of the advance. Had they realized how much consternation they caused the drivers of the tanks, who did not relish the thought of injuring French civilians—particularly on such an auspicious day in their lives—the people might have stuck to the pavements. By 9 o'clock the Group were skirting the old battlefields at Mons and an hour later they were approaching Pont-a-Marcq.

There was a large cross-roads in this village at which the Group was supposed to turn right in the direction of Lessines, but, when they were still half a mile from it, anti-tank guns opened fire—the first to do so since the Somme—and the two leading tanks were knocked out. The first tank to be hit was Major F. J. C. Bowes-Lyon's (No. 2 Squadron), but, although three shells landed on it, it did not start to burn until the third hit, and the gunner, Gdsm. Binns, was able to destroy two of the enemy guns before bailing out. This successful opening invited the belief that the rest of the opposition would disintegrate as soon as fire was brought to bear, but, when a troop of tanks (Sergt. Willcox) tried to force their way up the main road and discovered that there were infantry in support of the offending anti-tank guns, there could be no doubt that the progress of the entire Group was threatened. The King's Company were therefore ordered to debus and the troop commanded by Lieut. M. Stoop were sent round the left flank to silence another gun. Lieut. Stoop's mission met with every success, but, when the Brigade Commander, Brigadier N. W. Gwatkin, drove up in his jeep to confer with Lieut.-Colonel E. H. Goulburn, it was decided that if Brussels was to be reached that night the whole Group could not be spared to deal with the opposition. The only solution was to leave the King's Company and No. 2 Squadron behind and to find a way round Pont-a-Marcq for the rest of the Group.

Another route was soon discovered and within half an hour, having reshuffled their positions and re-marked their maps, all except the King's Company and No. 2 Squadron set off once again for Brussels. Thus not only did the King's Company and No. 2 Squadron miss the excitement of the entry into Brussels but they went through some very unpleasant fighting as well. Sunday, the 3rd of September, 1944,

1944 will be recorded as the day on which Brussels was liberated, but Grenadiers will also remember it as the day on which their senior company and its supporting armour fought and won one of the most difficult of the many actions in which the three Battalions of the Regiment were involved during the campaign.

By 12 o'clock, when the rest of the Group left for Brussels, Major N. E. W. Baker had led the King's Company through a thick wood which ran to the right of the road and was firmly established on its northern edge. From here he could spot at least three enemy defensive positions. In two of these there were anti-tank guns, and the third, a factory, afforded its occupants excellent observation over the flat country to the south. Over this piece of open country No. 2 Squadron could not advance, as it was being swept by anti-tank-gun fire, so Major Baker ordered the Leicestershire Yeomanry to fire a barrage on the cross-roads in Pont-a-Marcq while he advanced north with two platoons to destroy the enemy positions on the edge of the village. As the company moved off out of the woods they were greeted by machine-gun and mortar fire as heavy as they had ever experienced, and later the enemy opened up with rapid-firing 20-mm. anti-aircraft guns. There was little cover to protect the company and they suffered heavy casualties, but they pressed on relentlessly, and by skilful use of 2-inch mortars and supporting fire from carriers managed to close in on the enemy and overrun two 88-mm. guns as well as a number of infantry.

This costly manœuvre enabled Major Baker to call up the reserve platoon, which passed through and drove the Germans out of the factory. From the factory roof further enemy positions could clearly be seen, and with the help of No. 2 Squadron, which knocked out more anti-tank guns and a large quantity of enemy transport, several parties were able to sally forth and start clearing the village. For two hours the tanks and infantry wrestled with the Germans, driving them out of house after house and riddling them with bullets when they tried to flee. By 7 o'clock the enemy was so demoralized that the combined efforts of the company and squadron and a battalion of the 50th (Northumbrian) Division, which had been sent up as soon as the strength of the enemy in Pont-a-Marcq had been discovered, experienced little difficulty in ousting the Germans from their last hide-outs in the village.

When the final count was taken it was discovered that the company and squadron had captured one hundred and twenty-five prisoners, killed twenty-five Germans, and wounded about the same number. But their own casualties had not been light: the King's Company had lost fifteen men killed and twenty-five wounded, and No. 2 Squadron

N

TO LILLE

PONT-
A MARCQ

The Factory

C

B A

Merignies

Molpas

Cappelle

TO BRUSSELS

FROM DOUAI

Remainder of Group's detour

Scale in Yards

0   500   1000   2000

A — Limit of advance up main road
B — Lieutenant M. Stoop's troop
C — King's Company No 2 Squadron
Q — Anti-tank guns

PONT-A-MARCQ

Face page 110

seven killed and six wounded. Major N. E. W. Baker and Lieuts. **1944**
M. B. Akroyd and N. G. J. H. Stiff had been wounded. Many of the
inhabitants of Pont-a-Marcq were killed or maimed, as the Battalion
was reminded later when the Mayor sent photographs of the funeral
procession that took place when the bodies of the fallen were transferred to a special cemetery in the village. It was subsequently discovered that Pont-a-Marcq was a strongly held hedgehog position,
part of the defences of the approach to Lille, containing altogether
some twelve 88-mm. guns and two hundred men. Had the Grenadier
Group been given a route farther south, as might well have happened,
no opposition would have been met because the Germans were not
making any concerted attempt to block the road to Brussels.

By a strange sequence of events, the Battle of Pont-a-Marcq
probably saved the lives of a number of other Grenadiers the next
morning. At the start of the advance on Brussels the L.A.D. and
Technical Department had set off behind the Group, and as a result
of attending to several minor breakdowns and accidents they had
lagged slightly behind. Capt. A. J. Shaughnessy, the Technical Adjutant, therefore decided to spend the night of the 3rd of September in
Lessines, and the party settled down to a good night's sleep. Early the
next morning they were woken by the excited cries of local patriots **Sept. 4**
warning them that a German column, containing anti-tank guns and
liberally equipped with automatic weapons, was rapidly approaching
the town. The Maquis were not very well organized, but they managed to make enough noise to divert the enemy's attention while the
L.A.D. flung aside spanners, files and oilcans and searched for their
long-forgotten weapons of personal defence. The few available Bren
guns were tactically sited in upper windows and the fitters quickly
took up positions of advantage. Their long preoccupation with mechanical matters had evidently not detracted from their skill-at-arms,
because as soon as the Germans came into sight they greeted them
with a tremendous fusillade which was sufficiently accurate to make
some of them leap for cover. The Germans, however, had a considerable advantage in both numbers and equipment, and, although they
were as keen to get to Germany as the British, they might have proved
troublesome had it not been for the timely arrival of the King's Company and No. 2 Squadron on their way to rejoin the Group after the
battle at Pont-a-Marcq. The Sherman tanks and the Motor Company
gave the Germans small mercy and in a very short space of time
seventy prisoners were taken for the loss of only one man wounded.
The L.A.D., who had acquitted themselves nobly in an unpractised
role, complicated by the difficulty of communications with the Maquis,
were thus safely relieved in the nick of time, and only because the

Germans had decided to defend Pont-a-Marcq. Such are the vicissitudes of war.

Perhaps at one time the enemy contemplated defending Lessines because the only comparatively large force of Germans that the main body of the Group encountered after leaving the King's Company and No. 2 Squadron during the battle at Pont-a-Marcq was in this town. Their journey from Pont-a-Marcq, over the Belgian frontier and through Tournai resembled in every way the triumphal progress of the past few days, and it was only as they were approaching Lessines, which is some twenty miles south-west of Brussels, that the first suspicion of trouble arose. Civilians came running towards the tanks shouting that there were about two hundred Germans with horse-drawn vehicles in the eastern half of the town and that the local contingents of l'Armée Blanche, the Belgian underground army, were being hard pressed. The tanks slackened their pace and the reconnaissance troop was sent on into the town to investigate. The civilians, however, had grossly exaggerated the danger, because the Germans were in a state of hopeless confusion and a few bursts from the reconnaissance troop were enough to make them surrender. A number of the Germans had already been hustled into prison by l'Armée Blanche and their horses were now quickly separated from the wagons and killed. It gave the well-fed Grenadiers a grim reminder of Belgium's privations to see the local butchers cutting up the horses where they lay on the roadside.

By the time they had passed through Lessines the Group had already covered over sixty miles since leaving Douai and the tanks needed refuelling. The Motor Battalion therefore went speeding on and left the tanks to catch up as soon as they could. Lieut.-Colonel J. N. R. Moore went on ahead with the 1st Battalion control vehicle and one or two scout cars, and, much to his amazement, he suddenly met two lorries, crammed with German infantry, driving along the road in the opposite direction. A few revolver shots sufficed to persuade the infantrymen to dismount and surrender without more ado, and they turned out to be the last even remotely organized Germans whom the Group were to see that day. By 7 o'clock the tanks and half-tracks had joined up again and, as they were already almost in the suburbs of Brussels, Lieut.-Colonel E. H. Goulburn called a halt to give out orders for the occupation of the city.

The Welsh Guards were on the point of entering Brussels from the south, so the Group Commander decided to set up his headquarters in the grounds of the Palace of Laeken and to protect all vital bridges and road junctions west of the palace from any German counter-attack from the north. No. 4 Company and No. 1 Squadron were told to park themselves on the first main road junction; No. 2 Company 1944 were made responsible for guarding two canal bridges farther east, elements of No. 3 Company were to defend another bridge; and Group Headquarters and the remainder of the 2nd Battalion were told to make for the grounds of the Royal Palace. Sniping was feared and this plan avoided the narrow, tortuous streets in the heart of the city farther south.

The Household Cavalry, in front as usual, had reported that two anti-tank guns were blocking the main road into the city. But when the Group got under way they were forgotten amid all the excitement and were never seen or heard of again.

It was 9 o'clock in the evening when the column finally moved forward again and drove out from a small lane into one of the great main roads leading into Brussels. Here, in the gathering darkness, were the first lights that anyone had seen since leaving England, the first signs of common, everyday life, the first hint of normality—so soon to be dispelled. At first the column pounded down the wide cobbled main road carefully, keeping a sharp look-out for Germans everywhere. They did not know whether the enemy had already left or if the loud bark of an anti-tank gun would suddenly muffle the shouts of the civilians lining the road, and crown with tragedy the long advance so nearly completed. But a German motor-cyclist who came tearing down the road towards them, only to end up a mutilated wreck in a ditch, was crowning evidence that the Germans were in a state of utter chaos, and from that moment on the whole column let itself be carried forward on the tide of hysteria which was rapidly rising to a crescendo among the citizens of Brussels.

How they ever reached the rendezvous at the Palace of Laeken few members of the Group can understand. They found themselves surrounded by the biggest, densest crowds they had ever seen, who used every conceivable mode of expression to show their joy at being liberated. A violent passion, utterly uncontrollable, had overcome the million people of Brussels. From cafés, shops and houses they poured forth, forcing the tanks to slow down to walking pace, and then seizing the opportunity to jump up and embrace the crews, kissing them, showering gifts into the turrets and even, sometimes, baptizing the commanders with whole bottles of champagne. It was Beauvais and every other town from the Seine onwards all over again, on a scale a thousand times greater.

What happened in Brussels that night has probably never happened in England—except possibly on Armistice Night in London in 1918—and never will. For the Bruxellois this night meant the end of nine

I

1944 years of occupation—not four as it had for the French.* They were as determined to blot out the memory of occupation in the revelry of this one night as they were to exult in liberation. Men and women who had collaborated were shown no hint of mercy: paraded through the streets, dragged, kicked, and handcuffed. Soon bonfires were started in front of bookstores, and Nazi literature and portraits of Hitler were hurled down from neighbouring windows into the blaze. The Germans seemed to have disappeared completely and left the victorious army free to taste the joys of liberation unmolested. Down in the modern quarter of the town German officers who apparently thought that the troops had passed through were apprehended carrying away cases of champagne, brandy and cigars. Capt. A. G. Heywood, the Adjutant of the 2nd Battalion, mistook one of these cars for a Grenadier vehicle. He started to run alongside it and had shouted "Next left for the echelons" when he was greeted by a shot from inside which, luckily for him, bounced off his collar-bone and did no damage. He drew his own revolver and fired into the interior of the car, causing it to stop, and out jumped four German quartermasters on their way out of the town with all they could gather in the way of last-minute loot.

Amid these scenes, which varied from high tragedy to low comedy, the various companies and squadrons somehow managed to find their way through the streets. Directed by guides of doubtful sobriety and competence, they eventually converged on the Château Royal, where Queen Elizabeth, the Queen Mother of the Belgians, was waiting to greet them. When the Brigadier and the two Commanding Officers arrived they were invited to dinner and afterwards they spent the night in the palace. The tank crews harboured between the avenue of plane trees in the grounds outside.

All through the night the people of Brussels danced in the streets, sang songs and drank toasts in champagne to their liberators. When the Grenadiers finally went to bed, it was the end of perhaps the most memorable day of their lives. Not only had they witnessed one of the most extravagant displays of mass human emotion that have ever been known, but they had also been in the forefront of the longest opposed advance that any division, in any army, had ever before undertaken in a single day.

---

*Belgium is the only country to have suffered German occupation during two world wars.

The Grenadiers enter Brussels, 3rd September, 1944.

Brussels, 4th September, 1944.   Major-General Allan Adair, D.S.O., M.C., Commander of the Guards Armoured Division, enters the city.

2

BRUSSELS TO NIJMEGEN

*Grenadier Group liberate Louvain—British advance slowed down—
Advance across Albert Canal—Resistance at Bourg Leopold and
Hechtel—Guards Armoured Division force crossing of Escaut Canal
—Plan for the airborne operations at Arnhem, Nijmegen and Eind-
hoven—Guards Armoured Division's role—Rapid advance through
Eindhoven and Grave to Nijmegen*

Brussels the next morning was in holiday spirit. As soon as it was **1944** light the women donned their best clothes and hats, the men put **Sept. 4** flowers in their buttonholes, and every family in Brussels strode out into the streets to celebrate. In the old part of the town, along the cobbled streets which wind up the steep hill to the Cathedral, the vendeuses sat behind huge baskets of fruit, rocking with raucous laughter as they made their sales. In the Napoleonic town, with its classical vistas and graceful arches, people filed in thousands past the Tomb of the Unknown Warrior. In the modern quarter of boulevards, big shops, cafés, kiosks, cinemas, theatres and night clubs the crowds in the streets were even bigger and rowdier than the night before. And in the grounds of the Royal Palace people swarmed among the tanks and vehicles, getting acquainted with the Guardsmen and parading their families for inspection.

Most of the speedometers in the tanks had registered more than a hundred miles since leaving Douai, and the Group confidently ex-pected to remain in Brussels for at least another twenty-four hours to do some maintenance. But at 11.15 a.m. the Group Commander went to a conference at Brigade Headquarters and returned with the dis-quieting news that the Group was to leave Brussels at 1.30 p.m. and capture Louvain, some eighteen miles to the east. The rest of the morning was therefore spent in rounding up the crews and giving out orders for the complicated move out of Brussels.

Two good roads run east out of Brussels to Louvain. From a mili-tary point of view the northern road is the better of the two because it runs through open, undulating country and is inordinately wide. The southern route is a few miles longer and twists and turns through thick woods most of the way, besides passing through the town of Tervueren. The Grenadier Group were told to take the northern route, but soon after moving off from Laeken a warning came from the Household Cavalry that the road was covered by anti-tank guns pro-tecting Brussels aerodrome. The Group Commander immediately

1944 obtained permission to use the southern route, and after a slight delay, caused partly by the necessity of re-sorting the vehicles and partly by the antics of the civilian onlookers, the column started off along the tree-lined avenues towards Tervueren.

Fate was kind to the Grenadiers in handing them the chance of liberating Louvain, because it was from this town, after the invasion of the Low Countries, that they had been forced to start their retreat to Dunkirk in 1940. Then the civilians lining the road back to Brussels had worn on their faces the distracted look of men and women about to undergo life imprisonment. For the Grenadiers it had been a ghastly experience, too, like abandoning a sinking ship in the full knowledge that there were people still on board who could not swim. But much water had passed under the bridges since then, and when the Grenadiers drove back to Louvain four years later the scene was reversed. In every village which the Group passed through the civilians came bursting out of their houses to wave a welcome instead of a farewell, and their faces were lit up with smiles. Not a single German fired at the tanks between Brussels and Louvain, a fact which was noted with satisfaction by the civilians, one of whom said in broken English to an officer what amounted to "When you were in the same predicament as the Germans you put up a better show."

In Louvain itself the main garrison had fled and the Group seized the big bridge over the River Dyle with little difficulty, although there was a switch on the far end which would have exploded a 500-lb. bomb. One platoon inflicted severe casualties on a large group of Germans at the railway station who were apparently waiting for the next train home, but, apart from an occasional group found hiding in houses, snipers appeared to be the only other Germans left behind in Louvain. As luck would have it, the leading brain specialist of Belgium was at hand and he immediately operated on a victim of a sniper, a sergeant who was badly wounded in the head and who, under normal battle conditions, would have stood no chance of recovery.

Sept. 5-6   The Grenadiers remained in and around Louvain for the next twenty-four hours, carefully clearing each street and sending patrols backwards and forwards across the surrounding fields and woods to round up a number of Germans who had hoped to evade being captured. Wireless communication with Brigade Headquarters in Brussels was very bad indeed, and at about 11 p.m. on the second day in Louvain Lieut. D. W. Fraser, the Liaison Officer of the 2nd Battalion, was sent back to Brigade Headquarters at Brussels to find out what the situation was. Reports had been coming in from all sides, including the Brussels radio itself, that the war had come to an end, but when Lieut. Fraser returned he brought no confirmation of any such news. He had been told that the Division was to advance east- **1944** wards to the Albert Canal the following morning, the 32nd Brigade going via Diest to seize a crossing near Beeringen, and the 5th Brigade travelling farther north via Aerschot, to cross near Bourg Leopold. The Grenadier Group was to lead the 5th Brigade and to be followed by the Coldstream Group.

This move, as well as the one that followed it—up to the Escaut Canal—was conducted in quite different circumstances from those to which the Division had grown accustomed during the past two weeks. There were no lightning dashes, no sensational liberations; frequent orders were equally frequently cancelled, and progress was made only by small steps. The reason for this was that the Germans were making a very determined effort—considering their resources—to slow down the British advance so that it would be overtaken by winter weather before it reached Germany. They had few cards up their sleeves, but those they held were aces—a whole string of ports, stretching from Brest to Antwerp. Without these the British High Command was finding it increasingly hard to keep the forward troops supplied, and for the time being no more units could be sent up to assist the Guards and 11th Armoured Divisions which were well in front of the remainder of the Second Army. Supplies still had to be landed on the beaches of Normandy or at Cherbourg, several hundred miles away. Ten thousand trucks covered this distance each day, and the most urgent supplies were flown over in Dakotas from England, but they were naturally unable to fulfil the needs of the whole of the Second Army, which, had the ports been free, would have been sent forward towards Germany straight away. The 11th Armoured Division and the Guards Armoured Division had therefore to be left to fight their way across the Albert and Escaut Canals as best they could.

The move from Louvain to the Albert Canal went without a hitch. **Sept. 7-** At Aerschot No. 4 Company and No. 1 Squadron, who had been sent **9** on ahead to capture the bridge and had spent two nights there, took over the lead and the advance proceeded uneventfully. But at the canal the situation deteriorated. A patrol of the Household Cavalry were about to cross the bridge when it was blown up in the face of the leading armoured car, and enemy in considerable strength could be observed on the far bank. The Commanding Officer immediately made a plan to cross by a railway bridge about half a mile south which, according to civilian reports, was passable to troops on foot, but, shortly afterwards, news arrived that the 32nd Brigade on the right had won a small bridgehead at Beeringen and that the 5th Brigade were to suspend all operations until the damage to the bridge had been repaired and the 32nd Brigade were across. The effect of this was to

1944 prevent the Grenadiers crossing for another forty-eight hours because early the next day reports were received that a German armoured column was approaching from Liege and the Grenadiers were ordered to move ten miles south to stand between the column and the bridge. Although they never saw any sign of the column, the move over the bridge did not take place until 6 p.m. the following night, because the 32nd Brigade, which had been reinforced by the Dutch Princess Irene Brigade, met much stronger opposition than had been anticipated in the bridgehead. The crossing lasted well into the night, as there were no fewer than two other brigades on their way over at the same time, but a bright moon assisted the reconnaissance parties, and the Group were settled in defensive positions by 2 o'clock in the morning.

Sept. 10   At 10 a.m. the Group started to move slowly north up the centre of the bridgehead, picketing all cross-roads and road junctions, and sending patrols out to the north and west. As the day progressed the news coming from the Welsh and Coldstream Groups, who were attacking the two centres of enemy resistance at Hechtel and Bourg Leopold, became increasingly pessimistic. It was evident that these two towns would be hard nuts to crack, and the Grenadier Group were ordered to harbour for the night just south of some big woods near the main road, to be available to help either the Coldstream or Welsh Guards if need be. This entailed a cross-country move by night, with the moon hidden and little time for adequate reconnaissance. The leading vehicles set off at 9.30 p.m. and, although the distance they had to cover was only some three miles, they did not reach the woods until after midnight. Half the squadrons missed the road and plaintively called up on the wireless for instructions, and wheeled vehicles were bogged in the tank tracks; but time, as always, smoothed out the troubles.

Sept. 11   The plan for the next day was that the 5th Brigade should capture a bridge over the Escaut Canal. It was to be done in the following way: while the 32nd Brigade pinned down the S.S. troops in Bourg Leopold and Hechtel, the 5th Brigade were to go between the two towns, cut the main road running north from the latter, and then advance up it to the Escaut. A comprehensive smoke and artillery programme was arranged because not only was the ground between the two towns very open—it had been used by the Belgian Army as a tank training ground—but it was also bounded on the north by two big woods from which well-sited Panthers and anti-tank guns could easily hold up any number of advancing tanks.

The day dawned mistily, but by the time the Group had moved forward to a road joining Bourg Leopold and Hechtel, at which the advance was to begin, the sun was shining brightly. The smoke screens **1944** were brought down at 10 o'clock and shortly afterwards the leading troops crossed the road unhindered. No. 1 Squadron and No. 4 Company were in front and, despite the smoke screen, they soon ran into anti-tank-gun fire. One of the first tanks to be hit was Sir Howard Frank's and, as he jumped out, machine-gun fire wounded him fatally. Two further tanks were bogged in the sandy soil of this treacherous country and the situation rapidly grew serious enough to call for a change of plan. It was decided to send No. 3 Squadron and No. 2 Company round by a different route and they very soon found the party of enemy that had been causing the hold-up. The Germans were on the far side of a small stream over which there was a railway bridge, dilapidated but capable of bearing the weight of tanks. At the sight of the approaching Shermans the enemy quickly surrendered, whereupon No. 2 Company and No. 3 Squadron were able to traverse the remainder of the open country and cut the road leading north from Hechtel to the Escaut.

The Group's progress up the main road was neither fast nor spectacular. After advancing a thousand yards a Household Cavalry patrol was fired on by a self-propelled gun, and as there were thick woods on either side of the road further progress except on foot was out of the question. Patrols were sent out, but as soon as the gun was ranged or a patrol approached it, it pulled back, the squadron moved forward, the gun fired and the whole process started all over again. Eventually the patrols reached the northern edge of the wood, but as soon as the tanks moved up the road they were again fired on from a long way away. As the country was now very open and an attack straight up the road would have proved very expensive, Lieut.-Colonel E. H. Goulburn sent the King's Company and No. 2 Squadron in a wide sweep to the left in an attempt to cut in behind the enemy and if possible to seize the main cross-roads about a mile south of the bridge over the Escaut Canal. The country was difficult and they were forced to make quick dashes across rides in the woods which were covered by anti-tank guns from one end. By degrees, however, they made their way round and ended up on the railway line which ran close to the main road, about three miles short of the bridge. Here the Motor Company left its vehicles, and the platoons moved off along the railway lines, supported by the tanks. As they approached a level-crossing about two miles ahead they saw a considerable number of enemy both on the road near the crossing and at the main cross-roads nine hundred yards to the north. The enemy's attention was clearly distracted by No. 2 Company farther down the road, and the King's Company, ably supported by No. 2 Squadron, dashed in and did great damage to a

1944 completely unsuspecting enemy with no loss to themselves. One Mark III tank, two 88-mm. anti-tank guns, one self-propelled gun, one 20-mm. heavy machine gun and all the towing and ammunition vehicles for the guns were destroyed and the crews either killed or taken prisoner. This happened just as darkness fell, and the sky was lit up for miles around by the blazing vehicles.

Closely following on this success came news of another. While the Grenadier Group had been slowly forcing their way up the main road, the Irish Guards had been able to advance unchallenged up a smaller road to the east, and in a very gallant tank charge in the twilight had secured the bridge over the Escaut Canal intact. Thus, after a long and complicated day's fighting, the Division was across the third big water barrier it had captured since the Seine.

Sept. 12-16 For the next five days, while the bridgehead was being strengthened and supplies were rushed up, the Grenadiers remained near the Escaut. On the 12th the King's Company (Capt. The Hon. V. P. Gibbs) cleared the village of Lommel, and later the same day the Support Company (Major G. Thorne) crossed over the canal to hold a position astride the main road leading to Eindhoven. A patrol from this company, led by Lieut. W. J. R. Jarvis, were the first British troops to cross the Dutch frontier. On the 13th Lieut. F. C. H. Fryer took out a patrol in the hope of finding a new way across the canal, but just as they reached the water's edge the bridge which they were expecting to use was blown up in their faces. The Group were relieved of patrolling duties on the following day and they settled down to a peaceful routine which included anything from courts-martial to visits to Brussels.

During this period the Higher Command were coming to a very important decision. For some time they had been toying with the idea of dropping a British and two American airborne divisions at strategic points in Holland, and of then sending a flying column of tanks and infantry through the airborne troops to turn the Siegfried Line and clear the way for an attack on the Ruhr. The dangers confronting the scheme were so immense—airborne operations are always a risky business because, like the harvest in Scotland, they are subject to the whims of the weather—that, until the middle of September, the Higher Command had not considered it to be practicable. But now, with the crust of German resistance rapidly hardening, the winter approaching and no prospect of Antwerp being opened up to shipping for at least another month, they were on the horns of a dilemma: either they could continue the advance at the same slow rate—which would definitely mean that the war would go on until the spring—

or they could swallow the risks involved in an airborne operation at **1944** this time of year and perhaps finish the war by Christmas. The problem really amounted to this: if the airborne operation took place, would the saving of life caused by a speedy end of the war compensate its probable cost? While the Grenadiers waited near the Escaut, the Higher Command thrashed out the problems and about the 14th of September they reached a decision: the gamble was worth taking.

The operation was given the name "Market Garden," "Market" denoting the airborne part and "Garden" the land operation. Briefly the plan was as follows: the 101st American Airborne Division were to drop at Eindhoven, the 82nd American at Grave and Nijmegen, and the 1st British at Arnhem; between them they were to seize crossings over the Maas, the Waal and the Neder Rhine, and then open the way for an advance by the British Second Army. The XXX Corps, consisting of the Guards Armoured Division, the 50th (Northumbrian) Division, the 43rd (Wessex) Division and the 8th Independent Armoured Brigade, were to lead the Second Army, and the Guards Armoured Division were to lead the XXX Corps. Within the Division the 5th Brigade, consisting of the Grenadier and Irish Groups, the Leicestershire Yeomanry and the 14th Field Squadron, R.E., were to lead; and the Irish Guards Group were to lead the 5th Brigade, the onus of breaking out of the bridgehead over the Escaut thus falling on them. The column was to pass through the following places: Valkensvaard, Eindhoven, Zon, Veghel, Grave, Nijmegen and Arnhem. If Arnhem was reached, the Division were to advance to Appeldoorn, some twenty miles to the north, and then swing east in preparation for an advance into Germany. D Day, if the weather was suitable, was to be the next day, the 17th of September.

A long armoured advance often starts badly. The enemy almost always receives word beforehand that an attempt is to be made to break through his lines. Only when by sheer doggedness the armour forges a passage through the iron curtain of anti-tank guns does the advance begin to take shape. But once through, the armour gathers momentum and then only the very strongest measures on the part of the enemy will stop it.

This was indeed the case during the advance from the Escaut Canal **Sept. 17** to the Neder Rhine. Although the sky on the 17th of September was overcast, there was no wind, and punctually at 1 p.m. the airborne armada soared over Holland and dropped its cargoes near the country's three big waterways. But back at the Belgian-Dutch border the tanks experienced the greatest difficulty in forcing their way out of the Escaut bridgehead. The pine forests north of the canal were bristling with anti-tank guns and bazooka-men, and although several

1944 squadrons of Typhoons attacked anything they saw in front of the tanks it was heavy going. One squadron of the Irish Guards lost nine tanks three miles north of the frontier post. The burning vehicles and exploding ammunition blocked the road so that the rest of the Irish Guards could not pass by. But eventually they found a way round and by nightfall had taken Valkensvaard. The Grenadiers, prevented from crossing until 6 p.m., hurried through the bridgehead and harboured for the night four miles south of them.

Sept. 18   The second day of the advance was as hard as the first. The Irish Guards were again held up, this time at Aalst, a small village three miles south of Eindhoven, and the Grenadiers were ordered to bypass the town to join up with American parachutists at Zon to the north. This turned out to be a wild-goose chase, because, although no enemy were encountered, every time the advance seemed to be progressing, a canal or stream would intervene with a bridge that invariably broke after a couple of tanks had crossed. Eventually, just before nightfall, the Brigadier ordered the Group to return to the main road, as the Irish Guards had succeeded in reaching the American paratroopers in Eindhoven—the home of the giant Philips radio works, which had supplied the Germans with much of their electrical equipment. The Group had to reverse a considerable distance to get into the main road, but they made fast progress after that. In Eindhoven the streets were decked with orange bunting and the plump, homely citizens were singing songs and cheering. But there was no time to stop, as a position had been chosen for the Grenadiers to harbour just south of the Wilhelmina Canal at Zon. The bridge over the canal was blown, but the Americans held both banks securely and the Divisional engineers were able to erect a temporary structure during the night. By now the column was deep into Holland, and the initial period of breaking through the enemy defences was over. The necessary momentum had been gathered and it seemed that, with a little luck, the airborne divisions should be relieved.

Sept. 19   The engineers made excellent progress with the bridge building and by 6.15 the Grenadiers were under way. They were now in the lead and they were told that, come what may, they must reach Nijmegen that night. It was a cold morning, but the spirit of the chase had been amply aroused and they drove forward oblivious of the pathetic attempts of German stragglers to hold them back. In every village and at every road junction parties of American paratroopers were waiting to welcome them, cheering wildly and beckoning the way to the next American strong-point. Canals and rivers flashed by and the column sped on through St. Oedenrode, Veghel and Uden, until, at 10 a.m., the great bridge at Grave loomed into sight.

HOLLAND, BELGIUM AND NORTHERN

Route of 1ˢᵗ & 2ⁿᵈ Battalion Grenadier Guards

Scale of Miles

0   10   20   30   40   50   60

N O R

S E

Southampton

Brighton

Portsmouth

ISLE OF
WIGHT

STRAIT OF DOVER

E N G L I S H   C H A N N E L

Somme

Carb

Amiens

Beauvais

Auneuil

Bayeux

Les Andelys

Gisors

Caen

St Lo

Vernon

Seine

F   R   A   N

Condé

Argentan

Laigle

Flers

Verneuil

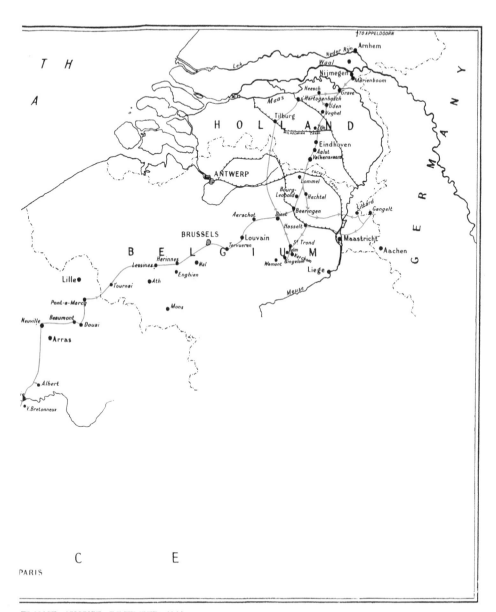

FRANCE, AUGUST—DECEMBER, 1944

Here the column halted to allow the tanks to cross the bridge well 1944 spaced out. A moment later an American liaison officer arrived with a message from Lieutenant-General F. A. M. Browning, the Deputy Commander-in-Chief of the Airborne Forces—and a distinguished Grenadier—saying that he wished to see the Commanding Officers. They set off immediately and found him waiting by the roadside in Overasselt. Soon they were joined by Major-General Allan Adair and Brigadier N. W. Gwatkin. It was a great occasion, as less than a month ago they had all met near Caumont, never expecting to meet again so soon—and at that in Holland.

General Browning's summing up of the situation in Nijmegen was hopeful: the 82nd U.S. Airborne Division were holding the high ground south-east of Nijmegen, their patrols had entered the town, and the road bridge across the Waal had not been blown. But he had no information about the situation at Arnhem, so it was vital that the tanks should link up with the 1st Airborne Division without delay. General Browning drove away to confer with General Gavin, the Commander of the 82nd U.S. Airborne Division, taking with him the two Commanding Officers, Major A. M. H. Gregory-Hood and Capt. The Duke of Rutland. While this conference was taking place the Group moved to the suburbs of Nijmegen by a route which General Browning had given them, and at midday they were halted outside the monastery at Marienboom. It was from this ancient building that they launched the most important attack of their career.

CHAPTER V

THE BATTLE OF NIJMEGEN

1ST AND 2ND BATTALIONS

*Description of town—Behaviour of Germans before the Allied advance—
The American parachutists drop at Nijmegen—Importance of the battle—
Grenadiers involved in fierce street fighting—Capture of the Valkhof—1st
Battalion clear approaches to the bridge and 2nd Battalion tanks dash
across to link up with American paratroops—Capture of the railway bridge
—Why did the Germans not blow up the bridges?*

1944 NIJMEGEN, about the size of the city of Oxford, is a town of some
100,000 inhabitants. Like most things Dutch, it is trim and clean, but
in every other respect it bears more resemblance to the towns of
Germany than those of Holland. There are no canals or shaded levels
to break up the rather depressing monotony of its rows and rows of
middle-class houses, and it is one of the few towns in the Netherlands
in which you can walk uphill. From the water-front on the Waal to
the big round-about in the middle of the town is a rise of some five
hundred feet, and the shopping centre is on a slope—unheard of for
Holland.

There are six roads leading out of the enormous round-about in the
centre of the town, one of which is a broad, tree-lined avenue leading
up to a smaller round-about three hundred yards from the huge single-
span bridge that links Southern Holland with Arnhem and the north.
From this second round-about the road curves sharply round to the
left along an embankment, on the left of which there is an old
medieval fort surrounded by sloping lawns and a maze of carefully
See Plan planted flower-beds, known as the Huner Park. On the right there is a
p. 140. sharp drop of about eighty feet on to a great expanse of flat pastureland which stretches as far as the eye can see. The bridge itself is one
of those majestic structures which are big enough to allow themselves
the luxury of rumbling deeply whenever a vehicle passes over. The
railway bridge is about half a mile down-stream. Between the two
lies the water-front of Nijmegen, and with its gaily painted houses and
its miniature wharves and jetties it looks more like the plage of a
fishing village in the South of France than anything one would expect
to see on such a cold and unfriendly river as the Waal.

The war for the inhabitants of Nijmegen had not been easy. In 1944 1940, just after the German invasion, Dutch forces had warded off German attempts to take the bridge for three whole days, and in the end the bridge, the pride of the town, had had to be blown, only to be rebuilt later by the German Army. Then in 1943 an American bombing force, evidently mistaking Nijmegen for Cleve or some other town in the Rhineland, had dropped a stick of bombs right in the centre of the town, which destroyed the shopping district and killed eight hundred citizens. On top of all this, there had been desperate food shortages, deportations to Germany and the many other horrors which the Germans imposed during the last two years of their occupation. By September, 1944, when the news of Brussels's liberation had sifted through to them, the inhabitants of Nijmegen had had only one ambition: to be liberated quickly and, if possible, without a fight.

The Germans, however, made no secret of the fact that they expected a battle to take place in Nijmegen. Early in September they did a curious thing. For over three months the giant hollow pillar which supported the Arnhem side of the bridge had been filled with dynamite and carefully wired so that it could be discharged at a moment's notice. There was a plunger in a concrete pillbox about twenty yards from the pillar, which, when pressed, would have caused the central span to crash into the river. The Dutch, remembering 1940, knew that this method was foolproof, and they were therefore considerably taken aback when early in September the Germans dismantled the charges in the pillar and, instead, placed a much less powerful set of explosive underneath the short section of the bridge joining the centre span with the Arnhem bank. It was a foregone conclusion that if this was let off it would be impossible for anyone to use the bridge; but, on the other hand, the centre span would be untouched and it would be no major operation to build a temporary structure in the place of the blown section. At the time the Dutch did not realize the full significance of what the Germans had done. They imagined that the charges had been changed and weakened because the risk to the man who would have to blow them—he could not, for some technical reason, be more than twenty yards away—would be too great. In actual fact, as will be shown later, the German decision to change the charges was made for a less humane reason. The motive becomes the most important clue in any diagnosis of the unexpected behaviour of the defenders of the bridge.

As September wore on, the Germans became increasingly purturbed and their attitude towards the civilian population became more threatening than ever. Their mounting anger expressed itself in three stages, each more cruel than the last. The first came in the form of a

1944 proclamation which the people awoke to find plastered on their walls on the morning of the 12th of September. Signed by the local Gauleiter, it was printed in red ink on white paper and was lined by a margin of black ink, larger and far more ominous than the traditional edging of *The Times* on the death of the reigning sovereign. For sheer barbarity the posters could not have been rivalled. They said, in effect: "Anyone suspected of sabotage of any kind or of aiding the Allies in any way will be shot without trial."

Sept. 16 The Dutch, as their history tells, are a brave people and they are not inclined to acquiescence in the face of threats. But a proclamation such as this would bend the will of the most courageous and it opened the way for the second stage of the German domination of Nijmegen. On the 16th they demanded that civilians should come forward to dig slit trenches on the banks of the canal which runs past the southwestern outskirts of the town. In the past these summonses had met with little response. The burghers of Nijmegen had resorted to countless subterfuges to absent themselves from such schemes, but on this occasion the Germans appended a threat which revealed the fundamental callousness of their nature. They warned the population that, unless they obeyed, the home of every teacher in the town would be burnt in reprisal. Nijmegen has a flourishing university, so the number of houses involved would not have been small. Yet, to the annoyance of the Germans, no one turned up and, that night, they started to dump all the teachers' furniture into the streets. If enough civilians did not come forward to dig the next day, warned the Germans, they would take action.

Sept. 17 Faced by this ultimatum, a sizeable number of citizens went out to the canal the next morning, the 17th of September. They had been working for several hours when suddenly the air-raid sirens began to wail and a moment later British fighter planes screeched down on to the town, riddling the anti-aircraft defences, many of which were on the canal itself just where the civilians were working. The attack was followed by several others and bombs began to land with increasing frequency on the anti-aircraft defences. One happened to hit the electric power station and the electricity for the whole town was cut out, including the power that ran the sirens. No "all clear" was therefore sounded and the people remained in their cellars long after the planes had departed.

At about 1 o'clock the drone of engines was again heard and soon the sky above Nijmegen was crammed with a vast concourse of Allied planes. There was nothing novel about this for the people of Nijmegen, as, for the past year, they had watched with delight the thousand-bomber formations flying overhead to bomb the Ruhr and other targets in Germany. The people therefore came out into the **1944** streets and watched the rather pathetic attempts of the few remaining anti-aircraft guns to shoot them down. Then, suddenly, word spread through the town that this was no ordinary bombing force. About four miles to the west, at Berg-en-Dal, the highest point in Holland, the aeroplanes had been seen dropping parachutes, and the parachutes did not just contain supplies but men as well. But still the people did not realize what had happened. They thought the parachutists were probably German and they ran to the telephone to find out more from the suburbs. For some time no news could be obtained, as the inhabitants of Berg-en-Dal were cowering in their cellars, but finally someone got through and found out the truth. The parachutists were Americans, real live Americans, and they had with them guns and food and even little cars which were bounding over the country in the most amazing fashion. (The Dutch had yet to become familiar with jeeps.) The town buzzed with rumours: "Why are the Americans landing in Nijmegen; have they come to take the town?" The general consensus of opinion was that they were there to take Cleve or Goch, as the advance parties of an American force which was about to enter the Rhineland. For some curious reason it apparently never occurred to them that the Americans might be there to capture the bridges.

The afternoon passed peacefully and Nijmegen began to think that its dream of not becoming a battlefield was coming true. The Americans were evidently heading east. At midnight, however, the people's worst fears were realized. Shots began to ring out from the area of the round-about near the bridge, sounding at first like the grumblings of a nervous sentry, but rapidly developing into a maelstrom of bangs and crackles. Strong American patrols with rubber soles on their shoes had crept right into the defences surrounding the bridge and had very nearly run the Germans off their feet. The battle for the Nijmegen road bridge had begun.

The next thirty-six hours seemed like an eternity to the people of **Sept. 17-** Nijmegen. Their quiet, ordered life was suddenly transformed into a **19** long, hideous nightmare, which became more terrible as the hours dragged by. First there was the fighting itself which made every street a potential death-trap and rendered a cellar a family's most treasured possession. Swooping into different parts of the town as unpredictably as forks of lightning, the Americans tried time and time again to get near the two bridges. Sometimes they overran a German strong-point, sometimes they were repelled with heavy losses. They fought brilliantly, but the Germans were well organized and, dug in behind the defences which they had taken weeks to prepare, were secure against

1944 any attack that the Americans with their limited resources could hope for the moment to stage.

Secondly, there were the German counter-measures which were conceived in colder blood than the most brutal reprisal during the occupation. At 6 o'clock on the night after the Americans arrived the Germans put petrol cans in five hundred houses near the bridges and then, sometimes before the occupants had fled outside, bowled hand grenades into them to start them burning. They purposely set fire to every third house so that in a matter of minutes the flames spread and gutted whole streets at a time. Disillusioned and terrified, hardly daring to leave their doorsteps for fear of coming between the cross-fire of the Germans and the Americans, the owners sat huddled in groups, waiting for someone, anyone, to come to their rescue. But as they watched their worldly possessions crackling in the inferno they knew that there could be no relief because not only had the Germans cut off the water supply but they had evacuated the fire-service personnel as well.

It is easy to imagine that by this time the people of Nijmegen were in a state of mind bordering on panic. Many of them could no longer have been responsible for their actions, and it is therefore hardly surprising that they fell into two traps which, wilfully or otherwise, the Germans had laid behind them. The first was in the form of a large dump of spirits which the Germans made no attempt to hand over to the local authorities. Tired and frightened, the people believed that the contents of this dump might deaden their suffering, and in a few hours they had drunk as much as they would normally have consumed in a month. Having satisfied themselves at the wine dump, many of the citizens then migrated to the railway station, where even greater temptation awaited them. In the station and on the sidings outside the Germans had abandoned two or three hundred railway trucks crammed with booty from France and Belgium. The temptation to grab what they could was too great for many of the burghers; they had been deprived of so many luxuries for so long that it seemed madness not to avail themselves of this long-awaited opportunity. But mass looting, as anyone who has seen it happening knows, is the most dangerous and demoralizing influence on even the most disciplined body. And in this case it led to irregularities which the people of Nijmegen would never have tolerated in their town at any other time.

It was known in Nijmegen that there was only one event which could quickly cut short this nightmare of fighting, arson, inebriation and looting. The magic word "tanks" loomed up in the red sky above Nijmegen like a giant question-mark. "When will the tanks arrive?" This vital question provided the people of Nijmegen with their sole topic of conversation for many a long hour. They found the answer **1944** later than many of them had hoped, but earlier than the vast majority had dared to believe was possible.

Such was the background to the arrival of the Grenadier Group at the old monastery of Marienboom on the outskirts of Nijmegen at midday on Tuesday, the 19th of September, 1944.

The fighting that took place in Nijmegen after the tanks had arrived was fiercer and more bitter than anything the Grenadiers had experienced in the campaign so far. It was described by one American correspondent, who was a veteran of the war in the Pacific, as "the most frightening yet the most thrilling battle I have ever watched." Anyone who was there will tell you that Nijmegen was the high-light of the whole campaign. Why? What was it that lifted Nijmegen above the average run of battles and stamped it with the seal of history so soon after it took place?

Two factors combined to give the Battle of Nijmegen its unique position in the record of the North-West European campaign. The first was, of course, the desperate importance that was attached to the capture of the big road bridge intact. Every Grenadier who took part in the battle knew that twelve miles away, at Arnhem, there were nearly five thousand Englishmen whose lives depended on the arrival of the tanks and that these men would be left stranded if the road bridge were blown up. The battle was thus given a more definite purpose than was usual; it was not just a question of fighting the enemy, driving him back and then exploiting the gains the next day. There was a prize, a big and valuable prize, and, as will be seen, during the whole battle the Grenadiers were seldom more than a stone's-throw away from it. It is easy to understand how this agonizing uncertainty about the fate of the bridge, which all the time was so near and yet so far, gave added impetus to their endeavours to take it.

The second factor which was responsible for giving the Battle of Nijmegen its intrinsic importance is perhaps more easily forgotten now that the sequel to it is so well known. It must be remembered that, to those who were fighting for them, the bridges at Nijmegen and indeed the one at Arnhem were not only prizes in themselves but also the instruments with which it might have been possible to end the war in a few weeks. Arnhem, Appeldoorn, the Ruhr and even Berlin were the goals if the Nijmegen bridge could be captured intact. In this knowledge, risks could be borne more easily, the sense of urgency was more acute and the fighting itself seemed more worth while than would have been the case had the bridge at Nijmegen been an end in

K

1944 itself. Never before in the whole campaign had so much seemed to depend on so uncertain an operation as the capture of the huge bridge which might be blown up at a moment's notice.

"Uncertain" is perhaps too weak a word to describe the situation at Nijmegen bridge when the tanks arrived at Marienboom. General Gavin, the Commander of the 82nd U.S. Airborne Division, believed that the Group had a fifty-fifty chance of capturing the bridge intact—and much less if they failed to reach it before dark. After the conference at General Gavin's headquarters the Commanding Officers **Sept. 19** therefore dashed to Marienboom and lost no time in drawing up their plan. Lieut.-Colonel E. H. Goulburn has described the scene at the café in which they gave out their orders:

> "It was a lovely sunny day and the café had already attracted the attention of the crowds. Groups of excited civilians were rushing wildly in and out, talking to anyone who was prepared to listen. The Underground supporters were being marshalled together in one room by the Dutch Liaison Officer, and Dutch guards, obviously impressed with the importance of the occasion, were ineffectively trying to prevent anyone coming in or going out. Outside a battery of American 75's were firing away as hard as they could, and as our tanks began to arrive still more excited and delighted spectators joined the crowds. Inside the café the owners were doing a roaring trade."

The plan that they decided upon required three columns to be formed from the Group's resources—one to capture the road bridge, another to take the railway bridge, and a third to make for the Post Office in the centre of the town, which, the Dutch insisted, housed the blowing apparatus of the main bridge. The column destined for the road bridge would be composed of No. 2 Company (Capt. The Duke of Rutland) except for one motor platoon and one section of carriers, No. 3 Squadron (Major A. M. H. Gregory-Hood), minus two troops of tanks, and all except one company of the 2nd Battalion 503rd U.S. Parachute Regiment (Colonel Vandovort). The column heading for the railway bridge would consist of elements of No. 3 Company and No. 2 Squadron, and the remaining company of the Parachute Battalion. It would be commanded by Capt. J. W. Neville. Major G. Thorne was given command of the Post Office column and his force comprised two platoons of No. 3 Company, a troop of tanks of No. 1 Squadron and a platoon of American parachutists picked off the road at random by General Gavin. They were all to set off simultaneously. The rest of the Group was ordered to follow the road-bridge column as far as some barracks about a mile short of the road bridge, and be ready to rush across should either of them be captured. The Leicestershire Yeomanry were ordered to bring their artillery into play against known enemy strong-points before the attacks began.

Nijmegen: The road bridge.

Nijmegen, September, 1944.   A Grenadier tank crossing the road bridge.

Typhoons swooped down on the German positions in Nijmegen at **1944** about 3.30 and shortly afterwards the column headed for the main bridge set off. Dutch guides had been provided and, not having to bother about map reading the column moved swiftly up Groesbeeksche Straat and into Dominicanen Straat. There were no civilians on the streets and the blinds were drawn in many of the windows— a sure sign that the enemy was about—but no shots rang out to impede the progress of the tanks. It soon began to look as if the enemy were waiting for the tanks to set foot on the bridge and then to blow it up.

At the top of Dominicanen Straat there is a large square called the Maria Plein, with six roads leading out, one of which, a short street with tall houses on either side, joins the Keizer Lodewijk round-about in front of the bridge. The leading troop of tanks, a section of carriers and a motor platoon dashed across the square and started moving up a street named after a Doctor Claas, which would have brought them out level with but to the right of the Keizer Lodewijk round-about. The remainder of the column, except for about fifty American paratroopers, who crossed under cover of smoke grenades, never set foot in the Maria Plein. Having missed the leading section of the column, the Germans swept the square with anti-tank-gun and small-arms fire and made it quite impossible for further tanks to cross. For the moment, then, the task of capturing the bridge devolved on the small force which had entered Doctor Claas Straat before the Germans awoke to the danger.

It turned out to be too big a commitment for so small a body, because, when they emerged into the open ground near the round-about, only three hundred yards from the southern end of the bridge, two self-propelled guns, several anti-tank guns and a great number of German infantry armed with automatic weapons started to fire at them. At least one anti-tank gun was destroyed, but the leading tank was knocked out and the troop leader, Lieut. J. A. Moller, was killed. Soon afterwards, the next two tanks were hit and badly damaged, and now only one tank remained. Cut off from the main body by the fire which swept the Maria Plein, and faced with a numerically much stronger force holding the southern approaches to the bridge from well-concealed and strong positions, the small detachment of Grenadiers were in no position to make a frontal assault across the open ground towards the bridge. There was left one hope. If the remaining motor platoon of No. 2 Company and another troop of tanks (Lieut. The Earl of Kimberley) could work their way round to the right and move down Barossa Straat into the open ground, they would be admirably placed to engage the enemy near the round-about from the

1944 rear. The manœuvre would undoubtedly be extremely hazardous, but, considering the important results it might achieve it was considered practical.

While the move was taking place, Lieut. M. Dawson, the commander of the platoon in Doctor Claas Straat, collected all the automatic weapons in one place and left only a skeleton force to guard the northern exits of the Maria Plein. He then organized a party to seize from the rear a large house in Graadt von Roggen Straat, the street bordering the open ground, from the top windows of which the Germans defending the bridge could be seen taking up positions. Settled in this house, the platoon were able to use their automatic weapons to great advantage as soon as the force working its way round the right flank engaged the enemy. For a brief spell it looked as if their combined efforts might make some impression on the enemy, but, although a considerable number of the enemy were killed or wounded, the Germans never really ceased to have the upper hand. For every shot that was fired at them they returned two. And in the end an 88-mm. gun scored a direct hit on the house. Luckily only three Americans and one Guardsman were wounded, but the platoon had no alternative but to withdraw, as by this time the force in Barossa Straat were held up and unable to engage the enemy near the roundabout. Light was failing, so the two parties formed strong-points in Doctor Claas Straat and Barossa Straat, where they spent an anxious night, though suffering no further casualties. The rest of the column, consisting of the company and squadron headquarters and two companies of Americans, remained south of the Maria Plein until the next morning.

Capt. J. Neville's column, heading for the railway bridge, met with no more success. As soon as they turned into Heessche Laan, about half a mile south of the bridge, a Panther fired at them and, although Lieut. G. R. Merton's troop forced it to pull back several hundred yards, they could not get near the railway bridge. To reach it they would have had to run a gauntlet of fire from the railway embankment on their right, then pass through a tunnel under the embankment which German infantry were defending and which heavy guns on the other bank of the river were covering, and finally climb up a ramp on to the bridge itself, being fired at all the time. It was obviously an impossible task, and when they had penetrated the belt of machine-gun fire as far as the factory on the left of Heessche Laan, Capt. Neville ordered the force to converge for the night near a church in Krayen-hoff Laan. The motor platoon of No. 2 Company, commanded by Lieut. J. C. Moller, formed a cordon round the tanks to protect them from raiding parties, but no precautions that Capt. Neville could take

could have warded off a serious German attempt to obliterate the 1944
force. The Germans were all around them, countless houses were on
fire, they were running out of ammunition and they were out of touch
with the rest of the Group by wireless. Capt. F. J. Jefferson, the 2nd
Battalion's Signal Officer, did manage to get a message through to
them in the middle of the night, but by the morning the force had lived
through only a portion of the forty-eight hours they were to spend
completely isolated from the Group.

Of the three columns, only Major G. Thorne's actually completed
the task it had been given. Guided by a vociferous Dutchman travelling in a tank, this column proceeded direct to the Post Office via
Goehorn Straat and the Juliana Plein. The tanks, ably led by Lieut.
J. W. Scott, blazed away at any building likely to contain Germans,
and the force soon reached the Post Office, having destroyed a small
anti-tank gun *en route*. The Post Office turned out to be unoccupied
and not even to be an enemy headquarters, let alone the hide-out of
some little man who could press a plunger to destroy the bridge. It
was a valuable building, however, and Major Thorne deployed his
force to defend it. At about 8 p.m. he was ordered to send a patrol
north-east up Gerard Hoodt Straat and attempt to establish a strong-
point on the Keizer Lodewijk round-about, which was the pivot of all
enemy positions guarding the road bridge and from which infantry
and anti-tank guns were blocking the advance of the column at the
Maria Plein. He used half his force for this task and led it himself,
leaving the remainder holding the Post Office. He managed to get into
the street when a self-propelled gun, concealed in the Huner Park,
north of the street, opened up at close range with high-explosive shells
and immediately caused several casualties. The force dispersed into
houses on either side of the street, but any movement on the street
itself brought down heavy and accurate fire, and it was impossible to
advance up behind the houses. At about midnight Major Thorne
realized that further progress with his small party was out of the
question and accordingly he ordered a withdrawal to the Post Office.
All casualties were successfully evacuated and the Post Office was not
attacked during the night. The remainder of the Grenadier Group had
spent the afternoon and evening at the barracks beside the road on the
road-bridge column's route. At 11 p.m. Lieut.-Colonel E. H. Goulburn
ordered No. 4 Company and a troop of self-propelled guns to go to
the Maria Plein, block all the entrances, and link up with Major
Thorne at the Post Office. Battalion Headquarters of the 1st Battalion
and the rest of the 2nd Battalion remained near the barracks for the
night. The Germans once again made a bonfire of many parts of
Nijmegen that night. This time their method was different—phos-

1944 phorus shells instead of petrol cans and hand grenades—but it was equally effective. Red-hot cinders spurted out into the streets, silhouetting anyone who ventured out into them.

If successes and failures are measured by the relative numbers killed on either side, then the fighting in Nijmegen on the 19th of September was successful. The columns near the bridges killed or wounded a large number of Germans with practically no loss to themselves, and the third column captured the Post Office. However, at no stage in the battle did the forces directed on the two bridges look like being able to rush them or even seriously disturb the German defences. It might appear to a casual observer that with half the Group not committed to the battle at all, greater efforts could have been made to take these two vital bridges. But it must be emphasized that it would have been madness to have employed more tanks in the maze of streets near the bridges, as there was no reliable information about the strength of the Germans. Besides, the Group had been led to believe that the Germans were far more disorganized than they actually were. That this appreciation had turned out to be erroneous was, to say the least, unfortunate, but it could be accepted without too much regret because, after all, the cardinal fact remained that the two bridges were still intact and might be won the next day.

During the night the two Commanding Officers conferred with Brigadier N. W. Gwatkin and they then worked out what one Grenadier company commander called "the best and simplest plan for capturing the main bridge that anybody could have asked for."* Its salient feature was to surprise the enemy by attacking the road bridge from the west via the Valkhof and not from the south via the Keizer Lodewijk round-about, as he obviously expected. To do this meant moving through a good portion of the town which had not yet been cleared, and the Group would run the risk of becoming involved in trouble which it need not really face; but it seemed to the Commanding Officers to be absolutely essential to clear enough of the town to have room to manœuvre for the final attack on the bridge itself, and also to make sure that the attack would not be molested by Germans advancing from the west. To prevent reinforcements entering the town the Group Commander therefore ordered Capt. J. W. Neville's column to clear a further area of the town near the railway; and to protect the left flank during the clearing operation and the rear of the Group during the attack on the bridge, pickets would be posted along a stretch of flattened houses as each company advanced north.

*General Browning had hoped that if the Grenadiers did not rush the bridge on the 19th another parachute brigade would be dropped at Nijmegen on the 20th to capture it. But the weather was too bad, and at 2 a.m. the Grenadier Group were told to do so instead.

Lieut.-Colonel E. H. Goulburn revealed the plan to the company
commanders at 4 a.m. An hour and a half later the motor companies
concentrated near the Juliana Plein and detailed orders were given to
the platoon commanders. Each motor company was given a troop of
tanks from No. 2 Squadron and also a section of machine guns to
support them. The 3-inch mortar sections were grouped in a platoon
under Lieut. I. R. Westmacott, and they and the 25-pounders were to
fire on to the approaches of the bridge during the whole of the
operation.

At 8.30 a.m. the attack was launched. It turned out to be considerably easier than anyone had dared to hope. Within an hour and a half
No. 4 Company had reached Koning and Marienburgsche Straats,
and only Hersteeg Straat was still being swept by Spandau fire from
the north. No. 2 Company immediately passed through and soon after
midday were established on the southern side of Burcht Straat. This
street was also under fire from the east, but the King's Company were
able to cross it by using smoke grenades and they very quickly captured the police station and the convent north of it which overlooked
the river bank. Progress on the left was slower in the maze of small
streets, but the Group Commander decided that enough progress had
been made for the main assault on the bridge to start. The clearing
operation had taken in all about five hours, but it had been thoroughly
carried out and had yielded some thirty prisoners in return for a few
casualties sustained by Nos. 2 and 4 Companies.

At 3 o'clock Lieut.-Colonel E. H. Goulburn held a hurried conference with the American commanders and decided upon the final
details of the big assault. It was to be a three-pronged attack, the
King's Company on the extreme left clearing the Valkhof—a large
wooded mound with a maze of subterranean tunnels underneath—
and then working their way forward on to the embankment leading
on to the bridge, No. 4 Company capturing the Huner Park and the
fort to the north of it, and the Americans, on the extreme right, clearing the open ground east of the Keizer Lodewijk round-about. No. 3
Company would send one motor platoon to the river bank to protect
the King's Company rear during the attack on the Volkhof, and
Lieut. M. Dawson's platoon (No. 2 Company) would fight with the
King's Company itself. All attacks were to go in simultaneously and
zero hour was fixed for 3.30 p.m. This left the company commanders
with scarcely a quarter of an hour in which to make their preparations.

Under ideal conditions it would have taken at least half an hour
to attend to the many problems arising out of so complicated an
attack as this. Liaison between the company commanders, a careful
study of the ground over which the attacks were to go in, issuing of

1944 detailed orders to platoon and section commanders so that each man would know exactly where to go and what to do—these were only a few of the details which would normally have been cleared up before the platoons started to advance. Under the circumstances, of course, all that the company commanders could do was to give their platoon commanders the bare outline of the plan and leave them to fill in the gaps as they saw fit. This state of affairs, which, according to textbook teaching, should have doomed the operation to failure, had excellent results. It meant that the intangibles of war, which lose and win battles, had unlimited scope. As one company commander later wrote: "From the first five minutes the fighting did not conform in any way to my original plan, but once we got our teeth into the enemy the men's spirit was so terrific—even laughing and joking—that nothing could have stopped us."

Capturing a well-fortified mound like the Valkhof would be an operation fraught with incalculable dangers under any circumstances. It was exceptionally difficult in this case, because the Germans had had time to surround it with a network of barbed-wire entanglements, slit trenches and dug-outs, all of which were fully manned. But they had evidently expected the Grenadiers to attack from the south and, by crawling up the embankment on the Lindenburg Straat side and cutting a hole through the barbed wire on top, two platoons managed to climb inside the Valkhof before the Germans realized that the attack had begun. This initial surprise put the Grenadiers in a very strong position. They were able to engage the enemy in hand-to-hand fighting and gradually close in on the dug-outs and winkle them out from the slit trenches.

But it was a costly beginning. Capt. The Hon. V. P. Gibbs, the company commander, was killed as the assault started—leaving Lieut. M. Dawson* in charge—and the two leading platoons suffered heavily. After five minutes of very bitter fighting the company were established on the eastern edge of the Valkhof, from where they were able to dominate the bridge and fire on the Germans dug in on the embankments south of it. Lieut. Dawson immediately sent a platoon round by the right to try to get on to the embankment under cover of fire from the leading platoons, but this platoon ran into heavy fire when crossing the Voer Weg and had to retire after suffering casualties. An attempt was next made to work round to the embankment by following the river bank and this proved extremely successful. One platoon established themselves on the embankment about only fifty

---

*Although Lieut. Dawson and his platoon ran the whole way to the Valkhof when Lieut.-Colonel Goulburn ordered them to join the King's Company, they arrived just as the attack was starting. Lieut. Dawson therefore had to command the company without knowing the details of the plan.

yards from the end of the bridge, but as their field of fire was very **1944**
limited and they could not get on to the bridge itself because of the
fire which No. 4 Company and the Americans were bringing to bear
on the bridge, Lieut. Dawson ordered them to retire to the Valkhof.
From here the company dominated the bridge, so they waited in the
dug-outs for No. 4 Company and the Americans to draw nearer.

No. 4 Company's attack in the centre started badly. Major H. F.
Stanley, the company commander, decided to advance on a two-
platoon front, each platoon supported by a tank. At 3.30 the left-hand
platoon, commanded by Lieut. L. W. Fazackerley, led off, fanning out
across the open ground known as Kelfkensbosch. They had not
advanced more than a hundred yards before the Germans opened up
with the most withering fire from the area of the bridge. Lieut.
Fazackerley was shot through the stomach, Lieut. P. G. A. Prescott's
tank was hit by an enormous shell and blew up, L./Sergt. Heawood
and his section were mown down and pinned by fire, and casualties
started to mount all round at a most alarming rate.* Major Stanley
decided at once that it would be useless to throw his company at the
enemy in this manner and came to the conclusion that the only possible way to move up the St. Jorisstraat and link up with the Americans would be through the houses. This was easier said than done.
Many of them were on fire, and the flames were spreading quickly.
After climbing innumerable walls, however, and making use of several
ladders which German snipers had used to escape, he managed to get
through to the Americans. They were in an equally difficult position,
being severely harassed by Spandau fire coming from the round-about
and from a high bank overlooking the gardens near the bridge, which
were part of the Huner Park. It was obvious that until the enemy were
moved from the fort which completely dominated the Americans' line
of advance no further progress was possible. Major Stanley therefore
decided that he would have to manœuvre his company across the St.
Jorisstraat. As all the doors of the houses on the north side of the street
were obviously locked and all the windows were shuttered, this would
mean that, once across, the company might be exposed to German
fire at point-blank range. This risk had to be taken, however, and, with
the aid of smoke, he took the company over in waves. The company
then worked their way through the gardens at the back and alongside
a high wall bordering the Huner Park until they were only thirty yards
from the fort. Lieut. P. B. M. Greenall and his platoon (ten strong)
immediately charged at it and succeeded in driving away the whole
force of Germans, killing many of them and taking about thirty

---

*Lieut. I. R. Westmacott was wounded while trying to evacuate them. Lieut. C. E.
Kevill-Davies and Gdsm. Meadows, of No. 2 Squadron, 2nd Battalion, also went
forward several times through intense fire to help.

prisoners. At the same time, Lieut. A. Slob's platoon surrounded a large house near by, covered the exits with machine guns and threw in phosphorus grenades which roasted alive about 150 Germans who were inside.

At this point all serious German resistance seemed to crack. They were overwhelmed by fire. The King's Company were pumping bullets on to the bridge from the Valkhof. Sergt. Waller, who had just returned to his post through heavy fire after delivering a message to Lieut.-Colonel E. H. Goulburn, was machine-gunning from the police station. The tanks, brilliantly directed by Major F. J. C. Bowes-Lyon, were spraying the countryside with 75-mm. and Browning fire. Lieut. The Earl of Kimberley had driven his tank into the gardens and was doing particular damage. Soon a patrol from No. 4 Company moved down on to the bridge and, apart from a considerable quantity of shell-shocked prisoners, found it clear. Unfortunately, the patrol leader, Lieut. P. B. M. Greenall, was killed by a German who dashed across the bridge in a side-car.

It remained for the 2nd Battalion to move over the bridge. At 6.30 a troop of tanks which had been held in readiness by the round-about edged forward along the embankment, but it was still too light: they were met by strong anti-tank-gun fire and forced to withdraw. By 7 o'clock it was beginning to grow dark and the troop, commanded by Sergt. Robinson, of No. 1 Squadron, moved out again, firing their guns into the gathering gloom round the bridge. They moved swiftly down the slope, dashed on to the bridge and disappeared from sight. Two tanks were hit by anti-tank-gun fire, but Sergt. Robinson and L./Sergt. Pacey, avoiding the missiles which the enemy dropped from their perches high up in the girders, reached the far end of the bridge, skidded broadside through a road block, and after knocking out two anti-tank guns by the side of the road came to a halt at a railway bridge a mile farther up the road. Here they met the remnants of a gallant body of American paratroops who had crossed the river earlier in the day some two miles down-stream.

They were joined a few minutes later by Sergt. Knight, who, having discovered that his tank was not on fire after being hit by a bazooka, had leapt in again and driven on. Shortly afterwards Capt. The Lord Carrington was sent over the bridge to control the situation and maintain communications. The Americans immediately manned the crewless tank and the position was hastily prepared for defence. The small, isolated party spent an anxious night there, for, although the Irish Guards passed over the bridge to form a bridgehead, they did not come up to the Grenadier position.

Morning came and found the precious road bridge, from which the

explosive charges had been removed during the night,* still intact. **1944**
Prisoners of all types and descriptions began to give themselves up,
bringing with them equipment which was even more varied—88-mm.
guns, 50-mm., 37-mm., a baby French tank, Spandaus, Hotchkiss
machine guns, new rifles and old 1916 long-barrel and long-bayonet
rifles, mines and bazookas, and shells of many different calibres, sizes,
shapes and vintages. As if this was not enough, at 9 a.m. Capt. J. W.
Neville's column, which had spent the previous day painfully edging
its way forward to the railway bridge, swept up the ramp leading on
to it and took possession without the loss of a single man. The miracle
had happened—both bridges were safely in Allied hands.

How had it come about? Why had the Germans not blown the
bridge as soon as they saw that they were going to be overwhelmed?
This is a question to which it is difficult to give a definite answer,
because it so happened that the Germans in Nijmegen came from
many different regiments and divisions and among the prisoners there
was no one in possession of all the facts. One theory, which perhaps
won more credence in America and Holland than in the British
Army, was that a certain Dutchman, a citizen of Nijmegen, van Hoof
by name, crept over the road bridge on the Monday afternoon and
tampered with the charges, so that when, at the last minute, the
Germans tried to blow them nothing happened. Van Hoof was killed
the next day and so there is no possible way of proving or disproving
this theory. But it is a little hard to believe. Surely no soldier or
civilian, however brave, could have hoodwinked the German sentries
and patrols, in broad daylight, over twenty-four hours after the Americans had dropped at Berg-en-Dal. Even if he swam across, which he
never claimed to have done, one look at the pillars is enough to show
that he could never have climbed on to the bridge.

No; the only logical explanation is that the Germans never had any
real intention of blowing the bridges. They must have thought that the
armoured division which they had concentrated thirty miles from
Arnhem would destroy the 1st Airborne Division—which it very
nearly did—and that the armoured division they had assembled near
's Hertogenbosch would cut off the Guards Armoured Division. Bank-
ing on this, it would have been folly for them to have blown the main
spans of either bridge, as once they had driven back the Second Army
they would need the bridges for bringing up their supplies through
Holland. At the same time, they probably thought that a situation

---

*A courageous young sapper officer, Lieut. Jones, accompanied the tanks across
the bridge to cut the wires and search the demolition chambers underneath each span.
To his astonishment, when he entered the first chamber he found it crammed with
Germans. They readily surrendered, and by the time he had searched each chamber
he had collected over sixty prisoners.

1944 might arise in which it would be to their advantage to stop the Second Army without actually destroying the main structures, and this, pre-sumably, is why they removed the charges from the big pillar and put them underneath the small span near the Arnhem bank.

To account for the fact that even the small span was not blown, one can only assume that, on Wednesday, the 20th of September, no German on the spot had sufficient courage to give the order in the absence of definite instructions from the Higher Command.*

---

*On the 21st German swimmers with fins on their feet blew the central span of the railway bridge. This fact has been marshalled by some to prove that the Germans really intended to blow the bridges. But surely by that time they must have realized that they had little chance of cutting off the Guards Armoured Division. and it was therefore to their advantage to blow it.

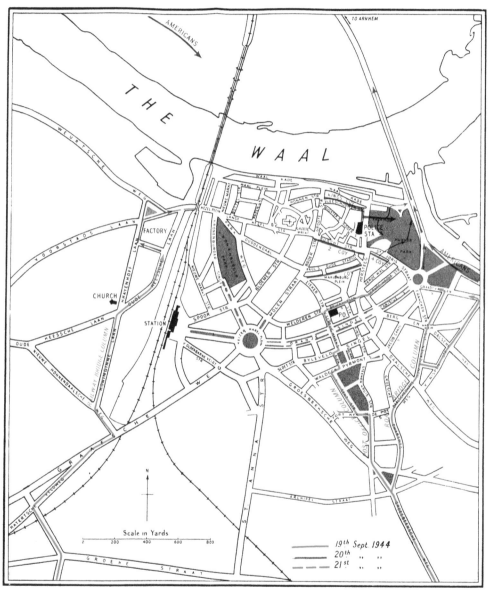

NIJMEGEN

CHAPTER VI

HOLLAND

1

REOPENING THE NIJMEGEN CORRIDOR

1ST AND 2ND BATTALIONS

Failure of the Arnhem adventure—German intentions in Holland—The enemy cut the road between Grave and Eindhoven in rear of the Guards Armoured Division—The Grenadier Group reopen the road near Uden— The Nijmegen corridor secured by driving the Germans out of Heesch— Temporary respite for Grenadier Group

THE highway from Nijmegen to Arnhem runs along an embankment 1944 raised high above the surrounding countryside. It fell to the Irish Guards to try to force their way along it to rescue the marooned paratroopers at Arnhem. For three days they struggled forward and by superhuman effort reached Elst, half-way across. But farther they could not go, for whenever the tanks drove off the embankment they became bogged and while on it they could not depress their guns sufficiently to hit the German batteries dug in, invincibly, behind the dykes. And so, after eight long days and nights of bloody fighting, the gallant paratroopers had to be brought back to Nijmegen.

No one will ever know for certain how soon the war would have ended had the Arnhem adventure succeeded. It is within the bounds of possibility that the Ruhr would have been encircled by the middle of October and the effect of this might have been decisive. But all that can be said for sure is that if it had been possible to link up with the airborne forces at Arnhem and to exploit the advance into Germany, the Allies would have been spared two of the most gruelling months of fighting of the whole campaign; for, at the worst, the winter months would have been spent in Westphalia or Hanover and not in Holland, which, with its never-ending canals and waterways and its susceptibility to flooding, could hardly have been a more unsuitable setting for the continuation of the war.

There were two factors, besides the failure to reach Arnhem, which determined that Holland should become the main battlefield of the

1944 British Liberation Army during the months of October and November, 1944. The first was the stubborn refusal of the Germans to leave the Scheldt islands which controlled the entrance to Antwerp. Without this great port, which was capable of handling all the supplies needed to maintain the 21st Army Group, the hands of the Higher Command were tied. So long as petrol, ammunition and food had to be hauled all the way from Normandy, there was not the slightest possibility of carrying the war forward to the Rhineland. The Higher Command were therefore determined to open up Antwerp whatever the cost, and by the end of September the whole of the First Canadian Army and a considerable part of the Second British Army were starting on this task. The terrible conditions under which this difficult amphibious operation was conducted need not be recorded here. It is enough to say that by November Antwerp was opened up to British shipping.

The second factor which kept the British Army in Holland was the need of expanding the extremely precarious corridor which the Guards Armoured Division had forged across the country as far as Nijmegen. In some places it was scarcely more than forty yards wide —the width of the road and the hedgerows on either side—and the Germans were making strenuous efforts to cut it. On the west of the corridor, the Allies' main object was to secure the valuable road which runs from Nijmegen through 's Hertogenbosch and Tilburg to Antwerp. On the east the idea was to drive the enemy back from the area of the Peel—a vast tract of boggy heath running from the village of St. Anthonis in the north to the Canal du Nord in the south—as far as the banks of the River Maas. All three Battalions of the Regiment were destined to take part in these operations.

Sept. 22 The 1st and 2nd Battalions had already dispatched parties to scour Nijmegen for suitable billets in which to rest when the first ugly rumours of the cutting of the corridor began to trickle through over the air. Somewhat naturally the fighting in Nijmegen had distracted their attention from the rear areas, and they were under the impression that the general situation was considerably better than it actually was. It was not until the rumours were confirmed at midday on the 22nd of September—they also heard about this time of the death of Lieut. J. N. Fielden, who had been badly wounded by a sniper the day before—that they realized what a very tight corner they were in.

Their plight was certainly fraught with danger. They, the Irish Guards Group and the remnants of the British and American paratroopers were the only fighting troops north of Eindhoven, and if the Germans succeeded in severing their contact with the Second Army for long, their supplies would run out and they might well find themselves in the same predicament as the 1st Airborne Division at

Arnhem. Indeed, their position might be even graver, because it would **1944**
be far more difficult to supply an armoured division with the necessary
petrol and ammunition for it to function than an infantry division
whose requirements can be dropped by parachute with relative ease.
The future which had seemed charged with wonderful possibilities
when the bridge was captured had suddenly turned sour.

Half-way between Grave and Eindhoven there are two small towns
called Veghel and Uden, and it was on the road joining these places
that the enemy had driven a wedge across the supply line. It was to
Uden, therefore, that the Group set off in the early afternoon of the
22nd of September. No. 4 Company and No. 1 Squadron were put in
the lead and the rest of the Group followed on behind soon afterwards.
The American parachutists, who had waved the Group forward when
it was dashing along the same road in the opposite direction, were
still holding the bridges, and the Group's journey to Uden was eventful only by reason of the little clusters of Dutch people who congre-
gated in the villages to watch the tanks go by, obviously believing that
liberation had come to an untimely end.

Uden was a strange sight. American parachutists, about a company
in number, had set up headquarters in the school, and small Stars and
Stripes fluttered from the windows; R.A.S.C. lorries, the tail-end of
convoys which had been hurrying back to collect more supplies to
bring up to Nijmegen and had been cut off, were parked in every
street; staff officers sat mournfully in their cars, waiting to take back
reports from the front line to their Generals. If they had been passengers on a Tube stuck between two stations this odd assortment of
stragglers from the British and American Armies could hardly have
looked more annoyed.

The American paratroops were in wireless touch with Veghel and
they believed that there was little likelihood of the Germans between
the two towns attacking either of them. But, wishing to find out the
real strength of the enemy force, the Group Commander immediately
dispatched a troop of tanks from No. 1 Squadron and a motor platoon
from No. 4 Company with instructions to go as far down the road as
the level-crossing about three miles south of Uden. This patrol sped
down the road without seeing any sign of the Germans and had just
reported the level-crossing to be clear when a scout car was shot at
by a bazooka. The tanks quickly took up defensive positions near the
railway line and the remainder of the Group put guards on all the
roads leading into and out of Uden. But the patrol was not attacked
again, and at midnight the Group Commander ordered it to withdraw. It did so by firing every weapon at its disposal into the hedges
and fields on both sides of the road, and arrived back at Uden to find

1944 the garrison fearfully awaiting an enemy counter-attack which so great a riot of noise had seemed to presage.

Sept. 23   The next morning an elaborate plan was made to clear the opposition between the two towns, but, as happened not infrequently, when it was put into effect it was found that most of the enemy had melted away during the night. A patrol, led by Lieut. The Hon. T. A. Corbett, which was making for Veghel by a roundabout route to the east of the main road ran into some of the retreating enemy and suffered ten casualties, and No. 1 Squadron met and destroyed three enemy tanks near the main road itself; but otherwise opposition was negligible. By 3 p.m. the leading elements of No. 2 Company and No. 3 Squadron had linked up with the American paratroopers from Veghel.

Sept. 23-24   The main supply route to Nijmegen was now open once again and the whole of the Grenadier Group except Nos. 2 and 4 Companies, who were stretched out along the main road, were able to spend a peaceful night in Uden. But the possibility of further German counter-attacks had by no means diminished, and during the next twenty-four hours strong patrols were sent out at all hours to explore the surrounding countryside. During this period strings of gliders, loaded with supplies for the paratroopers at Arnhem, were continuously passing overhead. Confused by the multitude of broad rivers and by the dearth of easily recognizable landmarks, the pilots frequently came down to a low altitude long before they were near their destination, and the German ack-ack gunners in positions on both sides of the main road were able to score many successes. Several gliders landed in the No Man's Land which lay between the British on the east of the road and the Germans still farther to the east, with the result that both sides would send out parties, the one to capture, the other to rescue, the stricken airmen.

Sept. 25   One of the patrols sent out to these gliders reported that the Germans were showing signs of activity to the north-west, and it was feared that the enemy might be sending a force along the main 's Hertogenbosch—Grave road to break across the corridor. So, at 6 p.m. on the 25th, the King's Company and No. 2 Squadron were ordered to send a troop of tanks and a motor platoon to the village of Nistelrode, some two miles to the north-west, and if this place was clear the patrol was to push on to Heesch, a larger village two miles farther on, through which ran the main 's Hertogenbosch—Grave road. As had been expected, there were no enemy in Nistelrode, but in Heesch the situation was entirely different. This village became the scene of a two-day battle which, it can with justice be claimed, was the turning point of this particular part of the campaign; for, once the Germans were driven out of Heesch, the future of the corridor to Nijmegen ceased to be a matter of dispute.

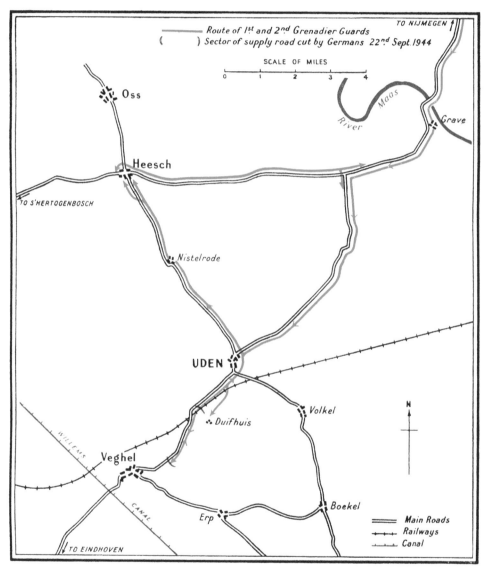

Route of 1ˢᵗ and 2ⁿᵈ Grenadier Guards
( ) Sector of supply road cut by Germans 22ⁿᵈ Sept. 1944

SCALE OF MILES
0   1   2   3   4

TO NIJMEGEN

Oss

Maas

River

Grave

Heesch

TO S'HERTOGENBOSCH

Nistelrode

UDEN

N

Volkel

Duifhuis

WILLEMS

Veghel

CANAL

Erp

Boekel

Main Roads
Railways
Canal

TO EINDHOVEN

UDEN

HEESCH

In the middde of Heesch there is a large cross-roads, and it was 1944 when they were only thirty yards away from it that the patrol first encountered Germans who were prepared to make a stand. A 37-mm. gun accounted for Lieut. R. F. Edward-Collins's tank, but the officer managed to crawl to a nearby house and was later rescued from under the noses of the enemy by a party commanded by Capt. M. G. T. Webster. It was obvious that this patrol alone would be unable to drive the Germans away from the cross-roads, so a stronger patrol, commanded by Capt. I. R. Farquhar, was rushed up at once. Exactly the same thing happened: the leading tank was knocked out and its commander, Lieut. R. Luff, had to hide in a haystack, surrounded by Germans, before making good his escape. By this time it was almost pitch dark, so both the patrols withdrew and even stronger measures were planned during the night for the capture of the cross-roads.

It was plain that a full-scale attack was needed, so during the morn- Sept. 26 ing all except No. 3 Company and Main Battalion Headquarters moved up to Nistelrode. The King's Company were the first to reach the village, and before the others arrived they cleared a large wood on the right of the road about half-way to Heesch. There were no Germans in the wood itself, but from its northern edge the company were able to spot the enemy in houses just south of the cross-roads. They killed or wounded a certain number of them with their mortars and also gave their Commanding Officer valuable information about the enemy positions.

As soon as they reached Nistelrode the Group Commander went forward to make a plan. He decided that all they could attempt that day was the capture of the eastern half of the village, so the Command Post, No. 2 Company and No. 3 Squadron were told to remain in defensive positions in Nistelrode while the remainder of the Group made an attack. It was to be on a two-company and squadron front, the King's Company and No. 2 Squadron on the left of the main road and No. 4 Company and No. 1 Squadron on the right. The former See Map p. 146 were to capture the cross-roads and push on another three hundred yards to the north, the latter being given as their objective a block of the village farther to the west. A short artillery concentration, to be fired by a battery of the Leicestershire Yeomanry and the 1st Battalion's 3-inch mortars, was to precede the attack to distract the enemy's attention. That it did so Lieut. R. Luff and a member of his crew were able to testify when they rejoined the Group that night, because they were hiding in a barn in the middle of the enemy outposts at the time and they both said that it caused them far more dismay than any of their previous worries.

L

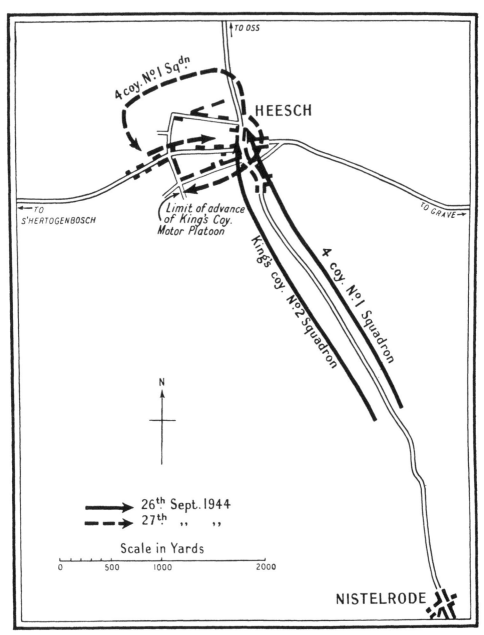

TO OSS

4 coy. No. 1 Sq.dn

HEESCH

TO
S'HERTOGENBOSCH

Limit of advance
of King's Coy.
Motor Platoon

TO GRAVE

King's coy. No. 2 Squadron

4 coy. No. 1 Squadron

N

26th Sept. 1944
27th ,, ,,

Scale in Yards

0   500   1000   2000

NISTELRODE

HEESCH

1944   Promptly at the appointed hour, 3.45 p.m., the attack started and
went in with all the smoothness of a carefully rehearsed exercise on
Salisbury Plain. The tanks moved forward slowly, with the infantry
spread out between them, and as they advanced they fired almost
uninterruptedly with small arms and their main armament of 75-mm.
high-explosive shells. The noise was shattering and the expenditure of

ammunition enormous, but it served its purpose well because hardly **1944**
any fire came back and the bewildered enemy emerged from ditches,
hedgerows and cellars to surrender in large numbers. Both companies
and squadrons reached their objectives with practically no casualties,
only two men being killed and four wounded during the whole battle.
One hundred and sixty Germans were taken prisoner and a fair
number were killed or wounded. It transpired from subsequent in-
terrogation that the enemy battalion holding the cross-roads had
arrived only some three hours previously and had no anti-tank
weapons with them, which accounted for the fact that not a single
Grenadier tank was even hit. That night the Group was not disturbed
by any enemy attempt at retaliation, but it was evident that the
Germans were still in the western half of the village and were not
going to leave without a fight.

To obtain surprise Lieut.-Colonel E. H. Goulburn decided the next **Sept. 27**
morning to attack from the north and not from the cross-roads, as the
Germans presumably expected. For this task he used No. 4 Company
and No. 1 Squadron, and he called up two motor platoons and a
machine-gun platoon of No. 3 Company to assist. The company and
squadron were to move north from their present position for about
six hundred yards, turn west for about one thousand two hundred
yards, then go south into Heesch and finally clear the western end of
the village back to their original position. The company were to
move as fast as possible, with a troop of tanks supporting each
platoon; and the two motor platoons of No. 3 Company were to
follow more carefully, clear the area thoroughly and look after any
prisoners that might be taken. The machine-gun platoon were to take
up positions where the company turned south after their western
advance, and were to protect the rear of the attack on the village. The
operation was to be preceded by a mortar concentration, and a mobile
observation post controlling the 4.2-inch mortars was to move with
the leading troops.

No. 4 Company and No. 1 Squadron started off on their round-
about journey to the western part of the village at 1.30. For them the
going was easy: there were a considerable number of the enemy
about, but they were completely taken by surprise and could offer
only belated and half-hearted resistance. The main burden of the
attack fell on the platoons of No. 3 Company following behind. By
the time they reached the German positions the enemy had recovered
from the shock of seeing a squadron of tanks charging towards them
and they fought bitterly. The two platoons kept going and gradually
forced the Germans to give ground, but it was a very costly business.
First, a faulty 4.2-inch mortar bomb landed in the middle of one

1944 platoon and killed the platoon commander, Lieut. R. E. Talbot, while later both platoons were caught in the open by mortar fire. This double misfortune accounted for the whole of one platoon except the platoon sergeant and drivers, and it made serious inroads into the other. In contrast, No. 4 Company and No. 1 Squadron suffered very few casualties—Lieut. J. W. Scott had been wounded—and by 3 p.m. reached the road junction at the western edge of Heesch.

Before the operation was continued into the village itself, Lieut.-Colonel Goulburn came up to confer with Major H. F. Stanley. In view of the serious casualties that had already been incurred, the Commanding Officer ordered a motor platoon (Lieut. N. W. Alexander) of the King's Company, who were still near the big cross-roads, to come up and assist No. 4 Company. This platoon, led by Major N. E. W. Baker himself—he had rejoined the Battalion a few days previously, having been wounded for the second time on a patrol near the banks of the Escaut Canal—did not follow the somewhat devious route taken by No. 4 Company earlier in the afternoon, but moved through the orchards just south of the village. There were a great many of these orchards, all surrounded by high hedges, and the tracks followed by the platoon wound their way past several houses not marked on the map, with the result that the platoon slightly left their true course. When a few hundred yards south of the rendezvous they ran into a most unpleasant ambush and several Spandaus opened up from three sides at very close range. The platoon were hopelessly pinned, whereas the enemy were firmly ensconced in houses. Major Baker, together with two or three others, decided to make a dash for it, and despite being fired at the whole time this party succeeded in reaching some cover about seventy yards away completely unscathed. Major Baker eventually contacted two tanks and four machine-gun carriers, which he took back with him in an effort to dislodge the enemy and rescue the helpless platoon. Unfortunately, however, the enemy had considered their cheap, unexpected success enough for one day and had made off westwards, having taken prisoner all the unwounded members of the motor platoon, including Lieut. Alexander.

By this time the fates had evidently decided that the Grenadiers had had their share of misfortune for the day, because No. 4 Company cleared the remainder of the village with ease and by 6 p.m. were back in their original position near the cross-roads. When the final count was taken it was found that the day had cost the 1st Battalion alone fifty-four men killed, wounded or missing. The Germans, however, must have suffered just as heavily, if not more so.

Shortly after midnight the enemy bombarded the cross-roads, and a few minutes later infantry could be heard moving into Heesch from

the west. Luckily, Major R. Hoare, who commanded the battery of 1944
Leicestershire Yeomanry supporting the Group, had registered the
road junction at the western end of the village very accurately, and
his battery immediately fired a tremendous concentration on this area.
Lieut. P. J. Brocklehurst ran his tank right through the German positions—it was knocked out, but he and one of his crew managed to
crawl back to safety—and the attack, which was ill-prepared from the
start, was completely broken up before it came to close quarters. No
more Germans tried to molest the Grenadiers either that day or the
next.

On the morning of the 30th of September the 7th Armoured Divi- Sept. 29-
sion, which had been operating on the left flank, reported that they 30
had cut the main road about two miles west of Heesch without meeting any opposition, and the Coldstream Group reported the bloodless
occupation of the village of Goffen, two miles to the north-west. The
Grenadier Group were therefore put in reserve in a counter-attack
role, and at about midday the 2nd Battalion moved back to a rest
area near Grave. The 1st Battalion were ordered to concentrate in
Heesch for a short rest, but this order was obligingly cancelled a few
hours later, and the Battalion were ordered to move back to the
road junction where the road south to Eindhoven met the Grave—
's Hertogenbosch road.

Just before the Battalion left Heesch a very agitated civilian reported that there were about fifty Germans hiding in a ditch near the
main road and about a mile west of the village. Lieut. The Hon. T. A.
Corbett, No. 2 Company, immediately took out a carrier patrol and
returned very soon afterwards with the fifty Germans. They were very
miserable specimens of humanity and lay in the ditch until picked up
like snared rabbits. Their officer tried to set a good example and ran
for home as fast as he could, but he was shot in the stomach for his
pains.

At about 5 p.m. the 1st Battalion left Heesch and drove back along
the main road towards Grave. September had in every way been a
hectic month for the Grenadier Group and, resolved into two separate
Battalions again, they gladly settled down to relax in the midst of this
dreary, autumnal Dutch landscape. Theoretically, they were there to
bar the way of the enemy should he decide to counter-attack across
the Maas. At the moment, however, the Germans were much more
concerned with getting as many men as possible back over the river
to the north, because, having lost three hundred prisoners besides
many killed or wounded in the Battle of Heesch, they had learned
that a break-out to the east, south of the river, would be a costly and
unpleasant undertaking.

2

WINTER BATTLES IN HOLLAND
4TH BATTALION

After a long wait in Normandy the 6th Guards Tank Brigade move to Holland—The Battle of Venraij—Fighting among the Dutch dykes—Liberation of Tilburg—The Battle of Meijel—Resting at Helmond

1944
Aug. 28-
Sept. 28 For the whole of September the Guards Armoured Division and the one or two other formations at the head of the advance across the Lowlands stole all the headlines; the rest of the British Second Army —the majority of its infantry divisions and its heavy tank brigades— were almost forgotten back in France. When the Arnhem adventure failed, however, the divisions and brigades which had waited patiently to be called forward came into their own again and during October the spotlight of attention was focused almost entirely on them. The fast-moving armoured divisions had had their say for the moment. It was now up to the infantry and the heavy tanks which supported them to grind their way towards the Rhine.

While the Guards Armoured Division had been dashing through Belgium and Holland, the 4th Battalion of the Regiment, as part of the 6th Guards Tank Brigade, had remained firmly rooted in France. It was galling for them to hear and read about all the great things that were going on farther north and not to take part in any of them. At times, in fact, they began to wonder if they had not already seen the end of their war service, because rumours of peace proposals were flying around and the Guards Armoured Division's continual successes made it seem quite possible that there was some truth in them. The Brigade's one idea was to get going again, but the shortage of tank transporters and the fact that almost all their trucks were being used to rush up supplies to the front line made it very difficult. Eventually, on the 7th of September, Brigadier W. D. C. Greenacre decided to move the Brigade nearer the Seine without tank transporters, and on the 12th of September, by pooling a number of trucks belonging to the services and the battalions, the Brigade crossed the river at Les Andelys. When across, they moved into billets on the main Paris —Rouen road,* and finally, on the 24th of September, definite infor-

---

*It was an interesting coincidence which brought the 4th Battalion to this area, for it was here in 1940 that the "Davies Rifles," commanded by and named after the Commanding Officer of the 4th Battalion, then Major Davies, took up positions during the retreat through France. Lieut.-Colonel H. R. H. Davies and Capt. P. R. Colville, who was also with him, paid a visit to the old positions and found that the remains of some of the trenches were still visible.

mation arrived stating that they were to move north and come under **1944** the command of the VIII Corps "somewhere in Holland."

The 4th Battalion left the Seine on the 29th of September, two days **Sept. 29** after the Battle of Heesch. The journey took the tanks the better part of three days, and it was a trip which few members of the 4th Battalion will ever forget. In every Belgian town which the tanks passed through the people came out from the houses and cheered and waved and shouted "Vive le Gardes" as they threw the tank commanders enormous bunches of grapes, tomatoes, apples and plums. The fame of the Guards had spread right through Belgium after the liberation of Brussels, and the Belgians, who are by nature hospitable, let nothing deter them from expressing their joy and gratitude at being once again free after four long years of occupation.

When the Grenadiers stopped for the night at Waterloo, where over a century before they had earned the name "Grenadier," the coffee-pots were on the boil and the gateaux on the table almost before the Guardsmen were off the transporters. The best wines were produced, the girls put on their gayest dresses, and everyone talked and laughed and drank until two or three in the morning. You would have had to go a long way to find a more sincere and spontaneous display of inter-national good will than this meeting of the British and the Belgians on the old battlefields of Waterloo during the evening of the 29th of September, 1944.

The 4th Battalion's destination was Geldrop, a small town a few **Oct. 1** miles east of Eindhoven, and they arrived there on the 1st of October. In common with the majority of Holland's smaller towns, Geldrop had suffered no damage from bombing, and for the first time since leaving England the Battalion were billeted in civilian houses with real beds to sleep in. But on active service a good billet is always the prelude to an early move. Sure enough, after twenty-four hours of the comparative luxury of Geldrop, the Battalion were called upon to set off for the big battles which were about to take place in Holland.

The 4th Battalion's introduction to warfare in Holland did not **Oct. 2-6** involve them in any heavy fighting. They were sent to Nederweert, a small town at the junction of the de Deurne and Nederweert Canals, where they took over the line from the Royal Scots Greys. For the first two days the Germans bombarded the area with mortar shells and sent patrols across the canal under cover of darkness, but after that the Battalion's positions were molested only by snipers concealed in pillboxes on an island where the two canals meet. Throughout their time at Nederweert, however, the tank crews had to keep very much on the alert because the country was perfectly flat and the odd tree and windmill dotted along the canal bank provided them with very little cover.

1944   The Germans' favourite target for their mortars was the church
spire in Nederweert. Luckily it was a stout stone construction, and
although it was hit several times when members of the Battalion, in
particular Major G. E. Pike, were observing the German positions
from it, no harm was ever done. From the spire it could be seen that
the German positions were behind the marshland on the farther side
of the canal, and civilians reported that the Germans were in the habit
of patrolling this area during the night. So on one occasion Lieut.
G. A. G. Selby-Lowndes took a small patrol of his reconnaissance
troop across the foot-bridge into No Man's Land. After crawling
about for some time, however, and interrogating the civilians, he
returned, having seen no sign of the Germans. The local Dutch
Resistance Movement also made several sallies across the canal and
threw all the ammunition they could find into the water.

These expeditions were far more successful than any that the
Germans attempted. One night Lieut. J. F. D. Johnston, whose troop
was guarding the front of No. 3 Squadron, was suddenly disturbed
by loud bangs and the crackle of bullets whistling past the house in
which he and half his troop were resting. But the shooting died down
almost at once and they did not discover until the morning that a
patrol of the Grassmehl Parachute Force had crossed the canal in a
rubber dinghy three hundred yards to the left and had crawled round
to attack the tanks from the rear. Lieut. Johnston had left his own
tank behind a bank close to the house, while his other two tanks were
on guard duty, and the Germans, evidently thinking that this tank was
manned, had fired a bazooka at it, which fortunately glanced off the
sloping rear plate without causing serious damage.

On the 6th the Battalion were relieved by the County of London
Yeomanry. As No. 1 Squadron were handing over to them, a German
sniper hit Major J. C. Gascoigne in the shoulder and wounded him
severely. Capt. R. R. Etherton then took over command of No. 1
Squadron.

With the 6th Guards Tank Brigade Headquarters, the Battalion set
off for Mook, a small town just south of Nijmegen. The Higher Command were directing their attention towards the Reichwald Forest and
were considering the possibility of seizing the ground between the
Maas and the Rhine, thereby improving their position for the eventual
attack on Germany itself. Mook was to be the forming-up point for
this attack—which was to be known as Operation "Gatwick"—and
the 4th Coldstream had already spent several days there drawing up
plans and exploring the ground. When the 4th Battalion and Brigade
Headquarters were half-way to Mook, however, they were met by a
harassed liaison officer from Corps Headquarters who stopped the

tanks and diverted them off the main road for the night. Operation 1944 "Gatwick" had been postponed indefinitely. When it finally took place, in February, 1945, a mere one thousand five hundred tanks and six infantry divisions were employed—among them the 6th Guards Tank Brigade and the 3rd British Infantry Division, who, in October, so nearly embarked on it alone.

For the moment the Higher Command were content to launch a less ambitious operation designed to clear the ground up to the Maas, south of Nijmegen, which the Germans were known still to be holding in considerable strength. The formations taking part in it were to be the 3rd British Infantry Division and the Grenadier and Coldstream Battalions of the 6th Guards Tank Brigade. Venraij, a village twenty-five miles south of Nijmegen and five miles west of the Maas, was the objective, and it was anticipated that the attack would start on Wednesday, the 11th.

This operation was the first of three battles in a miniature campaign which the 4th Battalion were to fight in Holland during the month of October. Like the rest, it was fought under conditions which were quite different from and far worse than anything the Grenadiers had experienced in the campaign so far or, indeed, than they had to contend with in the future. During the whole of October the German troops opposing them were the finest and fittest the enemy could then muster; the majority of them were paratroopers, good fighters anyway, and, defending as they were the very doorstep to their Fatherland, they were inspired by chauvinism to be even more stubborn than usual. But it was not the Germans, nor even the interminable mortaring, that made these battles seem like one long, bad dream. It was something far more terrible—mud.

When the Grenadiers reached Oploo, a small village north of Venraij from which the attack was launched, a violent gale was raging and in the course of a few hours the whole of the surrounding countryside was transformed into a sea of mud. From that moment on everything the Grenadiers did, everything they could do, was determined by this horrible concoction of nature. Everywhere there was to be mud, bogging the tanks, so deeply sometimes that even the recovery vehicles could not pull them out, putrefying anything that came in contact with it, seeping into the tank tents at night, making everybody cold and dirty and miserable from dawn until dusk. Holland in that bleak winter month was a far cry from the land of flourishing tulips and smiling burghers that many had imagined it to be. It was as desolate as an enormous Irish peat-bog in the depths of winter.

The Dutch landscape is not renowned for a super-abundance of Oct. 11 trees, yet, barring the way of the attack on Venraij, there was a large

1944 forest, so thickly planted that it proved a highly inconvenient obstacle for the tanks. In a large clearing on the northern edge of the forest, roughly half-way between Oploo and Venraij, stood the village of Overloon, and before the attack on Venraij itself could take place this small German outpost had to be captured. If all had gone according to plan, the 4th Coldstream would have undertaken this task on the 11th, but the appalling weather conditions caused the attack to be postponed for twenty-four hours. The incessant rain was playing havoc with the vital lines of communication and they were rapidly becoming impassable. During this delay, however, the Royal Engineers worked unceasingly, cutting rides through the woods and filling in dykes, to make it possible for the tanks to advance. They did this job so well that, although it was still pelting, at 12 o'clock on the 12th the Coldstream were able to move forward across the dykes and begin the operation.

Oct. 12   After a long and costly day of fighting, the Coldstream surrounded Overloon and reached the northern edge of the forest. The Grenadiers, in order to reach Overloon in time to exploit the Coldstream's gains, were obliged to have "Reveille" at 2.45 the next morning; as it was Friday the 13th the superstitious frowned on this combination. The Battalion succeeded, however, in harbouring successfully at the forming-up point, and various reconnaissances were carried out to discover where the tanks could best plough through the quagmire. The plan was for two squadrons of the Grenadiers and three of the Coldstream to push on due south in a five-pronged thrust into the woods south of Overloon.

OVERLOON AND VENRAIJ

Oct. 13   The Grenadiers were on the extreme right, No. 2 Squadron supporting a battalion of the King's Own Scottish Borderers down the western edge of the wood and No. 3 Squadron, with the Royal Ulster Rifles, heading through the wood itself, farther to the left. Before they set off, an exceptionally heavy artillery barrage poured shell after shell into the German positions—so many, in fact, that according to the law of averages few of the Germans should have survived. But something went wrong and as soon as the barrage began to lose its intensity the Germans came streaming out of their dug-outs to engage the tanks. They were in a very strong position because, for one thing, during the past few days they had sown an enormous number of mines along the northern edge of the wood, not just ordinary mines but a new type which had recently been invented and turned out to be sufficiently powerful to penetrate the heavy base plates of a Churchill.

For another, they had been issued with a number of new weapons, among them a viciously accurate 188-mm. bomb-thrower which fired *See Map p. 158* salvoes of six shells in rapid succession. Furthermore, needless to say, they did not hesitate to use to full advantage the apparently unlimited supplies of mortars which had been placed at their disposal. Thus, dug in behind almost impregnable minefields, exploiting the surprise value of their new weapons and showering the tanks with murderous mortar fire, they were admirably situated to stand up to the onslaught of the Churchills.

Where No. 3 Squadron were attacking, the opposition was particularly heavy. The squadron found it quite impossible to penetrate even the fringe of the wood and for their pains they lost three tanks, two men killed and three wounded, among the tank casualties being Lieut. J. H. Patrick's Churchill, which was hit three times by an 88-mm., miraculously without loss to the crew. No. 2 Squadron fared better. They inched their way down the western edge of the wood where the mines had not been so thickly laid, and soon after midday reached their objective. The Germans, however, did not cease to splatter the position with the most harassing machine-gun and mortar fire, and the infantry found it impossible to remain with the tanks. This was a calamity, because had the infantry been there the haul of prisoners would have been very large indeed. As it was, Capt. J. B. Currie rounded up over half a dozen fully armed members of the Battalion Hoffmann single-handed—a feat for which he was awarded the Military Cross.

On the Coldstream's front the fighting continued well into the evening. After a stiff battle in the forest two of their squadrons went on for about a thousand yards farther down the road towards Venraij. The drivers ploughed the Churchills through the bogs with great skill, but just as it was growing dark the leading squadron bumped into a detachment of enemy Panther tanks which completely held them up. The fact that they had made their way through the wood and advanced so far the other side was, however, a very creditable achievement in itself, and in conjunction with the advance the 4th Battalion had made on the right it meant that over half the distance to Venraij had been covered. That night, as on many other occasions during the next three months, the squadron sergeant-majors who were responsible for bringing up supplies to the forward squadrons had a very unenviable time. It required a great deal of ingenuity and often a lot of luck not only to find the squadrons in the pitch darkness but also to get the half-tracks safely through the rivers of mud to them.

The next day No. 3 Squadron of the 4th Grenadiers were detailed Oct. 14-15 to push on to the eastern edge of the next large wood, the Laag Heide,

1944 and manœuvre into suitable position for the final attack on Venraij. They moved out to join the Lincolns at 6.30 in the morning, but H hour was repeatedly postponed and the attack did not begin until 3.30 in the afternoon. They were given considerable artillery support and this time it proved far more effective. Within an hour they reached the Laag Heide, having suffered no casualties and having helped the infantry to take at least one hundred and fifty prisoners.

Earlier in the day No. 1 Squadron of the Grenadiers and a battalion of the South Lancs were diverted from the main attack on Venraij to push the enemy back from the east of Overloon towards the Maas. At 10.15 half the squadron, under the command of Capt. W. T. Agar, crossed the start line on the edge of the Overloon Wood with two companies of infantry. They reached Shaartven, the first village beyond the wood, without difficulty, but when Sergt. Ayscough moved on to the forward edge of the village his troop was immediately engaged by anti-tank guns. L./Sergt. Bowen's tank had its main gun barrel pierced, Sergt. Ayscough's had five bogies removed, and the third, L./Sergt. Grimshaw's, was hit through the turret and his operator, Gdsm. Garner, was killed. This last tank caught fire and the crew baled out, but as they had left it in reverse gear with the engine running it obligingly reversed itself, flaming, back into the wood, a distance of about eight hundred yards. At 1.15 the remainder of the squadron, commanded by Capt. R. R. Etherton, moved round the western edge of the village, missing, as it subsequently turned out, a large minefield by a few yards. Lieut. G. F. Rocke engaged the houses in the village with great effect, and a considerable number of prisoners were taken. A little later two Germans, more original than the rest, emerged from a house in front of his troop waving white flags and set off at high speed in the opposite direction, but a burst of Besa fire from Lieut. Rocke's tank soon rectified this breach of the Geneva Convention. By 5 o'clock the village of Halfweg had been captured and the squadron harboured on the eastern outskirts of Overloon. About a hundred prisoners had been taken, and the enemy killed were estimated at the same number—all from the Battalion Hoffmann.

Although both squadrons of the Grenadiers had an extremely successful day on the 14th, the final attack on Venraij did not take place as early as was expected. The reason was that on the 14th the Coldstream tried to cross the Molenbeek, a dyke some twenty-five feet wide in front of Venraij, and failed completely. It was more than obvious that the crossing of this dyke would be a major operation, and as the tanks were badly in need of maintenance it was decided that the infantry should be left to hold the line while the tanks went back to a triangular wood north of Overloon for a day's rest.

Holland, October, 1944.   A 4th Battalion Churchill stuck in the mud near Overloon.

St. Trond, Belgium, January, 1945.   2nd Battalion Shermans.

By this stage of the war the crossing of a water barrier like the 1944 Molenbeek had been reduced to a fine art. While the tanks supported them with fire, infantry would rush forward with rubber boats, launch them, paddle across and clamber up on to the other bank. The Avres would then move up to the near bank and deposit fascines—enormous bundles of brushwood—into the ditch. Finally, tanks would move forward, cross over on top of the fascines, and help the infantry on the other side. It was this method, slightly elaborated, that was considered most suitable for the crossing of the Molenbeek, as the only bridge in the neighbourhood had been destroyed and a crossing which the Grenadiers had hoped to be able to use had been cratered in five places. The very heavy rain which fell during the night, however, dislocated the plan to no mean extent.

At first everything went smoothly. No. 2 Squadron left their harbour Oct. 16 at dawn, proceeded to the south-western corner of the Laag Heide and helped the 7th Suffolks to cross the Molenbeek at 7 a.m. It was only when the Avres tried to deposit their fascines that things began to go radically wrong.

Between the Laag Heide and the Molenbeek the ground turned out to be thickly sown with mines, and one after another the Avres fell victim to them, suffering severe casualties in vehicles and personnel. Luckily, No. 2 Squadron had been provided with a troop of Flails, and they were sent forward at once to clear a lane through the minefield, but by the time they had done so the Avre troop had lost over half of its vehicles and was unable to function any longer. The 7th Suffolks and the King's Own Scottish Borderers had worked their way across the gap, under the invaluable covering fire of the tanks, and they kept the Germans occupied until an Avre bridge-layer could be brought forward. The bridge-layer, an invention which was to be of the greatest possible use to the tanks on many subsequent occasions, passed through the lane cleared by the Flails and safely deposited its charge about fifty yards north of the original crossing. The leading troop of No. 2 Squadron, commanded by Lieut. J. B. Sumner, immediately crossed over, but two of its tanks and the leading tank of the next troop (Sergt. Gilbert) sank in the mud soon after leaving the bridge, thereby blocking the route completely. Nothing more could be done. A carpet of Schu* mines had accounted for the infantry commanding officer and three company commanders; three tanks of No. 2 Squadron, four of the Avre troop and three Flails had either become casualties or sunk in the mud; and the Germans on the farther side of the Molenbeek were too strong for the infantry to tackle alone. So, having so nearly succeeded, the attempt to cross the Molenbeek

---

*German anti-personnel mine.

1944 at this point had to be abandoned. Higher up the beek two squadrons of the Coldstream were having an equally hard time, but they did eventually succeed in laying a bridge and by nightfall had helped the infantry to get into Brabander, a village on the outskirts of Venraij.

Oct. 17 The next morning they and No. 3 Squadron of the Grenadiers, who had been diverted from their Battalion the day before and sent round to cross the Coldstream bridge to join up with the East Yorkshires, continued pushing south on the western outskirts of Venraij. Although the weather was very poor, Typhoons gave excellent support and sprayed the church tower in Venraij, which it was thought was being used as an observation post, because shell and mortar fire had been heavy the whole day. In the afternoon No. 1 Squadron of the Grenadiers came round to take part in the final attack on Venraij, in preparation for which the infantry sent patrols into the town that night.

Oct. 18 At 6 o'clock on the morning of the 18th the tanks of No. 1 Squadron entered Venraij. After crossing the main square they were stopped by four or five priests, who stated that there were mines ahead. The Church proved correct, but as the infantry were meeting only an occasional sniper the fact that the tanks could not advance down the street did not impede the progress of the battle. Lieut. A. D. Winch was engaged by a 75-mm. anti-tank gun which secured a hit on the side of his tank and slowed it down, but this gun was soon knocked out and his troop quickly advanced to its objective on the open ground just south of the town. Here they faced a strong enemy platoon position which caused them a certain amount of trouble, but the infantry soon arrived to deal with it.

At the same time, a squadron of the Coldstream cut right across the northern part of Venraij, and, without meeting any serious opposition, captured the large monastery of St. Servatius, where they discovered an extremely powerful wireless set, which seemed an odd addition to the monks' possessions. No. 3 Squadron of the Grenadiers who had joined up with the Suffolks, had an excellent day: they pushed on south from the hospital area and reached the southern edge of the wood below Venraij early in the afternoon.

At 6 o'clock that night the B.B.C. announced that American tanks had entered Venraij!

TILBURG

Oct. 20- For the next twenty-four hours the Coldstream probed the enemy
25   defences south of Venraij, preparing the way for an attack right up to the Maas; but on the 20th of October the whole of the 6th Guards Tank Brigade was ordered to move to Bakel, a small town between

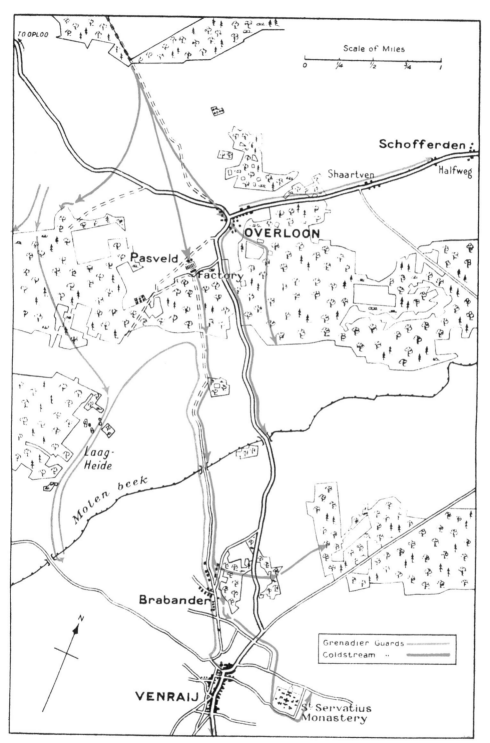

OVERLOON AND VENRAIJ

Gemert and Helmond, to await an attack in precisely the opposite 1944 direction towards Tilburg. This caused a certain amount of disappointment among the 3rd Division, the Grenadiers and the Coldstream, because there was now no doubt that their combined efforts had broken the back of the German line before the Maas. It was felt that if the enemy was not immediately chased to the other side of the river he would have time to reorganize his defences and the costly battles which had been fought at Overloon and Venraij would have been to a certain extent in vain—a feeling which turned out to be entirely justified a very few days later.

The 4th Battalion did not play a very spectacular part in the liberation of Tilburg, which is one of Holland's most important industrial centres. The 3rd Battalion of the Scots Guards, who had been out of the line during the Battles of Overloon and Venraij, did almost all the fighting, and although both the Grenadiers and the Coldstream were always just behind the Scots Guards, neither battalion had cause to fire their guns in more than a perfunctory manner. This did not mean, however, that the journey to Tilburg was a joy-ride for either battalion. In fact, for the Grenadiers it was very much the opposite. Tiresome incidents kept on recurring, which did little to boost their morale.

First of all, when the 4th Battalion were sent across the Wilhelmina Oct. 26 Canal to converge on Tilburg from the south the narrow towpath along which they were directed turned out to be sprinkled with mines and in a matter of seconds No. 2 Squadron lost a tank, an A.R.V. and a scout car. No lives were lost as a result of this debacle, but the Battalion had to spend a maddening forty-five minutes turning round on the narrow towpath, retrace their steps to the bridge and find another route towards Tilburg—all of which resulted in a very late night indeed. The second incident, which was really brought on by the first, was perhaps more irritating, although it did not lack a certain element of humour. The post truck, owing perhaps in part to the late arrival of the tanks but more to a slight miscalculation in map reading on the part of Sergt. Gregory and L./Cpl. Yates, went charging into a German outpost on the outskirts of Tilburg, with the result that the mail, which consisted mainly of parcels from England, was never seen again.

By far the most humiliating episode of the lot, however, occurred Oct. 27 on the 27th October, when the Grenadiers were ordered to enter Tilburg itself. They had not gone more than a few yards before a water main burst right in front of them, flooding the only road they could use so deeply that neither for love nor money could they proceed. They were therefore forced to remain on the outskirts of

1944 Tilburg experiencing the bitter-sweet sensation of listening to the extravagant jubilation coming from inside the town, where the Coldstream were proudly celebrating.

MEIJEL

Less than twenty-four hours after the liberation of Tilburg the 6th Guards Tank Brigade and the 15th (Scottish) Division were ordered to return across Holland to the very area they had left a week before. Their premonitions had turned out to be correct: on the other side of the salient, a few miles south of Venraij, in a sector held by the 7th American Armoured Division, the Germans had launched a counter-attack across the Canal de Deurne, captured Meijel, and were pressing on, through the Peel, towards the Second Army Headquarters in Helmond.

Oct. 29- The Brigade were warned to be ready to move early on the morning
31 of the 29th, but in the course of the day reports became graver and by 4 o'clock the Scots Guards had already started off. Two panzer divisions—the 9th and 15th—were said to be involved in the attack, but American reports, though sensational, were vague, and, in fact, the Scots Guards saw no sign of the enemy during the day. Second Army Headquarters, however, began to evacuate Helmond—a move which later had pleasant repercussions for the Brigade. The next day the Americans were withdrawn and the 227th Brigade, with the Scots Guards in support, took over their positions in front of Asten, a small town to the north-west of Meijel. While the Scots Guards kept the Germans pinned here, the Grenadiers and the Coldstream, who had arrived on the scene on the 29th, moved nearer the Deurne Canal, towards Liesel, a village six miles north of Meijel, which was as far as the German counter-attack had penetrated.

It took the Grenadiers and the Coldstream five days to drive the enemy back down the Liesel—Meijel road. First, they had to retake Liesel itself, as the Germans had firmly implanted themselves in the village and were extremely loath to leave. With pillboxes manned by infantry surrounding Liesel, and with heavy mortars and artillery firing from the other side of the canal to protect them, the Germans were able to fight a spirited rearguard action. Thick fog, which reduced the telescope vision of the gunners to often less than a hundred yards, impaired the fighting efficiency of the two Battalions to a large degree, but by 3 o'clock on the 31st Liesel had fallen.

Nov. 1-4 The Battalions' next task was to capture the three small villages on the main road down to Meijel. This they did in a series of leap-frogging movements which the Germans either opposed with self-

propelled guns or, equally effectively, with mines. They had mined **1944**
almost the whole length of the road, and were keeping it constantly
covered with machine guns and anti-tank guns firing from the opposite
side of the canal. After these monotonous little battles had been going
on for two and a half days, the enemy opposition grew fainter and it
seemed conceivable that the Germans might be withdrawing to the
other side of the Maas. But, on the afternoon of the 2nd, Nos. 1 and 2
Squadrons of the 4th Grenadiers ran into as heavy opposition as they
had ever met before. There could be no doubt that the Germans were
stubbornly holding on to a limited bridgehead on the western side of
the canal, with Meijel and the wood north-east of it as the main
position.

Before the final attack on Meijel could take place, it was essential
to know more about the enemy dispositions. So, at 7.30 on the morning of the 3rd, No. 3 Squadron supported three Flails in an attempt to
clear a minefield which had been preventing the 15th (Scottish) Reconnaissance Regiment from pin-pointing the enemy positions. In so
doing, the squadron had three tanks hit. Of these, two were commanded by troop leaders Lieuts. J. H. Patrick and P. N. Railing, both
of whom survived, together with their crews. The third, however, was
not so lucky, and both the commander, Sergt. K. White, and Gdsm.
Greenwood were killed. All three Flails were knocked out—two by
anti-tank guns and one by a mine—but not before they had accomplished their vital task of clearing the minefield. During this expensive
encounter Major I. J. Crosthwaite was shot at—and missed—by a
sniper at a range of three yards, an amazing lapse of efficiency in that
normally deadly effective branch of the German Army.

The plan for the big attack on Meijel involved the passing of No. 2
Squadron round the back of the enemy position, to the east and south-
east of Meijel Wood, and an assault by an infantry brigade, supported
by the remainder of the Grenadiers and a squadron of Crocodiles, on
Meijel itself. It was originally intended to be put into effect on the
morning of the 4th, but it was postponed for twenty-four hours, to
enable the artillery support to be more carefully arranged. The squadron which was to pass round east of the Meijel Wood would inevitably
come under considerable anti-tank-gun fire from the other side of the
canal, six hundred yards farther east, and as the country was extremely open and entirely flat Major C. M. F. Deakin, who was
commanding the Grenadiers after the departure of Lieut.-Colonel
H. R. H. Davies a few days before, requested that a comprehensive
smoke programme should be laid along the length of the canal.

After a wet night, during which all squadrons were shelled in
harbour (one tank, Capt. W. T. Agar's, received a direct hit), the

M

1944 weather took a turn for the better and the sun came out. Vast quantities of smoke shells were brought up and the M10 self-propelled guns attached to the Battalion knocked down several suspected German observation points in church towers and windmills, in preparation for the big attack on the morrow. It was to be the most difficult and by far the most costly action the 4th Battalion were to fight in North-West Europe.

Nov. 5   The attack began at 7.30 a.m. No. 2 Squadron moved off first, followed fifteen minutes later by No. 1 Squadron and the Royal Scots Fusiliers, slightly farther to the right. It was a crisp November morning with a clear, blue sky. Visibility was excellent, and as they started off the tank commanders could see the Germans running about on the other side of the canal, two thousand yards away.

Soon after starting, No. 2 Squadron lost a tank in a minefield. They pushed on and very nearly succeeded in reaching the north-eastern corner of the Vieruitersten Wood, but just before they had got far enough to turn south towards Meijel things began to go very badly indeed. They had driven straight into the middle of a mine-infested bog, and every effort they made to move, in any direction, resulted in a further loss of tanks. Anti-tank guns, heavy artillery and mortars were showering missiles on them, and the tanks could not manœuvre. The revolving tracks churned up the mud and merely embedded the tanks deeper in the morass. The drivers did their utmost to extricate the tanks, but the odds against them were too great.

The situation rapidly became so hopeless that the Commanding Officer ordered Major G. E. Pike to rally what tanks he could just behind the start line, approximately eight hundred yards back. Only four tanks out of the whole squadron came back, and of these only two were battleworthy. Of the tanks left out, five went up on mines, three were badly shattered by anti-tank guns, and the remainder were completely bogged in the mud.

All the tanks whose guns were still capable of firing continued throughout the day to support the infantry by shooting-up local farm-houses which still contained Germans. This gallant band, under the leadership of Capt. J. B. Currie, withstood the onslaught all day and killed a large number of the enemy. For ten and a half hours the artillery kept up a constant smoke barrage along six hundred yards of the canal—a performance which undoubtedly prevented the full fury of the German guns being unleashed upon them. Capt. Currie, Sergt. Berresford and L./Cpl. Dean were among the few tank commanders still able to fight their tanks. The remainder had to dismount and take what cover they could on the ground.

Lieut. Sheffield found a small ditch, about twenty yards away from

his tank. He leapt into it and discovered to his horror that it was so **1944**
deep that he could hardly keep his head above water. He waded along
it for some one hundred and fifty yards and then suddenly realized
that he was in full view of the remainder of his squadron, who might
easily mistake his steel helmet for that of a German. On looking back
at his tank, he was all the more horrified to see his driver and co-driver
calmly helping each other on with their equipment, apparently quite
unaware that in a wood less than two hundred yards away there was at
least a brigade of Germans. A smoke shell then obliterated them from
view and on looking over to the right he saw five Guardsmen disappearing down a shelter. He decided to follow them, but as he
approached a Sten gun was levelled at him. Happily, Sergt. Gilbert,
one of the occupants of the dug-out, recognized him just in time. He
had not been inside for more than a minute before five Germans came
running past the entrance. Sergt. Gilbert's Sten gun misfired, so he
proceeded to bellow at them with such ferocity that they put up their
hands at once and dashed into the dug-out. Two minutes later Sergt.
Gilbert repeated this performance, but just as five more Germans had
thrown down their machine guns and rifles a sniper, only fifteen yards
away, fired at him, missing his head by inches. This distracted Sergt.
Gilbert's attention and the five Germans slipped into a farm building
which faced the entrance to the dug-out, but a few seconds later a shell
landed on it and the five Germans dashed away. For the next eight
hours the six Englishmen remained in the dug-out with the Germans,
being all but asphyxiated by smoke shells exploding around them.
Finally, at 4 o'clock, they decided to make an attempt to return to
Battalion Headquarters. They set off at the double, Sergt. Gilbert leading, then two Germans, L./Cpl. Sprighton, then two more Germans
followed by Gdsm. Jaques and Bleakley, and Lieut. Sheffield. They
had not gone thirty yards when a Spandau opened up on them and
Lieut. Sheffield suddenly noticed that Gdsm. Bleakley was still carrying an enormous kitbag. He suggested that it was slightly superfluous,
but Gdsm. Bleakley replied that it contained a present for "the wife,"
and he was ——————— if he was going to leave it behind after having
brought it so far. After a series of miraculous escapes the whole party
reached safety, but Gdsm. Bleakley had had to abandon his kitbag on
the way.

As there were not enough tanks to support further infantry attacks
these were called off, and at about 3.30 the Commanding Officer
ordered the reconnaissance troop to fight their way to the rescue of
No. 2 Squadron. Under the command of Lieut. G. A. G. Selby-
Lowndes and supported by 95-mm. tanks of Major I. J. Crosthwaite's *See Map*
directed by Major G. E. Pike, the Honeys succeeded in reaching and *p.* **164**

1944 rescuing No. 2 Squadron. Out of the six Honeys, three became bogged on the way, but Lieut. Selby-Lowndes organized a ferry service of his remaining Honeys, and brought back all of No. 2 Squadron with the exception of Sergt. Berresford's party. It was now too dark for any further trips to be made by tanks, and the Commanding Officer ordered Major Pike to stop the rescue work, being confident that if Sergt. Berresford and his party were still alive they would make their way back after dark. Anxious hours were spent waiting for news of them, but at about 9.30 the leading infantry reported that Sergt. Berresford had succeeded in bringing his own crew and four other wounded back through the German lines, despite sniping, mortaring and shelling. A few days later Sergt. Berresford received the immediate award of the Distinguished Conduct Medal.

It had been a bad day for No. 2 Squadron, but, considering the number of tanks which had been blown up on mines, shelled and battered by anti-tank guns, the casualties had been miraculously light. They had not only got themselves, their codes and the vital parts of their tanks away under the noses of the enemy but they had also captured several German prisoners.

To go back to the morning. Fifteen minutes after No. 2 Squadron had tried to drive their way round the enemy left flank, No. 1 Squadron (Capt. R. R. Etherton), with the Royal Scots Fusiliers, headed direct for Meijel. Five tanks immediately went up on a minefield which the infantry had not been able to locate during the previous night. A further advance seemed suicidal, but two platoons of the infantry fought their way as far as Shans, a hamlet in front of Meijel. In order to help these two platoons, which were in a most precarious position, the Commanding Officer ordered No. 1 Squadron to try to break through the minefield with one more troop, on the chance that they might find a path where no mines had been laid, or, by pure luck, miss those which were there. This troop, under the command of Lieut. G. F. Rocke, pierced the minefield, but were put out of action by anti-tank-gun fire; by some miracle not a single man was lost. Lieut. Rocke then left his tank to see whether there was another way round, or if he could do any more to help the infantry. But just at that moment a carrier came by, blew up on a mine, sailed through the air, and crashed on top of him. He lay there, in agony, for a full hour until another carrier could be brought up to lift it off. Lieut. The Hon. M. R. V. Eliott had also been wounded, by a mortar.

By this time it had become obvious that in view of the anti-tank guns, the bogs and the mines no further tank advance was possible. On the right there was a bog and on the left a canal and more bogs; between the two there was an enormous minefield which left a gap of

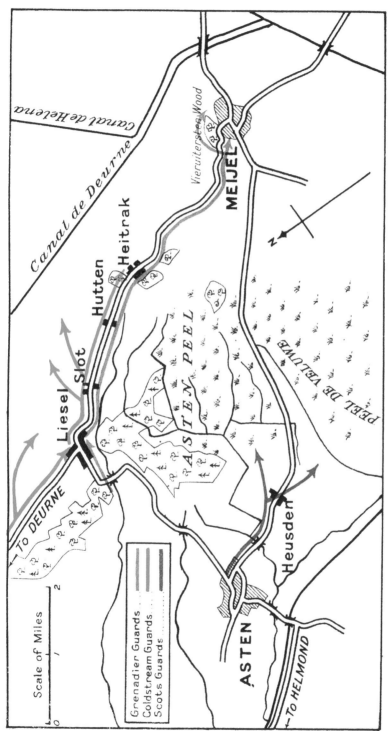

Scale of Miles

Grenadier Guards......
Coldstream Guards.....
Scots Guards..........

TO DEURNE

Liesel   Slot   Hutten   Heitrak

Canal de Deurne

Canal de Helena

Vieruitersten Wood

MEIJEL

FASTEN PEEL

PEEL DE VELUWE

ASTEN

Heusden

TO HELMOND

N

MEIJEL

Face page 164

only about one thousand two hundred yards, and this had been care- 1944
fully covered by machine guns. Furthermore, on the east of the canal
the Germans had complete liberty of movement and could bring round
their self-propelled guns to the left rear of the Battalion. Although it
was a perfectly fine day, there was no air support to obliterate these
well-sited and well-dug-in positions, and the amount of artillery available was not enough to overwhelm them on its own.

The shelling had been exceptionally heavy all day, and as the light
faded it grew worse. The Divisional Commander therefore decided to
call off the remaining phases of the attack. Brigadier W. D. C. Greenacre then ordered what was left of the Battalion to withdraw and to
proceed to Helmond. The infantry commanders were satisfied that no
enemy tank thrust was likely and they felt that they did not require
the Grenadiers' tanks to remain in a counter-attack role. Only No. 3
Squadron would have been available for this, and, although it was of
course offered it was decided that in view of the probable future
operations, or lack of them, they would not be needed.

And so, in the darkness and in pouring rain, the Grenadiers set off
for Helmond. "A" Echelon had arrived an hour or two before and
had managed to find some billets. By half-past seven twenty-five
Grenadier tanks, all that were left of the forty-eight which had started
out that morning, were rumbling over the cobbled streets of Helmond.

The 4th Battalion remained in Helmond for nearly six weeks, Nov. 6-
leaving it only once, for an attack, which never took place, on a village Dec. 12
near the Maas. This was the first time since the 6th Guards Tank
Brigade had landed on the Continent that the whole Brigade had been
together in the same town, and very soon the living arrangements for
the tank crews were organized on a most luxurious scale. Each man
was billeted with a Dutch family, often being given a bedroom entirely
for his own use. There were cinemas, a Churchill Club consisting of
rooms for writing and recreation and a canteen serving tea and cakes
in the evening, E.N.S.A. shows, varying in size and ambition, and
countless dances and parties arranged by the Dutch. An occasional
forty-eight-hour leave in Brussels rounded off the picture and made
the Battalion's six weeks in this small Dutch town seem more like a
holiday than war duty.

During the day time the tanks were overhauled and the damage
which the Germans had inflicted on the Battalion at Meijel was soon
repaired. Old battle-worn tanks were replaced with new ones, and the
hundred and one major and minor repairs needed after the strenuous
weeks in the Peel were ably attended to by the Battalion's mechanical
doctors, the men of its Light Aid Detachment.

1944   While the Battalion was thus occupied a sensational announcement was made to the tank crews: in the near future they were to leave their tanks behind in Helmond and take over part of the line as infantry. Having trained for so long, and fought for what was now a considerable time, as a tank brigade, the prospect of having to defend and patrol a swift-flowing, flooded and distinctly unfriendly Dutch river in mid-winter was alarming to a degree. That, in the end, they would be saved from doing so, no one could foresee at the time, so during the latter part of November the Battalion settled down to some very intense training to prepare themselves to play a double role—either as infantry or tank men.

3

GRAVE

1ST AND 2ND BATTALIONS

Leave in Brussels—Visit of His Majesty The King to Grave—The Grenadier Group ordered to Gangelt, just inside Germany

Oct. 1-5   While the 4th Battalion were fighting at Overloon and Venraij, the Grenadier Group remained near Grave, where they had moved after the Battle of Heesch. It was by no means an ideal spot in which to spend several weeks out of the line: the 1st Battalion had to live very uncomfortably in a huddle in the middle of a heath, and the 2nd Battalion were only slightly better off with an average of one farm-house per squadron and just enough stabling to allow everyone to sleep under cover. But the main joy was rest, and so long as that was secure no one was in the mood to complain.

The Group had been near Grave for only a few days when forty-eight hours' leave to Brussels began, at first only for officers but later for all. During October officers could be given rooms at the Hotel Metropole or one of the other hotels which were still running normally, but soon heating and lighting difficulties made it impossible for the Belgians to operate their hotels with large influxes of troops, and the majority of them were requisitioned by the Army, who supplied the necessary coal and food. For the officers of the Guards Armoured Division a special hotel, known as the Eye Club, was taken over in the Boulevard d'Anspach, and it quickly established a reputation for good food and good service that was to ensure its continuance after the war, when all the other hotels became derequisitioned.

Among the more expensive delights of Brussels right from the begin- 1944
ning were the restaurants. They were unashamedly *marché noir* and
were continually being closed by the police, but as soon as one was
closed another opened up, and it was always possible to have a meal
which would have put many pre-war English restaurants in the shade.
The prices were high, but a spirit of *carpe diem* was abroad and it
mattered little.

It was while Lieut.-Colonel J. N. R. Moore was on one such trip to Oct. 6
Brussels that it entered the head of the Higher Command to move his
Battalion, and when he returned on the evening of the 6th of October
to his late headquarters a scene of vacant desolation met his eye.
He searched the surrounding countryside for over an hour and a half
before he discovered their new whereabouts, in the woods some five
miles south-east of Nijmegen, whither they had been shifted to support
the 82nd Airborne Division. In this new position the 2nd Battalion
suffered a considerable amount of shelling of all types, and one
unlucky reinforcement officer, Lieut. G. R. M. Sewell, came up to his
squadron with the ration lorry, was wounded and had to be sent back
again on the same lorry. The expected counter-attack, however, never
materialized, and on the 10th of October the Battalion were relieved
by the 13th/18th Hussars and moved back to their original area near
Grave for a further rest.

On the day the 2nd Battalion were called out to the aid of the
Americans, radar installations reported that ten hostile gliders had
landed just south of the River Maas, near the 1st Battalion's positions.
It was feared that the enemy were attempting a suicide raid on the
vital Grave bridge, so the Commanding Officer was ordered to send
out strong patrols. Major L. S. Starkey, who was commanding the 1st
Battalion in the absence of the Commanding Officer, immediately
dispatched No. 2 and the King's Companies along the main 's Hertogenbosch—Grave road to investigate. The two companies had not
gone far when the leading section saw a figure wearing a parachutist's
helmet standing in a ride just off the road. The man was twice chal-
lenged, and as he replied in a foreign language heavy fire was opened
at once. It was only after several minutes had elapsed and a prisoner
had been taken that doubt was felt about the identity of the post.
Everyone was immediately ordered to stop firing, and it was discovered that the so-called enemy were not German parachutists, but
a detachment of the Supply Company of the Polish Airborne Brigade
which had been dropped at Arnhem. Although this most regrettable
incident cost the lives of two of the Poles, the King's Company were in
no way to blame, because they had been told categorically that there
were no Allied troops in the area whatsoever.

On the 12th His Majesty The King passed through the divisional area, and detachments from both Battalions paraded at Grave barracks for inspection. His Majesty spoke to several officers and other ranks on parade, and to all the senior officers in the Officers' Club afterwards. Four days later both Battalions were again ordered to move: the 1st Battalion to take up positions guarding bridges in the area of Grave, Battalion Headquarters itself going to Overasselt; the 2nd Battalion to assume a new counter-attack role in the area of Ewijk, a small village some five miles west of Nijmegen and just south of the Waal. In both places the enemy's bark turned out to be more formidable than his bite, and life soon resumed the normal tenor of training, amusement and periodic leave. All the men of both Battalions were under cover in good Dutch houses; E.N.S.A. shows, varying in size and ambition, played nightly in Nijmegen; there were cinemas and shower-baths in the Divisional Club at Grave; life, in fact, was normal—or as normal as it could be in Holland during the winter of 1944.

On the 26th of October the 1st Battalion received a painful surprise when their Commanding Officer, Lieut.-Colonel E. H. Goulburn, was removed and promoted to the command of the 8th Infantry Brigade in the 3rd British Division. Major The Lord Tryon, the Second-in-Command of the 2nd Battalion, was appointed to succeed him, but no sooner had he taken up his post than he was transferred to command the 4th Battalion, as that post fell vacant at the same time and a commanding officer with training in armoured warfare was essential. Major L. S. Starkey, who had been Second-in-Command of the 1st Battalion, took over from Lord Tryon, and Major C. Earle, O.B.E., came out from England to become Second-in-Command.* The only other change of note which took place during this period affected Capt. R. Steele, the Adjutant of the 1st Battalion. Shortly after he had returned from Paris, where he had gone with a party of twenty other ranks to provide ceremonial guards during Mr. Winston Churchill's visit for an Armistice Day ceremony, he left the Battalion to assume a staff appointment at Divisional Headquarters and handed over his duties to Lieut. M. Dawson.

As October passed into November the novelty of so long a period of inactivity began to wear off and no one in the Group was sorry when, on the 8th of November, Lieut.-Colonel J. N. R. Moore returned from a conference at 32nd Brigade Headquarters with the news that a major move was to take place on the 12th. The Nijmegen area was to be taken over by the Canadian Army, and the Guards

---

*When Lieut.-Colonel Goulburn left, Lieut.-Colonel Moore (2nd Battalion) assumed command of the Grenadier Group.

Armoured Division was to take over a sector of the line near the town 1944 of Sittard, in the Maastricht Appendix, from a cavalry brigade of the U.S. Ninth Army. The Grenadier Group, still under the command of the 32nd Guards Brigade, were to take over the sector north of the little town of Gangelt, just inside Germany and on the extreme right of the divisional area.

On the 10th of November the advance parties, shivering in their chilly scout cars, set off for Gangelt. The Group's "holiday" was over.

CHAPTER VII

ON TO THE RHINE

1

HOLDING THE LINE NEAR GANGELT

1ST AND 2ND BATTALIONS

Slow Allied progress during early winter—Occupation of Gangelt Line—Evacuation of German civilians—Patrolling against a clever enemy—Move to Birgden—A rest period near Sittard

1944 NOVEMBER and the first half of December, 1944, were a most unsatisfactory period for the Allied forces in North-West Europe. Plans, which had they succeeded might have brought the end of the war infinitely closer, never reached fruition, and the news bulletins from all parts of the front were as inspiring as a catalogue for a jumble sale. If there was ever a time when the morale of the Allied armies was sternly tested it was during these closing weeks of 1944. The intense cold, the continual rainstorms and the ubiquitous mud did little to make the vision of victory seem any more real than it had appeared after the withdrawal of the 1st Airborne Division from Arnhem.

On the surface, the outlook at the beginning of November was not altogether bleak. Antwerp had been captured, a feat which made all the difference to the supply position of the 21st Army Group. The railways through France and Southern Holland were beginning to operate again. Travel by road was becoming a less tedious and less lengthy business now that the majority of the vital bridges had been repaired. But, although superficially the Allied war machine was in a stronger position than at any time since D Day, fundamentally the wheels were becoming clogged. For, during October, the last vestige of the momentum developed in the drive to Nijmegen had vanished, and the Germans had had the necessary breathing space in which to throw up a network of defences from Switzerland to the North Sea.

It was hoped at S.H.A.E.F. that during November the seven Allied armies, also stretching from Switzerland to the North Sea, would gradually work their way forward and form bridgeheads on the farther banks of the Rhine. It was even deemed possible that the Ruhr might

170

be pierced. But setbacks occurred from the very beginning. First, 1944 General Patton and then General Patch (the Commander of the U.S. Seventh Army) got ahead, only to find that they had no strategic reserves with which to follow through. Then, when they came to advance again, they found that the Germans had closed in before them. One week followed another through November and still the seven armies, straining forward side by side, measured their gains in only thousands of yards and sometimes in only hundreds. The whole period was an example of the military truism that defence is always easier than attack when both sides have their forces drawn out on a long front.

The part played by the Grenadier Group during these colourless weeks was as dull as their dash across the Low Countries in September had been thrilling. Before they left Grave, on the 12th of November, they were warned that their role would be one of static defence and, for once, a Higher Command prediction about their future turned out to be true. "Static defence," however, is a somewhat double-edged expression. It does not necessarily connote remaining day after day in the same positions, waiting with sublime confidence for the next enemy attempt at attack. It usually means endless patrols, frequent swopping of positions and being constantly on tenterhooks for the slightest sign of enemy activity. At any rate, it was in this manner that the Grenadier Group interpreted the term during November, 1944.

Gangelt, the small town just across the German border from *See Map* Holland, to which the Group journeyed from Grave, lay on a small *p. 192* ridge overlooking open, rolling countryside which German farmers seemed to have made no attempt to cultivate. The contrast to the depressing flatness of the landscape around Nijmegen was striking, but any æsthetic pleasure it might have occasioned was nipped in the bud by the commanding positions which the Germans held on another ridge only three miles to the east; for the front line ran between the two ridges and the villages which the Group took over from the Americans—Hastenrath, Vintelen and Kievelberg—were as exposed to the vagaries of wandering eyes as a room in a small house over-looked by a block of flats. Furthermore, the German artillery had carefully sighted their guns on the three villages, and the Americans reported that whenever a vehicle left Gangelt to bring up supplies, however carefully or slowly it was driven, it had to run a gauntlet to reach the forward outposts.

Taking heed of this warning, the two Commanding Officers went to Nov. 13- great pains to cut noise down to a minimum when the Group took 24 over from the Americans. The motor companies moved up to Gangelt

1944 late in the afternoon, and as soon as it was dark proceeded to the villages on foot. The supporting arms, machine guns and anti-tank guns, were not sent up until the motor companies sent word back to say that they were safely dug in. Similarly, the tanks and company vehicles did not go forward until the anti-tank guns were in position; and the American tanks did not leave until each company was safely settled. This intricate time-table completely hoaxed the Germans and they had no idea that the change-over had taken place. Yet, by sheer coincidence, they happened to shell the north-eastern outskirts of Gangelt just as the King's Company were passing through, and in a matter of seconds one officer, Lieut. R. P. Letcher, was wounded and two other ranks were killed.

The German civilians were still living in their farms and houses when the Grenadiers arrived, and it was thought at first that there might be some connection between this fact and the shelling of the King's Company in Gangelt. So, very soon afterwards, they were evacuated to internment camps in Holland and Belgium. The removal of one problem, however, only created another, for the German civilians were allowed to take with them no more than what they could carry and they left behind flocks of beasts of all descriptions which had to be fed and cared for. Endless pursuit made some of the pigs as nimble as antelopes and some of the chickens fly like partridges in December, and the sight of R.S.M. Dowling, with blood-stained knife and smoking revolver, chasing the duck that would not die was one of many incidents which went to show that the Battalions were not in their element as farmers. Capt. E. M. D. Denny, who had been in the bacon business in peace time, took charge of the situation, but while he felt able to cope with the odd pig and fowl, when it came to some five hundred head of cattle it was a different matter; so Civil Affairs,* now in its metamorphosis to Military Government, stepped in to organize bands of Dutch farmers, and for three days they roamed the country over the border, driving in herds of cattle. During this time the traffic on the roads became impossibly congested, telephone lines were chewed and ripped to pieces by rampant bullocks; in fact, chaos reigned supreme until the last cow had mooed its way into Holland.

The companies in the forward villages did not let this bovine diversion distract them from their new responsibilities. First, a large number of cellars were cleaned out and made habitable so that as many men as possible could take shelter in them and rest during the frequent mortar bombardments. Then the slit trenches, which had to be manned each night, were steadily improved until they were impreg-

---

*The Civil Affairs officer in charge was Colonel R. S. Lambert, an ex-Grenadier.

nable against anything except direct hits. Finally, the companies 1944
started on their main task of patrolling which was to occupy many of
their days and nights as winter closed in.

There were various stumbling-blocks in the way of these patrols.
The greatest of these was a legacy left behind by the Americans.
During their tenure of this part of the line the Americans had worked
hard to shield the three outlying villages from German raiding parties.
Not only had they surrounded them with thick barbed-wired defences
but they had also planted anti-personnel mines both inside and outside
the wire as well as anti-tank mines on the roads and tracks leading
north from the villages towards the enemy positions. Admirable
though these precautions were, the Americans had unfortunately forgotten to keep an accurate record of the mines, so that the companies
had to spend several nights plotting them to find safe lanes through
which the patrols could pass.

The second problem to arise was that of communication between
the forward companies and Battalion Headquarters, for if some vital
piece of information is discovered by a patrol it loses half, if not all,
its value if it is not passed back immediately. Telephone lines were
laid to all three villages, but as even the lightest shelling seemed to
break the line the line parties of the signal platoon, working forward
from Gangelt, were permanently kept busy under conditions which
were often both unpleasant and dangerous. To ensure against com·
munication breaking down at a vital moment, the Group Commander
ordered that all telephone lines would be tested every fifteen minutes
and that wireless sets would be switched on as soon as a break in the
line occurred. All the wireless sets were checked three times a day, a
precaution which, combined with the others, prevented any ugly
situations arising through a breakdown of communications.

Then there was the question of rest. During the day, life in the three
villages was very dull because movement of any kind was discouraged
in case it should attract enemy attention; long patrols at night are
always tiring. It went without saying, therefore, that some form of
organized rest would be needed, the more so since there seemed little
likelihood of the Group being relieved for some time. At a conference
held by Lieut.-Colonel L. S. Starkey on the 14th it was decided that
the best way to arrange for this would be to open rest houses for each
company where the men could have a full night's sleep, be medically
examined and have a bath. The principle at which the Commanding
Officer aimed was that once in every five or six nights every man
should spend a complete night indoors. These rest houses, one in
Schinveld, one in Gangelt and the other in Hastenrath, were comparatively comfortable and they were much appreciated. The pit-head

baths at Brunsum, a mining village two miles from Schinveld—whither the rest houses were moved after the first fortnight—were particularly popular, as here boiling-hot baths could be had for the asking.

Once the mysteries of the minefields had been solved, adequate communications assured and the domestic life of the Group put on a firm footing, patrolling started in earnest. The Americans had estimated that the German defences roughly followed the line of a small stream which lay in low ground about half a mile north of Kievelberg, and that their company positions were based on three villages, Broichoven, Saefelen and Schummenquartier. It was seen at once that a raid on these positions would be a singularly hazardous business, because not only was there a small ridge to be crossed but, beyond it, the ground was so open that a body of men could hardly fail to make themselves conspicuous. The enemy defences were known to be as elaborate as the ones made by the Americans. In fact, the only encouraging aspect of the situation was the apparent absence of any kind of German anti-tank guns.

For the first few nights the company commanders contented themselves with sending out small patrols to pin-point the enemy positions and determine the strength of the opposition. After a while, more men were sent out each night and every possible approach to the enemy strongholds was carefully investigated. Several of these patrols were fired on and were able to locate enemy positions—one, led by Lieut. J. E. P. Grigg, confirmed the Americans' estimate of the enemy's strength in Broichoven. But the results were disappointing, as it was made quite plain that only really strong raiding parties could hope to penetrate the perimeter of the German defences—and these higher authority would not sanction. Faced by this situation, the Commanding Officer decided to change his tactics. Instead of sending out patrols night after night in the vague hope of finding a flaw in the enemy defences, he ordered the companies to lay ambushes for the German raiding parties known to be operating in the area, and endeavour to capture a prisoner. The Germans, however, showed a remarkable aptitude for steering clear of these traps.

Nov. 25   Each night the companies would take it in turn to contact the Group's neighbours on the right flank—the 5th Battalion Dorsetshire Regiment. On the night of the 25th the patrol set off as usual, contacted the Dorsets and then disappeared into the blue. A search was made in daylight the next morning, but no bodies, equipment or sign of a struggle could be seen. It later transpired that a strong enemy patrol had infiltrated through the leading positions, had watched the Grenadiers pass on their way out, and had jumped upon and seized the men on their return journey. The enemy succeeded in taking them

back to their positions, and the sergeant and Guardsmen were liber- 1944
ated five months later by the 7th Armoured Division from a prisoner-
of-war camp in North Germany. On the following night the company Nov. 26
commander of Headquarter Company, Major H. G. C. Illingworth,
gallantly offered to lead a similar patrol. Eye-witnesses reported that
shortly before the hour at which the patrol was to leave, the shout of
"Headquarter Company, get on parade!" echoed through the narrow
streets of Gangelt. Shortly afterwards a massed body of men rumbled
off through the town with the doughty major forming the kernel of a
solid phalanx.

As the month wore on and the enemy showed little sign of activity, Nov. 28
apart from patrolling, it was decided to force his hand (and, no doubt,
make amends for the capture of the two Grenadiers three days
previously) by a big daylight raid on Schummenquartier. The Group
Commander obtained the necessary permission and it was agreed that
the force would consist of two motor platoons and a section of carriers
of the King's Company, the tanks of No. 2 Squadron, and two troops
of Flails of the Lothians and Border Horse for clearing lanes through
the enemy minefield. A large proportion of the divisional artillery,
mortars and medium machine guns were to be in support. On the
afternoon of the 28th a dress rehearsal was staged which included a
sand-table conference for all the officers, and then everyone retired to
await reports from a patrol which was to go out that night and discover if Schummenquartier was, in fact, still held by the enemy. This
patrol, consisting of Lieut. J. H. W. Huggins and a Guardsman of
No. 3 Company, crept to within two hundred yards of the village and
then lay down and listened for signs of enemy movement. There were
no lights shining in the village and they could hear absolutely nothing,
so after a while they resorted to various subterfuges to try to attract
the enemy's attention. One of these was to fire mortar shells into the
village, a gesture which would surely have prompted the enemy to
retaliate sharply had they been present in force. But the enemy's
answer came in the form of a single red flare, fired some four hundred
yards away to the north, and some desultory mortar fire near the
patrol's position. These various experiments having drawn such
meagre reaction from the enemy, higher authority decided the next
day that there were insufficient grounds for the attack and withdrew
its sanction. The preparations, however, had given both Battalions
something to do and think about, so that although it ended in an anti-
climax the operation had served half its purpose.

It now seemed unlikely that the Group would ever identify the Nov. 29
enemy facing them, but on the very next night an ambush patrol of
No. 3 Company intercepted a German patrol east of Kievelberg. The

1944 enemy, numbering some ten men, outnumbered the Grenadiers by about two to one, but they were well and truly caught in the open and after a brisk fight two of them were taken prisoner, one seriously wounded. The unhurt prisoner was not a good advertisement for German education, but he was observant and only too willing to tell all he knew. During a three-hour gruelling administered by Lieut. J. R. M. Rocke, the 1st Battalion Intelligence Officer, he revealed a lot of valuable information, including the fact that the enemy facing the Group were more numerous on the ground than the Grenadiers themselves.

The 1st Battalion had captured its long-sought-for prisoner only in the nick of time, because, with the arrival of December, their stay in this part of the front was drawing to a close. Before they left, Field-

Dec. 1 Marshal Sir Bernard Montgomery held an investiture at Divisional Headquarters and several members of the Group received decorations: Brigadier E. H. Goulburn, D.S.O., a bar to his Distinguished Service Order; Lieut.-Colonel J. N. R. Moore the Distinguished Service Order; Major N. E. W. Baker, M.C., a bar to his Military Cross; Majors H. F. Stanley and F. J. C. Bowes-Lyon and Capt. The Lord Carrington the Military Cross; Sergt. Robinson the Distinguished Conduct Medal; and Sergeants Atkins, Taylor and Partridge the Military Medal. After the ceremony the Field-Marshal made a speech in which he praised the Division for its work in France, Belgium and Holland, and he also gave details of the 21st Army Group United Kingdom leave scheme, which was due to start on the 1st of January, 1945.

Dec. 4-7 The 1st Battalion were relieved of their commitments in the Gangelt area on the 4th. At dusk the companies in the outlying villages started to pull back and during the night the change-over, with the 3rd Battalion Irish Guards, was completed with as much care and with the same degree of success as it had been nearly a month before when the Group took over from the Americans. The Battalion were to spend only four days out of the line, so they were sent to Schinveld and billeted in surrounding villages. The 2nd Battalion remained in support of the Irish Guards.

Although Schinveld was well within range of enemy guns, the Germans seemed to have an affection for it and most of the houses, both in the town itself and in the outlying villages, were still intact. This did not prevent the accommodation from being extremely cramped, but at least the electric light was still working and every man was housed under cover. In Schinveld, and indeed whenever they were out of the line during the next few months, the Battalion fed like fighting cocks because the Germans always left behind in their cellars

vast quantities of bottled food, ranging from strawberries to sauer-
kraut and often whole hams or sides of bacon. No one felt any com-
punction about taking this food, because it was quite obvious that the
Germans had been living off the fat of the land for many years.

On the 8th of December infantry of the 7th Armoured Division
took over from the 2nd Battalion in Gangelt, and on the same day
the 1st Battalion moved forward again into the line, this time relieving
the Worcestershire Regiment, of the 43rd Division. This battalion
was situated near Birgden, holding a sector of the line adjacent on the
right to the one the Group had held at Gangelt. In the morning the
Commanding Officer and company commanders, accompanied by the
squadron leader of No. 1 Squadron and the Officer Commanding
No. 217 Squadron, R.A.F. Regiment, both of which were placed
under the command of the Battalion, explored the area and decided
where the companies were to go. The length of line for which the
Battalion were to be responsible was considerably shorter than before,
but the area was very built-up and the enemy were much closer than
they had been at Gangelt. It was decided, therefore, to keep three
companies in and near Birgden, one in Kreuzrath, a village about a
mile to the west, and the remainder of the Battalion in Stahe on the
Gangelt—Geilenkirchen road. Liberal quantities of anti-tank guns
were allotted to each company, and it was planned to plant a reserve
machine-gun platoon north of Stahe, both to protect Battalion Headquarters and to fire indirectly over Birgden in case of emergency.

Battalion Headquarters and No. 3 Company moved into Stahe in
the early afternoon, and two hours later the motor companies came up
in their transport through Gangelt and on to the main Geilenkirchen
road, where all but the essential transport, as it had been from Gangelt, was sent back to Schinveld. The companies then moved up to
their positions on foot, to relieve the Worcestershires, and when they
had done so the supporting arms came up too. The enemy were so
close to the northern outskirts of Birgden that the Worcestershires
left their 6-pounders to be taken over by the Battalion's gunners. The
enemy must have heard the transport of the leading companies, reduced to a minimum though it was, moving into position, but luckily
they made no attempt to interfere with the relief. The recent rains,
however, had covered the roads with mud, sometimes to a depth of
six inches or more, so that it was all the drivers could do to slog their
way up to the companies.

The long, straggling village of Birgden had been torn to pieces by
the war. The damage, which must have been considerable even before
the village had become part of the front line, had been accentuated by
artillery and mortar fire, and now Birgden was mutilated and scarred

N

1944 out of recognition. Doors swung idly to and fro, the plaster had been torn in great strips from the walls and ceilings, and uncared-for and unwanted dogs and cats prowled hungrily and noisily from house to house. The eeriness was increased by the fact that in the two forward company areas everyone had to speak in whispers and move stealthily from position to position, because in some places the enemy were only a hundred and fifty yards away and they were very quick to react with high-explosive or Spandau fire if they heard voices or movement. They also had a bad reputation for patrolling in this sector, and almost every preceding unit in the place had some story to tell of a section post which had disappeared in the night or of an enemy patrol which had infiltrated right through the company positions and captured supply vehicles on their way forward. The only compensation for the two forward companies was that the chief target for the enemy's indirect fire was the church in the middle of the village, which was at least two hundred and fifty yards from the nearest section post. At the southern edge of the village No. 217 Squadron, R.A.F. Regiment, were better placed, as there was not the same need for silence or concealment, but there was always the very real danger of enemy patrols infiltrating into the rear of the village, the only antidote for which was constant alertness. The King's Company in Kreuzrath were nearly a thousand yards from the enemy. Kreuzrath had not been badly damaged and there were still a number of geese and pigs in residence—a fact which gave the more culinary-minded members of the company ample scope to exercise their skill.

Dec. 9-11 On the day after the Battalion moved back into the line the Commanding Officers attended a conference at Brigade Headquarters on Operation "Shears." This operation, to be carried out by the XXX Corps, with the 43rd and 52nd Infantry and the 7th and Guards Armoured Divisions under command, aimed at rolling up the salient held by the enemy west of the River Roer. It was to start with an infantry attack on the right or eastern end of the line north of Geilenkirchen on the 12th of December, and on the following day the Guards Armoured Division were to pass through the 43rd Division and advance north-west towards Roermond, with the 7th Armoured Division operating on the left flank. The whole operation depended on the weather, and the Commanding Officers were warned that it would be postponed unless there was a hard frost. On the following day a reserve squadron of the 2nd Battalion carried out a training exercise and every single tank bogged, so no one was surprised when "Shears" was postponed indefinitely on the 11th. With the announcement of the postponement came the welcome news that the 1st Battalion were to be relieved that evening by the 1st Battalion Welsh Guards. A squadron of the 2nd Battalion remained with the Welsh Guards, and **1944** another squadron moved to another sector of the line to support the 155th Infantry Brigade.

As far as the Grenadiers were concerned, the Birgden area had not begun to live up to its blood-curdling nickname of "Hellfire Corner." The forward companies had only been asked to send out local reconnaissance and contact patrols, neither of which were ever disturbed by the enemy. The shelling had been so light and inaccurate that only one casualty had been sustained by the Battalion during the whole three days. Nevertheless, the Battalion were thankful to be relieved of their responsibilities and they drove back to Geleen, a mining town a few miles south of Sittard, in high spirits. Here, in congenial surroundings, it rested for over a week.

The Dutch spared no effort in making the men comfortable, and **Dec. 11-** thanks to the hard, dry roads a great deal of vital maintenance, which **15** had been scamped while the vehicles were parked in mud, was attended to. The area was very built-up, so training could be organized on only a modest scale, but a sniper's course was started by Lieut. K. C. Boles, and officers attended discussions on the best methods of employing various new weapons. After strenuous weeks in the front line, the life of the Battalion was gradually geared down from the tempo of the tropics to a more temperate calm.

Christmas was not far off. Leave to England would start with the New Year. The line was quiet. No one was in the mood to complain. Yet, considering that they had come to the Continent to do a job, it did seem a little surprising to many people in the three Grenadier Battalions that all three of them should be standing by idly at the same time, even though it was mid-winter. In Helmond the 4th Battalion were arranging Christmas parties for Dutch children. In the Sittard area the 1st and 2nd Battalions were keeping their fingers crossed, having been told that before long they might be moving back to Belgium for winter training. The situation seemed a little unreal. Was this the phoney war of 1939-40 all over again? To some it seemed as though it was, and they were unhappy about the future. To others the situation appeared perfectly normal. After all, during the last war, had not the Germans shown great respect for the Christmas season?

2

THE ARDENNES OFFENSIVE

*Rundstedt's supreme effort to win the war for Germany—Its early success
—Field-Marshal Montgomery's counter-measures—4th Battalion sent first
to Louvain to block Brussels road and then to Maastricht—Grenadier
Group of Guards Armoured Division sent to St. Trond—Neither involved
in the defeat of the German offensive—A happy Christmas*

1944   It was at this stage of the war that the world woke up one morning
Dec. 16- to receive one of the bitterest shocks it had been given for years. Ever
19
since the beginning of the war Germany had claimed to have a secret
weapon up her sleeve. So often had the claims been repeated that
people had become sceptical. But on a cold, foggy day in December,
1944, the dreaded object appeared, not in the form of a new aeroplane
which could fly to the moon or an improved Big Bertha, but, far more
disconcerting, as a complete army, of whose whereabouts at that time,
incredible though it may seem, not a single Allied staff officer was
apparently aware.

Investigations since the end of the war have revealed that General
von Rundstedt, the German Commander-in-Chief in the West, started
forming this force—it was known as the Sixth Panzer Army—in the
late autumn of 1944. In it were collected the cream of the German
Army—S.S. troops, panzer grenadiers and paratroopers. It was issued
with Tiger and Panther tanks, and trained under the most realistic
battle conditions at Paderborn in the Hanoverian Plain. Highly secret
courses were opened to instruct a special branch of it in the English
language and British and American customs, to act as a sabotage
force. And the best military brains in the country were switched on
to making the army the most efficient striking force Germany had
ever known.

Originally General von Rundstedt had intended to use the army as
a strategic reserve which could be brought forward to stem an Allied
spearhead towards the Rhine. But when he saw that the Allies were
maintaining an even pressure along the whole line and had no intention of mounting a large-scale offensive until after Christmas, he
decided to use it differently. His intelligence officers assured him that
almost every Allied division was in or near the front line. If, therefore,
the Sixth Panzer Army could crack a hole in the Allied line they could
shoot on to Brussels and the sea and possibly repeat the sweeping
victory over France of 1940. It was a gamble, but no less likely to
succeed than the Allied attempt to turn the Ruhr in September.

On the 16th of December General von Rundstedt gave the word **1944** "Go." The blow fell in the Ardennes, that favourite hunting ground of German tacticians since the time of Frederick the Great. German officers in American uniforms were parachuted behind the Allied lines. Flying bombs hurtled in front of the panzer army. A green American division defending Malmedy crumpled beneath the blow. An American armoured division was caught napping and quickly encircled. As the day wore on, other American divisions were caught by the avalanche and divisional and corps, and even army, head-quarters escaped being overrun only by the skin of their teeth. With incredible speed the Germans overran village after village. All through the 17th of December the battle raged, while fog prevented the Allied air forces from lifting a finger to stem the advance.

Never has the surprise element in a big offensive been crowned with so much success. No one at S.H.A.E.F. or headquarters lower down in the chain of command had the slightest idea how serious the situation was. Communications were cut from the start and it was up to the commanders on the spot to do the best they could. For the first three days a news black-out prevented those not actively con-cerned in the attack from obtaining any official information about it. Rumours spread like wildfire, however, the more depressing ones seeming the most reliable when the orders of the day of both von Rundstedt and Hitler came over the air, indicating that this was the German Army's last supreme effort to achieve victory.

At first the three Battalions of the Regiment remained unaffected by the storm. In Helmond training and preparations for Christmas went on as before. In the Sittard area the noise of enemy armour moving about behind the lines and the occasional revving of engines on what had been up to now a comparatively quiet area gave substance to fears that an offshoot of the offensive might break out opposite the 1st and 2nd Battalions. On the night of the 19th the noise of moving tanks became quite loud and the 1st Battalion were put on an hour's notice to move on to the high ground south-east of Sittard. But fortun-ately they were never called on to do so, and it was later revealed that the Germans were resorting to the well-worn trick of playing records and sound-tracks of martial noises as a cover for the offensive taking place elsewhere. Meanwhile, advance parties left for Diest and Louvain, where, it was said, the Group would spend the next few weeks.

Hopes of such a leisurely future, however, could not be reconciled **Dec. 20** with the mounting gravity of the situation. On the 20th of December General Eisenhower vested the command of the American Ninth Army in Field-Marshal Montgomery and drastic troop movements

1944 took place in the 21st Army Group to bar the way to Brussels to the German attackers. At 9 o'clock on the morning of that eventful day the 4th Battalion were told to be ready to move at once, and the Grenadier Group were instructed to send off another advance party, this time to Hasselt, for the more belligerent purpose of finding the Group suitable defensive positions in the path of the German advance. By midday the 4th Battalion had left Helmond *en route* for Bree, twenty-eight miles away on the Dutch-Belgian border, and before dark the Grenadier Group were under way for Belgium, with only the haziest instructions as to what they were to do when they arrived.

Dec. 21-23   During the next twenty-four hours, a period of hectic planning and counter-planning, the measures which were to be taken to deal with the crisis were gradually forthcoming. Having spent the night near Bree, the 4th Battalion awoke the next morning to find themselves being placed in, and rapidly taken out of, three different armies: first Canadian, then British and finally American. It was decided that the Battalion would go to Louvain, to help block the road to Brussels, but no sooner had the advance parties left than it was discovered that Second Army had rescinded the order for this move and that there was no need for them to have gone at all. Interesting captured enemy documents had revealed that Maastricht was one of the German objectives, and so the 6th Guards Tank Brigade were to go there to support the American Ninth Army. By this time it was too late to recall the 4th Battalion, and they drove the hundred miles to Louvain, remaining there for twenty-four hours—the officers' mess housed in a comfortable café, complete with orchestra and dancing girls, which, it was subsequently discovered, was a house of very doubtful repute. From Louvain the 4th Battalion proceeded to Maastricht, a distance of some seventy miles, with the tanks on transporters. Here, comfortably installed in billets, they awaited the word to drive out of the town and deal with a German attack which, it was thought, might develop in the country beyond Aachen, or from Sittard, where the Germans were erroneously believed to possess several divisions so far uncommitted. The 4th Battalion were also to be ready to support the 51st (Highland) Division in an attack southwards into the rapidly expanding enemy bulge, should it be necessary.

While the 4th Battalion were starting on their fantastically roundabout dash to Maastricht via Louvain, the Grenadier Group left the Sittard area, crossed the Maas at Maastricht and ended up at St. Trond, which is about thirty miles from Louvain. Although it covered a far shorter distance, the Group's journey did not lack incident any more than the 4th Battalion's. Both Battalions made the greater part of it in darkness over roads that were coated with a sharp frost and thick with traffic; from Hasselt to St. Trond they had to move against **1944** axis signs which all pointed in the direction of Diest, as the Provost had not had time to remove them; and at no time could they be certain that, in rounding a corner, they would not bump into the advance guards of the attacking Germans. When finally they arrived, cold, tired and covered from head to foot in dust, they were given just enough time to gulp down some breakfast and then had to set about digging slit trenches and putting the tanks into concealed positions, as the enemy were expected hourly.

For five days the situation remained agonizingly uncertain, but the **Dec. 24-** Germans never got as far as either Maastricht or St. Trond. The **29** Americans, upon whom the brunt of the attack fell, gradually regained the ground they had lost during the first grim forty-eight hours and the Germans began to suffer huge losses in tanks and men. Slowly but surely the scales were weighted down against them. The fog lifted, enabling the Allied air forces to swoop down on the tightly packed enemy columns and destroy the petrol lorries without which the huge Panthers and Tigers could not operate for long. Bastogne, where the American 101st Airborne Division made its famous stand, was relieved and General Patton's tanks began cutting the bulge in two. By the New Year it was estimated that von Rundstedt had lost between forty and sixty thousand men—a catastrophe which spelt instant doom for German operations in the Ardennes and was to prevent the Nazis from ever again taking the initiative on the Western Front.

During November and December the Allied High Command had been making plans for a large-scale January offensive designed to drive the Germans back across the Rhine. The 21st Army Group was to launch it, heading south-east from Nijmegen towards Wesel, and the American Ninth Army was to join in later and attack due east, meeting the British armies near the river itself. When Field-Marshal von Rundstedt started the Ardennes offensive these plans had, of course, to be postponed, as, in the resulting troop movements, the 21st Army Group became so spread out that it would have been impossible to concentrate it at Nijmegen in time. The earliest the operation could start was the beginning of February.

The 1st and 2nd Battalions spent the whole of the intervening period near St. Trond* and the 4th Battalion spent a large part of it at Maastricht. To be out of the line for so long a time, among kind and friendly people and in particularly comfortable billets, was indeed a

---

*The Group were spread out between the villages of Velm, Kerckom, Waasmont and Gingelom. (See map, p. 188.)

1944 break for all three Battalions. Before moving, the 4th Battalion had been bracing themselves for a dose of infantry work on the banks of the Maas, and the Grenadier Group had not expected to be left in peace in Belgium for more than three weeks at the most. After moving, all three Battalions had resigned themselves to the possibility of many weeks of heavy fighting in the Ardennes.

Dec. 24   Christmas was only two days off when they first arrived at Maastricht and St. Trond, and as the German offensive was still raging furiously the likelihood of their being able to celebrate in the traditional manner seemed very scant indeed. The Higher Command, with visions of men setting off to fight, replete and heavy with Christmas fare, had forbidden any Christmas dinners to be consumed without their express permission. But, unlike many units in the 21st Army Group, all three Battalions were lucky: on the 24th news arrived that they were free to go ahead with their original plans.

Dec. 25   During the past month the Quartermasters of the three Battalions, with their usual foresight, had been carefully collecting any kind of edible delicacy they could lay their hands on—swopping N.A.A.F.I. Eau de Vie for turkeys with American soldiers, and bully beef for eggs with the local inhabitants—and on Christmas Eve they goaded cooks, decorators and fatigue parties into frenzied action to prepare the food and the décor. Between them they worked miracles. Every single man sat down to Christmas dinner in a gaily decorated room, with plates instead of mess-tins to eat off and in some cases with civilian waitresses standing by to serve. There were pork, roast beef and tinned turkey, at least three vegetables, and Royal Christmas puddings, most kindly sent by Her Royal Highness The Colonel—all helped on their way by very liberal rations of beer. In the evening there were impromptu concerts and sing-songs, and each of the sergeants messes gave parties.* Considering that the Germans were less than thirty miles away and that nearly twenty-five per cent. of each of the Battalions had to be standing by in case the fighting came closer still, the three Grenadier Quartermasters—Capts. T. W. Garnett, F. E. J. Carver and E. R. Randall—had done a job which deserved only the highest praise.

After Christmas the situation in the Ardennes clarified itself and the three Battalions were soon allotted more definite roles than the rather vague one of sitting in the path of the offensive in case it spread to

---

*At the 4th Battalion's party at Maastricht an American guest was heard to remark that he would "sure like to meet de Lord." This was considered a most praiseworthy desire, but it transpired that the "Lord" referred to was the Commanding Officer and not the Deity. His wish was therefore more easily granted. He concluded his remarks to Lieut.-Colonel The Lord Tryon by stating that in his unit "we do sure hate our C.O."

their respective positions. On Boxing Day the 4th Battalion came **1944**
under the command of the 43rd Division and remained with them
until the end of January. Their first duty was to guard the huge dumps
on the eastern banks of the Maas upon which the American First and
Ninth Armies depended for the majority of their supplies. It was
thought that the Germans might easily try to seize them, so the
Battalion made endless reconnaissances with the Division, involving
daily journeys into Germany, to plan defensive positions for the tanks
and infantry around the dumps. The maps of the area were so inaccurate that all troop leaders and later all tank commanders spent a
day in the area learning the geography of the ground by heart. Each
squadron kept a troop ready to move to the defensive positions at a
moment's notice.

By the beginning of the New Year, however, the Germans were in **1945**
such a bad way that it seemed very unlikely that they would attack the **Jan. 1-11**
dumps or that Maastricht would see more of the war than occasional
buzz-bombs and minor bombing raids. So a sergeants' and a cor-
porals' drill course, a young officers' tactical course, and infantry tank
training with the 43rd Division were arranged, and, as far as the
weather would allow, carried out. In the New Year a good deal of
snow fell in the area and on the 8th and 9th of January it amounted
to a blizzard. The roads became very treacherous and chains had to
be fitted to all the vehicles. The frequent fogs covering the valley of
the Maas made the task of the drivers who had to bring up supplies
all the more difficult.

3

BATTLES IN THE MAASTRICHT APPENDIX*
4TH BATTALION

*Local Allied offensive to straighten the line—4th Battalion involved
in fighting west of the River Roer*

The Commander of the XII Corps, General Ritchie, paid a visit to
the Battalion during the first week of January, and from him they
learnt of a coming offensive by the XII Corps. It was to be a large-
scale, methodical, mopping-up operation designed to clear the enemy
out of the area bounded by the Rivers Roer, Wurm and Maas—in
other words, the ground which faced the 1st and 2nd Battalions when

---

*The name given to the narrow strip of Dutch territory which stretches south from
Roermond to Maastricht between the Belgian and German borders.

1945 they were in the line near Gangelt. Its sole aim was to economize in the number of men needed to hold the front line by straightening out the Corps front, and it was not intended either that the offensive should develop into a break-out or that large numbers of prisoners should be taken. Weather permitting, it was due to begin about the 15th of January.

As a preliminary measure the 43rd Division, which, with the 4th Battalion, had been in reserve for over a fortnight, were to take over that part of the front which the 52nd Division had been holding and the 52nd Division were to go slightly north-east. It was hoped that this move would give the impression that the main attack would be delivered due east so that the Germans would move a large amount of their strength from the Rheinsberg—Roermond district, where in fact it would be directed. This drive to the north was to be carried out by the 7th Armoured Division and the 52nd Division, supported by the 8th Armoured Brigade. The 4th Battalion and the other battalions of the 6th Guards Tank Brigade were to remain in support of the 43rd Division.

Jan. 12-19   The change-over of the two Divisions began on the 12th of January and the 4th Battalion left Maastricht for Rumpen, a small village near Brunssum, the next day. The roads were covered with a thin layer of frozen snow, so for the greater part of the journey the Battalion travelled across country. For the next six days preparations for Operation "Blackcock" (as the offensive was called) continued. The plans for it were extremely complicated, involving the control of many different units often attacking in many different directions on the same day. Careful reconnaissances, in some cases aerial, were made so that squadron leaders would be familiar with all the territory over which they might have to attack. A number of tanks were whitewashed and others were covered with old parachutes or liberated German linen, but, as so often happens in the Army, the main issue of white material did not arrive until a few days after the fighting had ceased.

On the 13th a minor attack was made by a unit of the 7th Armoured Division to test the enemy defences and this divulged what had already been suspected, that this sector of the line was held by only two divisions, the 176th and 183rd, both Volks Grenadiers. By the resistance which they offered to this "feeler," it was obvious that both formations were merely supporting listening posts to give warning of a major Allied attack. The Corps offensive opened in earnest on the 16th and the B.B.C. interrupted a programme to announce the news. It coincided with a spell of bitterly cold weather backed by a strong south-easterly wind which soon developed into a gale. The 7th Armoured Division and the 52nd Division were not deterred, and

by the 20th of January, when the fighting spread to the 43rd Divi- 1945
sional sector, they had made satisfactory gains to the north towards
Heinsberg.

Reports had reached the Battalion that the opposition encountered Jan. 20-
23
during the opening phases of the operation had come from small
bodies of infantry ably supported by self-propelled guns. On the 20th,
however, when the 4th Battalion opened up the road from Breberen
to Kievelberg, which was vital to future operations by the 43rd Division, they did not even see a self-propelled gun, opposition being
entirely confined to spasmodic and inaccurate mortar fire. In the
course of the next forty-eight hours resistance stiffened, but the operation went absolutely according to plan, and the 4th Battalion were See Map
called on to fight on only two more occasions. The first was on the p. 192
22nd, when No. 2 Squadron of the 4th Battalion, supporting the 4th
Wiltshires and supported by Crocodiles, Flails and self-propelled
guns, were ordered to take the village of Straeten, a strong-point into
which the 3rd Battalion Scots Guards had just pumped a total weight
of twenty-eight tons of shells. The village was almost completely flat,
and after the Crocodiles had set fire to what remained three hundred
Germans came out to surrender to Lieut. A. J. R. Davenport's troop,
who were in the lead. But as the rear half of the squadron were
approaching Straeten, self-propelled guns emerged from a smoke
screen which had been laid on the left flank and knocked out one
Honey and Sergt. Dye's tank, Sergt. Dye being killed. For a few
minutes the situation was very confused, but luckily as soon as Lieut.
The Hon. L. G. H. Russell's troop engaged the self-propelled guns,
they withdrew to Erpen. No. 1 Squadron followed them up at once
and patrols rushed forward into the village, which was captured by
the evening. That night Lieut. R. J. McCallum's troop remained with
the infantry, and were counter-attacked by the troop of self-propelled
guns. His tanks were silhouetted by the light of flaming houses, but by
expert manœuvring he staved off the attack—a performance which
earned him and his gunner, Gdsm. Stokes, the Military Cross and
Military Medal respectively.

By this time the enemy resistance west of the Roer was quietly
folding up and the Corps' total of prisoners was well over the two
thousand mark. Mines and the one encounter with a troop of self-
propelled guns had caused the only tank casualties in the Battalion.
By the 23rd the Corps line had been brought up to the River Roer and
to the main defences of the Siegfried Line, with the exception of two
small areas, one near Roermond and the other farther south.

It was to deal with this latter pocket that the 4th Battalion went into Jan. 24
action for the third and last time in Operation "Blackcock." In doing

1945 so they added Uetterath, Berg and Daumen to the long list of villages which the Brigade had already captured. Opposition was almost non-existent except for a number of short, sharp mortar bombardments, one of which killed Lieut. A. D. Winch before he had time to take cover, Capt. I. R. K. Swift, the Technical Adjutant, was slightly hurt by an exploding mine when recovering a tank, and M.Q.M.S. Oldfield, Sergt. Howarth (R.E.M.E.) and L./Cpl. Sprules were wounded at the same time.

Jan. 25-30   This small action put the finishing touch to the XII Corps' mopping-up operation. The Allied line now ran from Duren, along the River Roer to Heinsberg. Operation "Blackcock" was over. It was presumed, however, that the enemy, not knowing the limited objects of the attack, were still expecting to have to contend with a crossing of the Roer. Every possible precaution was therefore taken to encourage this belief, and whenever a forward squadron withdrew they were either covered by a smoke screen or moved before daybreak. By the 28th the whole Battalion were back in their original area around Brunssum and two days later, after a journey over icy roads to Waterschiede, in Belgium, they were taken on transporters to Tilburg. Here, basking in the glory which the 6th Guards Tank Brigade had won in the eyes of the inhabitants when it liberated the town some three months previously, they waited to go to Nijmegen for Operation "Veritable," which the 21st Army Group had hoped to launch a month previously to drive the Germans back across the Rhine.

4

ST. TROND

1st and 2nd Battalions

Inactivity during January—Intense cold—The Group move to Tilburg—
Waiting for the new offensive to start

Dec. 24-Feb. 1   While the 4th Battalion were at Maastricht, and later taking part in Operation "Blackcock," the Grenadier Group were leading a comparatively pleasant existence in the villages south of St. Trond, where they spent Christmas. As soon as the Ardennes offensive showed signs of petering out, they were relieved of the irksome duty of standing-to at dawn and dusk, and during the whole of January they were given only one operational commitment, that of guarding the road and railway bridges over the Maas at Huy for five days.

THE 4th BATTALION IN HOLLAND

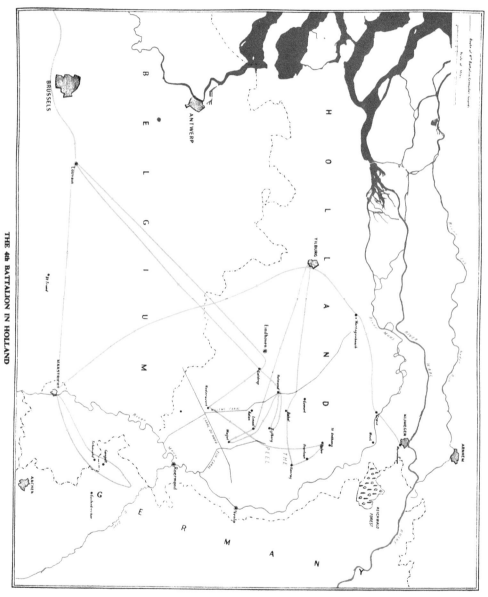

Although it was bitterly cold in January, and the roads were some- 1945 times almost unusable, both of the Battalions devoted this free period mainly to training. In the 1st Battalion another snipers' course was run by Lieut. K. C. Boles, the 3-inch mortar sections were given instruction by Lieut. A. P. St. C. Raynor, and the Battalion's anti-tank guns, which had so far had few opportunities to go into action, spent several days on a range at Lommel. In addition, each of the motor companies held discussions on tactics with squadrons of the 2nd Battalion, which were followed by demonstrations and small exercises. Then towards the end of the month the benefit they had gained from their training was put to the test in a scheme (called Exercise "Eskimo" in honour of the weather) which a number of tanks of the 2nd Battalion supported. It lasted for over thirty-six hours and more than lived up to its name, because three Guardsmen had to be evacuated suffering from exposure.

For the tanks the most urgent task at first was that of fitting end connectors to the tracks to enable them to get a better grip on soft ground. These gadgets took the place of the shoe that normally joins track links together on the outside edge, performing the same essential function, but sticking out a good three inches farther and therefore increasing the width of the track. Once this had been done troop training began and then wireless exercises, gunnery courses and trade tests were held. Finally, a team of new drivers were trained—a process which required an abnormal amount of patience and courage because the most expert driver ran the risk of suddenly turning a complete circle or skidding off the road into the ditches. Driving a jeep in these conditions was just as nerve-racking as it had been at Hemsley during the previous winter: the windscreens would gradually freeze up, becoming quite opaque, whereupon the unfortunate driver would be forced to steer by poking his head round the edge with all likelihood of having his nose frostbitten.

Although the cold was so intense that no one felt inclined to venture into the open air if it could be avoided, the Battalion's living quarters reminded people more of Antarctica than the jungle. Owing to the shortage of transport, neither the Belgian nor the Dutch coalfields were functioning properly and consequently the British Army coal ration was only three pounds per head per day, which was totally inadequate for both cooking, for which it was intended, and heating, for which no military provision was made at all, apart from malodorous oil stoves supplied for offices. Two steps were therefore taken to try to ease the position: first—which was official—to move any men who were still living in out-houses under proper permanent cover, and, second—which was unofficial—to obtain coal by judicious deals

1945 and exchanges. The immediate effect of the former was for the 1st
Battalion to move their headquarters and No. 3 Company from the
château and buildings at Velm to Wasmont, a village a few miles
farther south on the road to Namur, leaving the 2nd Battalion in sole
possession. As to the latter, Battalion Headquarters was unaffected,
chiefly from an inability to make suitable contacts. Nor did No. 2
Squadron and the King's Company have much success, for, as an
officer who visited their officers' mess wrote, "the ordeal of sitting for
an hour in the lofty stone room in the château where they have gained
a footing, staring at a sham fireplace with no chimney and holding my
shivering fingers over the black fumes of a paraffin stove, is something
to be remembered but not repeated. The other companies and squadrons, however, are maintaining a fierce standard of heat which is the
envy of us all." The Battalion's discomfort was further aggravated
for a time by the shortage of baths. There was a bath-house in a glue
factory near by, but few people could be persuaded to use it owing to
the powerful smell of decomposing bones that always pervaded it. The
mobile bath unit came to the rescue as usual and installed itself in a
factory which evidently manufactured a less evil-smelling product.

The social side of the St. Trond period was the most varied of the
whole campaign. With Brussels only an hour away by road, the
officers could, when the weather permitted, drive in for dinner and
out again the same night, besides taking their normal leave vacancies.
Near Diest, only ten miles away, there was a restaurant, La Vielle
Barriere, whose cuisine equalled anything that Brussels could offer
and which had a pleasant personal note that some of the smarter
restaurants lacked. For the men, there were frequent dances—which
had not been possible in Holland because of the restrictions of the
Church—but the roads were so often frost-bound that the companies
in Wasmont and the surrounding villages had to rely for additional entertainment largely on travelling E.N.S.A. shows and mobile
cinemas. Capt. A. J. Shaughnessy produced an excellent show which
toured the companies, and there were weekly cock-fights in the
villages, which always drew large audiences.

Feb. 2-6   On the 2nd of February the Group were warned to be ready to
move and on the 3rd reconnaissance parties* from both Battalions left

---

*Reconnaissance parties used to be of two sorts—operational or non-operational,
and sometimes a mixture of the two. The operational type was just a small party
consisting of a representative from each company or squadron who went off after the
day's fighting to find a suitable field in which to put the Battalions and to post
markers for the vehicles to drive in on when they arrived. The fully non-operational
type took in all the above, multiplied several times, with additional representatives
from every department who thought they could do themselves well by having their
emissaries there before the others. In point of fact, the more people a battalion could
send on in advance the smoother and more complete were the arrangements for the

for Tilburg. It was understood that they would have to find accommo- 1945
dation for the Battalions for two days at the most, as by that time
Operation "Veritable" would be well under way and the Guards
Armoured Division would be sent racing across the Rhineland to
seize the bridge at Wesel. With the prophetic vision of hardened cam-
paigners, they told themselves that this would mean that they would
be in Tilburg for at least a fortnight and persuaded the authorities on
the spot to let the Group have a working-class estate, built at vast
expense in the early days of the war by the Germans to house industrial operatives. How right they were to insist on good billets the
Battalions soon found out.

The Group left the St. Trond area on the 7th of February loaded Feb. 7
with the gifts and good wishes of the local people. The journey to
Tilburg, which was only fifty-five miles away, took them a full nine
hours, as the weight of the leading tanks on the frost-covered roads cut
the cobbled surfaces to threads and slowed down the tail of the column
to a snail's pace. Several Irish Guards tanks became completely
marooned for an hour or so, as the road collapsed behind them and
was impassable in front. But the 1st Battalion came off worst of the
lot, as they were travelling in the wake of the entire armour of the
Division and found the roads a churned-up mass of paving-stones,
mud and water. When they eventually arrived in Tilburg it was pouring with rain and past 7 o'clock.

The next day was D Day for Operation "Veritable" and from Feb. 8-
10 o'clock both Battalions were at one hour's notice to move, expect- 21
ing the final order to leave to come through late the same night or
early the following morning. But that day dragged on, everyone going
to bed practically fully dressed in case the order arrived; the next day
dragged on, and the next. Finally, on the 11th of February, the
Battalions were put at three hours' notice and on the 12th at six hours'
notice, after which they were allowed to walk outside the Battalion
compound for the first time since arriving in Tilburg. From then until
the 21st of February, when the move eventually took place, the routine
settled down to an unmistakably peace-time basis, with drill parades
and drill competitions* (in accordance with the Regimental custom
of spring drills) filling most of the morning, and cinemas or baths the
afternoons and evenings. Oysters and white-bait from the Scheldt

---

reception of the main body, which resulted in a continual fight between Brigade
Headquarters, who always sought to limit battalion advance parties to the barest
minimum to avoid congestion on the roads, and the Commanding Officers, who were
eager to get as many people ahead as possible. Usually a compromise of some sort
was arrived at agreeable to both parties, the Battalions always slipping in a few
vehicles at the last moment which they hoped would pass unnoticed. In this instance,
the reconnaissance party was of the latter type.

*The Guardsmen called Tilburg "Drillburg."

1945 filled a gap in the gastronomic world, the latter, however, being rather a deceptive fish, since they refused to produce any results when fried in the English manner. It was eventually discovered that they were pickled in onions and allergic to cooking and that the local inhabitants ate them raw out of a tub. But as this did not catch on, their popularity declined, leaving the messes with a large debt and small tubs of fish on their hands. The oysters, however, were a great success, despite dire warnings from the 4th Battalion that they had caused a heavy casualty rate when they had tried them. Capt. E. M. D. Denny in particular won much popularity with his recipe for oyster pie.

The only fly in the ointment was the persistence of the flying bombs which flew over the town on their way to Antwerp and England. None of them actually landed at Tilburg, though one day one cut out over a drill parade, causing great consternation to those in the ranks, as the Sergeant-Major was slightly deaf and carried on with his demonstration of the right turn quite unaware. Fortunately, the explosion took place well outside the town and nobody was hurt. But after this incident there were many members of the Group who breathed a sigh of relief when, on the 20th, the orders for the move to Nijmegen finally came through.

GANGELT

CHAPTER VIII

THROUGH THE SIEGFRIED LINE

1

NIJMEGEN TO GOCH

4TH BATTALION

Operation "Veritable"—4th Battalion selected to breach the Siegfried Line —An unexpected opportunity seized with great success—4th Battalion occupy a hill dominating Cleve—Capture of Goch—Heavy fighting beyond Goch—Desperate courage of German defence

OF the many offensives which the British Liberation Army launched **1945** between D Day and VE Day, Operation "Veritable" was fought on **Feb. 8** the grandest scale. Five hundred Halifax and Lancaster bombers made the preliminary bombardment, a thousand guns—many more than there were at El Alamein—gave artillery support, and the attacking force itself consisted of six infantry divisions and one thousand five hundred tanks. Over three hundred thousand men were involved. By the time it was over not only had the much-vaunted Siegfried Line been broken through but also the entire German forces between the Maas and the Rhine had been sent hurtling back into Germany in complete disorder.

This remarkable victory was won only after a month of some of the heaviest fighting of the campaign. The operation lasted for a whole month, which, considering that the distance covered, from Nijmegen to Wesel, was a bare forty miles and, considering the vast numbers of British and Canadian troops involved, seemed endless. Floods, which submerged parts of the battlefield for days on end; mud, as thick and viscous as it had been during the Dutch battles; seemingly endless belts of forest which had to be fought for inch by inch—not to mention the desperate resistance offered by the Germans, especially towards the end of the operation; these combined to slacken the pace of the Allied forces and, to a certain extent, to counter-balance their large superiority in numbers. Operation "Veritable," in fact, rivalled the Normandy campaign in the effort it required to bring it to a victorious conclusion.

1945　The 4th Battalion, with the rest of the 6th Guards Tank Brigade, sallied forth into the thick of the fighting on the very first day of the offensive, the 8th of February. The Higher Command, in hopes of winning tactical surprise by unleashing Churchills over the extremely bad tank country south of Nijmegen, had resolved to give the Brigade the highly important task of breaking through the Siegfried Line and, of the three battalions, the Grenadiers were chosen to do the actual breaching. For years the Nazis had been dangling the Siegfried Line in front of the Allies with the gloating confidence of a gangster brandishing a pistol at his victim; so, had a captured map not disclosed that the majority of the concrete works were personnel shelters and not fire positions, the thought of this mission would have been alarming to a degree. As it was, there was still reason for anxiety, because, six miles south of Nijmegen, running from the Reichwald Forest to Kranenburg, short stretches of anti-tank ditches, road blocks, anti-tank guns as well as minefields had been pin-pointed by Allied aircraft, and it was in the centre of these, near Frasselt, that the 4th Battalion were to attack.

The Battalion started to make their way up towards Frasselt in the early afternoon of the 8th, the offensive having begun at 5 o'clock that morning. Their attack was supposed to start shortly after midnight, but the road from Nijmegen was so congested and the mud so thick that they had gone only half-way by nightfall. At 10 o'clock the main route collapsed completely and the whole breaching force, consisting of a squadron of Flails, two troops of Avres and two half-squadrons of the 4th Battalion, had to proceed for the remainder of the journey up a single muddy track which became more impossible as each vehicle used it. All night long the column struggled on, the rain pounding down incessantly, bridge tanks overturning, and the tanks themselves frequently having to pull each other through the quagmire. Finally, at 4 o'clock, dead tired, soaked to the skin, and rather dazed, the head of the column reached the anti-tank ditch of the Siegfried Line—only to find that, for all their labours, the breaching force commanders had misunderstood an order and were nowhere to be seen.

Stuck out in the open in the middle of this wintry night, on the very threshold of the Siegfried Line, with the sky lit up by gun flashes, the odds seemed loaded outrageously against their ever getting across the ditch that night. But all of a sudden their fortunes took a turn for the better. It was discovered that, by a freak of chance, the Germans were not defending the immediate vicinity of this particular part of the Siegfried Line, and Major Pike—with immense initiative which was rewarded with the Distinguished Service Order—took the breaching

force under his wing, manœuvred them into position, arranged for 1945
two lanes to be spanned across the ditch, and got Nos. 2 and 3
Squadrons over in less than half an hour. Then, after a brisk encounter
with the enemy which ended in their capturing ten officers and two
hundred and thirty men, the two squadrons rushed on towards Cleve,
their objective, and by 5 o'clock were firmly ensconced on the Mater-
born Feature, a wooded hillock which dominated the town. Thus, in
the course of a single hour on that cold February morning, a hole was
punched in the Siegfried Line through which the remainder of the
force could pass for the attack on Cleve, the first large German town
to be threatened by the British Army in modern history.

The hopes of easy victory which this initial success held out, how- Feb. 9
ever, were soon squashed. Three days elapsed before Cleve was cap- 16
tured (by the 4th Battalion and 3rd Battalion Scots Guards, with their
supporting infantry), and in the interval the Nijmegen—Cleve road
became flooded to a depth of three feet. This disaster prevented the
very real gains of the first two days from being exploited soon enough,
as it meant that supplies and reinforcements had either to be brought
up in Dukws or else sent twenty-five miles round via the Reichwald
Forest—both totally inadequate processes. If it had been feasible for
the Guards Armoured Division to be passed through on D + 3 or
D + 4, as was planned, they would have caught the Germans on the
rebound and might easily have reached Wesel and the Rhine in a
single day. As it was, the enemy themselves were able to bring up
reinforcements and for the rest of the month battles followed battles
in monotonous succession.

The 4th Battalion remained out of the line for nearly a week after
the capture of Cleve while the 4th Coldstream and 3rd Scots were
fighting a series of difficult battles east of the town and the 43rd
Division were struggling forward towards Goch. Little was achieved
during this time, and as the situation gradually deteriorated plans of
many kinds were made to remedy it. These had a direct bearing on
the 4th Battalion, as they were the only battalion in the 6th Guards
Tank Brigade which had not been in action for several days and they
were consequently in great demand for the coming operation. In less
than twenty-four hours they were switched from the 15th (Scottish)
Division to the 53rd Division, to the 43rd Division, to the 51st (Highland) Division and finally back to the 15th (Scottish), and they were
detailed to take part in at least a dozen plans which had as their goals
such widely separated towns as Emmerich, Goch, Calcar and Udem.

On the 17th the die was cast for Goch and the Grenadiers moved to Feb. 17
a point just south of the Forest of Cleve, about two miles north of
Goch. It was known that Goch was a bulwark of the German positions

1945 between the Rhine and the Maas and that, besides the natural obstacle of the River Niers, anti-tank ditches were included among its defences. Elements of three divisions were believed to have been collected to man the defences in addition to the normal garrison troops, and it was considered that there was still likely to be a lot of fight in them, even though the town had been subjected to intense aerial and artillery bombardment for many days. Four British divisions were therefore to take part in the attack: the 51st (Highland) Division, to clear the town south of the River Niers; the 53rd Division, to hold their positions between the river and the Goch—Cleve railway; the 43rd Division, to seize eight crossings over the anti-tank ditch; and the 15th (Scottish) Division, supported by the 4th Battalion, to take the town from the north.

Feb. 18   Before the 4th Battalion and 44th Brigade moved towards Goch early on the morning of the 18th, the Brigade Commander and Lieut.-Colonel The Lord Tryon went right up to the anti-tank ditch to see how best it could be crossed. As their presence drew absolutely no reaction from the enemy, they concluded that he must have withdrawn a substantial part of his force, and before a full-scale attack was mounted they sent a company of the 8th Royal Scots forward on the off-chance that they might seize a crossing alone. But before long the company returned with the news that the enemy had done no such thing, and for the rest of the day the tanks did their utmost to help the infantry and the bridge-layers to force a crossing. First No. 1 Squadron and then No. 3 Squadron closed in on the obstacle, in the face of withering fire, but the infantry were kept almost permanently pinned to the ground by the mortaring, and the bridge-layers either slid into the ditch or else bogged in the mud. Finally, at about 4 o'clock, when the situation seemed almost hopeless, it was decided to make one last attempt before the light failed. The remaining bridge-layer, Sergt. Rigley's, was brought up, and to everyone's astonishment, instead of bogging or turning over, it calmly laid its charge over the ditch. Lieut. J. H. Patrick's troop promptly crossed over with a party of infantry, scattered the Germans on the other side, and by 5 o'clock were in possession of the factory area—a feat which, combined with the gains of the other divisions, sealed the fate of the defenders of Goch.

Feb. 19   They did not give in immediately, however, and during the whole of the next day No. 3 Squadron had to comb the north-western suburbs to dispose of them. Shells and mortar fire streamed into the town unremittingly, but the squadron took an enormous bag of prisoners: one tank, Sergt. Wheeler's, captured more than two hundred in one street alone, the majority of them paratroopers who had bicycled up from Venlo that day. By nightfall, apart from occa-

sional shelling and venomously accurate sniping, peace had been
restored to the town, so much of which had been destroyed that it
awoke memories of Caen. Some time later the Corps Commander said
that he had expected that the Divisional Commander would have to
use the whole of the 15th (Scottish) Division to capture the northern
half of this important communication centre, and that he had been
greatly surprised when news arrived that this had already been done
by the 4th Battalion and the 44th Brigade alone.

The 4th Battalion remained in Goch for four days, prevented from Feb. 18-
snatching hardly any rest at all by the perpetual barrages which were 22
put up by British artillery around them. After an exhausting period
of planning and counter-planning, it was eventually decided, on the
22nd, that, after a preliminary attack by the 46th Brigade just south
of Goch, the 4th Battalion would pass through and capture a small
wood on the way to Weeze, to prepare the way for an attack by the
53rd Division on Weeze itself. The 46th Brigade's preliminary attack
had involved a difficult day's fighting, during which Capt. Cannan,
who was with the Royal Scots Fusiliers when they were being heavily
mortared and shelled, was seriously wounded. It was already dark
when the 46th Brigade secured the start line for the attack by the 4th
Battalion the next morning, and as a result, when they moved out of
Goch early on the 23rd of February, there were certain misgivings
about the impending battle. The left flank would be completely
exposed, the wood itself housed unknown dangers, and it was evident
that the Germans were still well equipped with guns and mortars.

To everybody's delight, an intermediate objective was taken by Feb. 23
10.45, the ground opposition being very light, although on No. 3
Squadron's front the shelling and mortaring were possibly the most
accurate of the whole campaign. After a short interval the attack was
resumed and the wood was soon captured. On the way a self-propelled
gun was roused from its lair and Lieut. J. N. R. Hearne killed it
successfully. No. 2 Squadron, not to be outdone, immediately coun-
tered by claiming the capture of six self-propelled guns, but all of these
turned out to have been deserted. Nothing happened during the night
and no counter-attacks developed.

The next morning No. 3 Squadron reported that there was a self- Feb. 27
propelled gun a thousand yards to their left firing down the railway
line. What it was supposed to be doing there no one ever discovered,
but mediums were brought up and this and another gun in the same
area were soon disposed of. A little later Sergt. Berresford, who had
commanded a troop ever since landing on the Continent, had the
misfortune to step on a Schu mine and was severely wounded, losing
both feet. His courage was very great: he refused morphia, saying
that he had only a slight pain in his feet.

1945	The tanks remained stationary all day near the river across which the 44th Brigade had been forbidden to fire, for fear of hitting the 53rd Division, who were moving up for their attack on Weeze on the other side. Yet the King's Own Scottish Borderers saw Germans scurrying up and down the road on the other bank of the River Niers, just under their noses. It was hard to refrain from firing, but 15th (Scottish) Divisional Headquarters were adamant. Then a curious coincidence occurred. Another group started to use the same wireless frequency as the 44th Brigade, clearly an armoured formation and obviously attacking somewhere in the neighbourhood. They could be heard asking whether they could fire at a certain house or at a certain wood, and eventually they were identified as the leading squadron attacking with the 53rd Division. At last the commanding officer of the King's Own Scottish Borderers could control himself no longer, and, grabbing a microphone, explained that he was sitting on the hill on the other side of the river and could see all the German positions. Could he help? They assured him that he could. The first thing to come dashing down the hill was a self-propelled gun. This information was duly passed on to the squadron, who said they would be delighted if he could deal with it. He did—mediums finished it off very quickly. Then a German staff car came up. German officers climbed out and looked at the battle through their binoculars. Immediately the King's Own Scottish Borderers brought their mortars to bear on them, and so it went on—without the knowledge of either Divisional Headquarters.

Feb. 26	On the 26th the 44th Brigade were withdrawn and the 8th Brigade, of the 3rd British Infantry Division, took over the line from them. The change-over of the two brigades went very smoothly, although there was severe shelling going on all the time, especially on No. 1 Squadron's front. This was the last time the Grenadiers were to fight with the 44th Brigade, with whom they had trained in England and fought many battles since landing in Normandy. The respect and admiration felt by every man of the 4th Battalion for the 44th Brigade were very real indeed: they had come to regard them as their own infantry, and their association was always one of the happiest.

As part of the 15th (Scottish) Division, the 44th Brigade were being sent to Tilburg for a well-earned rest, and the 3rd British Infantry Division was one of the four formations which were being brought up for the remaining phases of Operation "Veritable." The others were the 11th, the 2nd Canadian and the Guards Armoured Divisions. On the 23rd of February the American Ninth Army had started its offensive across the Roer River, and this new threat was having a marked

effect on the Germans. It was evident that a final push by the 21st **1945**
Army Group was all that was needed to drive the Germans across the
Rhine. So plans were made for two new attacks—one by the Cana-
dians (called Operation "Blockbuster") to clear Udem, Calcar and
finally Xanten, and the other a steady advance due south through
Weeze and Kevelaer to join up with the American Ninth Army at
Geldern. It was on the latter operation that the 4th Battalion and the
Grenadier Group, who had come up with the Guards Armoured
Division, were employed for the next week.

On the 27th of February the 4th Battalion were put under the **Feb. 27**
command of the 8th Brigade, of the 3rd British Infantry Division, and
told to cut across the road linking Udem and Weeze. All three squadrons of the Battalion took part in this action, and for No. 2 Squadron
it was a comparatively normal day: they met surprisingly little opposition, and Sergt. Gregory's troop reached the main road by 11 o'clock
in the morning; the squadron's only casualty was Lieut. A. H. Gray,
who was wounded when a bazooka hit his tank. The other two had
one of the most eventful days of their lives.

Probably No. 1 Squadron had the most dramatic time. Half-way
between the wood they had captured on the 24th and the road they
encountered opposition from two hamlets, Geurtshof and Bussenhof,
and the fighting rapidly became so confused that the infantry had to
reorganize and only just managed to continue the advance. What
apparently happened was that as the tanks and infantry reached
Bussenhof white flags appeared from the houses. Two platoons immediately went straight up to the houses, but the Germans opened fire
and killed them all. The majority of another platoon had also been
lost, so that there was practically nobody left in the company to carry
on. On the left of No. 1 Squadron, however, the infantry fared better
and all went well until the reserve troop, Lieut. R. J. McCallum's, was
suddenly attacked by bazooka-men. Lieut. McCallum's tank began to
burn and, although the ammunition in it might have blown up at any
moment, he ordered his driver, L./Cpl. Lane, to reverse so that they
would have some chance of escaping alive. Their courage was rewarded, and after many adventures they rejoined their squadron,
which, in the meantime, had reached the main road.*

After reorganizing on the Weeze-Udem road, Lieut. I. C. Minnette-
Lucas's troop and the infantry moved farther down towards Weeze to
secure the bridge across the Muhlen Fleuth. They were subjected to

---

*It was thought that Lieut. McCallum's troop were fired at from the edge of the
wood, probably by Germans who had been kept down by the artillery barrage but
had emerged in time to shoot-up the reserve troops as they came past. This was the
case along the whole front that day; in spite of a heavy artillery barrage, the Germans
recovered in time to fight the tanks.

1945 intense mortar and machine-gun fire, but they pressed on with great bravery and eventually captured the bridge intact. Sergt. Ingham crossed over and continued along the road for about a hundred yards and was then ordered to come back. The ground opposition was not heavy, which, considering the importance of the bridge to the defence of Weeze, was surprising. It was discovered later that on the bridge Sergt. Ingham's tank squashed an "R" mine which was attached to aerial bombs, but for some reason these did not explode.

The troop remained covering the bridge until 6 o'clock at night. Just as they were turning round to come back, a counter-attack was heard forming up on the other side of the stream, but artillery fire was brought down on it and it was eventually dispersed. Two of Lieut. Minnette-Lucas's tanks became bogged, and their crews were brought back on Sergt. Ingham's tank to the forward edge of the wood, where the squadron were in a "hedgehog" position. Capt. I. R. K. Swift and Sergt. Quick tried hard to recover these tanks with an A.R.V., but the mortaring was so accurate that they had to leave them until the next day. As it grew dark the machine-gun fire did not die down and it was evident that the Germans were still very much on the alert. "Monty's moonlight"* was illuminating the battlefield and now and again the infantry could see figures moving about on the other side of the bridge. Then at 10.15 the Germans threw in a strong counter-attack. Sergt. Dillingham and L./Sergt. Higgin, who had remained less than thirty yards from the bridge all day, fired their Besas across the stream, but they could not fire their high-explosive because it would have been suicidal to let the Germans know that there were still tanks in the vicinity. The forward company holding the bridge-head on the farther side of the stream were nearly overrun, but they fought nobly and managed to repel the counter-attack. After this No. 1 Squadron were ordered to send a troop right up to the bridge, and Sergt. Dillingham was chosen for the task. Near his position was a farm, and the paratroopers inside kept on waving a lantern in front of a window, hoping that the tanks would fire at it, give away their position and thus become easy prey for stalkers. Luckily Sergt. Dillingham saw through this trick and held his fire.

There were a lot of eerie noises as the night wore on, but nothing developed until 4 o'clock, when the Germans hurled another furious counter-attack against the bridgehead. Almost at once Sergt. Dillingham was wounded by a bazooka, and as the infantry had slightly withdrawn, Sergt. Higgin and one self-propelled gun were left to defend the bridge by themselves. They fought hard and stubbornly and held their ground until Major R. H. Heywood-Lonsdale, the

---

*Artificial daylight produced by searchlights playing on clouds.

squadron leader, ordered them to withdraw. As communication with 1945 Battalion Headquarters was very bad owing to interference, a message which was passed back explaining the situation was interpreted as an S.O.S. and news soon spread that calamity had befallen the bridge-head, that enemy self-propelled guns were across the bridge and that the troop of No. 1 Squadron who were guarding it had been knocked out. The Infantry Brigadier went off to organize a counter-attack with a battalion of the 53rd Division who were near by, and everyone else at Battalion Headquarters bit their fingers in an agony of suspense. When dawn broke the next morning the situation turned out to have been less serious than had been expected. The bridgehead was still intact, it had never been overrun, no self-propelled guns had crossed the bridge—in fact, it was even doubtful whether enemy infantry had ever crossed it. The situation had been saved just in time by the bravery of the infantry and by the arrival of eight tanks of No. 1 Squadron commanded by Major R. H. Heywood-Lonsdale and Lieut. I. C. Minnette-Lucas. They had blazed away with their guns until the enemy withdrew, completely overwhelmed by the combination of Besa and Bren-gun fire. The next day at least three hundred German bodies were found lying about on the battlefield.

During the early stages of No. 1 Squadron's battle at Weeze bridge No. 3 Squadron, with the 1st South Lancs, were having a very un-pleasant time in a wood about a mile and a half to the left. It was very thick and swampy and the tracks which looked so inviting on the map turned out to be will-o'-the-wisps leading to impassable bogs. Battalion Headquarters heard nothing of this squadron for some time. The two leading troops were fighting their way on in silence—Lieut. S. C. Rolleston on the right and Lieut. R. J. Owen on the left. The former made good progress through the woods until his tank went up on a mine and he was forced to take over his troop corporal's tank. Shortly afterwards his driver, Gdsm. McCulloch, put his hand out of the hatch to throw away an empty Besa box at the same moment as a bazooka hit the turret. His hand was badly lacerated, yet he managed to put the tank in reverse and drove it back to safety. Lieut. Owen waited for some time for the infantry to appear and was then ordered to push on through the woods towards the Weeze—Udem road where he was told his infantry would be waiting for him. This turned out to be sheer optimism, because as he emerged into a clearing just in front of the road paratroopers from the 7th Parachute Division swarmed round his tanks and knocked out all three of them with bazookas. Gdsm. Rule was killed, and L./Cpl. Yerbury, Gdsm. Towells, Sergt. Hanks and Lieut. Owen were all seriously wounded. The troop were with-drawn by Sergt. Hanks (who subsequently was awarded the Military

1945 Medal for the great courage he displayed during the action) and a
new plan was drawn up. It had to be cancelled, however, as the
infantry had had so many casualties that they could not mount another
attack.

The 27th of February had been an exciting and, at times, an
awkward day for the 4th Battalion.* They had been up against probably the best troops in the German Army—fanatical paratroopers
who scorned death and who were willing to stand up in full view of
the tanks to fire their bazookas from a distance of often less than a
hundred yards. But it was the last time the Battalion went into action
in Operation "Veritable." They spent the next week, most uncomfortably, in a wood near Goch, and by the time they were called
forward again the fighting had ceased.

2

GOCH TO BONNINGHARDT

1ST AND 2ND BATTALIONS

*The Group take over part of the Goch salient—Leap-frogging through
the woods towards the Rhine—Germans retire to Wesel*

If "Veritable" had gone according to plan and the Germans had
not flooded the entire northern half of the battlefield, the Guards
Armoured Division would almost certainly have played a brilliant
part in the operation; they might even have captured the bridge at
Wesel and saved the Allies from having to fight their way across the
Rhine later. But the narrow, bog-infested front to which the battlefield was soon reduced by the flooding was no milieu for an armoured
division, and they were left milling around in Tilburg until the 20th,
the day the 4th Battalion captured Goch.

---

*It had been an exceptionally difficult day for the troop leaders. Even in a relatively
straightforward battle there are a hundred and one things a troop leader has to do.
He has to guide his tank, make full use of the ground, keep in constant touch with
his infantry, scan the landscape for the enemy, direct his gunner on to targets,
position his other two tanks, pass messages back to the squadron leader over the air,
and at the same time be on the alert for all the unexpected situations which might
arise in modern warfare. It is even harder when he has to fight in woods, for the
trees make ideal cover for snipers and bazooka-men, and he is suspicious all the
time. Besides, the trees are natural obstacles for tanks, so he has to guide his driver
with the utmost care. He has to protect his flanks and yet keep his gun from hitting
the trees. He feels curiously alone and unprotected, even though his infantry may
be all around his troop. It is dark and very frightening.

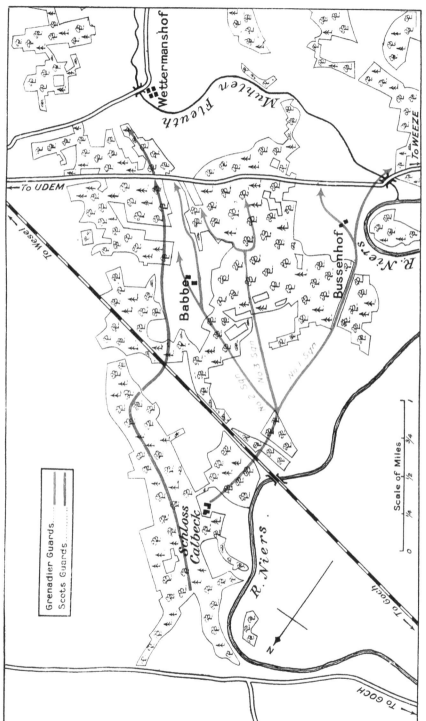

WOODS SOUTH-EAST OF GOCH

The Grenadier Group returned to the scene of their former triumphs in Nijmegen on the 21st and spent two days there, in extreme discomfort, before setting off for the battle area. There was a spate of conferences during these two days, and while Lieut. A. Slob, M.C., a Dutch officer who had joined the 1st Battalion a year before, was travelling in his jeep to one of them, a tank crashed into it, injuring him fatally. 1945 Feb. 21-22

The Group's first tank was to take over a short section of the Goch salient near the village of Halvenboom. To get there, the wheeled vehicles went by road, though the mud-caked surfaces hardly justified the name, and the tanks and carriers travelled along the Gennep—Goch railway—a shattering experience for the 2nd Battalion, as each time a tank hit a sleeper it shook violently. By 8 o'clock the column had reached the northern outskirts of Goch and as soon as the tanks relieved the congestion on the roads by pulling into harbour areas the 1st Battalion moved up to the front line to begin the change-over.* It was raining heavily and searchlights were blazing into the sky as the Battalion crept slowly forward through the thundering gun lines, climbed out of their vehicles, and then marched forward to take over their positions at half-hourly intervals. The 6-pounders sank deep into the muddy tracks and the trucks experienced the greatest difficulty in turning round, but by 2 a.m. the two forward companies, Nos. 2 and 4, were inside slit trenches watching for signs of an enemy counter-attack, and the reserves safely housed in cellars. Feb. 23

The next morning the two companies awoke to find that they were perched on top of a forward slope, exposed to enemy observation from the church towers in Udem and Kapellen. Mortar fire rained down on them all day, but they suffered only one fatal casualty, Sergt. Partridge, M.M., of No. 4 Company. That night a patrol was sent out under Lieut. E. F. Fairbanks-Smith to find out more about the enemy. The moon was shining, but the patrol crawled close enough to the enemy to hear the squeals of pigs being slaughtered, and it came back loaded with information which was of great value to the Canadians, who attacked through the Battalion's positions late the following night. Feb. 24

All the companies were warned to lie low during the first stages of this Canadian attack because an intensive barrage had been arranged and it was feared that the Germans would retaliate. More prisoners than shells came back, however, and the Battalion had a dress-circle view of the attack. The Canadians passed through at 4 a.m. to take Kapellen, and later the same day the Greys, of the 4th Armoured Brigade, followed suit to attack Udem. Feb. 25

---

*This was one of the few occasions in the campaign when all three Grenadier Battalions were in the same part of the line.

The Group were now no longer in the front line, and for the next couple of days the battle slowly drew away. Shells ceased to land with such monotonous regularity on the forward companies, but as the Canadians moved on, more and more guns were brought up, increasing rather than diminishing the thunder of war around them. Every company had at least a troop of guns in its area, and then, as a last straw, a battery of 150-mms. ponderously settled down beside them, leaving its mark on their eardrums for a long time to come.

As February changed to March a new plan was evolved for an advance to Bonninghardt, which was originally to have been one of the Group's objectives in the early days of the operation. Movement orders and postponements followed, hot on each other's heels during the 1st and 2nd, and it was not until the ungodly hour of 1 a.m. on the morning of the 3rd that the Group started to move. The night was very dark and so much of the road was blocked by rubble and other transport that, after passing through the bomb-shattered towns of Weeze and Kevelaer, the column became very split up. As daylight appeared, bringing with it a hailstorm, however, the vehicles were sorted out and, shortly before 7 a.m., the leading company and squadron were approaching Kapellen, which contained an important crossroads giving access to the high, wooded ground around Bonninghardt.

The 5th Brigade were supposed to pass through the 3rd Division just north of Kapellen and attack this high ground that morning, but the enemy in the area had been withdrawing under pressure, blowing craters and laying mines as they went, and the leading troop of No. 3 Squadron were told that the main road to Kapellen was well and truly cratered where it crossed a small but deep stream. It was known that at least a brigade was in or forward of Kapellen, but after a patrol of No. 2 Company had reported that the crater was not covered by enemy fire and that there was no possible way round the obstacle, a bridge-building party of sappers was sent out under the protection of a composite force provided by No. 2 Company and No. 3 Squadron. The gap to be bridged measured one hundred and ten feet across, and as the day drew on the prospect of launching the attack that day dwindled and died. The Irish Guards, who were just behind the Grenadiers, were therefore told to turn round and try to reach Kapellen by a different route. The Grenadier Group also turned round and harboured for the night in the middle of a large, boggy field about a mile west of Kapellen, knowing full well that they were overlooked by the enemy and that several vehicles were certain to be struck when pulling out in the morning. A few prisoners filtered back to the Battalion in the course of the evening, and from them it was learned that the Winkelscher Busch, the thickly planted wood on the high ground near

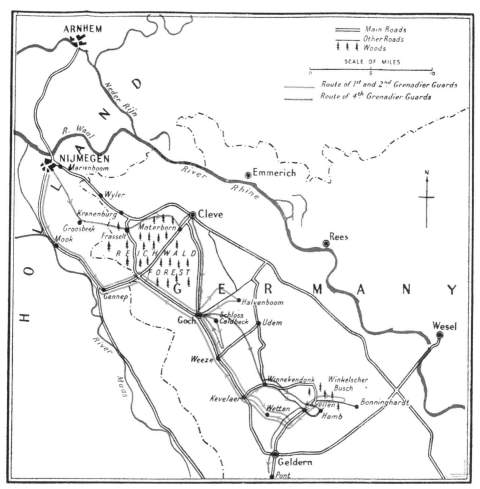

NIJMEGEN TO GELDERN

Bonninghardt, as well as the woods to the east, was held by an assorted 1945 selection of the 84th Infantry Division, supported by self-propelled guns and nebelwerfers—a hair-raising species of multi-barrelled mortar.

At 7.30 the next morning the 2nd Battalion pulled the 1st Battalion Mar. 5 out of the boggy field and No. 3 Company and No. 2 Squadron set off immediately, travelling through Kapellen, across a patch of rough, sandy heathland and then up the steep incline towards Bonninghardt. The south-western half of the Winkelscher Busch had already been cleared by two battalions of the 3rd Division, and the Irish Guards, who had taken Hamb the night before, were watching the eastern half of it. Yet, as No. 2 Company and No. 3 Squadron came to the top of the incline, they were fired at by Spandaus and mortared. They imagined at first that the fire must be coming from an isolated post, but as they started along the main road to Bonninghardt and the Rhine two large self-propelled guns appeared. So, as soon as 2/Lieut. A. Jones's tank had knocked them out, the Group halted to make a more precise plan.

Now that they were on the high ground, great woods stretched in every direction, cut in only a few places by belts of pastureland. The Group Commander therefore decided that the companies, assisted by the 5th Coldstream, should make a series of attacks, leap-frogging through the woods as far as Megzenrath, about one and a half miles away towards the Rhine. No. 2 Company, supported by No. 3 Squadron, would make the first attack and seize the south-eastern part of the Winkelscher Busch. No. 4 Company, supported by No. 1 Squadron, would then pass through and clear another large wood three-quarters of a mile farther east. Finally, the 5th Coldstream would come up and attack Megzenrath. The Leicestershire Yeomanry were to give strong artillery support throughout the battle.

No. 2 Company started to advance at 2.30 and in less than three hours the woods leading to Megzenrath and the village itself had been captured, all three companies having stuck rigidly to the plan and the time-table. The opposition had proved much lighter than had been expected, and had Spandaus not been lying in wait for No. 2 Company in a wood to the left of the Winkelscher Busch there would have been no casualties. But these solitary Spandaus caught Lieut. D. E. Pike's platoon in the open and he and three of his Guardsmen were killed.

That night the Germans started to withdraw, slowly but definitely, Mar. 6- to Wesel, and the Grenadier Group did not go into battle again in   11 Operation "Veritable." The Americans and the British 52nd Division on the right, and the Canadians on the left, gradually rolled up the

1945 front until they reached the western banks of the Rhine. While these last shots were being fired, the Grenadier Group made several moves, coming at times under severe shell fire which caused casualties, but on the 8th of March the Germans surrendered and on the 11th the Group retired to a rest area near Gennep.

CHAPTER IX

GERMANY

1

THE RHINE CROSSING

A new optimism in the Allied armies—The great operation for crossing the Rhine accomplished with surprising ease—4th Battalion cross the pontoon bridge at Wesel and link up with the American paratroops

WHEN, in August, 1944, the curtain was pulled down on the long struggle in Normandy, the armoured divisions in the 21st Army Group paused for two weeks in the bocage, then suddenly sprang to life and in one bold, impulsive stroke, raced across France, Belgium and Holland to German's western frontier. In the spring of 1945 this fragment of military history repeated itself. Only the setting was different: the long struggle (Operation "Veritable") took place in the Rhineland; the pause, on the banks of the Rhine; the race, across Germany to that country's frontier with Denmark. And to round off the happy repetition of events with a trace of poetic justice, in the spring of 1945 it was the 4th Battalion and not the Grenadier Group who, for a considerable portion of time, led the 21st Army Group's advance—the advance which brought the German Army to its knees.

1945
Mar. 11-
30

As they waited in the Rhineland for the great day when the crossing of the Rhine would begin, the three Battalions of the Regiment surmised that the penultimate phase of the war was over; and that whatever lay ahead could not be worse than what had gone before. A wave of contagious optimism swept through the Battalions, drugging their usual dread of a new operation, giving them a new, vital confidence in themselves. The weather jumped two months ahead. The sun shone, warm and brilliant every day. Daffodils came out to dance in a June breeze. It was a time for sun-bathing, and the clear, blue skies made it easy to forget the mud and slush and dirt which so recently had seemed the inevitable adjuncts of warfare on the Continent. Brussels leave started again; leave to Eindhoven, leave to Tilburg—every remotely civilized town within reach had some representative of the three Battalions snatching a quick holiday. Life was indeed worth living.

207

1945   Even the 1st and 2nd Battalions, billeted near Gennep in houses
that were pitted with shrapnel, windowless and often roofless, made
light of their discomfort and set about training with carefree enthusiasm. Gennep had been in the front line during the greater part of the
winter and anti-personnel mines lay dotted over the countryside as
thickly as weeds, but a course for young officers under Major N. E. W.
Baker, M.C., and one for snipers under Lieut. J. C. Duncan were
bravely carried through to the bitter end and resulted in only one
casualty—Lieut. G. B. Palau, who lost his left foot. The 4th Battalion
at Pont, an undamaged village two miles south of Geldern, cleaned
and painted and overhauled their Churchills until they were as spick
and span and in as perfect running order as at the beginning of the
campaign.

Meanwhile, the preparations for the crossing of the Rhine were
going full steam ahead. The surrounding countryside, over a hundred
miles from the sea, was being swiftly transformed into a sort of nauti-
cal wonderland. At all hours of the day and night gigantic transporters
carrying speed-boats, pontoons, Dukws, Buffaloes and Weasels, came
thundering down the road towards Wesel. From the south arrived
lorry-load after lorry-load of American supplies, driven by negroes
who, by the pace they went, looked as if they were heading back to
Alabam'. Bombers flew over every night to pummel strategic points
behind the Rhine, and artillery barrages dealt remorselessly with the
German positions on the river bank itself. By the 20th of March the
thousands of tons of supplies needed for a large amphibious operation
had been hauled up, and a false, expectant calm settled over the Allied
stations in the Rhineland.

During these last few days of grace before the final great plunge of
the war the Battalions quietly packed up, reducing to the barest
minimum the paraphernalia they normally carried in their vehicles
to make room for an ominously large issue of food, water and petrol.
Certain changes occurred in the orders of battle, the most important
in the 1st and 2nd Battalions. In the former, Lieut.-Colonel L. S.
Starkey left to take over a command in England and Lieut.-Colonel
P. H. Lort-Phillips arrived direct from the 3rd Battalion in Italy to
take his place; in the latter, Capt. P. J. Diggle rejoined his squadron
after an absence of nearly two years on sick leave. On the 23rd of
March Field-Marshal Montgomery visited the 4th Battalion on his
way to meet Mr. Churchill, who had just arrived in the Rhineland.
The Commander-in-Chief presented medal ribbons to a number of
officers and men who had recently been awarded decorations, and
then, standing on the bonnet of a jeep, gave a short talk. He let drop
no hint as to when or where the crossing would take place, but he

seemed so relaxed, so confident, that everyone was left with the im- 1945
pression that he felt the end of the war was really in sight. As a result,
the death of Capt. R. H. Monteith, who had been killed the evening
before when his scout car ran into the back of an unlighted tank
transporter, seemed all the more tragic; he was buried in the Guards
Armoured Division cemetery at Kapellen on the 24th—the day that
the 21st Army Group strode across the Rhine.

The Battalions did not know beforehand that the 24th had been
chosen as D Day. They had been kept completely in the dark about
the whole operation. There had been rumours, of course, rumours of
huge airborne landings, of tanks being prepared to float across the
Rhine on rafts, even one about the entire British armies being sent
south to cross the river at Remagen, where the Americans had just
captured a bridge. But the plan itself had been a well-kept secret.
When, early on the 24th, hours after the operation had begun, the
company commanders and squadron leaders held conferences and
unfolded the entire picture, the story they had to tell was rivalled in
dramatic quality only by the D Day of the 6th of June, 1944.

Their story ran roughly as follows. Late the previous night five
hundred British bombers had swooped down on Wesel and turned the
whole town into an enormous blazing inferno. Before the last planes
had passed over the target a thousand guns had opened a mammoth
barrage, also directed on Wesel and lasting for over half an hour. At
its height the 1st Commando Brigade, their faces blackened, had
climbed into Buffaloes, set sail across the Rhine and clambered up the
farther bank right in the centre of Wesel. At about the same time,
farther up the river, the 15th (Scottish) and the 51st (Highland) Divisions had also made assault crossings. Later, while it was still dark,
a Canadian division had fought their way across at Emmerich, com-
pleting a stretch of nearly ten miles of the eastern bank of the Rhine
that had been captured during the night. With the dawn the colossal
task of building pontoon bridges had begun.

But this was not all: the final punch was still to come. As the
squadron leaders and company commanders were talking, the drone
of planes could distinctly be heard in the distance. At 10 a.m. the
drone became a roar and a vast armada of Dakotas, skimming the
rooftops, crowded the sky for miles around. They were on their way
to the Dierfordter Wald, north-east of Wesel, to drop the 101st
American Airborne and the British 6th Airborne Divisions behind the
ranks of the German paratroopers defending the outskirts of Wesel.
For three hours there was no news of them, but when they were finally
picked up on the wireless fears that perhaps a second Arnhem would
occur vanished. After suffering many casualties on the dropping zones

P

1945 the paratroopers had quickly rallied and were already gaining the upper hand.

Such, in the barest outline, was the story of the crossing of the Rhine. The Rhine has always been Germany's great natural barrier against invading armies—surely it should have been one of the toughest battles of all? Yet there had been relatively little response from the Germans. The heavy fire had come from the west. The Germans' answer had been limp and mild. It remained to be seen whether it would continue that way.

The pontoon bridge at Wesel was floated scarcely twenty-four hours after the assault on Wesel ended. With no time to lose, the many divisions in the 21st Army Group which had not participated in the attack rushed across. Of the Grenadiers, the 4th Battalion were the first to go over. They, supposedly, were to join up with the paratroopers of the American airborne division and carry them on into the heart of Germany. Lieut.-Colonel The Lord Tryon and the three squadron leaders had already spent three days at the American Headquarters, when it was at Rheims, exchanging information about tanks and gliders and wirelesses and dropping zones, generally thrashing out the problems resulting from the co-operation of airborne and armoured forces. But after the Battalion had woven their way through the ruins of Wesel on the 27th they were informed that there had been a change of plan and that they were to spend the night on the outskirts of the town while their future was decided.

The Grenadier Group crossed the Rhine at Rees early on the morning of the 30th. They also were soon to strike deep into Germany, heading for Bremen—but not before the 4th Battalion were already well under way.

Men of the 6th Airborne Division on 4th Battalion Churchills passing through Billerbecke, where sheets, serving as white flags of surrender, wave from the windows.

Field-Marshal Montgomery addressing the 4th Battalion at Pont, Germany, March, 1945.

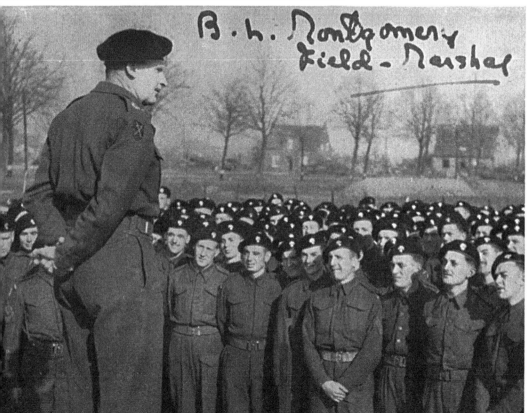

2

WESEL TO HANOVER

4TH BATTALION

The red and the black berets—First bound to Koesfeld—An exciting dash to the Ems—The bridge at Graven—Delay at Dortmund—Ems Canal—No. 3 Squadron at Osnabruck—The race for Minden—Forty-two miles in five and a half hours—Crossing of the Weser—Reaction of the German civilians—Dramatic capture of Leine bridge—Encirclement of Hanover

The 4th Battalion waited for twenty-four hours on the outskirts of Wesel before the Higher Command came to a decision about their future. It was a depressing period for them, as the rest of the 6th Guards Armoured Brigade* had gone ahead with the very Americans they had expected to carry themselves. When the 1 o'clock news of the B.B.C. announced that "the 6th Guards Armoured Brigade, carrying American paratroopers on their Churchills," had captured Dorsten—without them—they began to wonder if they had missed the boat altogether. _{1945 Mar. 27-28}

They need not have worried. When their turn came they entered into a partnership which exceeded their wildest expectations. They were to carry paratroopers after all—the British 6th Airborne Division, one of the most famous and most highly trained divisions in the British Army. The "Red Devils" had suffered heavily during the airborne landings in Normandy and again two days before, but in between they had had a priceless period of reorganization and rest. Unlike the majority of the infantry divisions on the Continent who had been fighting solidly for over nine months and were desperately tired, they were absolutely fresh and also eager to exact full retribution for the losses they had incurred, when heavily outnumbered, in Normandy. Everyone was convinced that the alliance of the red and black berets would be something the Germans would not easily forget.

When the call came the 6th Airborne were fighting alone about ten miles north of the fields outside Wesel where the 4th Battalion had been waiting. So in the early evening of the 28th of March the 4th Battalion moved off to join them. It had been dull and drizzly all day and as soon as the tanks got under way it began to pour with rain. They spent a wet and uncomfortable night in a cornfield at Rhade, just behind the 6th Airborne Division, formed up in a Normandy "hedgehog" because only the road itself had then been cleared. Early _{Mar. 29}

---

*After the Rhine crossing the Brigade was officially known as an "armoured" formation. With the new name came a new role.

1945 the next morning the headquarters of the Division arrived, together
with Field-Marshal Montgomery, General Dempsey and the American airborne commander, General Ridgeway. They conferred for a
few minutes, then General Ridgeway decorated certain of the paratroopers, and finally the Field-Marshal made a short speech congratulating the Division on the success of its landing and wishing it
well for what lay ahead. It was a simple, inspiring ceremony, and it
marked the end of the bridgehead period as well as the beginning of
the end of the North-West Europe campaign.

The night before, the Commanding Officer, Lieut.-Colonel The
Lord Tryon, had visited the Airborne Headquarters, where it had
been decided that each of the tank squadrons would be attached to a
brigade—No. 1 Squadron to the 3rd Parachute Brigade, No. 2 Squadron to the 6th Airlanding Brigade and No. 3 Squadron to the 5th
Parachute Brigade. Using these combinations, operations began that
afternoon.

See Map
p. 248 The objective was Koesfeld, an industrial town twenty-eight miles
to the north. The main road to it was allotted to No. 2 Squadron and
the Royal Ulster Rifles, while No. 3 Squadron with the 12th York
Parachute Battalion were given a route to the left, the first few miles
of which were nothing more than a track leading through a wood.
Neither squadron saw any enemy between Rhade and Koesfeld, and
had it not been raining hard for the past twenty-four hours both would
have been in Koesfeld by about 4.30. But half of No. 3 Squadron
became bogged getting through the wood, and No. 2 Squadron were
also delayed and had to leave two tanks behind, almost completely
submerged in a swollen stream which they were obliged to ford
because the only bridge had been blown.

No. 2 Squadron reached Koesfeld first and after dealing with a few
bursts of 20-mm. fire shot the Royal Ulster Rifles into the town. No. 3
Squadron arrived about an hour later, having successfully negotiated
the forests and swamps and having somehow found the way despite
totally inadequate and most inaccurate maps. Before they entered the
town No. 3 Squadron helped a company of the 13th Parachute Battalion to mop up a small enemy pocket slightly to the north, and they
were able to witness the amazing physical fitness of the paratroopers.
Although they had already marched twenty-five miles that day, the
company jumped barbed-wire fences and vaulted gates without showing the slightest sign of fatigue. It was a remarkable ending to a
remarkable day.

It had been an unforgettable experience for the tanks crews. After
nearly nine months of set-piece attacks, when an advance of two
thousand yards was a major victory, and half a mile was often a good

day's progress, they had suddenly found themselves taking part in an **1945** advance of twenty-eight miles in a single afternoon. They had become so used to moving over the brow of a hill to be met by a shower of 88-mm. shells and to emerging from a wood to be greeted by a company of infantry, that finding no Germans in an advance of twenty-eight miles seemed to wonderful to be true. It might happen once, but surely not the next day, the day after, and the day after that too.

The R.A.F. bombing raids had completely wrecked Koesfeld, and **Mar. 30** the rubble that littered the streets made it extremely difficult for the vehicles to get through the next morning. There was a delay of about an hour while a passage was cleared for them, but by 10 o'clock Nos. 1 and 3 Squadrons were through the town, preparing to make a lightning dash to capture a vital bridge over the River Ems at Graven, thirty-five miles distant. No. 1 Squadron were supporting the Canadian Parachute Battalion and were given the main road, No. 3 Squadron being once again allotted a rather precarious centre line along side-roads. In both cases the leading troop carried no infantry, so that their guns could be fired immediately opposition was encountered. The rest of the tanks in each squadron carried a company between them.

For the first few miles both squadrons raced forward as fast as the winding roads would allow. They were separated by a small range of hills from which the Germans could easily have fired on either squadron had they been there to do so. About five miles from Koesfeld the ridge turned north and, as No. 3 Squadron were about to cross it, they discovered that the road was barred by felled trees. It took a considerable time to drag these trees aside, as most of them were booby-trapped. Once they were through, a splendid Frenchman who had appointed himself as guide to the squadron warned Major I. J. Crosthwaite that there was a Hitler Jugend barracks ahead which was certain to give trouble. The squadron leader therefore ordered L./Cpl. Winstone, who was leading with a troop of Honeys, to have a quick shoot and return. Unfortunately, the Honeys stayed too long and L./Cpl. Winstone and all his crew except the co-driver were killed. The paratroopers immediately jumped off the tanks and, aided by the unorthodox but extremely effective manœuvres of the Frenchman, disposed of the Hitler Jugend. This last skirmish brought them to a main road, to discover a concrete road block, which Sergt. Kington demolished at ten yards' range with a 6-pounder. At about the same time, No. 1 Squadron were fired on by bazookas in Billerbeck, but with the Canadians acting as terriers and the tanks as guns the bazooka-men stood no chance. All these incidents, however, had

1945 caused delay, and it began to seem doubtful whether the tanks could reach Graven in time to capture the bridge intact.

Both squadrons therefore pushed on even faster than before, and No. 1 Squadron covered the next ten miles in seventy-five minutes. At first No. 3 Squadron, dashing along on a parallel road, kept abreast of them, but after about two hours they ran into a further road block at Darfeld. With the help of the local priest they eventually passed it, but by now it was obvious that they could never reach the bridge in time to capture it in daylight, and they remained at Darfeld for the night.

Everything now depended on No. 1 Squadron. In Altenburg, the last town before Graven, every house had its bits of white material strung out on a nondescript flagpole and all the windows were shuttered and barred. The deafening roar of the Churchill engines reverberated through the narrow streets, and the only sign of life came from the groups of paratroopers huddled together on the backs of the tanks. As they emerged on the eastern side of the town the light was fading, but they could just pick out the chimneys of Graven five miles away in the valley below.

There was a steep tarmac road leading down into the valley, and the tanks rushed hell for leather down it. As the leading troop were reaching the bottom, someone suddenly noticed a long column of enemy lorries fleeing for all they were worth along a road leading away to the north. In a flash the turrets of the whole squadron revolved round to the left and Besa fire streamed into the retreating Germans. But there was no time to stop. The tanks sped on through one village, then another, dealing on the way with an enemy staff car, fleeing bicyclists, and many other targets which the gunners could not resist. They never slowed down until they had reached the suburbs of Graven, five hundred yards from the bridge, where the paratroopers jumped off to rush forward and take it. In less than ten minutes it was in their hands—or so they thought, because only one bridge was marked on the map. But there were in actual fact two, and the one they had taken led on to an island in the middle of the Ems. Twenty minutes later there was a blinding flash, followed by a loud explosion, and the real bridge, three hundred yards up-stream, crashed into the water. They had been truly, if slightly prematurely, April-fooled! But, to a small extent, the column got their own back on the Germans that night, for, just after the bridge was blown, a passenger train came steaming into Graven carrying German soldiers on leave from the Russian front. The Canadians allowed them to kiss their wives and then promptly marched them off to spend their leave in a prisoner-of-war cage.

The Ems was the first of the three water barriers which stood in the way of the British Second Army as it struck across Northern Germany after the crossing of the Rhine. The second was the Weser, sixty miles to the east. Could the 4th Battalion repeat their triumph and lead the Second Army to that river too? It all depended on how quickly the sappers laid a Bailey bridge at Graven, and the next morning No. 1 Squadron waited impatiently for them to do so. Around midday, No. 2 Squadron, who had been left far behind by the previous day's advance, caught up again and No. 3 Squadron arrived soon afterwards from Darfeld. There was a certain amount of shelling going on and some refugees scared everyone by reporting that a strong party of Germans were lurking in the forest near by and were blacking their faces as if preparing for a night attack. In view of the fact that the nearest troops to the right were the rest of the 6th Guards Armoured Brigade driving on Munster and the 11th Armoured Division were a long way away on the left, this caused a certain amount of alarm. The paratroopers started to prepare defensive positions and in due course a party of Hitler Jugend made an attack on the Airborne Headquarters. It was about as effective as an exhibition patrol at a Boy Scouts' jamboree, and, apart from a few odd shells, nothing more formidable materialized.

There was a large factory in Graven and in it was an enormous quantity of stores, varying from small fur coats and cigars to household utensils. It was obvious that the Germans were highly trained in the art of looting, and the factory was soon seething with liberated prisoners of war from many countries, determined to have their share of these luxuries of which they had been deprived for so long. Battalion Headquarters had seen a lot of these prisoners during the previous two days and their party was now assuming Fred Karno proportions. They would enter a large farm or public-house and try to shove the German inhabitants into the cellar, while from another cellar would appear a cosmopolitan collection of liberated prisoners of war and everyone would stand in the middle of the room talking their heads off in their several languages, congratulating everybody, often including the Germans.

Early the next morning Nos. 1 and 2 Squadrons moved across the newly constructed bridge and went five miles farther on to the edge of the Dortmund—Ems Canal. All the bridges had been blown, and they had to wait for another twenty-four hours for the sappers to do their work. After three years' attention from the R.A.F. there was very little water left in the canal, but at this point it was about a hundred and twenty feet wide and the Bailey bridge was not ready before 10 o'clock the next morning. No. 2 Squadron crossed over immediately and went

1945 with all haste towards Lengerich, a large modern town about eight miles from the canal. They were fired on as they approached the town, but they continued and started to climb up a large wooded hill directly behind it. Here several self-propelled guns, together with the non-commissioned officers' wing of the Hanover Training School, shot at the squadron and knocked out two tanks, luckily without causing any casualties. The Germans were in such a strong position that by the law of the survival of the fittest they should have been able to rout the whole column. But the paratroopers were so fearless and so skilful that in less than an hour the majority of the non-commissioned officers from Hanover were on their way back to a prisoner-of-war cage.

Continuing the leap-frogging movement which had proved so successful previously, No. 3 Squadron then passed through to capture the high ground slightly farther east. Before they could do this, however, they had to destroy an 88-mm. gun which had been holding up No. 2 Squadron. Major I. J. Crosthwaite decided to give Sergt. Huxley's troop this task, and, supported by fire from self-propelled guns attached to the squadron, he moved off towards it. He had not gone more than a hundred yards when the German gun hit his tank right in the centre of the turret. Another equally well-aimed shot arrived a few seconds later—luckily both were high explosives—so Sergt. Huxley and his crew immediately baled out, just before another four shots completely knocked out the tank. It was obvious that No. 3 Squadron could not go on, so Lieut.-Colonel Darling, the Commanding Officer of the 12th Parachute Battalion, led an attack on the 88-mm. himself, while the squadron fired on another gun which had opened up to the right. Colonel Darling's attack went perfectly and not only knocked out the 88-mm. and a 20-mm. gun but killed seven Germans and took fourteen prisoners. After this Colonel Darling said he did not need the tanks any longer and they harboured for the night while he led a patrol another six miles towards Osnabruck.

At 7 o'clock in the evening the Devons, of the 6th Airlanding Brigade, were counter-attacked on the outskirts of Lengerich by the remainder of the Hanover non-commissioned officers. At first the Germans made some progress and Lieut. The Hon. L. G. H. Russell's troop had some hard fighting, but they were eventually held. When No. 1 Squadron moved up to Lengerich during the afternoon, half of the squadron went across a bridge which they mistakenly took to be Class 40. It was a remarkable structure and withstood the strain of the first few tanks, but when Lieut. A. MacR. Collie was half-way across it snapped and deposited the tank and its crew into the stream. This was exceedingly amusing for everyone except the five dripping objects which emerged from the sinking ship.

The squadrons were now eighty miles from the Rhine, and it had 1945
become quite obvious that the Germans had been completely engulfed
by the speed of the advance and had no hope of organizing a defensive
line before the next water barrier, the Weser. And so, on the 3rd of
April, Nos. 1 and 3 Squadrons led off towards Osnabruck, No. 1 going
south to bypass it and cut off the southern escape routes, and No. 3
to threaten it from the west.

No. 3 Squadron carried the 13th Parachute Battalion up to where Apr. 3
the 12th Battalion had advanced the night before—a point about
fifteen miles from Osnabruck. As soon as they arrived Lieut. J. N. R.
Hearne's troop helped the infantry to clear up two small positions
which had been causing trouble during the morning, and when this
small action was over the column started off for Osnabruck. It was
reported that two thousand Germans were attempting to defend the
road to Osnabruck, and so the tanks were spread out across the main
road with two companies of infantry on either side. Although the
ground was soft and the going difficult, the tanks moved forward with
great speed. Except for one small pocket of resistance which was soon
dealt with, no trouble arose until the squadron were approaching the
outskirts of Osnabruck. Here the tanks were forced to revert to the
road and soon afterwards they ran into a road block. It was very
lightly defended, and the paratroopers proceeded to tear it down.
This they did remarkably quickly, and the column was soon under
way again on the last lap of the day's march. As soon as they reached
the built-up area, however, they were met by volleys of 20-mm. fire.
This was gradually cleared, but when Major-General Bols (6th Airborne Division) arrived on the scene he decided that it would be
necessary to bring up Brigadier Mills-Roberts's Commando Brigade
to take Osnabruck during the night. Plainly the Germans intended to
make some sort of a stand in the town, and the narrow streets were
totally unsuitable for tank fighting. Lieuts. J. N. R. Hearne and J. H.
Patrick continued for a while to help the paratroopers in the western
suburbs, but at 5 o'clock they were called back. The squadron requisitioned a nearby hotel and remained there for the next thirty-six
hours.

While No. 3 Squadron had been fighting on the road to Osnabruck
No. 1 Squadron with the 3rd Parachute Brigade were making swift
headway farther to the south. Their route carried them through hilly,
wooded country along lanes as narrow and twisty as they are in
England. The squadron were shot at about five times by anti-aircraft
88's which had once defended the perimeter of Osnabruck, but the
guns were inaccurate and it was always their swan-song. Just as it was
growing dark and the squadron had already advanced about thirty

1945 miles, they overran some Germans fleeing pell-mell in horse-drawn carts. A few bursts of Besa soon brought this hurried withdrawal to an end, but as the road was very narrow and the axles of the carts had collapsed the squadron were delayed for some minutes. The paratroopers, however, lost no time in shoving the carts off the road and by 8 o'clock in the evening the Group had reached Wissengen, where they halted for the night, after an advance of thirty-five miles. It was an ink-black night and the half-tracks which had to return for petrol and ammunition had a terrifying journey back through the lanes which twisted through the woods. A single error of map reading might have been fatal, as only the route which the tanks had taken was known to be clear of the enemy. They would have been easy prey for enemy ambushing parties.

Apr. 4   At 9 o'clock on the 4th Nos. 1 and 2 Squadrons and Battalion Headquarters started off *en route* for Minden, a distance of forty-two miles. The two squadrons were separated by a long, wooden ridge, on either side of which the country was richly cultivated and studded with freshly painted farms, and here and there the remains of great medieval castles. No. 1 Squadron covered the first ten miles in fifty-eight minutes. The only opposition came from odd Germans who took a pot-shot at the tanks and then either fled down a side-road or slipped into a house for protection. Consequently, quite a number of houses were demolished—a few bursts of Besa directed at the roofs soon reduced them to smouldering ruins. Every now and then little boys of thirteen and fourteen sniped at the infantry and, having injured a few Englishmen, came running out with a white handkerchief expecting to receive surrender terms. Very often they were half-dressed in civilian clothes. At first their youth had protected them, but now that they had taken to firing bazookas they were dealt with in the same way as any other person using these weapons.

After making steady progress for about twenty miles, the leading troop of No. 1 Squadron saw some figures working frantically on a large bridge across the main road to Minden. The drivers accelerated and, on reaching the bridge, a German engineer unit was discovered to be trying to blow it with a 500-lb. bomb. They offered no resistance and helped the paratroopers to disconnect the fuse wires. While this was going on, Brigadier Hill, the Commander of the 3rd Parachute Brigade, saw a German in a neighbouring house talking on the telephone. His driver whisked out his revolver and shot the man through the arm, thus obviously preventing the enemy authorities in Minden from being informed of the sudden arrival of the tanks. After this incident all telephone wires were cut as soon as a place was taken, because otherwise any German in occupied territory could pick up the telephone and pass back valuable information to the German 1945 Army.

Having saved the bridge, the squadron then turned right and carried on with all speed to Lubbecke,* a small manufacturing town in which not a single German put in an appearance. The shops were full of goods and there were cars parked in the streets—it all seemed so peaceful that it was hard to believe that this town was now in the front line. A few minutes after the squadron had left Lubbecke on the last lap to Minden, No. 2 Squadron came through the town, having emerged from the other side of the ridge. Early in the morning they had encountered a strong enemy position, but, after a sharp engagement, had broken through and come on at record speed to catch up with No. 1 Squadron. They now proceeded in a northerly direction to Alsleden, where they prepared to advance early on the 5th to seize a bridgehead over the Weser at Petershagen.

No. 1 Squadron made straight for Minden. There were rather more machine-gun nests in the houses on either side of the road now (even though many of them were sporting white flags), and so rather more houses went up in flames. There were also two road blocks in their path, but in each case a way was found around them. On the right there was a steep range of wooded hills stretching to the Weser, and a single 88-mm. firing down from them might have caused havoc among the thin line of tanks speeding along below. But the risk had to be taken, and the squadron hurried forward to the outskirts of Minden. As they came over the brow of a small hill overlooking the valley of the Weser, they saw four self-propelled guns and a Panther bolting back into the town from a factory. They engaged them and then pressed on.

About four hundred yards from the Weser itself there was a bend in the road with houses on either side, and when Lieut. I. C. Minnette-Lucas's tank came round it one of the self-propelled guns opened fire. He was just starting to reverse when, by the most unlucky shot in the world, he and the crew of his turret were killed. The self-propelled gun, which was a short-barrelled 75, had fluked a shot right on to the turret ring; as the tank was a Mark VII the shot could have hit any-where else and the occupants would have been safe. When this happened it was only about 2 o'clock in the afternoon, but Brigadier Hill ordered the tanks to halt. Having reached the objective for the day so early, there was no point in risking further lives on the last three hundred yards, especially as an infantry attack at dusk would almost certainly capture the town itself without any difficulty. They had

---

*Lubbecke was later to become the headquarters of the British Control Commission.

1945 come forty-two miles in five and a half hours—the swiftest opposed advance ever made by a Churchill squadron. The "experts" who had claimed that Churchills could never compete with an armoured division had been proved manifestly wrong.

While the Group were waiting on the outskirts of Minden, an American liaison officer arrived at Brigadier Hill's headquarters in a jeep, having driven over the range of hills on the right. He was from the American First Army and reported that American tanks also were preparing to enter Minden from the south. There was a story which was circulated in the British Press that the Americans had arrived in Minden and were opening negotiations with the Burgomaster for the surrender of the town when Churchills started firing into it and broke up the proceedings. Needless to say, the story is quite untrue; but, if it had been, it would have provided a curious example of history repeating itself, because one hundred and eighty-six years before, on the very same spot, the British Army was guilty of bad liaison with its allies. At that time British forces mistook an order from a German general and instead of merely moving close up to the French cavalry line, they dashed straight at it, attacked and overthrew it. This move, according to the ideas of the time, was sheer tactical lunacy and succeeded only because of the valour of the infantry, three thousand of whom were killed. The British Army must have profited from this lesson, because when it captured Minden that night for the second time in history not a single man was killed.

Now that a crossing was assured over the Weser even the gloomiest pessimist knew at the bottom of his heart that the Germans could not hold out much longer. Like a giant octopus with its tentacles gripping anything within reach, General Eisenhower's armies were rapidly squeezing the life out of the few German divisions which could be spared from the Russian front. In the north the Canadian Army was wheeling to cut off the German garrison in Holland. The British Second Army was heading for the great ports of Hamburg and Bremen and eventually Denmark. The American Ninth and First Armies, having cut off the Ruhr, were making a dash due east for the Elbe. General Patton's Third Army was streaking towards Bavaria. The American Seventh Army and the French under Tassigny were cutting deep into Hitler's mythical Southern Redoubt. And along the whole of the Eastern Front the Russian steam-roller was pounding steadily forward.

In Northern Germany the warm spring sun poured down on the advancing divisions. They were plunging into one of the most rural parts of Germany. Once Munster and Osnabruck had been taken,

Hanover and the ports were the only large cities between them and 1945
the Baltic. The country was thickly dotted with small villages composed of gaily painted, half-timbered farmhouses which the inhabitants shared with their livestock. The people had obviously had an
easy war; the R.A.F. had paid little attention to them until just recently, and even then they had not suffered heavily, because railways
had been the chief objectives and the resulting chaos had left more
food for the villages. Now the inhabitants had merely to put up a
liberal display of white flags, retire to their cellars while the tanks
came through, and, with any luck, they would emerge to find their
homes unscathed. They seemed to treat the invasion of their country
so casually that at first it was difficult to believe that they had been
even indirectly connected with the war.

But very soon it turned out that for several years they had been
enjoying the fruit of former Nazi victories. In nearly every village
which the tanks passed through there were waiting for them on the
roadside little groups of men and women who cheered and waved
and threw flowers in a manner which brought back memories of the
welcome received when France and the Low Countries were liberated. At first our men were suspicious, anxious not to acknowledge
the greetings of any fawning Germans, but soon suspicion turned to
sympathy and sympathy to action as it became evident that these
people were not Germans but slave workers transported from every
country in Europe to toil for German masters. They were a pathetic
sight, ill-clothed and emaciated, pitifully grateful for their liberation.
These "displaced persons," as they were called, were later to become
one of the major problems facing the British Army. For the moment,
together with thousands upon thousands of released Allied prisoners,
they crowded the roads, getting away as fast as they could to the
dispersal points from which they hoped to be taken back to their
homes.

It was against this background of a prosperous and seemingly
innocent agricultural country, revealing at every turn of the road
further evidence of Nazi crimes, that the 4th Battalion fought their
last battles with the 6th Airborne Division. Compared with Normandy, Holland and the Ardennes, it was easy going. At times it was
a joy-ride for everyone except the leading troop. For them the danger
and suspense were never-ending. They never knew that round each
bend of the road and over each hill an 88 was not waiting for them.
And whereas previously every tank in a squadron had run an almost
equal chance of being hit, the leading troop now knew only too well
that it would be they and they alone who would suffer whenever a
German gun position was approached.

1945 Perhaps the greatest burden of all during these swift advances fell on the echelons. No matter how far a squadron advanced in a day, petrol and ammunition had to be brought up to them at night. It was only by the greatest ingenuity and hard work that this was done. On one occasion Major J. P. T. Boscawen, who was responsible for the 4th Battalion's supplies, was heard to remark : "Well, there is nothing else for it: the tanks simply must not fire today and, what is more, they must not move far either." But never once were the tanks let down.

Apr. 5-6 After taking Minden, the Battalion had to wait for two days near the banks of the Weser while a bridge was being constructed across it. During this pause, No. 3 Squadron came up from Osnabruck, covering the sixty-seven miles in under eight and a half hours. On the 7th of April, in glorious spring weather, the advance began again. No. 3 Squadron broke out of the bridgehead which No. 2 Squadron had helped to effect just north of Minden two days before and set off on the first stage of the journey to the Elbe. Their objective was the high ground overlooking the River Leine near Neustadt, and they had been given orders to patrol to Bordenau, three miles to the south, where they were to make an attempt to seize the bridge. If they could manage to do this, probably a day's delay would be avoided, as it would take the sappers at least that amount of time to build a new one. Bordenau was nearly thirty-five miles away.

Apr. 7 The day started unpropitiously. Four tanks broke down before crossing the Weser, another fell out later, and only two troops and the squadron leader's tank were left to take part in the day's work. There was a delay at the bridge and the tanks carrying the last two companies of the 12th Parachute Battalion took a wrong turning. Everything seemed to be going wrong.

As soon as the tanks passed through the paratroopers who had been defending the bridgehead perimeter they were met by Spandau fire coming from houses scattered along the road. Lieut. J. N. R. Hearne, who was in the lead, set fire to the houses one by one and the leading platoon dealt with the occupants when the heat forced them to evacuate their hide-outs. About forty prisoners were taken, but valuable time had been lost in doing so.

As soon as they could the paratroopers climbed back on to the tanks and the column set off again. The next village provided a few rifle shots and apparently instilled caution into the reconnaissance unit in front, who had never had experience of this type of fighting before. The expedient of bumping the leading tank into their last vehicle was tried and resulted in a desperate gain of fifty yards.

Finally, the squadron leader walked in front of their leading vehicle 1945 and made it perfectly plain that he was determined to carry on through the village whether they wanted to or not. The effect was electrical. From that moment the ball started to roll. With Lieut. Hearne in the lead, the column swept through village after village, going faster the whole time. On two occasions the leading platoon were dismounted at the threat of opposition, but none materialized except in the form of a mass of surrendering Wehrmacht. Wunsdorf was skirted amid cheers from French prisoners, and the column led on to the aerodrome, two miles north of the town. Here one of the armoured cars got into trouble and Lieut. Hearn rushed up to their help. The opposition consisted of small-arms fire, 22-mm. flak guns and some form of bazooka. These were quickly routed out by the leading platoon and by Lieut. Hearn on his feet bowling hand grenades.

It was then discovered that the armoured cars had overshot a turning which the squadron should have taken and the whole column was turned about, with Lieut. P. D. Ault and Sergt. Byron in the lead. By now the slow start of the morning had been handsomely redeemed and it was decided that the tanks, with the leading company of infantry on board, should go flat out for the bridge. The column set off at full speed along the winding road, the tanks almost skidding into the ditches because they were going so fast. Suddenly the bridge loomed in sight six hundred yards ahead. It was intact, so the drivers accelerated. Lieut. Ault was a hundred yards ahead, and the rest of the squadron was bunched together behind the squadron leader. A lorry appeared on the bridge, a man jumped out, to be met by a curtain of fire from the tanks. Everyone shouted and yelled, particularly Colonel Darling, who was perched on the back bin of Major Crosthwaite's tank. The wireless was a babble of entreaties to go faster. Lieut. Ault roared and twisted round the corners. Major Crosthwaite was doing eighteen miles per hour and not gaining an inch. Tracer was flicking up and down the bridge. At any moment it might go up. In a flash two tanks were over. Colonel Darling leapt down, charged at a pile of aerial bombs in the centre and wrenched away the demolition wires. The bridge was safe!

In ten minutes the village on the other side of the river had been cleared of the enemy, the crossing secured and renamed "Grenadier-Yorkshire Bridge." Although not as large, but quite as attractive architecturally, as the other Grenadier Bridge at Nijmegen, it was none the less taken without the loss of a single man. Leaving the troops to hold it, No. 3 Squadron dashed to the assistance of the 7th Parachute Battalion, who were in trouble on the airfield near by. A collection of Hitler Jugend and a few rather antiquated ground personnel

1945 were putting up an astonishingly spirited display of small-arms fire. With the arrival of the tanks, however, their zeal was somewhat damped, and in a few minutes they had been rounded up. The aerodrome was very modern and there were a number of the latest types of German fighter planes parked on it. But by far its most surprising characteristic was a brothel equipped with a war establishment of eight Lithuanians!

Apr. 8 Early on the 8th No. 1 Squadron captured Wunsdorf with the Canadian Parachute Battalion. The tanks remained in the town while the Reconnaissance Regiment went about two miles farther on to take a bridge over a tributary of the Leine which flowed down to Hanover. As was expected, the armoured cars found the bridge undefended and they settled down quite happily to await the arrival of an American armoured division which was to cross the river and encircle Hanover from the north. After they had been waiting for about two hours it was suddenly discovered that between them and the tanks there was a German tank and a self-propelled gun and some German infantry. How the armoured cars had missed them remained a mystery. No. 1 Squadron immediately went in to the attack with the Canadians. One of the Canadian sergeants was overheard giving out his orders: "I guess we gotta get this bridge and if we hit anything don't you guys sit around. Let's go." They certainly did not sit around and the Germans reluctantly retreated. In so doing, however, they overran the armoured cars and the occupants had to hide in the woods until the tanks arrived. Happily no lives were lost as a result of the incident, but it was a perfect example of how the Germans used a couple of tanks and a few infantry to slow down for a short time the advance across Germany.

Apr. 9-10 The 4th Battalion were now only about ten miles north-west of Hanover, and it was intended that they should remain where they were until the Americans had captured the city. The tanks were in great need of maintenance, as they had come nearly two hundred and fifty miles with only the most minor adjustments being made to them each night. So Battalion Headquarters and the Headquarters of the 6th Airborne Division took up residence in two hotels on the shore of the Steinhude Meer and the squadrons soon made themselves comfortable in villages round about. Four days' rest had been promised, and many tank crews began to strip down gearboxes and final drives which take a considerable time to put together again. Inevitably, on the evening of the second day Nos. 1 and 2 Squadrons were suddenly ordered to go forward another six or seven miles the following morning to enlarge the bridgehead over the Leine. The remainder of the 6th Guards Armoured Brigade, with the 15th (Scottish) Division, was expected

at any moment to take over the advance, and it was considered essen- 1945
tial that they should have more room to form up when they arrived.

By working hard for part of the night the tank crews managed to Apr. 11-
17
have their tanks ready in time for the bridgehead to be expanded early
the next morning. Their task proved to be an easy one. Only a handful
of Germans put in an appearance and by midday both squadrons had
reached the main road running due north from Hanover. Here they
settled down to continue with their interrupted maintenance. Major-
General Bols, the Commander of the 6th Airborne Division, paid
visits to all the squadrons during the next two days and thanked them
for everything they had done to help the paratroopers. It looked as
if the 4th Battalion and the 6th Airborne would soon part company,
but as it turned out this did not happen for some considerable time.
Nevertheless, they now ceased to lead the advance of the British
Army. Having covered two hundred and forty miles in twelve days,
and having been the first to reach the Ems, the Dortmund—Ems
Canal as well as the Weser, they now handed over to the Coldstream
and the Scots Guards battalions of the 6th Guards Armoured Brigade,
who were to carry the 15th (Scottish) Division on to the Elbe. They
deserved a rest.

3

REES TO THE APPROACHES TO BREMEN

1ST AND 2ND BATTALIONS

*Contrast between operations of the Guards Armoured Division and the
6th Guards Armoured Brigade—Hold-up at Aalten—Slow advance to
Enschede—Attack on Bentheim—Crossing of the Ems at Lingen—
Advance through wooded country to Kloppenburg*

There were two wars raging in Northern Germany during April,
1945. One was the type the 4th Battalion were fighting, a war of
infrequent casualties, of long, stimulating, daily advances, immensely
exciting, almost enjoyable, the sort of warfare that captures the imagination of the masses. The other was neither exciting nor stimulating,
not a light-hearted adventure but a calculated slogging match, the kind
of fighting that wastes lives and, because it is so unspectacular, receives scant attention from the Press. It was in the latter that the
Grenadier Group became involved after they had crossed the Rhine,
and the curious thing about it was that the route they followed gener- *See Map*
p. **248**
ally ran parallel to the 4th Battalion and was seldom more than
twenty or thirty miles to the north.

Q

1945   Why there should have been so much difference between the resistance the Germans offered on the two axes is easy to explain in the light of past events. In the first place, whereas the 4th Battalion had been confronted by the tattered remnants of the parachute divisions caught by the airborne landings behind Wesel, the Grenadier Group were up against the I Parachute Corps, which, although severely depleted, was still sufficiently well organized to fall back according to a preconceived plan. In the second place, the countryside through which the road to Bremen passed was ideal for defence: instead of being flat and open, as it was to a large extent between Wesel and Hanover, it was heavily wooded and, what was more important, so close to sea-level that once the tanks moved off the road they ran the risk of sticking in the fields, most of which were water-logged by irrigation. But when they crossed the Rhine the Group were still living in a fool's paradise: they had been led to believe that they would soon break the crust of the German resistance, and that then their journey to Bremen, nearly two hundred miles away, might rival in speed their dash from Normandy to Nijmegen of the previous year.

Mar. 30   The Group had a foretaste of what they were to go through during April on the very day they crossed the Rhine. Brimming over with enthusiasm, they threaded their way through the tumbled chiaroscuro of Rees, struck north though Anhalt, swung east behind the front line held by the 51st Division, and then turned north again at a cross-roads just west of Bocholt (which was still being hotly contested). So far there had been hardly a mutter from the Germans and they bounded forward again in the sanguine belief that they would reach their goal for the day—Enschede, a large Dutch manufacturing centre—with equivalent ease. They had come nearly fifteen of the thirty-five miles to Enschede already and, after all, the 4th Battalion, during their first day in Germany proper, had covered twenty-eight miles without a scratch only a short distance to the south-east. But soon the Group caught sight of the first example of the German delaying tactics with which they were shortly to become so well acquainted—a hefty road block, cunningly protected by a carpet of felled trees and mines. They had no sooner plodded through a muddy field round this object than something much worse loomed up four hundred yards ahead—a trinity of huge craters spanning the entire breadth of the road just where the country on either side was particularly boggy. So it went on. After four miles of chasing the elusive frontier as it weaved its way backwards and forwards across the road, they arrived at the small township of Aalten, just inside Holland, to find that most of the bridges leading into it were blown and that there was yet another gaping crater blocking the main road.

The situation looked bad, but Major N. E. W. Baker soon found a 1945
bridge still partially intact and he led the King's Company across it,
into the town itself. They had not gone more than two hundred and
fifty yards, however, before they came under intense 88-mm. fire
which made it almost impossible for the platoon commanders to
control their men. In the course of a few minutes four officers fell
victim not only to this weapon but to snipers and mortars as well:
Lieuts. R. B. Joly and J. A. C. Duncan were killed, and Major Baker
and Lieut. M. S. Bayley were seriously wounded. There could have
been no object in leaving the company in this valueless death-trap, so
the Commanding Officer ordered Capt. The Hon. S. D. Loch, M.C.,
who had taken over command of the King's Company, to withdraw
slightly to the bridge and then send a patrol east of the town, while
No. 4 Company did the same on the west.

The original plan for the day had miscarried so thoroughly by now
that the Group resigned themselves to spending the rest of the day
outside Aalten. When news arrived that the Irish Guards, who had
been trying to find a way round to the left, had not got farther than
the river either, further progress that day seemed more unlikely still.
But during the late afternoon the Commanding Officers heard from
civilians that, although there was still a small enemy garrison in the
town, the main route through it was not being defended. They therefore decided to rush through Aalten in the hope of seizing the high
ground about a mile to the north on the main road to Groenlo. In this
manœuvre the Group were not impeded. Lieut. M. Stoop, of No. 2
Squadron, captured a small bridge in the north of the town just as the
Germans were leaving for Winterswrjk, and after sweeping through
a howling arcade of civilians lining the streets the Group were soon
established on the hill.

From Aalten the main road to Enschede sweeps north-east in a Mar. 31
wide arc through Groenlo and Eibergen. Early on the 31st the Grenadier Group set forth along it, still hoping to make a real dent in the
enemy line. Their tanks were again leading the armour of the Division, the Household Cavalry being the only troops in front. As on the
previous day, craters and road blocks made a smooth journey impossible, but partly because the obstructions were situated in less
awkward places and partly because the Group had by now reduced
circumnavigating them to a fine art, it did not at first lack speed. By
10 o'clock they were approaching Groenlo, a quaint medieval town
surrounded by a pentagonal moat.

They had been warned that the Germans had formed a thin defensive crust round the town in thick woods on the southern outskirts and
that most of the bridges over the moat were blown. But the Group

1945 were not to be detained for long in Groenlo: the Germans in the woods willingly surrendered, a bridge was soon found over the moat, and No. 4 Company and No. 1 Squadron sped through the narrow streets with only desultory fire from snipers detracting from the welcome of the Dutch burghers. After they had fought their way across a bridge in the northern suburbs, a German gun suddenly opened up and Lieut. T. H. Birchall and a Guardsman were wounded, but even this did not cause a bottleneck in Groenlo because the Household Cavalry had explored the byroads to the east and the whole Battalion was able to slip past the guns and follow the Household Cavalry round to rejoin the main road two miles north of the town.

It was at Eibergen, the last big town before Enschede, five miles farther on, that the Group ran into really serious opposition. Here, on the southern outskirts, an anti-tank gun destroyed the leading tank of No. 3 Squadron, and although they jockeyed for position for a good ten minutes trying to find a way round, by the time the rest of the Group came up the advance had been brought to a standstill. Light was failing fast, so the Group Commander immediately sent the King's Company and two troops of No. 2 Squadron round to the east of the town, hoping that they would seize bridges over the river and relieve the pressure on No. 2 Company. As they edged their way forward the enemy observed them and they were heavily mortared, Capt. The Hon. S. D. Loch, M.C., being wounded in the thigh and having to relinquish his shortly held command to Capt. W. M. Robson, second-in-command of No. 3 Company. After a while the enemy calmed down and at nightfall the King's Company were firmly established on No. 2 Company's right, the richer for seventy-five ill-assorted prisoners. But the setbacks which the Group had experienced both that day and the day before had convinced the Commanding Officers that it was no longer any use trying to crash through opposition without careful plans being made beforehand. The Group had not been able to "break out" in the sense that they had after crossing the Seine in 1944, and speed would have to give way to a more plodding method of advance. It was disappointing, but there was no alternative if serious casualties were to be avoided.

After their engagement at Eibergen the Group set about finding harbour areas. No sooner had they done so than a carrier arrived from the 5th Brigade Headquarters with news that cut short their hopes of a good night's rest. That afternoon the 32nd Brigade, who had been moving parallel with the Group, had swung west of Eibergen and were already well beyond it, thereby threatening the rear of the enemy in the town, and making it practically certain that they

would withdraw to their native land during the night. The Irish 1945
Guards, whose turn it was to lead, were therefore to set off at the crack
of dawn to chase them. First, to make sure that the chase began on
the right foot, the crossings over the river would have to be secured,
and this task was given to the Grenadiers early that evening.

River crossings, however small the stretch of water, are seldom
simple and they require a lot of detailed planning if they are to progress smoothly. Rubber boats have to be brought from the echelons,
the men who are to travel in the various waves have to be chosen, and
the timing has to be synchronized down to the last second. To arrange
a crossing at such short notice as the Grenadier Group were given on
this occasion was therefore no easy matter, and it was further complicated by faulty wireless communication and the late arrival of the
boats. The attack was supposed to start soon after midnight, but there
were so many delays that it did not go in until 2.45 a.m. on the 1st of
April—the day of April Fools—in pouring rain. At first it seemed as
if the Irish Guards would never get through the following morning
because No. 3 Company found the main road bridge a tumbled ruin
and No. 4 Company could give no more encouraging report about a
bridge over a minor road in the west of the town. It had been thought Apr. 1
that these were the only possible places where the Irish Guards could
cross, but by a stroke of good fortune No. 2 Company, after paddling
across the river three hundred yards east of the town, came upon a
bridge beside a sluice-gate, unmarked on the map and undamaged by
the enemy, which was capable of bearing the weight of the heaviest
tank. With this crossing safely in their hands, the Group had accomplished their mission and they were able to settle down for the rest of
the night, dug in around their respective bridges in the comforting
knowledge that the Germans had already beaten a hasty retreat.

The Irish Guards passed through early in the morning heading for Apr. 1-2
Enschede and the German border, and the Grenadier Group fell in
behind to enjoy a comparatively peaceful two days. With time to look
around them, the Group noticed with admiration the speed with which
Corps Headquarters were following the leading troops: the Group
were never far behind the Irish Guards, yet the Corps telephone lines
were always laid ahead of them. Another novelty was the presence of
Military Government officers who were attached to the Battalions,
charged with the task of distributing pamphlets and proclamations as
soon as a town was occupied. Amongst their impedimenta was a half-
track carrying a battery of loud-speakers, which were used for a
multitude of purposes, from calling on the enemy to surrender, to
haranguing the local populace as the vehicle toured the streets of a
newly won village. At this particular juncture they had little to do, as

1945 the advance was still cutting through Holland, but when it emerged once more into Germany they were immensely busy.

The first of these two days in reserve was pleasantly uneventful, although it ended in a slight contretemps. The Irish Guards had decided that Enschede was much too big a town to be cleared in the few available hours of daylight, especially as there would be a brigade of the 3rd Division available for this purpose on the following day, and so the Grenadier Group were allowed to harbour early about three miles south of the town. Harbour parties were called for at dusk, and an hour later the main bodies followed up, met their guides, and turned off the road into the fields. It was only after all the vehicles had driven in that the appalling discovery was made that the ground was a peat bog. It was too late to do anything that night, but the next morning it took over four hours to pull all the vehicles out.

The Group's second day in reserve was less prosaic. They started off by following the Irish Guards again, but half-way through the morning they were suddenly ordered to send a force into Enschede to clear a road for priority bridging material. After what seemed a lifetime of backing and turning, a composite group of tanks and infantry were banded together, extricated from the column and sent dashing off to the very town that the Group had hoped to capture the day they crossed the Rhine. There had been reports of heavy opposition inside Enschede, but the force heard no cries for help and some time later it emerged on the farther side of the town, delayed a little, certainly, but by the liberated Dutch, not by the enemy. While Battalion Headquarters were waiting to hear the result of this foray into Enschede, they had lunch in a Dutch doctor's undamaged home. Some of the officers played with the electric-light switches like small boys, as it was the first lighting they had found in working order since Nijmegen in mid-February.

Meanwhile, the Irish Guards had quickly passed through Oldenzaal and were swinging east towards Germany. Over the border they found the road dominated by high ground to the east, near Gilderhaus and Bentheim, and the enemy soon showed every intention of selling his frontier very dearly. As they were approaching Gilderhaus the Irish Guards lost several tanks to well-concealed self-propelled guns and fanatical paratroopers extravagantly equipped with bazookas, and throughout the day they were locked in bitter combat trying to force their way into the village. It was 4 a.m. before Gilderhaus was finally reported clear, by which time the Grenadier Group had long been safely harboured just inside the German frontier, ready to pass through the Irish Guards in the early morning and take over the lead.

Apr. 3   The Group had been over the Rhine for four days now and they had covered nearly fifty miles. But still the River Ems, the first big water 1945 barrier they would have to cross during the journey across Germany, was a few miles away. As the first Grenadier tank wound its way through the streets of Gilderhaus on the morning of the 3rd of April, heading for the Ems, the commander looked down at his map and, remembering the difficulties of the past few days, wondered how long he would follow the route marked on it, before the crash of an anti-tank shell shattered the sides of his turret.

Trouble came soon. Three hundred yards beyond the leading sections of the battle-weary Irish Guards, the first three tanks of Lieut. A. R. Harding's troop were knocked out by self-propelled guns and the Commanding Officers had to cope with the problem of two vehicle-bound Battalions strung out like a snake for several miles to the rear. The King's Company, nearest to the scene of the trouble, at once leapt out of their vehicles and drove the enemy out of two small woods in front. But in the copse near the railway on the right they met a self-propelled gun firing at point-blank range which forced them to retire. After this encounter the battle raged all morning, and before long Capt. W. M. Robson* had been wounded by a shell. Every time a new line of approach was tried a self-propelled gun popped up and took aim at the nearest tank. An officer in the 2nd Battalion had the misfortune to meet one such self-propelled gun round the corner of a wood. He hastily backed his tank, but he did not notice a ditch behind and the Sherman slid into it and overturned. Just at that moment the gunner fired the 75-mm. by mistake, and the rest of the crew, thinking that the tank had been hit, jumped out, only to land in six feet of icy water.

The Commanding Officers decided soon after midday to attack Bentheim, a town just to the east, built on an eminence, and surmounted by an impregnable-looking castle which would overlook any attempt the Battalions might make to reach the Ems. It was evident that the enemy were going to put up a stiff fight while they evacuated their troops over the river, so the Commanding Officers naturally expected that they would furiously defend this very defendable bastion. They therefore drew up a plan for a powerful attack on the town: No. 4 Company, on the right, with a troop of tanks in support, were to advance on either side of the road leading into Bentheim; No. 2 Company, on the left, with tanks also, were to move through the orchards on either side of the Enschede—Bentheim railway. The companies were to pause three times during the attack to allow the Leicestershire Yeomanry to fire barrages, the Wasp platoon were to be ready to burn

---

*Capt. Robson was the third company commander of the King's Company to be wounded in four days.

1945 down troublesome buildings, and the rest of the Group were to follow behind and block the western exits.

But for reasons best known to themselves, the Germans decided to give up Bentheim after offering only token resistance at its western approaches. The attack began at 3 p.m. and until they were six hundred yards from the town they saw no sign of the enemy at all. On the right, when No. 4 Company emerged from the shelter of the woods into open country, a number of tanks bogged and they met considerable Spandau and rifle fire from the houses in front. But Major T. Tufnell, the company commander, sent the carrier platoon, under Lieut. R. G. S. Gerard, down the road to engage the enemy in the houses and the company were soon able to advance over the open ground to the buildings in the south-western outskirts of the town, suffering only a few casualties. No. 2 Company, on the left, slipped through the orchards into the town with even less difficulty and henceforward it was plain sailing for them both. The Wasp crews, hitherto thwarted of an opportunity to commit arson, let their imagination run riot and set fire to building after building. Then the 25-pounders took up the tune, the tanks came up, and within twenty minutes Bentheim was taken. The only serious casualty in either of the two forward companies after they entered the town was No. 2 Company commander, Capt. The Duke of Rutland, who inadvertently released his captured automatic pistol at his foot and had to be evacuated. All told, the casualties amounted to only fifteen—among them Lieut. J. K. Daniel, of the 2nd Battalion, who was wounded—yet the Group had killed twenty-four Germans and captured fifty-two prisoners. That night, as the Group made good their gains, Bentheim glittered luridly: pin-points of fire dotted every part of the town, and the crackle of burning timber could be heard in each street.

Apr. 4 The next morning, after the King's Company and two troops of No. 2 Squadron had cleared the eastern half of Bentheim of its last remaining Germans, Combined Group Headquarters moved into the castle. It was built of granite and rose impressively above the town. The massive gateways were very narrow, so the tanks had to be left outside the main entrance, but all the other vehicles of the Headquarters were driven in and each Battalion took over a wing. It was discovered that there was a Prince von Bentheim, who had left in 1934, and his correspondence revealed that he had been a frequent visitor to court functions in England, but where he was at that moment remained a mystery. Huge packing cases full of china, silver, glass and linen lay littered all over the public rooms, but only the wine in the cellars was claimed as booty of war. From the towers and rooftops of Bentheim the world seemed at peace: thinking they would remain in Bentheim for some time, the officers felt free to indulge in some **1945** sorely needed local government, and the Guardsmen sun-bathed. As they looked out for many miles over the flat country to the east they could pick out the white flags of surrender already fluttering from the windows of Schuttorf, a town on the banks of the Ems four miles away.

The Group had known for some time that the 154th Brigade, of the 51st (Highland) Division, would be brought up for the actual crossing of the Ems, and as they could see the white flags in Schuttorf, where the crossing was to take place, they imagined that they would be allowed to stay in Bentheim until it was over. But the Higher Command wanted to make quite sure that the 154th Brigade would not be detained in Schuttorf, and late that afternoon the Group received orders to advance into the town the next day. A Typhoon attack was timed to go in at dusk and a crowd of spectators from both Battalions gathered on the castle tower to watch the familiar black-smoke trails of the rockets criss-crossing over the sky, as machine after machine screeched down on the helpless town.

The castle tower was also put to good use when No. 2 Company and **Apr. 5-6** No. 3 Squadron set off for Schuttorf the next morning. Telephone lines and wireless cables were laid to the very top so that the Commanding Officers would be able to control the tanks like pawns on a chessboard. These grandiose preparations were soon thought to have been worth while, because when the Group disappeared from sight into some woods in front of Schuttorf, a call came over the air asking for artillery aid in dealing with an anti-tank gun. The 25-pounders quickly opened up and the column was seen to move on. But some minutes later the force commander, Capt. The Hon. W. N. Berry, was picked up on the air, revealing, much to his chagrin, that the anti-tank gun had turned out to be an ornamental cannon which had probably last seen service in the eighteenth century. And, a little later, he reported that, emboldened by this discovery, the Group had moved on to find the whole town a mass of white flags. The enemy troops had completely vacated the place, blowing the bridges over the Ems in their wake.

Soon after midday the Highlanders arrived for the assault crossing, and the force that had taken Schuttorf drove back to Bentheim to rejoin the Group. Within a few hours the Highlanders were safely across and infantry units of the XXX Corps were poured into the bridgehead. The 5th Brigade were supposed to go over on the 5th, but the bridgehead soon became so overcrowded that their departure was postponed for another twenty-four hours. They spent this extra day of leisure exploring the amenities of Bentheim, which counted among

1945 its luxuries a badhaus and a kurhaus for those who felt the urge to take the waters. Finally, early on the 7th, the Group, now last in the divisional column, left Bentheim and crossed over the turgid waters of the Ems.

Apr. 7-8   From Lingen, where the Grenadier Group and the majority of the XXX Corps crossed, there is a main road leading direct to Bremen, sixty-five miles away: it passes through only one big town, Kloppenburg, forty-five miles from Lingen, and it was to this place that the Guards Armoured Division were ordered to proceed. But instead of being sent north-east straight up the main road, they were made to go due west for about thirty miles and then strike north towards Kloppenburg—a journey of little less than a hundred miles.

This indirect approach to Kloppenburg involved the Division in some very close fighting. From the start, every advantage of terrain lay with the enemy: south of the main road the country was as flat as the Fenlands, and the great expanses of forest were relieved only by a plethora of small farming villages and by a few deep, lazy streams. There was little about the countryside that would have appealed to a lover of scenic beauty, but small detachments of soldiers intent on temporarily holding up an armoured advance could have asked for nothing better.

It took the Division six days in all to reach Kloppenburg. Of these the Grenadiers spent three in reserve, one sun-bathing and only two actually in action—a schedule which might invite the conclusion that they were subjected to no great strain. But quite apart from the fact that advancing through heavily wooded country is seldom less dangerous for the rear of the column than the head, or that the scorching sun and resulting dust were far from pleasant, or even that the two days in action were both expensive and exacting—quite apart from all this, the advance to Kloppenburg had a most unsalubrious effect on the Battalions' morale, for the simple reason that it rankled with them to know that in other parts of Germany other units were still speeding forward unhindered without hardly even having to fire a gun.

For the first two days of the advance, the 7th and 8th of April, the Irish Guards were in the lead and except for No. 2 Company and No. 3 Squadron—who were sent off late on the second afternoon to bypass Furstenau (where the 5th Brigade were to veer north-east towards Kloppenburg) and had to harbour prematurely because small bands of German infantry started popping into and out of the woods as it grew dark—the Group had no encounters with the enemy. On the 9th of April, however, the Group took over the lead and plunged into an exceptionally busy day.

They had three tasks in front of them: the first, which was given 1945
to No. 2 Company and No. 3 Squadron, as they had started on it the Apr. 9
night before, was to take Dalum and Bippen, both north-east of
Furstenau; the second was to take Schwagstorf, a village due east
of Furstenau, through which ran the main road to Bippen and See Map
Kloppenburg; the third was to cut this Schwagstorf—Bippen road p. 236
by advancing across country from Furstenau. It was hoped that this
three-pronged thrust would be completed by midday and that the
advance could then be continued towards Kloppenburg. But in Dalum
No. 2 Company and No. 3 Squadron ran into severe trouble which
balked the plans for the day.

They had been warned to expect trouble in Dalum, so when the
Spandaus opened up in the outskirts of the village Lieut. J. C. Moller,
the leading platoon commander, jumped on to the leading tank commander's Sherman to co-ordinate a plan. This was the normal proce-
dure on such occasions and it should not have been filled with any
particular danger. But just at that moment a hidden party of enemy
fired at Lieut. Moller and he was mortally wounded. And a moment
later Lieut. A. R. Ryan, whose tank Lieut. Moller was on, met
exactly the same fate. Having lost two officers in such rapid succession, Major A. M. H. Gregory-Hood (No. 2 Squadron) immediately
worked out a plan for a full-scale attack on Dalum. This progressed
very smoothly and the Group were soon established in Dalum, with
seventeen prisoners to look after. But the enemy had by now cut right
across the road behind the Group, and Major Gregory-Hood felt that
it would be unwise to go on towards Bippen. So the Group remained
in Dalum, completely isolated, until the following morning, by which
time Bippen had been captured.

No. 4 Company and No. 1 Squadron's attack on Schwagstorf was
a complete success. As they entered it from the west—No. 4 Company
commanded by Capt. J. R. M. Rocke in the absence of Major T.
Tufnell, on leave—they met a German force which had just arrived
in the village from the south. But they soon disposed of it, with a
profitable haul of prisoners, and set forth for Bippen. They had hoped
to go even farther on to Eggermuhlen, a village three miles to the
south-east, but dusk fell when they were still on the outskirts of
Bippen. As there appeared to be a considerable number of enemy
self-propelled guns in the vicinity, they were told to join the rest of
the Group in Klein Bokern, a small village on the Schwagstorf—
Bippen road which the King's Company and No. 2 Squadron had
captured during the morning without any untoward incidents. Here,
in constant trepidation lest the Germans in the surrounding woods
should decide to counter-attack, the Group spent the night.

1945
Apr. 10   At dawn the next morning the Group set to work to drive the Germans away from a further series of these troublesome villages north-east of Furstenau, so that the rest of the Guards Armoured Division would be able to pass through towards Kloppenburg. After a sharp struggle in the misty half-light, Bippen fell to No. 4 Company and No. 1 Squadron, and then, told by two foot-weary Germans that the enemy had withdrawn eastwards, the Group turned their attention to Eggermuhlen, No. 2 Company and No. 3 Squadron striking across country from Dalum, and No. 4 Company and No. 1 Squadron keeping to the road leading out of Bippen. After a still sharper struggle, Eggermuhlen fell too, but not before the troop commanded by Lieut. A. Jones had been caught in the open by a carefully concealed Jagd Panther, the officer and a number of his troop being killed.

These operations were completed by 1 o'clock and the Group then tackled their third task of the day, that of clearing Kettenkamp, a village two miles to the north, to which, prisoners reported, the enemy (of the 3rd Gross Deutschland Division) had made a hurried withdrawal. There was a large wood running just west of the road up to Kettenkamp, and when the King's Company were four hundred yards away from it they were met by intense small-arms fire as well as a few shots from an anti-tank gun which set fire to a tank of No. 2 Squadron. The weight of supporting fire from the tanks and the Leicestershire Yeomanry was sufficient for the company to close on the enemy, but it was nearly 6 o'clock before they were in possession of the wood. It took them so long because, for some reason, the Germans in the wood took it upon themselves to fight with uncommon stubbornness: several had to be evicted from fox-holes at the point of the bayonet, and two even went so far as to commit a European form of hari-kiri by pressing ignited grenades to their chests. These Germans, however, had no compatriots behind them to bolster their self-sacrifice: that night, harboured on a barren hillside near the wood, the Group sent patrols into Kettenkamp and found it deserted.

Apr. 11-
14   The attack on Kettenkamp was the Group's last major operational commitment on the road to Kloppenburg. The 51st (Highland) Division passed through on the 11th to continue the advance, and the Group spent the day lolling in the sun. Then, on the 12th and 13th, they fell in again behind the Irish Guards, who were fighting their way through another long list of drab villages nearer Kloppenburg— Berge, Menslage, Essen and Hemmelte by name. For a time it looked as if the Irish Guards would reach Kloppenburg by nightfall on the 13th, but at 5 p.m. they became hopelessly held up at Bevern, less than five miles south of the town. To make sure that this unexpected delay would not give the Germans falling back in front of the 32nd

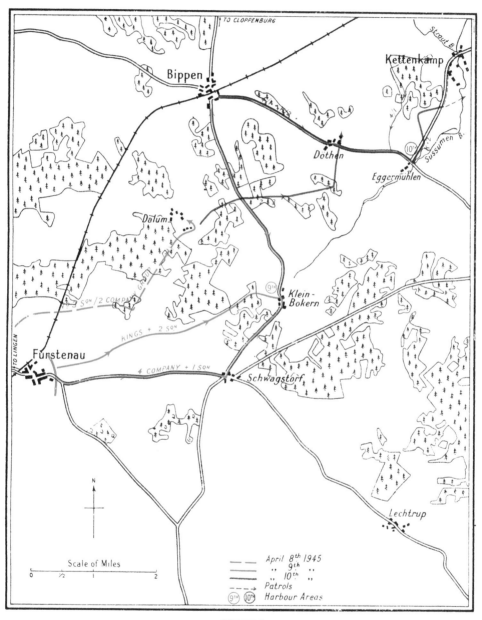

TO CLOPPENBURG

Kettenkamp

Scout 8.

Bippen

Dothen

Eggermuhlen

Sussumen B.

Dalum

Klein-Bokern

KINGS + 2 SQN

SQN / 2 COMPANY

TO LINGEN

Fürstenau

4 COMPANY + 1 SQN

Schwagstorf

Lechtrup

N

Scale of Miles

0   ½   1   2

April 8th 1945
  ,,   9th ,,
  ,, 10th ,,
Patrols
9th 10th Harbour Areas

BIPPEN

Brigade time to retreat northwards, the Grenadier Group were imme- 1945
diately ordered to send a force across country to cut the main Kloppenburg—Minden road at Schneiderkrug. This force, composed of the
King's Company, No. 2 Squadron and No. 2 Company, and commanded by Lieut.-Colonel P. H. Lort-Phillips, set out about an hour
before darkness. As they were nearing Schneiderkrug the leading
troop of No. 2 Squadron bumped into a small enemy anti-tank detachment which, having finished its day's work, was making a hurried
withdrawal. The squadron destroyed two of the anti-tank guns as well
as a lorry and three horse-drawn carts, but, as the burning and exploding wreckages effectively blocked the route, Lieut.-Colonel Lort-
Phillips decided that it was too late to reach Schneiderkrug and he
ordered the force to harbour where they were. When, the next morning, they pushed on to Schneiderkrug, the enemy had disappeared,
without sound or signal, into the blue.

4

THE END OF THE JOURNEY

The German Army crumbles—Strategy of the final phase—4th Battalion
encircle Uelzen—Reach the banks of the Elbe—The Guards Armoured
Division ordered to cut off Bremen from Hamburg—Attack on Zeven—
Liberation of the concentration camp at Sandbostel—4th Battalion reach
Lubeck—Link-up with the Russians—The end of the war in Germany

The arrival of the Grenadier Group in the Kloppenburg area coincided almost to the day with the end of the 4th Battalion's unbroken
advance with the 6th Airborne Division, and until the 16th of April
all three Battalions were left out of the line—the 1st and 2nd in two
villages south of Kloppenburg, called Halter and Garthe, and the 4th
Battalion in the villages they had captured about ten miles north of
Hanover. The strain on the Grenadier Group's fighting vehicles which
so many days in action had imposed had been equalled in the 4th
Battalion by sheer length of mileage, and there was hardly a Sherman
or a Churchill which was not in need of drastic maintenance. But it
was not really on this particular account that the three Battalions were
given time off in the middle of the campaign: it was for the more
general and infinitely more satisfactory reason that the German Army
in Northern Germany was showing signs of crumbling, and, like an
athlete nearing the end of the course, the 21st Army Group was busily
engaged in making sure of its second wind.

From the moment the 21st Army Group crossed the Rhine until

1945 just about this time, the overall direction of the advance had been fluid: within the limits imposed by Corps and Army boundaries the various divisions had been encouraged to race forward through Germany, deciding for themselves, as they came upon opposition, where and when to go next. The Higher Command had been feeling their way—and the results could hardly have been better. Now, three weeks after the Rhine crossing, the 21st Army Group was across the Ems and the Weser, and at no one point had the enemy resistance been powerful enough to hold up the advance for more than a few hours. In other words, so much had already been achieved that, like the needle on a weighing machine which fluctuates at first and then decides upon a definite number of avoirdupois, the planning for the final overthrow of Germany could now be carried on with more clear-cut intentions in view, and in less general terms than it had been before.

In reality, the Higher Command's scheme for this final phase of the war had as its primary object an early link-up with the Russians, who had renewed their offensive on the 15th of April and were already making handsome advances towards Berlin. But as there was still a sizeable German army left in Holland and as there was not the slightest reason for supposing that the great ports of Hamburg and Bremen would fall without a fight, the whole of the 21st Army Group could not be spared for this task. The Canadian Army had to be left behind west of Emden to seal off the Germans' Dutch garrison, and the 7th Armoured Division and the Guards Armoured Division had to be directed towards the Bremen—Hamburg area, leaving only the 11th Armoured Division, the 6th Guards Armoured Brigade and four infantry divisions for the link-up with the Russians. As events were to show, however, superiority in numbers counted for little at this stage of the campaign.

Apr. 16-
17   Indeed, the Germans were in such a hopeless position by now that their only hope of staving off an Anglo-Russian link-up was to make a firm stand on the Elbe. Already they were making frantic efforts to withdraw their troops across it, and even at Uelzen, the last big town on the western side of the river, where the rest of the 6th Guards Armoured Brigade had been fighting bitterly for several days, the German garrison was at last beginning to retreat. In order to forestall these German attempts to withdraw from Uelzen, the 6th Airborne Division, once again with the 4th Battalion of the Regiment, were ordered, on the 16th, to throw a steel ring round the town. This they did, with the help of the 11th Armoured Division, linking up with them on the evening of the 17th at Molsen, a small village three miles along the main road to the Baltic.

Surprisingly enough, the Germans hardly contested the encircling **1945** movement at all. In one or two villages which the 4th Battalion passed through bazooka teams put in fleeting appearances, but the self-propelled guns which had been left to support them were all found abandoned. The Germans seemed to have given up caring about their plight, as was shown by the attitude of a German colonel whom Lieut. McCallum found sun-bathing in his garden inside the ring. He did not bat an eyelid when the troop of Churchills drove on to his front lawn and lost no time in explaining how delighted he was to meet the Brigade of Guards again, as he stayed with the Coldstream for six months in 1911. He claimed to have sat on the board which examined the Churchill tanks captured at Dieppe, and reached the conclusion that the Germans had nothing to learn from British tank design. There was a certain irony in the fact that now, almost three years later, he was being taken prisoner by the very same tank, improved in no small measure by the experience gained at Dieppe.

Uelzen fell on the 18th of April and the 6th Guards Armoured **Apr. 18-** Brigade were given a short breathing space. Then all three Battalions **22** rushed on to the Elbe, the Scots Guards heading north, the Coldstream north-east, and the 4th Battalion, leaving the 6th Airborne Division* behind and joining up with the 5th Division, who had just arrived from Italy, going east. Fanning out in a large semi-circle, the nine squadrons of the Brigade had orders to deposit their infantry along a thirty-mile stretch of the River Elbe between Artlenburg and Dannenberg. By the afternoon of the 22nd they had accomplished their mission. Nowhere was there any really strong opposition, but the whole area was covered with woods which made perfect lairs for small parties of fanatics and sometimes enabled them to hold up a squadron for a few hours.

Probably No. 2 Squadron of the 4th Battalion suffered most from these groups—they consisted largely of Volkssturm† but quite often included civilians and even women—because they were advancing along the main road to the Dannenberg ferry, which was the last escape route open to the Germans. There were five well-concealed 88's on this road, and one of them, manned by female flak gunners, fired eight times at Capt. F. E. Clifford's tank without scoring a single hit! Sergt. Gardner, L./Cpl. Little and Gdsm. Stevens were killed during the operation and Lieuts. J. F. D. Johnston and A. J. R. Daven-

---

*The 4th Battalion hoped and expected to return to the 6th Airborne Division, but this was not to be. During the long journey from the Rhine to the Elbe there had been forged a bond of mutual friendship and respect which could scarcely have been stronger. The memory of the men in the maroon berets will linger for many years to come in the minds of the Grenadiers who fought with them, and the Pegasus flag which the Division later presented to the Grenadiers will remain as a permanent reminder of the days they had lived through together.

†The German equivalent of the Home Guard.

1945 port were wounded, but, as it turned out, they were the last casualties the Battalion were to suffer during the campaign. For, with the western banks of the Elbe firmly in the hands of the infantry, the Battalion were sent back to rest for over a week in Bevensen, and when finally they crossed the Elbe the German resistance had become completely innocuous.

Apr. 15-18 While the 4th Battalion were waiting in Bevensen for the infantry to cross the Elbe, the Grenadier Group were fighting in the Bremen—Hamburg area. They had expected to take part in an assault on Bremen with the XXX Corps, directed from Kloppenburg, but on the evening of the 15th of April plans were changed and the Guards Armoured Division were ordered to switch to the XII Corps and help it to prevent the Germans in Bremen from slipping out of the city to the north-east. The Grenadier Group were to cut the autobahn linking Bremen and Hamburg, and then capture Zeven, the only large communications centre in the Hamburg—Bremen peninsula, ten miles beyond the autobahn. This involved a move of some hundred miles, first south-east to Nienburg, on the main Bremen—Hanover road, where there was a bridge intact over the Weser, then north-east to Rethem to cross the Aller; and, finally, north-east again to Soltau, where they were to pass through the 7th Armoured Division, who had outposts just beyond. Long treks across country were nothing new to the Group by this time, however, and they arrived in Soltau on the evening of the 18th, little the worse for wear.

Apr. 19 The Group set about cutting the autobahn early the next morning, and it turned out to be a comparatively simple task. The great majority of the Germans in the area appeared to be withdrawing over the Elbe, and those who had been cut off by the 7th Armoured Division's advance were retreating rapidly into the Hamburg—Bremen peninsula. In fact, until they were almost in sight of the autobahn, the Group saw no Germans at all, although, thanks to the usual sequence of blown bridges, rotten road surfaces and indifferent opportunities for detours, their progress was slow. At Gross Sittensen, the last village before the autobahn, the two leading platoons took fifty-four prisoners, but by far the most important capture was that of the local telephone exchange. The line to Zeven was unfortunately cut, but a protracted and animated conversation with the postmistress of Gross Meckelsen, just across it, elicited the fact that the enemy had withdrawn to Zeven on the first approach of the tanks. Armed with this encouraging news, the Group swept across the autobahn and on to Gross Meckelsen, where, to their surprise, they discovered that the postmistress had been speaking the truth—anyhow, as far as her own village was concerned. Even more encouraged by this discovery, the

Group continued to Weertzen, four miles farther on, before total **1945** darkness brought their day's work to an end. By the time they harboured for the night they had not only cleared half of Weertzen but had also liberated a labour camp filled with French deportees.

Although the 19th of April had been an exceptionally profitable **Apr. 20** day for the Group, German resistance had been growing steadily stronger; so, before making a direct attack on Zeven, the Group were ordered to seize Heeslingen and Wiersdorf, the former two and a half miles north-east of the town and the latter two miles east of it. The attack on Wiersdorf was made by No. 2 Company and No. 3 Squadron, and it involved them in a very fierce battle that lasted for most of the day. Up to within scarcely a hundred yards of the village the going was easy, and it was only when the company were starting to clear it that trouble arose. The Germans had laid a trap with great cunning and as soon as the troop of tanks supporting the leading platoon approached the houses, all three were knocked out in rapid succession. In the crucial period that followed, Capt. T. P. A. Davies risked his life to save the crew of the leading tank, which was on fire, and every effort was made to continue forward. But a detour to the left was impossible owing to a thick wood, and so the next troop and two motor platoons had to make a wide sweep to the right in the hope of entering the village along the road leading down from Heeslingen. This manœuvre eventually led to success, but not before yet another tank had been knocked out.

The King's Company and No. 2 Squadron's attack on Heeslingen followed much the same pattern. The Germans had self-propelled guns in the village and, in the course of driving them away, Lieut. P. G. A. Prescott's tank ran over a mine, the officer himself being wounded. It was well into the afternoon before both villages were clear and even then they were hardly fit for habitation, as the enemy were pouring mortar shells into them with gradually increasing intensity. Wiersdorf soon presented a particularly sorry spectacle. Most of the houses had been hit by shell fire and some, which had been burnt out, were still smoking, while an odd flame licked an unconsumed beam. It was a dead village, and, as death can sometimes be, looked peaceful; but it was a false peace, for at frequent intervals self-propelled guns which had retired a mile or two towards Zeven opened up with a quick dozen shells which brought leaves fluttering down from the trees that grew amongst the gardens.

When evening came, the Group occupied a triangular position, with two firm feet in Wiersdorf and Heeslingen, and headquarters and reserves at the apex back in Weertzen. The Group's neck was well stuck out among the enemy; hostile sounds came from all sides, and it

R

1945 would have required only a little daring to slit their throat. Yet the worst that happened that night was that Lieut. R. King, who was bringing up the 2nd Battalion's forward supplies, rounded a corner and bumped into a Tiger tank; but the surprise was evidently mutual, as he escaped without damage to himself or his jeep.

Apr. 21-23   When the position was reviewed the next morning it was decided, for a variety of reasons, that it would be safer for the Group to postpone their attack on Zeven. The Irish Guards were having trouble on the left or southern flank, and farther to the south-east the 32nd Brigade were having a difficult time around Rotenburg; besides, the divisional artillery was not available, as it was all supporting the 32nd Brigade. But, in order not to waste time in the interval, the Group were ordered to find out as much as they possibly could about the enemy in and around Zeven.

The Irish Guards and the 32nd Brigade did not reach the Zeven area until the 23rd, so the Group had three days in which to investigate the enemy positions. Patrols were sent out every night and the information which they brought back was of great use when the time came to make the plan for the attack. They were able to confirm that the enemy was digging in on the railway embankment to the north-east of Zeven, and they found out exactly where the enemy were laying mines. More than one patrol reported having heard tracked vehicles in Zeven itself, but until a German ration lorry, driven by a master cook from the 115th Panzer Grenadier Regiment,* drove into Wiersdorf by mistake, there was some doubt about the Germans' armoured strength. This man was only too willing to talk and revealed that there were altogether fourteen armoured vehicles in the town, all manned by his own regiment. The same man also reported that there was an underground factory in the woods just south-west of Wiersdorf, so on the night of the 22nd a patrol was sent out to investigate. It ran into a strong enemy position in the woods, and the patrol leader, Lieut. T. C. Reeves, was hit and severely burned. The patrol was unable to evacuate him and he lay in the open for several hours before the Germans took him to hospital, where he died two days later.

Apr. 24   Promptly at 11 o'clock on the 24th of April the attack on Zeven began. The 5th Battalion Coldstream Guards, supported by tanks of their 1st Battalion, broke out from Wiersdorf, and the 1st Grenadiers, supported by No. 1 Squadron of the 2nd Battalion, went forward from Heeslingen—but not before the artillery had given their accus-

---

*Lieut.-Colonel P. H. Lort-Phillips flew over Zeven to observe this regiment's positions. The summer before, he had flown over the same regiment for the same purpose at Arezzo, Italy. (See Volume II, p. 456.)

tomed foretaste of things to come. The Coldstream, with their force 1945 split up on either side of the Wiersdorf—Zeven road, had the advantage of firm ground to travel over, but the country was very open and they suffered casualties from mortars and small-arms fire. On the right the Grenadiers, with the King's and No. 4 Companies leading the way through the woods north of the Heeslingen—Zeven road, had the advantage of a more covered approach, with the result that the enemy's defensive fire was late in arriving and casualties were negligible. On the other hand, a great number of their carriers and tanks became hopelessly bogged in the mud, so that the Coldstream were always slightly in front. Luckily this could not have mattered less, as the opposition from the enemy on the ground was literally non-existent.

The reason for this pleasant but unexpected state of affairs soon became evident when the first parties of prisoners began to drift in. Apparently, on the previous evening, the well-tried 115th Panzer Grenadier Regiment had been withdrawn north-west towards Bremervorde, and their place had been taken by the 2nd Battalion of the Gross Deutschland Regiment, a very moderate collection of individuals who had been denuded of their tanks and had had little time to take stock of their surroundings. They were delighted to be taken prisoner, and by 4 o'clock in the afternoon had surrendered the entire town to the 5th Coldstream and Grenadiers.

Capt. M. R. R. Marriott, of the 2nd Battalion, was fatally wounded during the attack and five men of the 1st Battalion received minor injuries; but the casualties were so much lighter than anyone had dared to hope that No. 4 Company immediately set off to seize a bridgehead over a small stream in the western suburbs of the town. All the bridges were blown and there was a large enemy tank on the far side, but after being assiduously stalked for a quarter of an hour it withdrew. A "scissors" bridge was then thrown across the stream, whereupon a carrier patrol from No. 4 Company crossed over, set their course along the Bremen road and returned only when they were fired on by enemy in some woods well outside the town.

Over three hundred shells landed in Zeven during the three hours following the arrival of the Group, and it looked as if the enemy might launch a counter-attack. But, thanks to some very accurate shelling on the part of the divisional artillery, the enemy's plans were frustrated before they had time to bear fruit. As the evening wore on, the shelling died away, and by nightfall all was quiet. When, that night, the final count of prisoners was taken, it revealed that the Group had taken one hundred and twenty-four during the day—not to speak of the four hundred wounded Germans in the military hospital or, in-

1945 deed, of the four British naval prisoners whom they found in the hospital too.

With Zeven safely in their hands, the Guards Armoured Division had virtually completed their mission in the Hamburg—Bremen peninsula. They had robbed the Germans of their last escape route from Bremen. But, viewing the situation from a narrower angle, there were still a number of minor tasks to be fulfilled before victory in the peninsula could be said to be complete.

Just before the attack on Zeven began an armoured-car squadron of Household Cavalry, under Major J. Ward, and No. 2 Squadron of the 2nd Battalion, set off north-east to cut the main road from Zeven to Bremervorde. The main motive of the expedition was to reach a concentration camp near Sandbostel, from which two Frenchmen had escaped with a letter from the senior officer, begging the British Army to bring urgently needed supplies of food and medicine. The German guards had apparently fled, and it was felt that by taking advantage of the enemy's preoccupation with the attack on Zeven the two squadrons might be able to reach the camp.

Apr. 25-28 "Ward Force," as the composite group were nicknamed, spent four days roaming around the countryside—two of them completely isolated from their supplies—but they could not get as far north as the camp. They cut the Zeven—Bremervorde road, they played havoc with numerous parties of Germans who had no idea that they were anywhere in the vicinity, and they captured several useful bridges; but, once they tried to penetrate the woods north of Selsingen, they were brought to a stop for want of infantry. And the unfortunate part of the matter was that, until the 29th, the rest of the Group, in Zeven, were powerless to help them.

The reason for this was that the Germans, now desperately short of equipment and information, were relying on widespread demolitions to delay the British advance long enough for them to escape over the Elbe into Schleswig-Holstein. The sappers worked untiringly to bridge the vast craters blown by the aerial bombs and sea mines from the dockyards of Bremen, but for four days the Group had to remain in Zeven. When, on the 29th, they were at last able to move, the road north to Bremervorde was reported to be still cratered in no fewer than ten places.

Apr. 29 The first task allotted to the 1st and 2nd Battalions (the former now commanded by Major C. Earle, O.B.E., as Lieut.-Colonel P. H. Lort-Phillips had left on long-overdue leave to England) was that of capturing the important bridge over the River Oste in Beven, a village about three miles south of Bremervorde. No. 2 Company, the force chosen for this job, had no time to lose, as it was known that the bridge was 1945 guarded and prepared for demolition. When, therefore, the company encountered a small wooden bridge on the way, over which their supporting tanks from No. 3 Squadron could not pass, they pressed on alone and, after a brief encounter with four unsuspecting German guards, seized the bridge in Beven intact. This was a creditable achievement, but it was dwarfed both in importance and difficulty by the second task that the Group were allotted—that of liberating the concentration camp at Sandbostel, where typhus had broken out and was reported to be causing over three hundred deaths a day.

A quick glance at the map was enough to show that Sandbostel camp would be a difficult place to take should the Germans decide to defend it. Between the village of Sandbostel and the camp flowed the River Oste, and the river bank on the camp side was steep and wooded. The Group were told, however, that there were only the prison guards left in the camp, and the King's and No. 2 Companies, who were put in the lead, set out on their errand of mercy confident that it would be quickly executed. As they left Selsingen a convoy of relief workers arrived on the scene with a few medical supplies and a great deal of paper with which to index the internees.

The company and squadron covered the four miles to Sandbostel village at high speed, and it was not until they were within sight of the Oste that the enemy, evidently in more formidable array than a party of prison guards, began to take notice of their approach. A self-propelled gun firing across the river from the high ground north of the camp knocked out the leading tank of No. 2 Squadron and then heavy mortar fire from the woods west of the camp started to rain down on Sandbostel itself. The leading platoons did not suffer heavy casualties, but as they could see that all the bridges over the river were blown there was very little that they could do. An assault crossing was clearly impracticable during daylight, as there were no assault boats handy, so Majors G. Thorne and The Hon. G. N. C. Wigram decided to withdraw their force behind the high ground east of the village. The artillery kept the enemy's heads down during the withdrawal and the company and squadron were soon safely installed beyond the enemy's reach in Gildhus. Only one platoon and one troop were left near the river to keep watch on Sandbostel.

During the late afternoon and evening large quantities of collapsible Apr. 30 boats and a bridging party of sappers were rushed up to Gildhus, and when it grew dark the plans for the night crossing were worked out in detail. By midnight all was ready, and soon afterwards the King's Company left the farm buildings where they had been sheltering and climbed into the boats. It was a bitterly cold, moonless night, and

1945 heavy rain was lashing down on the water, but the enemy did not add to the discomfort of the soaked occupants of the boats by firing down on to the river. Nor did they interfere as the first platoon to cross started digging in a hundred yards from the river bank, nor even when the next two platoons rushed up on to the high wooded ground to the south-east of the camp. It began to look as if the company would be in a strong position to attack the camp the next morning, but when dawn broke it was discovered that the bridge was still only half completed. It would have been foolhardy to expect them to remain where they were without tank support, so, in the cold half-light the two platoons nearest to the river were withdrawn, leaving only the platoon on the high ground to cover the bridge-building. When it became fully light the enemy at once spotted the sappers labouring with the bridge and they mortared it heavily, causing all the work to stop. At the same time, the platoon across the river, endeavouring to shift their position to less marshy ground where they could dig properly, came under very heavy small-arms fire from the camp, and the platoon commander, Lieut. N. S. Farquharson, and a number of non-commissioned officers were wounded. The survivors withdrew at once across the deep, fast-flowing river, but they got caught in the enemy cross-fire and only twelve men, frozen and soaked to the skin, came back to rejoin the company, one man having been drowned.

It was obvious now that the Germans were intent on holding the river and, though they perhaps would not have minded the Group reaching the camp, they were not going to let them cross without a fight. During the morning a plan was drawn up for a more powerful assault crossing some way down-stream, in order to give the sappers a chance of working on the bridge. It began at 2.30 in the afternoon, and of all the many battles which the Grenadier Group fought in the campaign it was without doubt the most unorthodox. As Nos. 2 and 4 Companies worked their way slowly across the river, supported by fire from the 2nd Battalion, the inmates of Sandbostel stood on the roofs of the huts and cheered themselves hoarse. And when the Grenadiers started climbing up the banks on the camp side the cheers became a deafening roar. In fact, but for the firing and for a sharp tussle with S.S. guards near the camp—during which Lieuts. D. B. Ryott and R. V. N. Surtees were wounded—the Grenadiers might have been the players and the internees the spectators on Cup Final day at Wembley.

At nightfall the fantastic battle for Sandbostel came to an end, mercifully for the loss of only a few lives. All through the night the Grenadier companies had to grapple with waves of civilian prisoners who kept breaking out of the camp in search of food, but by 4 o'clock in the morning the sappers had finished building the bridge and the

tanks came up to help to restore order. Meanwhile, a doctor and an 1945
interpreter had been sent into the camp to investigate conditions and
in the morning the prisoner-of-war and displaced-persons relief detachments arrived to take over. It did not take them long to sum up the
size or the urgency of the appalling job that confronted them—for
Sandbostel was a minor Belsen.*

As far as the Grenadier Group were concerned liberating Sand- May 1-8
bostel was their final mission of the war. For, although on paper the
conflict went on for another seven days, and a few patrols which they
sent north during the next twenty-four hours did make contact with
enemy rearguards, as regards serious fighting it was the end. On the
1st of May they moved to Mulsum, a village twenty miles east of
Bremervorde, and it was here that they heard the official announcement of victory on the 8th of May.

For the 4th Battalion one dull and one dramatic day still lay ahead. Apr. 30-
The 15th (Scottish) Division had forced a crossing over the Elbe at May 1st
Lauenberg on the 29th, and the Battalion had moved from Bevensen
into the bridgehead two days later. Now, with the 6th Airborne Division on their right making for Wismar to link up with the Russians,
and the 11th Armoured Division on their left heading for Lubeck,
they were to head for the Baltic.

The Battalion did not make very startling progress on the 2nd of May 2
May because in nearly every village the Germans had collected small
parties of desperadoes who would not give in without a fight. They
reached a point about twelve miles beyond the Elbe, however, which
was as far as the 11th Armoured Division had got, so it was touch and
go the next morning as to who would reach Lubeck first.

The war was still technically in progress, so, taking no chances, May 3
they started off by rounding each corner gingerly and keeping their
heads well inside the turrets in case of snipers. By midday all caution

---

*Lieut.-Colonel J. N. R. Moore, Lieut. A. Breitmeyer and Major The Hon. F. F.
Hennessy, of Divisional Headquarters, made a tour of Sandbostel Camp, accompanied by visitors from all levels of military dignity. Flags of the United Nations
were flying at the gate when they arrived and the self-appointed French Commandant,
Colonel Albert, had provided a guard of honour composed of prisoners from Great
Britain, the United States and France. The party were told that originally Sandbostel
had been a French prisoner-of-war camp; that after the crossing of the Rhine
prisoners of all nationalities had been sent there; and that on the 5th of April about
a third of the camp had been taken over by the S.S. for political deportees, among
them some French university professors, a Danish minister and a cardinal. There
were now eight thousand prisoners of war in the camp and fourteen thousand deportees, although two thousand five hundred people had died since the 5th of April.
The party were informed that conditions in the military portion of the camp had
been fairly good, thanks largely to Red Cross parcels. They could see for themselves
that in the concentration side of Sandbostel conditions had been just as bad as in the
more notorious camps at Belsen and Buchenwald.

1945 had been thrown to the winds. The drivers held their feet firmly on the accelerators and the tank commanders had their heads and shoulders well out of the turrets. At times it was almost impossible for No. 1 Squadron to keep going, as they were travelling along narrow country lanes chockfull of surrendering Wehrmacht. A troop leader would accept the surrender of a major-general and three minutes later would have to plough his way through a swarm of Germans to catch up with the rest of the column. No. 3 Squadron captured Molln without firing a shot, and a little farther on two perfectly sited 88's paid no attention to them at all. But about eight miles beyond Molln they were suddenly ordered to halt.

There was no apparent reason for this order, and as it probably meant that their hopes of being first into Lubeck would be dashed to the ground they were not a little annoyed. Russian voices could distinctly be heard on the wireless, and the squadron could only conclude that the 11th Armoured Division had linked up with the Russians ahead of them. But this was not so, and after waiting for two hours, conversing with liberated Dominion prisoners from a camp near by, they were allowed to proceed. There still seemed just a hope that they might still win the race, but about eight miles beyond the prisoner-of-war camp they came upon a village which a company of Germans had decided to defend. It took them a considerable time to get through and they did not reach Lubeck until 10 o'clock at night—four hours after the 11th Armoured Division.

The news that greeted them was better than the glory attached to winning any race. The Germans in Italy and Holland had surrendered, the 6th Airborne Division had already met the Russians in Wismar, and the Germans between Lubeck and the Danish frontier were suing for peace. In other words, the war in Europe, unofficially at least, was over.

THE LAST PHASE IN NORTH-WEST EUROPE. FEBRUARY—MAY, 1945

Route of 4th Battalion Grenadier Guards
Route of 1st & 2nd Battalion Grenadier Guards

Scale of Miles

CHAPTER X

FAREWELL TO ARMOUR

1

THE OCCUPATION OF GERMANY

VE Day in Germany—Occupation areas of the three Battalions—Disarming the Wehrmacht—Problems of German civilians—Displaced persons—Decision to reconvert Guards Armoured Division and Guards Armoured Brigade to infantry—"Farewell to armour" parade at Rotenburg

THE surrender of the German Army in 1945 was not as sudden as in 1918. Admittedly the final act of surrender only needed to legalize a *fait accompli* and give the semblance of authority to a situation that was frankly farcical. But the fact remained that nearly a week elapsed between the Germans' last coherent attempt to stave off the inevitable and their official laying down of arms. 1945
May 3-7

The Grenadier Group at Mulsum, and the 4th Battalion in Lubeck, spent these last few days of the war removing some of the after-effects of their long trek across Germany. The Quartermasters started sending in enormous indents for polish, and soon rifles and equipment began to shine and trousers to be creased in a manner reminiscent of the Guards Depot. The vehicles were given similar treatment and before long they too began to lose some of the imprints which the past six weeks had left on them. In fact, by VE Day there was little to show that any of the Battalions had ever taken part in a campaign at all.

VE Day itself was rather an anti-climax: victory had been in the air for too long for anyone to feel really elated. In Mulsum a brave attempt was made to mark the importance of the occasion, and, after some neighbouring gunners had emptied their guns in a last outburst of vindictiveness, four old and untrained drummers sounded the "Cease Fire." But owing to a slight miscalculation on the part of the Sergeant-Major the drummers drummed a quarter of an hour too early—with a remarkable lack of unison—and the borrowed Union Jack that was run up a flagpole afterwards was far too battered to do justice to the occasion. May 8

For all three Battalions, however, VE Day had a special significance. It marked the end of their service as fighting troops and the

249

1945 beginning of their new role as occupation troops. Before the day was up they had all moved, or started moving, to take over their new responsibilities: the 1st Battalion to Stade, near the west bank of the Elbe, the 2nd Battalion to the small port of Freiburg on the Elbe estuary, and the 4th Battalion to some villages a few miles south-east of Kiel.

May 8-
June 9
The 1st and 2nd Battalions remained in Stade and Freiburg for only a fortnight. On the 20th of May they left the Cuxhaven peninsula and took over fresh areas south of Bremen, centring round Twist-ringen and Martfeld. But whether a battalion was in the Kiel or the Bremen or the Cuxhaven area mattered little. The life they led and the problems they had to face were almost identical.

The areas for which the Battalions were responsible were almost all as large as a small British county. From Freiburg the 2nd Battalion had to radiate over three hundred square miles of German territory and the 1st Battalion's area around Martfeld contained no fewer than fifty-four small towns and villages. It would obviously have been impossible to exercise control over such vast stretches of country with the whole Battalion settled in one town, so from the start the areas were sub-allotted into squadron and company zones. This meant, in effect, that five or six officers, gifted possibly in other ways but new to the ins and outs of local administration, had to run the affairs of the equivalent to ten different local government departments in England. They were helped a great deal by their respective Intelligence Officers —Lieut. J. Howe (1st Battalion), Lieut. A. N. Breitmeyer (2nd Battalion) and Lieut. P. N. Railing (4th Battalion)—but they were dealing with a situation entirely without precedent and it required a great deal of patience and constant ingenuity to cope with it successfully.

For the first few days chaos reigned supreme. This was inevitable because when the Battalions arrived in their areas they had no clear idea of how widespread the disorder was. Before the patient could be cured, the disease had to be diagnosed. This took time, but once it had been done half the battle was over. A plan could be drawn up and put into action.

In their efforts to restore law and order to the communities in their zones the companies and squadrons soon found that they were con-fronted by three major problems—all of which had to be tackled simultaneously. The first, and by far the most important, problem was that of the German Army. In the last weeks of the campaign literally thousands of German soldiers had flocked into the Cuxhaven penin-sula and the stretch of country between Lubeck and Kiel. Most of them were fugitives, retreating in front of the Allied advance, but many had only recently arrived from Denmark, too late to join in the fighting. They all had to be disarmed, collected into workable groups, 1945 and then demobilized.

Disarming the Wehrmacht turned out to be a relatively easy task, because long before the Battalion arrived the German soldiers had been busy loading their arms, equipment and ammunition into various dumps scattered all over the countryside. Collecting them into groups and demobilizing them, on the other hand, were a nightmare. Whole battalions were sometimes discovered hidden away in obscure villages and it was rare to find even a company with all its men from the same regiment. Besides, there were any number of itinerant soldiers to be dealt with and check points had to be set up on all the main roads to rope in Wehrmacht personnel who were trying to make their way home without being thrown into prisoner-of-war camps. The job eventually became so complicated that a large stretch of the Baltic coast was set aside as a mammoth prisoner-of-war cage, and nearly a million prisoners were poured into it. But before this happened the Battalions spent many weary hours trying to sort out the muddle.

The second major problem concerned the German civilians themselves. Unlike the majority of their countrymen, the Germans in the Battalions' areas had seen nothing of the war at first hand. They had not experienced the soul-destroying sensation of cringing in their cellars while a battle raged above them, and there could be no guarantee that their reaction to occupation would be altogether helpful. One of the first measures the Battalions took, therefore, was to send troops of tanks through every village and along every passable road to provide "displays of strength." After hearing the menacing roar and clank of the Churchills or the Shermans, little doubt can have been left in the minds of the inhabitants of the efficacy of civil disturbances.

The next step was to make contact with the local Burgermeisters. They were ordered to arrange for the handing in of all weapons and Nazi literature and to prepare lists of Nazi party members in their districts. Then houses were searched and hundreds of identity documents were carefully scrutinized. Finally certain hours of the day were set aside for dealing directly with the local populations. These "question times," as they used to be called, soon became a considerable burden: hordes of people would assemble each day for an interview and the unlucky officer in charge would have to listen to discourses ranging from the application of the local midwife for a pass to go to a neighbouring hamlet, to some enthusiastic German's denunciation of a fellow-citizen. But they were worth their while, because gradually, but very thoroughly, the inhabitants had the meaning of total defeat brought home to them—through the medium of their own personal affairs.

1945 The third, and most urgent, problem from a humane point of view was that of the displaced persons. In each of the Battalions' areas there were thousands of these unfortunate foreigners whom the Germans had used as slave labour. They were mostly Russians—there were at least three thousand in the 4th Battalion's area alone—but there were hundreds of men and women from other countries as well. Stuffed into barracks without any thought of sanitation or privacy, they had led a miserable existence for years, divorced from any semblance of civilized society. It was only natural that now that their long-hoped-for hour of liberation had come they expected to receive all the good things in life and to be sent home immediately. They were too overjoyed to be able to appreciate the difficulties they presented, and they had to be handled with immense tact. Nevertheless, in ten days all the Frenchmen had been evacuated and a large proportion of the Russians had been handed over to the Red Army at Wismar. Within a month only a few hundred remained: these were mostly Poles and Yugoslavs whose future was controlled by high politics.

At times the Battalions' occupational duties savoured a little of musical comedy. A Commanding Officer would spend one hour interviewing a dozen white-haired, bespectacled Burgermeisters and the next giving out orders to a group of German colonels, dressed ostentatiously in Prussian finery and glistening leather. Once, at Martfeld, the 1st Battalion were suddenly asked to send a picket to guard a women's hospital, because the matron complained that there were so many bicycles belonging to male displaced persons parked in the halls that it was becoming impossible to keep the hospital clean. Many of the duties which the Battalions were called upon to perform were equally unorthodox, but there was nearly always a humorous side to them.

When they first moved to their occupation areas the Battalions were kept so busy that their normal peace-time activities were largely neglected. After the first fortnight the initial rush of commitments subsided, and drill parades and room inspections began creeping back into the daily curricula. When they reached Martfeld the 1st Battalion even started an educational course and now and again cricket matches were staged. E.N.S.A. shows made fleeting appearances and there was ample opportunity for swimming. In fact, housed in comfortable billets with beds to sleep in, electricity to see by, and proper mess-halls to eat in, the Battalions were finding occupation a congenial pursuit.

Soon after the war ended it became known that the Guards Armoured Division and the 6th Guards Armoured Brigade would lose their tanks sooner or later and once again become infantry.

Infantry was the crying need of the army of occupation, and it was as 1945 such that the Brigade of Guards had established its tradition. Towards the end of May a definite date was set for the change-over, and it was announced that in the middle of June the Guards Armoured Division and the 6th Guards Armoured Brigade would amalgamate into one body—to be known as the Guards Division—and move to a joint occupation area in the Rhineland.

Major-General Allan Adair at once decided to hold a "farewell to armour" parade to signal the end of the Guards Armoured Division and to herald the era of the new Division. The aerodrome at Roten-burg, a town midway between Bremen and Hamburg, was chosen for the parade, and as it was too far away from Kiel for the Churchills of the 4th Battalion to take part, a small detachment of men were sent instead.

The General let it be known that no trouble was to be spared in making the parade one that would long be remembered, and, from the 1st of June onwards, bodies of men and tanks from each of the Bat-talions in the Division lived in temporary billets near the aerodrome. Battleship paint from German naval stocks was procured to repaint the tanks, emery paper was produced to burnish the guns: everything that could make iron and steel gloss and glisten was at hand. There was one dress rehearsal and the day of the great parade came.

Early in the morning the crews drove out to the tanks, which had June 9 been parked the night before in their positions on the parade ground. From the grandstand at the eastern end of the aerodrome to the slight ridge opposite, there were row upon row of Shermans and Cromwells glinting battleship grey in the fresh sunlight. The gun muzzles, bright after hours of hard work, caught the light and reflected back a million suns across the turf. Between the two facing phalanxes of tanks stood, at the western end of the ground, vehicles of the Division's other mobile regiments: armoured cars of the Household Cavalry, Bofors guns from the 94th Light Anti-Aircraft, and self-propelled artillery from the 153rd Regiment and 21st Anti-Tank Regiment, R.A.

As time moved on to mid-morning the distinguished spectators started to arrive, some by road, some by air. At length Field-Marshal Montgomery's aeroplane landed and the Field-Marshal was driven to the grandstand. A moment later Brigadier N. W. Gwatkin, command-ing the 5th Brigade, gave the order to the tank crews to mount. There was a quick scurrying as drivers tumbled into their hatches and com-manders and operators scrambled into the turrets. The order was given to start up, and with one sound two hundred and fifty engines rumbled into life. Then each Battalion led off in one long column, so that there were four columns of tanks criss-crossing over the parade

1945 ground. As each tank passed the saluting base, the turret swung out-wards and the commander saluted. On led the columns until they reached the ridge at the far side of the area, where they wheeled away out of sight, to the strains of "Auld Lang Syne." Finally, the massed bands broke into the first of the regimental marches to welcome the black-bereted infantry who came marching back over the ridge.

Thus, four years almost to the day after the entry of the Brigade of Guards into the field of armoured warfare, the Guards Armoured Division and the 6th Guards Armoured Brigade passed into history.

2

BERLIN

1ST BATTALION

The Battalion form part of the British occupation force in Berlin—A series of Victory Parades—Arrival of Mr. Churchill for the Potsdam Conference —Culminating parade before Mr. Churchill through the heart of Berlin

When the Russian Army stormed into Berlin in April, 1945, they came face to face with death. R.A.F. bombing raids, Russian artillery, Russian tanks and Russian infantry had scarred Germany's capital out of recognition; they had sapped its life-blood. What once had been houses and shops and cinemas was now a grotesque, mountainous rubble-heap. Streets once thronged with happy, purposeful people contained only an occasional hausfrau searching for food. In the Tiergarten the lawns and flower-beds were littered with mangled engines of war. The Reichstag was in ruins and beside the battered, flooded Reich Chancellery the grass was black, marking the spot where Hitler's bodyguard had burned the dead body of their Fuehrer.

For nearly three months the Red Army ruled the stricken city alone. Then, in accordance with an agreement made at Yalta in 1943, troops of the other victorious Allies arrived to take over their occupational sectors. From France came a division under General Beauchesnes, from America the 101st Airborne Division, and from Great Britain the 7th Armoured Division, detachments from the services—and the 1st Battalion of the Regiment. For a month, amid the ashes of the enemy's capital, they staged parades and ceremonies to herald the new era of peace.

July 4-   The Grenadiers were quartered in the Hermann Goering Barracks
Aug. 3 in the suburb of Wedding—a grim, half-destroyed building which

15th July, 1945.   Mr. Churchill inspecting a Guard of Honour of the 1st Battalion at the Tempelhof Airport, Berlin.

20th July, 1945.   The 1st Battalion march past Mr. Churchill in Berlin.

swarmed with flies and at first had no sanitation. It took them two **1945**
weeks to make it habitable and even then there was a serious shortage
of furniture and fittings. But what they lacked in comfort they made
up in interest, for the month of July, 1945, was one of the most remarkable pages in the long history of Berlin.

The Battalion had not been in the capital for more than forty-eight
hours before they took part in their first ceremony—the hoisting of a
flag on the Grosse Stern, a monument in the Charlottenburg Chaussée, which commemorated the German victory in the Franco-Prussian
War. A flamboyant Frenchman, flouting ceremony, had already
hoisted a Tricolour and it was fluttering triumphantly when the Battalion presented arms for the Union Jack. But, not to be outdone, the
7th Armoured Division had produced a flag with particularly appro-
priate associations—the Union Jack which they had flown outside
their headquarters during the Battle of El Alamein.

Once begun, the parades seemed never to end. On the 12th of July
Field-Marshal Montgomery came to Berlin, and in the broad western
approach to the Brandenburg Gate, which formed the boundary
between the Russian and British sectors, he invested Marshal Zhukov
with the G.C.B. and Marshal Rokossovsky with the K.C.B. While he
did so armoured cars lined the shattered Tiergarten, glistening Cromwells formed the side of a box round the dais, and the 1st Battalion
provided a guard of honour. On the following day the whole Battalion
took part in a big parade with the 7th Armoured Division, marching
past the four Allied commanders of Berlin: Major-General Lyne
(Great Britain), Major-General Baranov (Russia), Major-General
Floyd Parks (America) and General de Beauchesnes (France). Then,
on the 15th of July, Mr. Churchill arrived for the Potsdam Conference
and was greeted by a guard of honour from the Battalion, drawn up
on the scorching turf of the Tempelhof aerodrome. Finally, five days
later, the most impressive of all the Berlin parades took place—a full-
dress Victory March of the entire British garrison in front of Mr.
Churchill.

It was held in the Charlottenburg Chaussée, the long, tree-lined
avenue in the heart of the German capital. The Germans had been
cleared from the streets, but a few inquisitive faces could be seen peer-
ing round the tree stumps of the Tiergarten. In the background, away
to the right, was the heavy, square Reichstag, its dome a tangle of
twisted ribs, and its blackened walls hung with a giant Union Jack
and a giant Red Flag. Huge placards depicting the faces of the "Big
Three" swung from the neighbouring buildings. Flags and bunting
decked the stands along the route. The sun was shining.

When the Prime Minister and his entourage arrived they were

1945 greeted by salvo after salvo from the guns grouped round the Grosse Stern. Then, almost before the echoes had died away, the party climbed into four half-tracks—the same shining vehicles which had carried Field-Marshal Montgomery and his attendant Generals round Rotenburg aerodrome a month before. They drove slowly past the long line of guns, tanks and infantry, reviewing the ten thousand men on parade.

The inspection over, the columns of armour and infantry began the march past. The massed tanks, painted a deep green, headed the procession, four abreast. Then came the armoured cars, six abreast, and after them a complete searchlight battery, an artillery formation with their guns, and a naval detachment led by the Chatham Band of the Royal Marines in white, spiked helmets. Next were the 1st Battalion, and as they drew level with the Prime Minister the massed bands opposite the saluting base broke into "The British Grenadiers."

No peace-time Nazi parade through an undamaged Berlin could have equalled in splendour the sight of these victorious Englishmen marching past their leader. For Mr. Churchill it marked the climax of a career; for the Grenadiers, not only of the 1st Battalion but of all battalions scattered throughout Europe, it symbolized the end of the Second World War.

INDEX

i

Lightning Source UK Ltd.
Milton Keynes UK
UKHW020335260319
339893UK00001B/3/P